DATE DUE

THE
WG&L TAX JOURNAL
DIGEST

2002

A digest of tax articles appearing in
THE JOURNAL OF TAXATION
PRACTICAL TAX STRATEGIES
ESTATE PLANNING
THE JOURNAL OF INTERNATIONAL TAXATION
THE JOURNAL OF MULTISTATE TAXATION AND INCENTIVES
TAXATION OF EXEMPTS
BUSINESS ENTITIES

Edited by

DANIEL E. FELD

Member of the New York Bar

WARREN
GORHAM
&LAMONT

A Thomson Company

How to Use
This Book

The 2002 *WG&L Tax Journal Digest* is a reference to all major articles published in *The Journal of Taxation, Practical Tax Strategies, Estate Planning, The Journal of International Taxation, The Journal of Multistate Taxation and Incentives, Taxation of Exempts* (formerly *The Journal of Taxation of Exempt Organizations*), and *Business Entities* during 2001. Of use to specialists in taxation, as well as attorneys and accountants in general practice, the *Digest* provides concise, dependable summaries of federal tax articles in these seven leading publications.

The digests are organized under a system of alphabetical topic headings to lead the reader quickly to the latest ideas on a given tax problem. The reader need only consult the Index at the beginning of the *Digest* to determine the area of interest and then the boldface heading at the top of each page to find the digest within the appropriate section. The digests have been placed under the Index topic entry or entries thought most likely to come first to mind in the course of one's research. Extensive cross-references are also used to reflect varying conceptual approaches to the material. Within each Index topic, the digests appear alphabetically by title.

Also included is a Table of Articles, placed at the end of the *Digest*. This index lists every article published in *The Journal of Taxation, Practical Tax Strategies, Estate Planning, The Journal of International Taxation, The Journal of Multistate Taxation and Incentives, Taxation of Exempts*, and *Business Entities* in 2001. In addition, a Table of IRC Sections enables the user to locate all articles relating to a specific Code section.

Acknowledgments

Several people contributed digests to this volume, including Jeanne O'Neill and Diane W. Green.

An important contribution was also made by Ken Feinleib, the book editor, and Carole Brandi, the copy editor, who diligently edited a large manuscript in a short period.

Index

A

ABANDONMENT

(*See* Losses)

ACCELERATED DEPRECIATION

(*See* Depreciation and Amortization)

ACCOUNTING METHODS

(*See also* Compensation for Personal Services; Depreciation and Amortization; Estates and Estate Tax; Interest Paid; Partners and Partnerships; Reorganizations)

In General

"IRS should not force continued use of incorrect accounting method" (2001). In FSA 200102004, the IRS has concluded that a taxpayer should not be forced to return to an incorrect method of accounting. (94 Journal of Taxation 250.)

"Lump-sum payments made at lease inception were rent to lease purchaser" (2001). In ILM 200048001, the IRS examined five situations to determine whether capital cost reduction (CCR) payments made by a lessee at the inception of a vehicle lease were rental income to the financial institution that acquired the lease, and if not, whether the CCR payments reduced the financial institution's basis in the leased vehicle for depreciation purposes. (66 Practical Tax Strategies 122.)

"New proposed revenue procedures on accounting periods" (2001). On May 11, 2001, the IRS released two proposed revenue procedures that, when finalized, would liberalize certain of the rules applicable to tax years. (3 Business Entities, No. 4, 54.)

"Overpayments not income in year of receipt" (2001). A distributor of health care products was not required to include in income under the claim of right doctrine the amount of customer credit balances attributable to customer overpayments that remained outstanding as of the close of the tax year, the Tax Court held in *Smarthealth, Inc.* (2001). (67 Practical Tax Strategies 114.)

"Proposed Regulations on mid-contract changes in taxpayers" (2001). The IRS has issued Proposed Regulations concerning a mid-contract change in taxpayer of a contract that has been accounted for under a long-term contract method of accounting. (66 Practical Tax Strategies 236.)

Accrual Method

"Full prepaid annual fees were income in the year billed" (2001). The Federal Circuit affirmed the Court of Federal Claims in *American Express* (2001), holding that the IRS properly construed the term "services" appearing in Revenue Procedure 71-21 to exclude annual cardholder payments and therefore all the revenue from the fees was properly required to be reported in the year it was received. (67 Practical Tax Strategies 306.)

"Upfront cash payments are taxable income upfront" (2001). An accrual-method business had to recognize in the year of receipt upfront cash payments it got from manufacturers in exchange for promising to purchase their products over a period of years, according to the Tax Court in *Westpac Pacific Foods* (2001). (67 Practical Tax Strategies 179.)

Cash Method

"Cash in on expanded opportunities to use the cash method" (2001). Under the cash method of accounting, income is recognized in the tax year it is actually or constructively received. Actual receipt requires the receipt of cash or its equivalence. Cash equivalence has been judicially defined relatively narrowly. Obligations received from a solvent debtor that are transferable, marketable, and trade at a discount no more than the prevailing time value of money are deemed the equivalent of cash. Income is constructively received if it is credited, set aside, or otherwise made available to the taxpayer and could be obtained by mere notice. Deductions are taken into account in the year paid.

After providing an overview of the cash method of accounting, the author discusses limitations. Two broad types of limitations are imposed on the use of the cash method of accounting. The first type co-exists with the overall cash method of accounting and limits its flexibility. The second prohibits the use of the method entirely.

Then, the author addresses Section 448, which prohibits the use of the cash method by certain types of taxpayers. Section 448 provides that C corporations, partnerships that have a C corporation as a partner, and tax shelters (defined by reference to Section 461(i)(3)) are precluded from using the cash method of accounting. A partnership that has a C corporation as a partner at any time during the partnership's tax year is subject to Section 448, even if the corporation owns the interest momentarily. Exceptions to the general rule are made, however, for certain farming businesses, qualified personal service corporations, and entities whose average annual gross receipts do not exceed $5 million.

Finally, the author turns to small business relief. The passage of the Tax Relief Extension Act of 1999 raised the stakes on the ability of taxpayers to qualify for the cash method of accounting. Among the provisions of this legislation was a prohibition, for sales or other dispositions entered into after December 17, 1999, on the use of the installment method of accounting by accrual-method taxpayers.

Significant criticism has been leveled at this provision, particularly by small business proponents, and congressional noise about repeal has been heard. On December 28, 2000, President Clinton signed Pub. L. No. 106-573, the Installment Sales Correction Act of 2000, which retroactively restored the ability of accrual-method taxpayers to use the installment method. In a significant victory by small business, the IRS issued Revenue Procedure 2000-22, which, pursuant to the IRS's discretionary power, provides a blanket exception for certain small businesses from the requirement to maintain inventories and account for purchases and sales on the accrual method of accounting. (M.A. Melone, 66 Practical Tax Strategies 142.)

"Flooring installer wins right to use cash method" (2001). The Tax Court has held, in *Smith* (2000), that the IRS abused its discretion in preventing a flooring installation business from using the cash method of accounting. This continues the recent string of cases in which the court has found that materials used by various businesses were not merchandise that had to be inventoried. (66 Practical Tax Strategies 54.)

"IRS will not challenge contractors' use of the cash method" (2001). The IRS Office of Chief Counsel, in CC-2001-010, has announced a change in its litigating position regarding the requirement that certain construction contractors must use inventory accounts and an accrual method of accounting. (66 Practical Tax Strategies 309.)

Change of Accounting Method or Accounting Period

"Guidance on adopting and changing accounting periods" (2001). The IRS has issued Proposed Regulations that update, clarify, and reorganize the rules and procedures for adopting, changing, and retaining a taxpayer's annual accounting period. (67 Practical Tax Strategies 115.)

"IRS could require taxpayer to change accounting method" (2001). The IRS did not abuse its discretion when it required a taxpayer to change its overall method of accounting from a hybrid method to an accrual method, according to the Tax Court in *Nemetschek North America, Inc.* (2001). (67 Practical Tax Strategies 366.)

"IRS liberalizes tax year change requirements in two draft Revenue Procedures" (2001). The IRS has issued the drafts of two proposed Revenue Procedures with respect to the adoption, change, or retention of tax years. Notice 2001-34 contains a non-automatic procedure, requiring the IRS's approval to change a tax year. The other draft procedure, found in Notice 2001-35, provides automatic consent. Both proposed Revenue Procedures were issued concurrently with Proposed Regulations under Sections 441, 442, 706, and 1378.

First, the authors discuss Notice 2001-34. When finalized, Notice 2001-34 will provide the procedures under Section 442 and its regulations to establish a business purpose and request the IRS's consent to adopt, change, or retain a taxpayer's annual accounting period. This proposed Revenue Procedure will apply to taxpayers that are outside the scope of other automatic consent Revenue Procedures to adopt, change, or retain a tax year.

Then, the authors consider Notice 2001-35. This Notice updates and modifies Rev. Proc. 87-32, which provides the means by which a partnership, S corporation, corporation electing to be an S corporation, or personal service corporation can obtain expeditious approval to change its annual accounting period. (C. Conjura & C. Ossen, 95 Journal of Taxation 27.)

Installment Sales

"IRS okays revoking election out of installment method" (2001). Notice 2001-22 provides that an accrual-method taxpayer that disposed of property in an installment sale after December 16, 1999, and filed a federal income tax return by April 16, 2001, reporting the gain on the disposition using an accrual method of accounting rather than the installment method, has the IRS's consent to revoke its effective election out of the installment method. (66 Practical Tax Strategies 236.)

ACCOUNTING PERIODS

(*See* Accounting Methods)

ACCUMULATED EARNINGS TAX

"Retention escapes accumulated earnings tax" (2001). The Tax Court found that a corporation did not have accumulated earnings and profits for the purpose of helping its shareholders avoid tax and, therefore, was not liable for the accumulated earnings tax imposed by Section 531, in *Knight Furniture Co., Inc.* (2001). (66 Practical Tax Strategies 247.)

ACQUISITIONS

(*See* Reorganizations)

ACTIVITIES NOT ENGAGED IN FOR PROFIT

(*See* Business Expenses; Losses; Partners and Partnerships)

ADDITIONS TO TAX

(*See* Interest and Penalties)

ADJUSTED GROSS INCOME

(*See* Gross Income)

AFFILIATED CORPORATIONS

(*See also* Allocations Among Related Taxpayers; Dividends and Distributions; Interest Paid; Reorganizations; S Corporations; Tax-Exempt Organizations)

"Applying Section 382 to loss corporation affiliates of exempt organizations" (2001). R.J. Mason, M.V. Rountree & H.A. Levenson, 12 Journal of Taxation of Exempt Organizations 139. (*Digested under* Tax-Exempt Organizations—Hospitals and Other Health Care Organizations, page 237.)

"Consolidated return election offers tax advantages—with complexity" (2001). Corporate taxpayers meeting the statutory definition of "affiliated group" are generally entitled to file consolidated federal income tax returns. The consolidated regulations contain various rules for computing a single, consolidated federal income tax liability. The calculation of a consolidated group's tax liability begins with the calculation of separate taxable incomes for each member of the group. Then, the regulations provide a series of adjustments to be made to the separate taxable incomes before aggregation. Each listed adjustment has a reference to the portion of the consolidated regulations that addresses that particular adjustment.

Once the members adjust their separate taxable incomes in accordance with the regulations, the group aggregates the separate taxable incomes and incorporates the consolidated tax items, such as net operating losses (NOLs) that are computed at the consolidated level. The consolidated group computes the tax liability on its consolidated taxable income as if it were a single corporation.

First, the authors discuss common transactions, including the sale of a subsidiary's stock and the sale of property. The election to file a consolidated return invokes the consolidation regulations as an overlay to the primary tax provisions that govern common business transactions. Generally, the consolidated regulations add an additional tax effect to the tax treatment mandated by the general tax provisions of the Code, such as the deferral of income or loss recognition generated by an intercompany transaction. In a limited number of circumstances, the regulations override the general corporate rules and impose their own treatment, such as the creation of an excess loss account. The consolidated regulations have an impact on the tax treatment of almost every business transaction engaged in by a member of a consolidated group.

Then, the authors consider using a new member's NOL carryover. Whether a corporation generates an NOL prior to joining the consolidated group, after departing a consolidated group, or as part of the consolidated group, the consolidated regulations guide the allocation and use of that loss between consolidated years and separate return years. Different rules apply according to when the NOL was generated.

Finally, the authors address the consolidated return election. Section 1501 allows an affiliated group to file a consolidated federal income tax return. To qualify as an affiliated group, the group must include a common parent corporation that is an includable corporation and at least one other includable corporation in which the parent owns at least 80 percent of the voting power and total value of its stock. The affiliated group also includes any other includable corporation if its stock is owned by members of the group under the same 80 percent ownership tests. All corporations, other than those listed in Section 1504(b), are includable corporations. (J.C. Warner & A.T. Frias, 67 Practical Tax Strategies 148.)

"Dual consolidated loss rules applied to bar use of foreign NOLs" (2001). 94 Journal of Taxation 186. (*Digested under* Net Operating Loss, page 131.)

ALIMONY

(*See* Husband and Wife—Divorce and Separation)

ALLOCATIONS AMONG PARTNERS

(*See* Partners and Partnerships—Partnership Allocations and Distributions)

ALLOCATIONS AMONG RELATED TAXPAYERS

"Applying Section 482 to third-party lease-strips—has the IRS overreached?" (2001). M.M. Levey & W.S. Garofalo, 12 Journal of International Taxation, No. 12, 12. (*Digested under* International Taxation—In General, page 90.)

"Will U.S. standardization erode key flexibility in APAs?" (2001). R.E. Ackerman, 12 Journal of International Taxation, No. 2, 12. (*Digested under* International Taxation—In General, page 97.)

ALTERNATIVE MINIMUM TAX

"Beware of AMT on incentive stock options" (2001). Taxpayers may be better off without the regular income tax deferral of incentive stock options (ISOs) in order to avoid the alternative minimum tax (AMT) consequences of these options. Nonqualified stock options (NQSOs) do not subject the employee to AMT on grant or exercise of the option.

If the employee chooses to exercise an ISO, the employee should be aware of the potential AMT consequences. For instance, an employee could unfortunately face a substantial tax liability simply from exercising an ISO, despite no disposition of the stock and no receipt of any "real money" to pay the tax. An employee who has an ISO should be aware of the benefits of making a disqualifying disposition in the same year as exercise to avoid the AMT adjustment.

An NQSO is generally the preferred option for both the employer and the employee. The NQSO provides flexibility with issues such as pricing, permissible time of exercise, employment status, and transferability. Although the employee realizes compensation income on grant or exercise, the employee is, importantly, not subjected to AMT on account of that income. In addition, the employer realizes a corresponding deduction when the employee includes the compensation in gross income. (L.M. Kaplan, 67 Practical Tax Strategies 260.)

"Section 381 limitation on NOL carryovers also applies to AMT NOL carryover" (2001). 94 Journal of Taxation 118. (*Digested under* Net Operating Loss, page 131.)

AMORTIZATION

(*See* Depreciation and Amortization)

ANNUAL EXCLUSION

(*See* Gifts and Gift Tax)

.APPEALS

(*See* Procedure)

ASSESSMENT AND COLLECTION

(*See also* Interest and Penalties; Procedure)

In General

"Assessment in single-member LLC's name is valid against owner" (2001). 67 Practical Tax Strategies 182. (*Digested under* Limited Liability Companies, page 123.)

"Collection statute held to be exclusive remedy" (2001). In a case of first impression, the Ninth Circuit, in *Shwarz* (2000), held that the Section 7433 unauthorized tax collection provisions are the exclusive remedy for a cause of action related to a wrongful disclosure of tax return information under Section 6103 and, therefore, a cause of action under Section 7431 for unauthorized disclosure of tax return information was precluded by Section 7433. (66 Practical Tax Strategies 109.)

"Court analyzes whether remittance is a payment or deposit" (2001). A New York federal district court in *Tate & Lyle North American Sugars, Inc.* (2001) denied summary judgment relief and ordered a trial to determine the facts and circumstances, but described the relevant inquiry to determine whether a remittance by a taxpayer to the IRS is a payment of tax or a cash bond deposit. (67 Practical Tax Strategies 300.)

"Court explains assessment procedures" (2001). The Tax Court explained in *Nicklaus* (2001) the necessary assessment procedures required prior to any collection action. (67 Practical Tax Strategies 299.)

"District court cannot determine tax liability or set time limits" (2001). The Tenth Circuit held, in *Sterling Consulting Corporation* (2001), that a district court lacks jurisdiction to determine a corporate tax liability in a receivership case and may not set a time limit for the IRS to conduct its examination of the tax return or its ability to assess a deficiency. (66 Practical Tax Strategies 372.)

"IRS memo explains requirements for offer in compromise" (2001). ILM 200128054 explores the process of accepting an offer in compromise of a tax liability. The memo was written in response to an associate area counsel asking whether a compliance area director could accept an offer that the counsel opposed. (67 Practical Tax Strategies 182.)

"Liens and levies are separate collection actions" (2001). The Tax Court held in *Parker* (2001) that liens and levies are separate collection actions and that the IRS is considered to have initiated collection action after it initiates each of these procedures. (67 Practical Tax Strategies 245.)

"Partners must be individually assessed prior to collection activity" (2001). A California federal district court affirmed a bankruptcy court's decision in *Briguglio* (2001), which held that an assessment must be made individually against a partnership's partners prior to the IRS being able to collect the tax liability, and this assessment must be made prior to the expiration of the three-year limitations period. (66 Practical Tax Strategies 373.)

"Surviving corporation subject to transferee liability for tax debt" (2001). The Tax Court held in *Eddie Cordes, Inc., Transferee* (2001) that a surviving corporation of a merger was subject to transferee liability for the full tax liabilities. (67 Practical Tax Strategies 359.)

"Tax assessments against a partnership not binding on partners" (2001). A California federal district court in *Galletti* (2001) held that a general partner must be assessed individually under Section 6203 before the partner can be held liable for the partnership's debts. (3 Business Entities, No. 6, 37.)

"Transferee liability imposed based on a fraudulent transfer" (2001). The Tenth Circuit affirmed a Tax Court decision in *Scott*

(2001), finding that transferee liability existed because the substance of the transaction is that the transferee received assets of the corporation that owes the tax liability. (66 Practical Tax Strategies 181.)

"Transfer tax liens and transferee and fiduciary liability" (2001). An analysis of transfer tax liens and transferee and fiduciary liability helps fit these concepts into the larger picture—the tax collection system—and thus helps estate planners advise clients faced with lien and liability problems.

First, the author discusses transfer tax liens, including special liens for estate taxes, and release of lien or discharge of property. In general, a lien attaches to all property held in a decedent's estate; the purpose is to ensure collection of any estate taxes that might be due as a result of the decedent's death. While a comparable lien exists for gift tax purposes, it is the estate tax lien in its various forms that is more likely to concern most estate planners. The reason is that the estate tax lien can be an issue even when an estate is solvent and there is no question about the amount of taxes to be paid or the ability to pay them.

In particular, the lien can interfere with the sale of estate assets to pay taxes and administration expenses or the distribution of estate assets to the appropriate beneficiaries, although the extent to which it will do so varies greatly from state to state. Thus, it is important to keep in mind the different forms that the lien can take and the means for dealing with the lien where property is to be sold or where special tax elections are made.

Then, the author addresses transferee and fiduciary liability, including transferee liability for gift tax and estate tax, transfer of assets from a transferee to a third person, and fiduciary liability under federal law. Transferee liability is most likely to arise in the gift and estate tax context: (1) when a gift or bequest is revalued for gift or estate tax purposes at a higher value than the transferor had anticipated or (2) when a transaction that the transferor or his executor did not consider to be a gift or bequest is determined to result in a full or partial gift or bequest, although transferee liability can also occur

(3) when a transferor or his executor simply does not pay the tax owed, whether due to inability to pay, ignorance, or otherwise.

While aspects of transferee and fiduciary liability can arise in planning, these issues are frequently important to consider in the context of an audit or litigation with the IRS that grows out of an audit. Finally, the author considers the means available to the IRS for collecting tax from a transferee. (E.R. Turner, 28 Estate Planning 147.)

Notice of Deficiency

"Deficiency notice valid even though date omitted" (2001). The Tax Court held in *Rochelle* (2001) that the IRS's notice of deficiency issued to the taxpayer was valid even though the notice did not contain the mandatory "Last Day to File a Petition with the United States Tax Court" date. (67 Practical Tax Strategies 44.)

"IRS provided sufficient detail to make deficiency notice valid" (2001). The Tax Court held in *Sunik* (2001) that the IRS's notice of deficiency was sufficiently detailed, indicating that the IRS made a valid determination of the taxpayers' liability. (67 Practical Tax Strategies 176.)

Statute of Limitations

"Due process hearing extended collection period" (2001). The Tax Court held in *Boyd* (2001) that a collection due process hearing pursuant to Section 6330 tolls the limitation period for collections. (67 Practical Tax Strategies 359.)

"Equitable tolling of limitations period available only after RRA '98" (2001). A California federal district court held in *Pritchett* (2001) that the equitable tolling of the limitations period provision enacted as part of the Restructuring and Reform Act of 1998 (RRA '98) is not applicable for tax years whose limitations period expired prior to July 28, 1998. Also, the court held that equitable tolling was not permitted under common law. (67 Practical Tax Strategies 45.)

"Fraud may extend employment tax return assessment" (2001). The Tax Court held in *Neely* (2001) that the elements of fraud may exist in the employment tax context, as it does in the income, estate, and gift tax areas. If the elements of fraud are proven by clear and convincing evidence, the limitations period for assessments will be indefinitely extended. (66 Practical Tax Strategies 240.)

"Individual partners must be assessed for limitations period to run" (2001). A California federal district court held in *Galletti* (2001) that the statute required an assessment against the individual partners and not just the partnership before the IRS may collect the tax. (67 Practical Tax Strategies 246.)

"Limitations period and latches did not prevent transferee liability" (2001). The Tax Court held in *Fridovich* (2001) that the limitations period had not expired and the doctrine of latches did not apply to prevent the IRS from assessing and collecting transferee liability for estate taxes that the estate owed. (66 Practical Tax Strategies 241.)

"Limitations period overrode by duty of consistency" (2001). The Ninth Circuit affirmed a Tax Court decision in *Estate of Ashman* (2000), holding that a taxpayer who had falsely reported that a distribution from a pension plan had been rolled over into a qualified account within the sixty-day period required to defer taxation was barred by the duty of consistency from claiming after the limitations period had expired that the distribution had been untimely. (66 Practical Tax Strategies 51.)

"Limitations period strictly construed for wrongful levy suit" (2001). The Seventh Circuit affirmed a district court holding in *LaBonte* (2000), ruling that the taxpayer's suit to recover levied property was untimely

and his letter to the IRS was not a proper "written request for a return of property" in order to qualify for an exception to the general nine-month limitations period. (66 Practical Tax Strategies 108.)

"No statute of limitations on penalty for failing to register a tax shelter" (2001). In ILM 200112003, the IRS determined that there is no statute of limitations for assessing a Section 6707 penalty for failing to register a tax shelter. (94 Journal of Taxation 375.)

AT-RISK RULES

"At-risk analysis" (2001). In *Pledger* (2000), the Sixth Circuit affirmed the at-risk analysis applied by the district court below. After analyzing the three-party sale-lease-back transaction at issue, the Sixth Circuit concluded that the taxpayer was not at risk because any debts it owed would be canceled out by another party's guarantee. Therefore, the taxpayer was not allowed to deduct losses from the transaction. (3 Business Entities, No. 2, 54.)

"Share of nonrecourse liabilities for purposes of Section 752 and the at-risk rules" (2001). In Letter Ruling 200120020, the IRS addressed a partner's share of nonrecourse liabilities for purposes of Section 752 and for purposes of the at-risk rules of Section 465. (3 Business Entities, No. 4, 54.)

AUDIT OF RETURNS

(*See* Procedure—Audit of Returns)

AUTOMOBILES

(*See* Business Expenses)

B

BAD DEBTS

"Discharged unsecured debt is bad-debt deduction for parent corporation" (2001). In TAM 200101001, the IRS ruled that a taxpayer should treat the unsecured debt of a subsidiary that was discharged in a Chapter 11 bankruptcy proceeding as a bad-debt deduction under Section 166 and not as a contribution to capital. (94 Journal of Taxation 251.)

BANKRUPTCY

"Claim not subordinated despite failure to collect from third party" (2001). A bankruptcy court in Indiana held in *White Trailer Court* (2000) that the IRS's claim should not be subordinated to other creditors because of its failure to collect these funds from a third party. (66 Practical Tax Strategies 179.)

"District court let bankruptcy court decide who gets funds" (2001). A California federal district court in *Richard E. Shaw and Associates, Inc. v. De Sante* (2001) transferred an interpleader action to a bankruptcy court to determine the priority of competing liens. (67 Practical Tax Strategies 112.)

"Erroneous tax abatement may be reversed" (2001). An Indiana federal district court adopted a magistrate's finding in *Buckner* (2001) that a tax abatement of a pre-bankruptcy assessment and levy may be reversed after a bankruptcy discharge because it was caused by an "unintended error." (66 Practical Tax Strategies 372.)

"IRS can set off otherwise exempt property" (2001). A bankruptcy court in Texas held in *Martinez* (2000) that the IRS may offset the debtor's 1992 tax liability, interest, and penalties against an otherwise exempt 1999 tax refund. (66 Practical Tax Strategies 178.)

"Limitations period tolled during back-to-back bankruptcies" (2001). The First Circuit joined a majority of circuits by holding that the limitations period is automatically tolled during back-to-back bankruptcies, in *Young* (2000). (66 Practical Tax Strategies 110.)

"Parent company's bankruptcy does not convert partnership items of subsidiary to nonpartnership items" (2001). 3 Business Entities, No. 4, 54. (*Digested under* Partners and Partnerships—Partnership Audits and Proceedings, page 151.)

"Right to setoff trumps right to exempt property" (2001). A bankruptcy court, adopting a minority view, held in *Kadrmas* (2000), that the creditor's right to setoff trumps the debtor's right to exempt and protect property in a bankruptcy proceeding. (67 Practical Tax Strategies 244.)

BASIS OF PROPERTY FOR GAIN OR LOSS

(*See* Capital Gains and Losses; Losses; Reorganizations; S Corporations)

BONDS, DEBENTURES, AND NOTES

"IRS takes hard line on Section 501(c)(3) bonds and exempt status" (2001). Over the past decade, as responsibility for monitoring the tax-exempt municipal bond requirements has shifted within the IRS, commentators and IRS representatives have warned of increasing enforcement actions. Statutes and regulations have become more limiting in the types of tax-exempt bonds that may be issued, and more detailed concerning requirements and procedures. In a sense, the municipal bond tax world is maturing.

Two recent technical advice memoranda—TAM 200006049 and TAM 200107020—issued by the IRS on different aspects of a particular case illustrate the hard-line approach the IRS is taking to application of the technical rules and the procedural difficulties that can arise—with potentially disastrous consequences—from a failure to meet them. (E.M. Mills, 13 Taxation of Exempts 45.)

"'Pervasively sectarian' institutions may now qualify for tax-exempt financing" (2001). S.J. Lark, 12 Journal of Taxation of Exempt Organizations 173. (*Digested under* Tax-Exempt Organizations—Religious Organizations, page 242.)

BOOKS AND RECORDS

(*See* Business Expenses; Interest and Penalties)

BOOT

(*See* Reorganizations)

BUSINESS EXPENSES

(*See also* Compensation for Personal Services; Depreciation and Amortization; Dividends and Distributions; Fringe Benefits; Partners and Partnerships; Passive Loss Rules)

Deduction Versus Capital Expenditure

"Acquiring corporation may not deduct target's contingent liabilities" (2001). An acquiring corporation may not deduct contingent liabilities of a target corporation, where the liabilities accrued before the target's acquisition (in a stock purchase treated as an asset purchase under Section 338) and were paid by the selling corporation after the acquisition under an indemnity agreement, according to FSA 200048006. (94 Journal of Taxation 121.)

"Aircraft heavy maintenance expenses found deductible: Is IRS retreating from *INDOPCO*?" (2001). The IRS, in Revenue Ruling 2001-4, allowed a current deduction under Section 162 to a commercial airline for its costs of conducting a "heavy maintenance visit" of an aircraft airframe. This heavy maintenance is required by the Federal Aviation Administration (FAA), and can take the aircraft out of service for more than forty-five days. The ruling will be useful to taxpayers in other lines of business to establish that the cost of regular major maintenance of equipment, not just aircraft, does not need to be capitalized.

The IRS in Revenue Ruling 2001-4 has gone a long way toward eliminating any residual fears practitioners may have had after *INDOPCO* that items properly treated as deductible repairs would become a bone of contention. Scheduled maintenance of equipment, designed from the outset to preserve an asset's estimated useful life, should not require capitalization even if the costs are substantial and the maintenance is required by a government agency with regulatory power. (D. Culp, R.M. Brown & C. Conjura, 94 Journal of Taxation 86.)

"Aircraft maintenance can be deductible or capital cost" (2001). In Revenue Ruling 2001-4, the IRS considers three situations and explains whether aircraft maintenance costs are deductible business expenses or must be capitalized. (66 Practical Tax Strategies 190.)

"Business buyer must capitalize assumed liability" (2001). A corporation that assumed liability for a patent infringement lawsuit against a business that it acquired had to capitalize the payment it made in satisfaction of that suit, according to the Tax Court in *Illinois Tool Works, Inc.* (2001). (67 Practical Tax Strategies 178.)

"Capitalize salaries but not overhead for contract acquisition" (2001). In a divided opinion, the Tax Court held that salaries and benefits paid by a corporation to acquire automobile financing installment contracts had to be capitalized in *Lychuk* (2001). On the other hand, the corporation could deduct related overhead expenses. (67 Practical Tax Strategies 48.)

"Commissions paid to external agents currently deductible" (2001). Residual commissions paid to third-party sales agents are currently deductible as ordinary and necessary expenses under Section 162 and should not be capitalized under Section 263, according to FSA 200114008. (67 Practical Tax Strategies 49.)

"Court offers 'capital' test for characterizing expenses" (2001). The debate over whether to capitalize certain corporate takeover expenses or treat them as current deductions continues to rage. For the acquiring company, the tax treatment of merger and acquisition (M&A) costs is reasonably clear—generally the costs are nondeductible capital expenditures. For the acquired or target company, however, correct application of the rules has been more difficult because the lower courts and the IRS often have arrived at different interpretations regarding which expenses should be capitalized and which ones qualify as current expense deductions. The continued proliferation of mergers and acquisitions has exacerbated the problem.

First, the authors discuss legislative and administrative interpretations. Section 162(a) contains the basic criteria that most expenses must meet in order to be claimed as deductions. Because of the wide scope of Section 162, its practical application has evolved largely from the vast body of case law over the years. As a further complication, many business expenses that would be allowable deductions under Section 162(a) are limited or disallowed by other Code provisions, including Section 263(a), which provides the general rule for expense capitalization.

Then, the authors address the Supreme Court's decision in *INDOPCO, Inc.* (1992) and related cases. The Supreme Court's holding in *INDOPCO* is often cited in determining whether expenses qualify as current deductions or must be capitalized. In large part, *INDOPCO* was decided by the Supreme Court to clear the disagreement among circuit courts in their interpretations of an earlier Supreme Court opinion, *Lincoln Savings and Loan Association* (1971). The disagreement and confusion continues, however, fueled by the IRS's more aggressive pursuit of capitalization since the *INDOPCO* ruling. Now an Eighth Circuit case, *Wells Fargo & Co.* (2000), appears to have identified the primary source of the confusion and provides a reliable methodology for determining whether an expenditure should be capitalized or expensed. Although some gray area remains, the Eighth Circuit appears to have removed a great deal of ambiguity regarding the deduction versus capitalization issue.

In *Wells Fargo*, the Eighth Circuit designed a flow-chart model to facilitate the evaluation of an expense to determine whether it should be capitalized or deducted. The court's model for evaluating expenditures to determine whether they should be capitalized or expensed proceeds in a progression of three distinct layers:

Layer 1. Did the subject expenditure result in a benefit beyond the tax year?

Layer 2. Did the expenditure create or enhance a physical capital asset?

Layer 3. The court plainly states that at the third layer of evaluation there are no easy answers. Taking into consideration all the facts and circumstances of each case, the evaluation becomes much more qualitative in nature. (E.C. Hume & A. Canales, 66 Practical Tax Strategies 260.)

"Court requires corporation to capitalize several expenditures" (2001). The Sixth Circuit, in *United Dairy Farmers, Inc.* (2001), has affirmed a district court decision by requiring that soil remediation costs, corporate reorganization accounting fees, and site study payments be capitalized. (67 Practical Tax Strategies 307.)

"Deducting the costs of implementing a new information system despite IRS objections" (2001). Separating the component cost elements as carefully as possible will be the key to deducting as much as possible of the costs of an enterprise resource system or other new type of information system. The IRS has issued no formal guidance for taxpayers but has instructed its agents to deny deductions and require capitalization for anything other than internal software costs. Taxpayers must be careful to justify various elements, and in particular to avoid the fatal badge of "re-engineering processes."

First, the authors discuss software costs, including IRS assumptions and treatment of related costs, such as training and consulting fees. The tax recovery rules for computer software create a major distinction between purchased and self-developed software. Purchased software must be capitalized, whereas the costs of self-developed software may be deducted. The IRS has allowed a deduction for self-developed software for many years, principally because it resembles research and development (R&D) expenditures deductible under Section 174.

Nevertheless, the IRS takes a narrow view as to what constitutes software development. Purchased software is capitalized and amortized over thirty-six months unless it is purchased as a package with hardware. If the software is packaged with hardware and the cost is not separately stated, it should be depreciated over the life of the hardware. The distinction between purchased and self-developed software turns on which party is at risk for the functional utility of the software.

The primary ambiguity is what actually constitutes software development. It is instructive to compare the IRS approach to this issue with the accounting rules. The AICPA notes that internal software development normally occurs in three stages. In the first or preliminary stage, the project is conceptualized and alternatives are evaluated. In the second or application development stage, the source code is written and installed into hardware. The third stage consists of training and maintenance activities. Only costs incurred during the second stage are to be capitalized because future benefits become probable only at that point. Costs subsequent to application are in the nature of maintenance costs and are expensed.

The IRS's approach is radically different. The preliminary or conceptual stage is not recognized at all. Internal software development is narrowly construed as simply writing source code. Costs that cannot be specifically identified with writing source code may be capitalized.

Then, the authors advise on planning for deductions. Prudent planning suggests segregating the component costs of information systems upgrades for two reasons. First, field agents are instructed to view the deduction possibilities more favorably for certain components and proper segregation could thus shrink the amount at issue in an audit. Second, lumping the costs of upgrades into large accounts, such as "consulting," invites the IRS to place the burden on the company to show that a major portion of the total is not re-engineering. (L. Maples, R. Finegan & L.D. Maples, 95 Journal of Taxation 267.)

"INDOPCO: a tiger, a pussycat, or a creature somewhere in between?" (2001). In the years since the Supreme Court decided *INDOPCO, Inc.* (1992)—the capitalization-versus-expense controversy in the context of a friendly takeover—predictions about the dire consequences for taxpayers have proven to be somewhat overstated. Neither the courts nor the IRS has taken the presumption in favor of capitalization and future benefits reasoning to the lengths that practitioners once feared.

After providing background on the case, the authors discuss the IRS's position since *INDOPCO*. In Revenue Ruling 94-12, the IRS clarified that the National Office's position on *INDOPCO* was that nothing had changed with respect to repairs of tangible assets. In many areas, including advertising, employee training, ISO 9000 certification, and business investigations, either the IRS has conceded deductibility or the courts have affirmed such treatment. Where the IRS has taken a harder line, it has not met with much success at the appellate level.

Then, the author considers the impact of *INDOPCO* on case law. The elimination of the "separate and distinct asset" test comes as no surprise, since logically the Supreme Court in *Lincoln Savings & Loan Association* (1971) never created one, as demonstrated by the Eighth Circuit in *Wells Fargo & Co.* (2000).

Perhaps the most favorable result from the progeny of *INDOPCO* has been the universal agreement that the expenditures to expand an existing business are not subject to capitalization under the future benefits theory. The only case in which this settled principle was not available to the taxpayer was in the Tax Court decision in *FMR Corp.* (1998), where the IRS was able to relate business expansion–type expenditures to specific contracts. Perhaps that will be the IRS's approach in the future.

Another taxpayer-friendly result of recent cases is the courts' reluctance to allocate costs to intangible assets. Perhaps we are in a period comparable to the period before the full absorption costing regulations and the uniform capitalization rules for tangible assets, and the courts are slow to proceed in attaching costs to the intangibles, especially where the costs do not fluctuate widely and allowing the deduction will not distort income. (W.E. Seago & D.L. Crumbley, 94 Journal of Taxation 14.)

"Section 179 speeds up deductions for equipment purchases" (2001). S.C. Colburn, 66 Practical Tax Strategies 361. (*Digested under* Depreciation and Amortization, page 34.)

"Sixth Circuit affirms capitalization of expenses relating to S election" (2001). 3 Business Entities, No. 6, 42. (*Digested under* S Corporations, page 189.)

"Tax Court rejects de minimis expensing rule" (2001). The Tax Court, in *Alacare Home Health Services, Inc.* (2001), rejected a corporation's policy of expensing all items costing less than $500, regardless of the items' useful life. (67 Practical Tax Strategies 110.)

"Tax Court requires capitalization of payment for relief of a burdensome lease" (2001). D.L. Surkin, 95 Journal of Taxation 298. (*Digested under* Depreciation and Amortization, page 35.)

Personal Expenses Versus Business Expenses

"Attorney's fees incurred to protect employment deductible" (2001). A taxpayer who incurred legal fees in connection with the termination of his employment and the pursuit of a civil rights action was entitled to deduct the portion of the fees that was attributable to the protection of his employment status, in *Remkiewicz*, a 2001 Tax Court case. (66 Practical Tax Strategies 182.)

"Rental deductions are more restrictive at home" (2001). Even those with a bona fide, year-round rental use of portions of their residence can be subject to the deduction limits of Section 280A, according to the Tax Court in *Morcos* (2001). (67 Practical Tax Strategies 184.)

"Renting home office to employer can reduce deductions" (2001). A taxpayer who rents a portion of his or her home to his or her employer and uses it in performing services as an employee may deduct home mortgage interest, real property taxes, and personal casualty losses, but not other home office expenses, according to ITA 200121070. (67 Practical Tax Strategies 184.)

Travel and Entertainment

"Automobile standard mileage rates rise for 2001" (2001). Taxpayers who use their automobiles for business, medical, or moving purposes and calculate their deductions using the standard mileage rates are in line for bigger deductions in 2001, according to Revenue Procedure 2000-48. (66 Practical Tax Strategies 117.)

"Drive up tax benefits for a variety of travel costs" (2001). Travel, including commuting in some instances, can be the source of deductions, provided substantiation is adequate and not too much personal recreation is added into the trips.

First, the authors discuss mixed business and pleasure travel expenses. Section 162 allows a deduction for all the ordinary and necessary expenses paid or incurred in carrying on a trade or business. Travel expenses are deductible only if a valid business reason exists for the travel. The tax law looks to whether the trip is primarily for business or pleasure. A business reason can be established through either Section 162 or Section 212.

Second, the authors consider education. Section 274(m)(2) specifically disallows deductions for expenses of travel as education.

Third, the authors address conventions and cruises. When the mode of travel is considered entertainment, the tax law places restrictions on the deductibility of the travel expenses even when the travel was primarily for business.

Next, the authors explain the substantiation requirements for travel expense deductions, placement on the tax return, and the difference between reasonable and lavish or extravagant expenses.

Then, the authors turn to charitable contributions and medical expenses. Some travel expenses may qualify as charitable contributions or medical expenses.

Finally, the authors discuss commuting expenses. (S. Burnett & D.P. Smith, 67 Practical Tax Strategies 328.)

"Employer's deduction can exceed income to employee for jet use" (2001). In a case of first impression, the Eighth Circuit ruled in *Sutherland Lumber-Southwest, Inc.* (2001) that a corporation's deduction for providing its employees with nonbusiness use of a corporate jet was not limited to the compensation imputed to the employees. (67 Practical Tax Strategies 127.)

"IRS revises per-diem rates for travel reimbursements" (2001). The IRS has raised the per-diem rates that employers may pay employees on business-travel status while still qualifying for simplified substantiation rules, according to Revenue Procedure 2001-47. (67 Practical Tax Strategies 315.)

"Mass transit commuting exclusion has mass appeal" (2001). T.A. Cardello, 67 Practical Tax Strategies 349. (*Digested under* Fringe Benefits, page 67.)

"Pack tax deductions into employee relocation programs" (2001). Provided distance and minimum-period-of-employment tests are met, favorable tax treatment is available for work-related moves; the precise rules depend on who is footing the bill.

First, the authors discuss the deductible versus nondeductible moving expenses when the company is not footing the bill. Even if a company is not paying for its employees to relocate, employees can still save money on the move. The Code permits employees to deduct certain relocation expenses for an employment-related move from their gross income. For a move to qualify as employment-related, the move must bear a reasonable proximity both in time and place to the commencement of a job. The "job," however, may be a new job, the same job, or a first job. Accordingly, all employees—including those who are returning to the workforce or entering the workforce for the first time—are eligible for the deduction.

Then, the authors address situations in which the company is footing the bill. Sections 82 and 162 generally permit employers to claim any reimbursements for employee moving expenses as ordinary and necessary business expenses. (M.S. Melbinger & D.B. Hoetger, 67 Practical Tax Strategies 10.)

"Purchase versus lease: directions for business car users" (2001). Many factors need to be considered, but differences in marginal tax rates have little impact on whether a taxpayer is better off purchasing or leasing a car.

First, the authors provide background on Sections 162(a) and 280F. Taxpayers are permitted under Section 162(a) to annually deduct ordinary and necessary expenses paid or incurred in carrying on a trade or business. Expenses associated with using an automobile for business purposes qualify under this rule. Purchased autos are depreciable under MACRS. Section 280F, however, imposes annual limits on depreciation deductions for passenger automobiles.

Then, the authors discuss the model developed for the article to determine whether to purchase or lease. The model takes into account numerous variables that are important in the lease or purchase decision. Relevant variables under one or both options include: (1) purchase price of the automobile; (2) interest rate on loan to finance the purchase (purchase option); (3) term of loan (purchase option); (4) term of lease (lease option); (5) amount of down payment; (6) date of purchase or lease; (7) capital gains rate; (8) pre-tax earnings rate on alternate investment opportunities; (9) percentage of business use; (10) marginal federal income tax rate; (11) residual asset value at end of lease; and (12) depreciation method (purchase option).

Finally, the authors consider the results from using the model to evaluate various assumptions regarding the lease versus buy decision as it relates to automobiles used for business. It would be an unusual situation in which the taxpayer could negotiate a lease that would be more advantageous than a purchase. (S.J. Baxendale, W.D. Stout & R.M. Walter, 66 Practical Tax Strategies 215.)

"Resort owned by shareholders avoided entertainment facility rules" (2001). Expenses incurred by a corporation in connection with the use of a resort for business meetings were not disallowed under Section 274(a)(1)(B) because they were not items with respect to a facility used in connection with an entertainment activity, according to TAM 200041001. (66 Practical Tax Strategies 55.)

"Staying away from home too long changed tax home" (2001). The Tax Court, in *Harris* (2001), held that the taxpayer could not deduct living expenses incurred while working at a "temporary" job in a distant city because the job lasted longer than a year. (66 Practical Tax Strategies 312.)

"What's wrong with a free lunch? Employers may be surprised when the 50 percent limit applies" (2001). The Code mandates a series of requirements that must be analyzed and satisfied if the employer wishes to deduct the full cost of the mundane box lunches served to employees at a business meeting. The employer has to consider that the tax cost of the meals will be increased by the application of the 50 percent deduction limit for meals and entertainment mandated by Section 274(n)(1). The taxpayer needs to put a procedure in place to identify those meals that satisfy statutory exceptions to the 50 percent deduction limit to avoid the statutory reduction. Unfortunately, plenty of tax ingredients go into serving a "free" business lunch.

After reviewing the rules regarding deduction for entertaining clients or employees, the authors discuss TAM 200030001. In TAM 200030001, the IRS addressed the three criteria for determining whether meals provided by a taxpayer at a business conference were de minimis fringe benefits: (1) the frequency with which the benefit is provided; (2) the value of the benefit; and (3) the administrative impracticability of accounting for the benefit.

In the TAM, the IRS ruled that the cost of food and beverages provided by the taxpayer (a brokerage firm) to its independent contractor representatives (brokers) at national and regional meetings was not a de minimis fringe benefit and was therefore not excepted from the 50 percent deduction limit under Section 274(n)(2)(B).

Then, the authors discuss social activities for employees. An argument for complete deductibility of employee meal expenses could be based on the exception to

15

the 50 percent deduction limit under Section 274(n)(2)(A) for recreational and social activities primarily for the benefit of employees who are not highly compensated. In TAM 200030001, the IRS found that the meals and cocktail parties provided by the taxpayer to the brokers "served a significant business purpose" and were not recreational or social in nature. Thus, the exception was not available. (H.W. Hans & A.S. Kurtz, 94 *Journal of Taxation* 151.)

C

CANCELLATION OF INDEBTEDNESS

(*See also* Bankruptcy)

"**Courts follow Supreme Court lead on effect of COD income on S corporation basis**" **(2001).** 3 Business Entities, No. 3, 56. (*Digested under* S Corporations, page 185.)

"**Farmer recognized discharge-of-indebtedness income on debt payoff**" **(2001).** In *Jelle* (2001), the taxpayers were involved in agricultural enterprises, including the operation of a dairy farm. In 1991, the taxpayers no longer were able to make monthly mortgage payments to the Farmers Home Administration (FmHA) due to falling milk production. They ultimately entered into an agreement with the FmHA to buy out the loans at ''net recovery value'' (i.e, the amount that would be received from liquidation, reduced by certain liens and other costs). They also agreed to pay additional amounts to the FmHA if they subsequently sold the underlying collateral for more than the recovery value during the next 10 years. The agreement, however, did not require an interest charge, current payments, or a certain amount due. The Tax Court agreed with the government that the taxpayers recognized discharge-of-indebtedness income as of the payoff date. (3 Business Entities, No. 2, 56.)

"**Supreme Court hands taxpayers a victory in *Gitlitz*, but will Congress take it away?**" **(2001).** R.M. Lipton, 94 Journal of Taxation 133. (*Digested under* S Corporations, page 189.)

"**Supreme Court hands windfall to owners of insolvent S corporations**" **(2001).** M.R. Martin & J.E. Tierney, 66 Practical Tax Strategies 202. (*Digested under* S Corporations, page 190.)

"**Supreme Court, reversing Tenth Circuit, holds that excluded COD income increases stock basis of S corporation shareholders**" **(2001).** 3 Business Entities, No. 1, 53. (*Digested under* S Corporations, page 191.)

"**The subchapter S discharge of indebtedness issue: Supreme Court picks law over equity**" **(2001).** R.A. Shaw, 3 Business Entities, No. 3, 4. (*Digested under* S Corporations, page 193.)

CAPITAL EXPENDITURES

(*See* Business Expenses—Deduction Versus Capital Expenditure; Depreciation and Amortization)

CAPITAL GAINS AND LOSSES

"**Carryover basis: planning and drafting issues**" **(2001).** D.R. Hodgman, 28 Estate Planning 611. (*Digested under* Estate Planning, page 42.)

"**Deemed-sale election can lock-in capital gain treatment**" **(2001).** The Taxpayer Relief Act of 1997 (TRA '97) created a limited opportunity election to treat a capital or Section 1231 asset as if it had been sold and reacquired as of January 1, 2001. The purpose of the election was to create a post-2000 holding period so that any post-election appreciation could be eligible for the special 18 percent tax rate provided for in Section 1(h)(2)(B).

First, the author discusses election mechanics. The election is made in the manner specified by the IRS and, once made, is irrevocable. The instructions to the 2000 Form 4797 indicate that the election process involves doing the following: (1) including the gain from the deemed sale on the tax return for the year that includes the date of the deemed sale and (2) attaching a statement to the return that states the taxpayer is making an election under Section 311 of TRA '97 and specifying the assets for which the election is made.

Then, the author considers the tax consequences of controlled-entity land sales and deemed-sale elections, including advantages and constraints on using the election. (J.R. Hamill, 67 Practical Tax Strategies 4.)

"Landlord's lease termination payments to tenant were capital gain" (2001). In Letter Ruling 200045019, the IRS determined that payments made to a tenant to terminate certain leasehold rights were capital gain. (94 Journal of Taxation 118.)

"Lease surrender payment is taxed as capital gain" (2001). 66 Practical Tax Strategies 53. (*Digested under* Real Estate, page 172.)

"No gain on guarantor's transfer of pledged stock" (2001). The Tax Court held that a taxpayer did not realize gain on the transfer of stock that he pledged to a bank to guarantee loans made to his son's corporation because the transfer was not in satisfaction of his own liability, in *Friedland* (2001). (67 Practical Tax Strategies 311.)

"On-line transactions intensify trader versus investor question" (2001). The Internet has expanded the ranks of day traders, who may be subject to some different—and often more favorable—tax rules than run-of-the-mill stock investors.

First, the authors discuss the classification of the taxpayer. If the scope of the taxpayer's activities is sufficient to be a trade or business, the next determination is whether the taxpayer is a trader or a dealer. A dealer expects to earn a profit from finding a buyer who will purchase from the dealer for more than the dealer's cost. This excess or mark-up represents remuneration for the dealer's labor as a middleman. In contrast, a trader depends on a rise in value or an advantageous purchase price to profit from a transaction. Thus, although both the trader and the dealer are engaged in a trade or business, only the dealer has customers.

Then, the authors address income and expense treatment and the mark-to-market (MTM) election. Based on case law, committed day traders can reasonably be classified as engaged in the business of being a stock trader. "Committed day traders" are those who trade often, hold stock a short period, and trade consistently throughout the year. The business classification brings with it not only the ability to claim deductions for adjusted gross income (AGI), but also the avoidance of the potential loss of many deductions by those investors who are subject to the alternative minimum tax.

In addition, the business classification comes without the usual burden of the self-employment tax and the loss of capital gains rates on long-term transactions. Traders, however, are still subject to the $3,000 capital loss limitations and the wash-sale rules, although even these may be avoided by electing MTM treatment.

Electing MTM is not a costless election. It involves potential IRS scrutiny when the election is filed and requires that long-term investments be identified as such on the day of their purchase if the advantage of the long-term capital gains rates are to be obtained.

Tax advisors should also be wary as clear guidance is lacking on how the IRS and the courts will react to a potentially large influx of taxpayers being classified as stock traders. (J. Robison & R.S. Mark, 66 Practical Tax Strategies 80.)

"Potential reduction in capital gains tax rate requires new planning and new recordkeeping now" (2001). Thanks to changes Congress made in the Taxpayer Relief Act of 1997, there is suddenly a new capital gains bracket for taxpayers in the 15 percent income tax bracket, and a new election for other taxpayers, who get their own new bracket beginning in 2006.

First, the author discusses assets eligible for the 18 percent maximum long-term capital gains rate. In order for the "upper income" taxpayer to be eligible for the 18 percent maximum long-term capital gains rate instead of the 20 percent rate, the following requirements must be met:

(1) The asset must be held for more than five years (i.e., at least five years and one day) so that the gain will meet the Section 1(h)(9) definition of "qualified five-year gain." Since the new holding period became effective January 1, 2001, the earliest year that an individual can benefit from the new lower capital gains rate is 2006.

(2) The asset must have been acquired (purchased, inherited, etc.) after 2000, i.e., January 1, 2001, or later. A special election, to treat certain assets held on January 1, 2001, as sold and then reacquired on the same date, may be made on the tax return for 2001. For publicly traded assets, the key date for revaluation is January 2, 2001, the first trading day in 2001.

Next, the author considers the election. The election to report the deemed sale is made on the taxpayer's 2001 return filed in 2002. The "sales price" used for publicly traded stock is the closing price (not an average price) on January 2, 2001. Although the election is irrevocable, an individual taxpayer will have the benefit of hindsight, i.e., the movement in value throughout 2001 and most of 2002 (with extensions of time to file).

Then, the author addresses tax planning issues. Since all of this planning is to save 2 percent sometime in the future, is it worth it? The answer is "yes" if the potential tax savings are foreseen to be significant, or if the fair market value on January 1, 2001 (January 2, 2001, for publicly traded stock) approximates the taxpayer's adjusted tax basis (generally its cost), or in some other instances. The answer would be "no," however, if the current tax cost or transactional costs (including professional fees) are projected to be significant.

Finally, the author turns to the 8 percent long-term capital gain tax rate rules for individuals and married couples in the 15 percent tax bracket. (A.E. Weiner, 94 Journal of Taxation 156.)

"Sales or exchanges of interests in pass thrus" (2001). D.M. O'Leary, 3 Business Entities, No. 1, 34. (*Digested under* Partnerships—In General, page 143.)

"Single sale generates multiple types of capital gains" (2001). Final regulations offer guidance on segregating capital gain from the sale or exchange of an interest in a partnership, S corporation, or trust into several potential tax rate baskets.

First, the author discusses partnerships. In general, Section 741 provides that the sale or exchange of a partnership interest is treated as a sale or exchange of a capital asset. Such a sale or exchange, therefore, yields capital gain or loss to the selling partner, except to the extent Section 751 applies. Section 751(a) provides that any money or the fair market value of any property received in exchange for a transferor partner's interest attributable to unrealized receivables or inventory items of the partnership are an amount realized from the sale or exchange of property other than a capital asset. Thus, the transaction yields ordinary income or loss. Unrealized receivables and inventory items are collectively referred to as Section 751 property.

Next, the author considers S corporations. A shareholder selling shares in an S corporation must recognize as collectible gain the gain that would be allocable to the transferred shares if the S corporation's collectibles were transferred in a fully taxable transaction for cash immediately prior to the sale of the S corporation shares. The collectible gain is taxed at no more than the maximum rate in Section 1(h) for such types of gain, 28 percent. The shareholder then has residual long-term capital gain equal to the gain that the shareholder would have on the sale of the shares, less the collectible gain. The selling shareholder does not have to take into account the Section 1250 capital gain that may be inherent in the assets of the S corporation.

Then, the author addresses trusts. Just as with partnerships and S corporations, the new regulations provide that a seller of an interest in a trust held for more than one year must recognize collectible gain, taxable at the 28 percent rate, equal to what would be allocated by the trust to the seller if the trust sold for cash its collectibles. The residual long-term capital gain, taxed at a maximum 20 percent, is the total long-term capital gain the beneficiary would recognize on the sale or exchange of an interest in the trust, reduced by the collectible gain. As with S corporations, the requirement imposed on partners and partnerships regarding Section 1250 gain does not apply to gain recognized on the sale or exchange of an interest in a trust.

Finally, the author turns to the holding period of the partnership interest and the contribution of a Section 751 asset. (J. Walsh, 67 Practical Tax Strategies 14.)

CARRYBACKS AND CARRYOVERS

(*See* Capital Gains and Losses; Net Operating Loss; Reorganizations)

CASUALTY LOSSES

(*See* Losses)

CHANGE OF ACCOUNTING METHOD

(*See* Accounting Methods—Change of Accounting Method or Accounting Period)

CHARITABLE CONTRIBUTIONS

(*See also* Tax-Exempt Organizations; Trusts and Trust Taxation; Valuation of Property)

"Charitable estate planning with retirement benefits" (2001). Federal tax laws that grant tax advantages for contributions to retirement plans are intended to encourage savings. These laws are designed to defer, rather than eliminate, federal income taxes. The corollary requirement is that income tax must be paid on retirement assets when received by the taxpayer or his or her

beneficiary. The combined effect of federal income tax and estate tax on retirement assets held until death can be devastating.

After providing background on income in respect of a decedent, estate taxes, and the combined impact of the taxes, the authors discuss planning techniques. The potentially confiscatory taxation of retirement assets held until death is a serious estate planning concern. The planning techniques discussed in this article may defer and/or minimize such taxes. These techniques ultimately involve diverting at least a portion of the retirement assets from non-charitable beneficiaries to charity. In some circumstances, though, life insurance (such as insurance on the life of the spouse or another individual beneficiary, or insurance on the life of the plan participant) can be a practical way to replace the wealth that will pass to charity. (S.J. Schlesinger & D.L. Mark, 28 Estate Planning 390.)

"Charitable fundraising involves more tax complexity than meets the eye" (2001). This first part of a two-part article discusses charitable fundraising tax issues viewed from the charity's perspective and primarily focuses on the charity's tax-reporting obligations. It covers issues ranging from the relatively simple tax reporting requirements of cash contributions to the more difficult issues arising from property donations and fundraising events that include raffles, auctions, and door prizes.

First, the authors address general reporting rules and rules for property worth over $5,000. Two of the most recent significant changes in charitable fundraising tax reporting were the enactment of Sections 6115 and 170(f)(8). Both provisions have placed the initial reporting responsibilities with the charity. Under Section 6115, when a charity provides a benefit to a donor in return for a donation, the charity must advise the donor of the value of the benefit received. Under Section 170(f)(8), a charity that receives $250 or more in cash or property must issue an acknowledgment statement to the donor before he or she files a tax return. If it fails to do so, the donor will not be able to claim a charitable deduction.

Regulation § 1.170A-13(c) provides that a donor will be denied a deduction under Section 170 for the contribution of any single item or group of similar items (other than cash or publicly traded securities) with a value in excess of $5,000 unless certain substantiation requirements are met. The first of these is that the donor must obtain a qualified appraisal of the donated property.

Then, the authors consider transfer reporting responsibilities. One of the "checks" Congress designed to help ensure that the value donors placed on donated property does not exceed fair market value was to institute the two-year disposition rule in Section 6050L.

Finally, the authors turn to application of tax shelter abuse rules, quid pro quo reporting rules, disregarded benefits, part gift/part benefit situations, and raffles. (J.V. Woodhull & V. Jones, 12 Journal of Taxation of Exempt Organizations 213.)

"Charitable gift planning after the 2001 Tax Act" (2001). The Economic Growth and Tax Relief Reconciliation Act of 2001 (the Act) is a very odd tax act, particularly with respect to its estate and gift tax provisions. It is touted as the repeal of the estate and generation-skipping tax. That is true for 2010, but only for 2010.

First, the author discusses the effect on charitable planning through 2009. The Act really is a nonevent when it comes to charitable planning through 2009. There may be fewer individuals who will need to plan because the exemption amount is larger, but there will still be a need for charitable planning by many wealthy individuals. Indeed, many of the charitable giving vehicles are used for income tax planning as well, and the Act will not affect that use, even with its lowered income tax rates. Given that the repeal of the estate tax is only to last for one year and that the gift tax is to remain, the Act is unlikely to have any effect on charitable testamentary planning.

Then, the author considers planning after 2009. Should future legislation make the 2010 regime permanent, the effect would be far more pronounced. Charitable planning will survive, but the bulk of the planning will

revolve around income taxes. (C.D. Duronio, 13 Taxation of Exempts 146.)

"Charitable giving tax bill leaves the House for an uncertain Senate future" (2001). On July 19, 2001, the House of Representatives passed the Charitable Solutions Act of 2001 (H.R. 7) by a near party-line vote of 233-198 (only fifteen Democrats and four Republicans breaking ranks). Controversy over the bill's "charitable choice" provisions, however, make its chances in the Senate problematic. (13 Taxation of Exempts 92.)

"'Charitable lid' formula used in connection with FLP disregarded" (2001). In FSA 200122011, the IRS did not respect the use of a formula gift in which increased valuations arguably would be offset by a corresponding charitable deduction. (95 Journal of Taxation 116.)

"Charitable remainder trusts: Final regulations on prevention of abuse of CRTs" (2001). S.J. Schlesinger & D.L. Mark, 28 Estate Planning 185. (*Digested under* Trusts and Trust Taxation, page 247.)

"Charitable remainder trusts require more than good drafting" (2001). C.J. Langstraat & A.M. Cagle, 66 Practical Tax Strategies 94. (*Digested under* Trusts and Trust Taxation, page 247.)

"Charting the interacting provisions of the charitable contribution deduction for individuals" (2001). This article is organized around an updated version of a flow chart published in 1974, 1985, and 1988. The flow chart reflects the changes made to the Code since then. Among the more important provisions passed by Congress are the following: (1) unrealized gain on certain charitable contributions of appreciated capital assets is not treated as a tax preference item after 1992; (2) numerous adjustments have been made to both ordinary and capital gain tax rates; and (3) Congress has stiffened the recordkeeping and valuation requirements for charitable contributions.

First, the authors discuss the rules regarding the recipient organization, the type of property donated, and interrelationship of percentage limitations. The flow chart in the article provides a step-by-step approach to determining the deduction allowed an individual for a contribution of cash, long-term capital gain (LTCG) property, or ordinary income property to either a public charity or a private nonoperating foundation.

The distinction between the public charity and the private nonoperating foundation is important because it may affect the total contribution a donor can deduct from adjusted gross income in arriving at taxable income. The tax treatment afforded the public charity is generally more favorable than that afforded the private nonoperating foundation.

The most common gift is one of cash. The two general categories of property contributed to charity are LTCG property and ordinary income property, with the latter category including short-term capital gain property.

The flow chart in the article is based on the premise that an individual contributes property (in any one year) to either a public charity or a private nonoperating foundation. Should an individual contribute property to both types of charities in the same year, an additional rule must be considered. The deduction generated by a contribution to a private nonoperating foundation is limited to the lesser of: (1) 30 percent (20 percent for LTCG property) of the donor's adjusted gross income (AGI) or (2) the excess of 50 percent of the donor's AGI minus the amount of the donation qualifying for the regular 50 percent deduction ceiling for public charities. This additional rule does not affect the tax treatment of contributions to a public charity, but it may reduce the deduction allowed for contributions to a private nonoperating foundation.

Then, the authors consider tax-planning strategies involving bargain sales, sales versus gifts of appreciated property, sales versus gifts of loss property, and determining the donee.

Finally, the authors address recordkeeping and valuation requirements and quid pro quo contributions. There are a range of recordkeeping and, in certain cases, valua-

tion requirements, that become more extensive as the size of the contribution increases.

A quid pro quo contribution is a transfer to a qualified charitable organization made partly as a contribution and partly in return for goods or services provided to the donor. If the quid pro quo contribution exceeds $75 in value, the charitable organization must provide a written statement informing the donor of the limit on the amount of the deduction and providing a good-faith estimate of the value of the goods and services provided to the donor by the charity. (J.L. Wittenbach & K. Milani, 13 Taxation of Exempts 9.)

"Charting the provisions of the charitable contribution deduction for corporations" (2001). In 1975, 1983, and again in 1988, the authors developed and then altered a flow chart that illustrated the impact of cash and property gifts made by corporations. This article is organized around an updated version of that flow chart. The chart reflects the changes made to Section 170 since passage of the Tax Reform Act of 1986. One such change is that the appreciation on contributed long-term capital gain property is no longer treated as a tax preference item when computing the alternative minimum tax.

First, the authors discuss three components that are critical in measuring the amount of the charitable deduction: (1) the type of recipient organization; (2) the accounting method used by the donating corporation; and (3) the type of property donated. When using the flow chart, the type of organization receiving the donation must be considered first. For purposes of the contribution deduction, a corporation is either a cash-method or an accrual-method taxpayer. The rules on contributions of property cover two main types of property: long-term capital gain property and ordinary income property. The latter category includes short-term capital gain property.

Then, the authors address the overall limitation on the allowable deduction. (K. Milani & J.L. Wittenbach, 13 Taxation of Exempts 125.)

"Diversification and other investment issues of charitable and other trusts" (2001). S.J. Schlesinger & D.L. Mark, 28 Estate Planning 87. (*Digested under* Trusts and Trust Taxation, page 247.)

"Divorce can permit division of CRUT without adverse tax consequences" (2001). 95 Journal of Taxation 117. (*Digested under* Trusts and Trust Taxation, page 248.)

"FASB sets financial accounting standards for gifts through agents and intermediaries" (2001). In its June 1999 pronouncement, Financial Accounting Standard (FAS) 136, Transfers of Assets to a Not-for-Profit Organization or Charitable Trust That Raises or Holds Contributions for Others, the Financial Accounting Standards Board (FASB) clarified the long-standing practice of accounting for assets contributed to a not-for-profit organization or charitable trust, and delineated standards for similar situations that should not be characterized as contributions. With these clarifications and revisions, the new standards are designed to establish a consistent vocabulary and structure for contribution discussions. (M.L. Thomas, 12 Journal of Taxation of Exempt Organizations 229.)

"IRS issues new regulations for charitable trusts" (2001). C.D. Duronio, 12 Journal of Taxation of Exempt Organizations 226. (*Digested under* Trusts and Trust Taxation, page 249.)

"Let the donor beware of the charitable family limited partnership" (2001). C.D. Duronio, 12 Journal of Taxation of Exempt Organizations 272. (*Digested under* Partners and Partnerships—Family Limited Partnerships, page 146.)

"Measuring life for charitable lead trusts restricted" (2001). 66 Practical Tax Strategies 184. (*Digested under* Trusts and Trust Taxation, page 250.)

"New regulations sanction 'accelerated' charitable lead trusts" (2001). R.D. Van Dolson, 28 Estate Planning 162. (*Digested under* Trusts and Trust Taxation, page 250.)

"Planning to meet a range of donor needs with 'flip' charitable remainder unitrusts" (2001). M.A.W. McKinnon, 12 Journal of Taxation of Exempt Organizations 253. (*Digested under* Trusts and Trust Taxation, page 251.)

"Pledge of stock options provides charitable deduction for corporation" (2001). 95 Journal of Taxation 374. (*Digested under* Stock Options, page 227.)

"President Bush presents his tax plans for charitable giving" (2001). President Bush has proposed four tax law changes to increase charitable contributions.

First, the authors discuss the nonitemizer charitable deduction. Enacting the nonitemizer deduction would encourage giving by the tens of millions of lower- and middle-income Americans who currently receive no tax incentive for their charitable gifts.

Next, the authors consider the IRA charitable rollover. The IRA rollover would encourage middle- and upper-income Americans who have excess retirement savings to share their good fortune with others through increased charitable giving.

Then, the authors address the targeted charity tax credit. President Bush stated that he will propose federal legislation that would encourage states to provide tax credits for charitable contributions addressing poverty and its impact.

Finally, the authors turn to the corporate percentage limit. President Bush has proposed increasing the limit on corporate charitable deductions.

President Bush has also proposed repeal of the federal estate and gift tax. However, preserving the estate tax, with its incentive for charitable bequests, would encourage the wealthiest Americans to continue to provide the leadership gifts so important to the continued vitality of the charitable sector. (R.A. Boisture, C.E. Livingston & K.A. Gurdin, 12 Journal of Taxation of Exempt Organizations 235.)

"Settlement of nondeductible bequest got deduction" (2001). A transfer directly to a municipality under the terms of a settlement agreement between the charitable and non-charitable beneficiaries of a trust qualified for an estate tax charitable deduction, in TAM 200128005. (67 Practical Tax Strategies 303.)

"Taxation and the human body: an analysis of transactions involving kidneys" (2001). Given the innovative nature of the living donor registry program (as well as its non-commercial character), it is not surprising that the courts and the IRS have yet to address the income tax treatment to be accorded living kidney exchanges. One finds a threatening analogy, however, in the cases and rulings that deal with sales and donations of blood and breast milk. A review of the law as applied to these transactions presents a good contextual reference for the tax consequences one might anticipate from a living kidney exchange.

After providing background on organ donations in the United States, the author discusses kidney exchanges and gross income, including analogies to cases and rulings dealing with blood and breast milk. The tax law has alternatively characterized the sale or donation of a body product, such as blood, as either the performance of a service or the transfer of property. Although irrelevant for purposes of determining the existence of gross income in the case of a sale, this distinction is intrinsic to the question of whether the transferor may claim a charitable contribution deduction where no consideration accompanies the transferee.

Then, the author considers kidney donations and charitable contributions. Regardless of whether a business purpose is involved, transactions in human body parts may have unexpected tax consequences. The conflicting theories—Is the taxpayer performing a service or donating or selling property?—might generate the same result for blood or other renewable items, but not where a solid organ such as a kidney is involved. Medical advances simply have not been met with appropriate changes in tax law. (F.R. Parker, Jr., 94 Journal of Taxation 367.)

"The tax consequences of accepting charitable contributions through a single-member LLC" (2001). C.E. Livingston, 13 Taxation of Exempts 107. (*Digested under* Limited Liability Companies, page 124.)

"The who's who and what's what of charitable fundraisers" (2001). This is the second installment of a two-part article. The first part discussed charitable fundraising tax issues viewed from the charity's perspective and focused on the charity's tax reporting obligations. This part examines motivations for giving that may make a charitable contribution deduction unavailable, the issue of charitable events promoted with for-profit organizations, and unrelated business income.

Section 170(a) provides an income tax deduction for charitable contributions made during the tax year. Generally, the term "charitable contribution" is defined as a contribution or gift to or for the use of an organization exempt from tax under Section 501(c)(3) or a governmental entity.

After providing background on the definition of charitable contribution, the authors discuss the earmarking requirement. A contribution is made "to or for the use of" a charity under Section 170 only if: (1) the charity has full control of the use of the donated funds and (2) the contributor's intent in making the payment is to benefit the charity itself, and not an individual recipient. Similarly, a donor that makes a contribution to a charity, but requires that the charity use the funds for a noncharitable activity, likewise lacks charitable intent and will be denied a Section 170 deduction.

Then, the authors consider the promoter issue. Just who is in receipt of the funds is critical in determining the tax consequences of a fundraising activity. A typical situation that involves the promoter issue occurs when a for-profit business teams up with a charity to raise money through some means that is publicized as either wholly or partially benefiting the charity. For example, the charity and an exclusive golf club can organize a golf outing, with the charity receiving the net proceeds. The relationship of the parties, and their involvement in the fundraiser, will determine whether the gross amount received through the conduct of this activity will be income to the for-profit business or the charity for federal income tax purposes.

Finally, the authors address charities' unrelated business taxable income (UBTI). Section 511(a) imposes a tax on the UBTI of organizations described in Section 501(c)(3). (J.V. Woodhull & V.R. Jones, 13 Taxation of Exempts 23.)

"Transfer of punitive damages to charity does not avoid all tax" (2001). 66 Practical Tax Strategies 250. (*Digested under* Trusts and Trust Taxation, page 256.)

CHARITABLE ORGANIZATIONS

(*See* Tax-Exempt Organizations)

CHURCHES

(*See* Tax-Exempt Organizations)

CIVIL FRAUD

(*See* Interest and Penalties)

CLOSING AGREEMENTS

(*See* Procedure)

COLLECTION OF TAXES

(*See* Assessment and Collection)

COMPENSATION FOR PERSONAL SERVICES

(*See also* Accounting Methods; Business Expenses; Deferred Compensation; Dividends and Distributions; Fringe Benefits; Partners and Partnerships; Pension and Profit-Sharing Plans; Stock Options)

"Adjustments to option prices did not affect status as performance-based compensation" (2001). In Letter Ruling 200051018, adjustments to stock option prices did not cause the options to fail to be performance-based compensation under Regulation § 1.162-27(e)(2). Accordingly, the IRS concluded that the taxpayer could deduct compensation in respect of the options without regard to the limitations of Section 162(m). (94 Journal of Taxation 184.)

"Are amounts paid to shareholder/employees wages or dividend distributions?" (2001). In *Pediatric Surgical Associates, P.C.* (2001), the Tax Court recharacterized a portion of the amounts paid as wages to the shareholder/employees of a C corporation conducting a medical practice as nondeductible dividend distributions. (3 Business Entities, No. 5, 55.)

"Backpay award creates current FICA tax liability" (2001). The Supreme Court, in *Cleveland Indians Baseball Co.* (2001), has held that a backpay award is subject to FICA and FUTA taxes for the year the wages are paid, rather than the years for which the wages are awarded. (67 Practical Tax Strategies 54.)

"Big compensation was reasonable under independent-investor test" (2001). In *Damron Auto Parts, Inc.* (2001), the Tax Court held that an auto parts salvage company could deduct more than double what the IRS said was reasonable compensation for its owner-employee. (67 Practical Tax Strategies 249.)

"Court rejects aggregate assessment of FICA on tips" (2001). The Ninth Circuit affirmed a district court decision in *Fior*

D'Italia, Inc. (2001), holding that the IRS is not authorized to assess an employer's share of FICA taxes on unreported tip income based on an aggregate method without first determining the amount underreported by individual employees. (66 Practical Tax Strategies 306.)

"Deductible performance-based compensation in a short tax year" (2001). In Letter Ruling 200044007, the IRS ruled on whether certain compensation paid by the taxpayer was qualified performance-based compensation and whether the taxpayer's officers with respect to a short tax year were covered employees. (94 Journal of Taxation 122.)

"Employer's deduction can exceed income to employee for jet use" (2001). 67 Practical Tax Strategies 127. (*Digested under* Business Expenses—Travel and Entertainment, page 14.)

"Formula-based compensation included disguised dividend" (2001). The Tenth Circuit in *Eberl's Claim Service, Inc.* (2001) affirmed a Tax Court decision that permitted a closely held corporation to deduct only part of the compensation paid to its shareholder-president. (67 Practical Tax Strategies 126.)

"Grant under stock incentive plan met the requirements for performance-based exception" (2001). A corporation's grant of non-statutory stock options to an executive under a stock incentive plan met the exception for "performance-based compensation" under Section 162(m)(4)(C), in ILM 200133014. (95 Journal of Taxation 313.)

"Income distributed to owner was compensation" (2001). The Tax Court issued two decisions in 2001 regarding the employment tax status of payments made to S corporation owners. *Veterinary Surgical Consultants, P.C.* involved an incorporated veterinarian practice, and the taxpayer in *Yeagle Drywall Co.* was a drywall construction business. In both cases, the court rejected the corporations' attempts to treat all payments to its owners as a distribution of earnings rather than compensation for services. (67 Practical Tax Strategies 373.)

"Payment from former employer was FICA-taxable severance" (2001). A $4.5 million payment received on leaving employment was classified as a fully FICA-taxable severance payment, despite the employee's signing a non-competition agreement in order to receive the funds, according to the Court of Federal Claims in *Donnel* (2001). (67 Practical Tax Strategies 314.)

"Planning helps avert employer tip tax woes" (2001). Circuit courts disagree on whether the IRS can assess the employer portion of the Federal Insurance Contributions Act (FICA) tax on aggregate unreported employee tips without determining how much individual employees underreported.

First, the author reviews the applicable rules, including employee tax, withholding and employer reporting, employer tax, and tip credit rules. The Code requires both employees and employers to pay FICA tax on tips. Employees are required to routinely report their tips to employers. So, in theory at least, employers know what amount to pay employer FICA tax on. Yet, history shows that substantial tip income can go unreported to employers.

Then, the author addresses audits and tip litigation. The IRS in recent years has stepped up its audit scrutiny in the tip arena. Somewhat ironically, though, it is not underreporting employees that the IRS is pursuing. It is employers, who unsurprisingly see this as a misguided law enforcement strategy. Particularly objectionable, from their standpoint, is the IRS examination approach. Lacking employee-specific information, the IRS is content to estimate the unreported tips largely based on aggregate employer sales data mixed with a dose of judgment. The result has been occasionally substantial employer FICA tax assessments and, in response, a spate of employer lawsuits that threaten to spill into the U.S. Supreme Court. Meanwhile, perhaps to blunt criticism, the IRS has developed a tip program that allows participating employers to mitigate employer FICA tax exposure on unreported tips.

The Seventh and Federal Circuits expressly disagree with the notion that the potential imprecision of the IRS's methodology is inimical to an employer-only FICA tax determination or, in general, the IRS's assessment authority. In their view, imprecision merely goes to the proper amount of tax owed.

In contrast, the Ninth Circuit, the only other circuit to rule on the legality of employer-only FICA determinations, rejects the current IRS position. Expressing concern over the potential inaccuracy of the IRS approach, it recently declared in *Fior D'Italia* (2001) that nothing in the Code gives the IRS the authority to use estimates in the FICA tax context.

Finally, the author explores planning considerations and the IRS tip program. At least until the U.S. Supreme Court speaks, employers outside the Ninth Circuit that have tipped employees in their employ risk employer-only tip examinations. To avoid uncertainty, employers, such as restaurant chains, with substantial operations, multiple locations, and many employees may wish to participate in the IRS tip program—the Tip Rate Determination/Education Program. (R.A. Stein, 66 Practical Tax Strategies 337.)

"Reasonable compensation" (2001). Two recent Tax Court cases present marked contrasts in approach to what constitutes reasonable compensation. In *Wagner Construction, Inc.* (2001), the Tax Court determined that compensation paid to two officer/shareholder brothers owning, respectively, 75 percent and 25 percent of the taxpayer's stock, was only deductible as compensation to the stockholders as follows: In 1995, $635,000 of the $1,294,888 claimed; and in 1996, $635,000 of the $1,099,765 claimed. In contrast, the Tax Court in *Damron Auto Parts* (2001) allowed 90 percent of the compensation to the corporate officer/100 percent shareholder to be deducted. (3 Business Entities, No. 5, 52.)

"Sale of goodwill partly converted into deductible compensation" (2001). To the extent a contract for the sale of goodwill was modified to require personal services, the buyer can get current deductions, rather than having to amortize payments, according to

FSA 200106006. This field service advice serves as an example of the benefits available from tax planning. It also implies importance of adequate documentation. (66 Practical Tax Strategies 191.)

"Shareholder-employees' compensation included disguised dividends" (2001). A portion of the salaries paid to shareholder surgeons by a personal services corporation exceeded reasonable allowances for services actually rendered and, therefore, was a disguised dividend rather than deductible compensation, according to the Tax Court in *Pediatric Surgical Associates P.C.* (2001). (67 Practical Tax Strategies 54.)

"Stock buy-back was compensation—not redemption" (2001). A corporation's purchase of its own stock from employees was treated as tax-deductible compensation, rather than as a redemption, for which no deduction would be allowed, in *Riverton Investment Co.* (2001), a Virginia federal district court case. (66 Practical Tax Strategies 318.)

"When are payments from an employer to an employee not 'wages' subject to employment taxes?" (2001). There are various conditions under which employees can earn compensation that is not wage income and, consequently, not subject to federal income tax withholding or FICA and FUTA taxes. Most people understand that interest earned on their bank accounts and rents collected for leasing out an extra room are income to the recipient, but are not wages. What is somewhat less well understood is that employees can receive such non-wage income from their employers under certain circumstances.

The IRS, in its published guidance, has outlined a number of scenarios in which amounts paid to an employee are not wages. Nonetheless, the IRS appears uncomfortable with its published guidance and routinely resists characterizing as non-wage income amounts paid by an employer in accordance with that guidance. This IRS tendency to narrow the published guidance by distinguishing it in ways difficult to predict makes

27

it hard for a taxpayer to determine and comply with the legal authorities. Perhaps the most recent and alarming example of this IRS backtracking can be found in the litigation position taken in *North Dakota State University* (8th Cir. 2001), in which the government argued that a taxpayer-favorable revenue ruling was both of questionable authority and distinguishable.

The courts have contributed to the confusion by applying inconsistent principles to the specific issues brought before them. Consequently, taxpayers struggle to find answers from the limited published guidance, contradictory judicial principles, and the ever-present threat of a new IRS theory for distinguishing the published rulings. The good news is that the IRS's formal guidance exists and taxpayers should be able to rely on reasonable interpretations of that guidance in deciding whether to impose employment taxes. (M.B. Hevener & A.G. Batter, 95 Journal of Taxation 349.)

COMPUTERS

"A framework for conducting state tax research on the Internet" (2001). In our interconnected and information-laden society, lackluster and haphazard approaches to information gathering simply will no longer suffice. The availability of inexpensive new resources on the Internet not only enhances the traditional services provided by tax professionals to their clients but may fundamentally alter the kind of services and standard of competence expected of such professionals.

The Web is one of several important tools for the modern professional. Learning the skill of Internet searching enhances the value of tax professionals to their clientele. This article presents a detailed framework for research that includes Web addresses of important research sites, categories of information research problems, and examples of home pages for several states with websites. (P.D. Callister, 11 Journal of Multistate Taxation and Incentives, No. 7, 26.)

"A platform for international e-commerce tax rules" (2001). W.L. Andrews III, 12 Journal of International Taxation, No. 1, 44. (*Digested under* International Taxation—In General, page 89.)

"A platform for international e-commerce tax rules (Part 2): What should the new rules look like?" (2001). W.L. Andrews III, 12 Journal of International Taxation, No. 8, 10. (*Digested under* International Taxation—In General, page 90.)

"*Cowles Trust Plus* and *TrusTerminator*, Version 10.1, handle estate planning documents with ease" (2001). *Cowles Trust Plus* is software for drafting documents related to an estates and trusts practice. The documents it produces include: (1) individual and joint living trusts, irrevocable trusts, and wills; (2) state-specific supporting documents, such as durable powers of attorney, health care powers and directives, community property agreements, and pour-over wills; and (3) documents related to the dispositive document, including routine client correspondence, Crummey letters, SS4 applications, itemized invoices, customized document covers, and correspondence to trustees, insurance companies, and the IRS.

Trust Plus is designed to be a comprehensive estate planning practice system, and therefore also includes various marketing and estate planning product delivery materials.

The Cowles companion product, *TrusTerminator*, Version 10.1, is a system for automating the documents related to the closing and distribution of trusts and estates. (D.H. Kelley, 28 Estate Planning 508.)

"Deducting the costs of implementing a new information system despite IRS objections" (2001). L. Maples, R. Finegan & L.D. Maples, 95 Journal of Taxation 267. (*Digested under* Business Expenses—Deduction Versus Capital Expenditure, page 12.)

"Information statements can now be provided to taxpayers electronically" (2001). N.J. Foran, 13 Taxation of Exempts 100. (*Digested under* Procedure—In General, page 164.)

"Internet guidance should reconcile old law with a new medium" (2001). R.A. Wexler & A.M. Anderson, 12 Journal of Taxation of Exempt Organizations 187. (*Digested under* Tax-Exempt Organizations—In General, page 231.)

"*Intuitive Estate Planner*, Version 4.2, offers a wealth of helpful estate planning features" (2001). The *Intuitive Estate Planner*, Version 4.2, (IEP) software program, a well-designed and functionally robust software program, was conceptually intended to integrate property inventory and estate tax calculations related to the estate planning practice. It produces its outputs both graphically and in a format that closely resembles the look and feel of spreadsheets. (J.G. Hodges, Jr., 28 Estate Planning 244.)

"IRS OKs e-filing of W-9s by QIs" (2001). After September 3, 2001, the IRS will allow a payor with an electronic system to electronically receive a Form W-9 (Request for Taxpayer Identification Number and Certification) from an investment advisor or introducing broker (qualified intermediary (QI)) authorized to transmit that form as the payee's agent. (12 Journal of International Taxation, No. 5, 11.)

"No-cost Internet resources for estate planners" (2001). The Internet offers a plethora of resources useful in an estate planning practice, that may be accessed free of charge. Available from various government and private websites are tax forms, legal research materials, and even computational programs. (D.H. Kelley, 28 Estate Planning 45.)

"On-line fee-based services for estate planners" (2001). This article examines a number of fee-based on-line services that supply valuable help and information to estate planning practitioners.

First, the author discusses *Leimberg Information Services, Inc.* (*LISI*). *LISI* is a service that provides extensive reports and commentaries on recent legislation, cases, and rulings by nationally recognized practitioners.

Then, the author considers *North American Deed Co.* (*NADC*). *NADC* is a national document preparation and recording service specializing in the preparation and filing of deeds in all jurisdictions.

Finally, the author addresses fee-based appraisals and valuation. The valuation of publicly traded stocks and bonds is addressed online by several services. (D.H. Kelley, 28 Estate Planning 349.)

"On-line transactions intensify trader versus investor question" (2001). J. Robison & R.S. Mark, 66 Practical Tax Strategies 80. (*Digested under* Capital Gains and Losses, page 18.)

"Privacy issues may add to the debate over state taxation of e-commerce" (2001). P.W. Gillet, Jr., 11 Journal of Multistate Taxation and Incentives, No. 6, 12. (*Digested under* State Taxes—In General, page 201.)

"Tax treatment of website development costs: not exactly point and click" (2001). The simplest website is an "information site." This kind of site is cheap to build and maintain, and can be up and running in a few hours. Much more complex, and infinitely more expensive to create, is the "e-commerce site." A functioning e-commerce site can take six to nine months to become fully operational.

First, the author provides background on website components and general accounting issues. Then, the author discusses software costs. Some view all costs related to the development of a website as software development costs. This position is usually favorable to taxpayers because software development costs are currently deductible by an active business under Revenue Procedure 2000-50. If software costs qualify as Section 174 research and experimental (R&E) expenditures, they are deductible even if incurred by a startup company subject to Section 195.

Nevertheless, websites are made up of many components, some of which are software but many of which are not. These components fall into two broad categories: (1) software—including text, data, graphics, sound, and video that are integral to the functioning of the software and (2) content—components that are not integral to software, e.g., graphics, sound, and video files, data (or a database), and text.

When a company pays another to develop its website software, the payment is a development cost only if the company making the payment bears the development risk. Otherwise, the payment represents the purchase of software.

The goal of a website software development project is to create an asset with a useful life extending beyond the year in which development costs are incurred. Under general tax accounting rules, these costs ordinarily would be capitalized under Section 263. Capitalized software costs are amortized over thirty-six months, starting in the year in which the software is placed in service.

Despite this general rule, taxpayers can elect to currently deduct software development costs. Development costs that are R&E expenditures under Section 174 are deductible currently. Even if software development costs do not meet the requirements of Section 174, however, Revenue Procedure 2000-50 says they can be accounted for under rules similar to those of Section 174. That is, they can be deducted currently or capitalized at the option of the taxpayer. (D.E. Hardesty, 94 Journal of Taxation 140.)

"The Internet brings 'cyber-accountability' to the nonprofit sector" (2001). C.K. Craig, 13 Taxation of Exempts 82. (*Digested under* Tax-Exempt Organizations—Disclosure and Information Reporting, page 235.)

"Web resources for tax professionals: update 2001" (2001). Tax professionals can gain quick access to a vast array of tax information on the web, provided they know where to look. This article contains a useful list of web addresses.

Tax professionals frequently need to research particular topics of interest when engaged in tax compliance or tax planning work. Fortunately, several topical indexes exist on the web that allow practitioners to locate information about specific issues

quickly. A listing of some of the more popular topical indexes appears in this article. A good place to start is *Tax Resources on the Web*, a website maintained by Alan Kalman. This site lists more than eighty tax topics in alphabetical order. Clicking on a topic takes the user to a list of resources related to that topic, such as IRS publications, applicable tax forms, and pertinent articles. A screen shot of *Tax Resources on the Web* appears in this article.

Then, the authors address tax news and updates, IRS resources, federal tax research, state and local tax, on-line preparation, e-commerce taxation, professional organizations, mailing lists, newsletters, discussion groups, setting up a firm's website, and other resources. (D. Schmidt & W. Yancey, 66 Practical Tax Strategies 349.)

"What guidance is needed—and not needed—for political and lobbying activities on the Internet" (2001). R.A. Wexler & A.M. Anderson, 12 Journal of Taxation of Exempt Organizations 260. (*Digested under* Tax-Exempt Organizations—Political Organizations and Activities, page 239.)

"What nonprofits should look for as states consider Internet taxation" (2001). N.H. Wright, 12 Journal of Taxation of Exempt Organizations 155. (*Digested under* State Taxes—In General, page 209.)

CONDEMNATION

(*See* Losses)

CONSOLIDATED RETURNS

(*See* Affiliated Corporations)

CONTRIBUTIONS

(*See* Charitable Contributions)

CONTROLLED FOREIGN CORPORATIONS

(*See* Foreign Corporations, Persons, and Partnerships)

CORPORATE DIVISIONS

(*See* Reorganizations)

CORPORATE REDEMPTIONS

(*See* Redemptions)

CORPORATE REORGANIZATIONS

(*See* Reorganizations)

CORPORATIONS

(*See* Affiliated Corporations; Dividends and Distributions; Foreign Corporations, Persons, and Partnerships; Professional Corporations; Redemptions; Reorganizations; S Corporations)

COST OF GOODS SOLD

(*See* Inventories)

CRIMINAL PROSECUTION

(*See* Interest and Penalties; Procedure)

D

DEDUCTIONS

(*See* Business Expenses; Charitable Contributions; Depreciation and Amortization; Interest Paid; Passive Loss Rules; Trusts and Trust Taxation)

DEDUCTIONS FROM GROSS ESTATE

(*See* Charitable Contributions; Estates and Estate Tax; Marital Deduction; Trusts and Trust Taxation)

DEFERRED COMPENSATION

(*See also* Compensation for Personal Services; Fringe Benefits; Pension and Profit-Sharing Plans)

"Deferred compensation rewards and retains key employees" (2001). The drafting of a nonqualified deferred compensation agreement requires the effort of a team of financial advisers—the accountant, tax attorney, and life underwriter—to properly protect the business, tax, and retirement needs of the employer and senior key management employee. This team must give special consideration to issues of tax deferral, the timing of deductions, funding flexibility, the risk of bankruptcy or insolvency, and the protection of trust assets from creditors. By doing so, they can choose the best trust arrangement to support the deferred compensation plan and meet the objectives of the employer and key employee.

First, the authors discuss the advantages of deferred compensation plans. Nonqualified deferred compensation arrangements offer flexibility and advantageous tax treat-

ment that can assist in attracting and retaining talented employees.

Nonqualified deferred compensation payments are deductible to the employer in the year an amount attributable to the contribution is includable in the employee's gross income. Thus, if the closely held corporation is in a lower tax bracket than its high-income senior key management employee, the employee's election to defer compensation means that this deferred income will be taxed at the lower corporate rate rather than at the employee's higher marginal personal tax rate in the year the services are rendered. A high-level employee is likely to be in the 39.6 percent marginal tax bracket when the services are rendered.

Then, the authors consider pitfalls. Drafters of deferred compensation plans must be careful to avoid three major pitfalls that could result in the employee losing the valuable deferral of income taxes for services rendered and compensation payable later: (1) constructive receipt; (2) economic benefit; and (3) formally funding a nonqualified deferred compensation arrangement.

Finally, the authors address rabbi trusts, secular trusts, and FICA taxes. (J.R. Pozzuolo & L. Kaplan, 66 Practical Tax Strategies 85.)

DEFICIENCIES

(*See* Assessment and Collection; Interest and Penalties; Procedure)

DEPENDENTS

"Requiring Social Security number for exemption is constitutional" (2001). The Tax Court held in *Cansino* (2001) that the Code's requirement that all dependents eligible for the dependency exemption must have and report a Social Security number is constitutional. (67 Practical Tax Strategies 110.)

DEPRECIATION AND AMORTIZATION

(*See also* Accounting Methods; Business Expenses—Deduction Versus Capital Expenditure)

"Amortization of noncompete covenant connected with stock redemption" (2001). In a case of first impression, *Frontier Chevrolet Co.* (2001), the Tax Court held that a company must amortize over fifteen years the payments it made for a five-year covenant not to compete entered into in connection with a stock redemption. (67 Practical Tax Strategies 117.)

"Election lets taxpayers avoid mid-quarter convention for depreciation" (2001). The IRS has announced in Notices 2001-70 and 2001-74 that it will issue regulations permitting many taxpayers to elect out of the Section 168(d)(3) mid-quarter convention rule in 2001. This special election is intended as a relief for taxpayers whose equipment acquisition plans were changed by the September 11, 2001, terrorist attacks. (67 Practical Tax Strategies 362.)

"Governmental agency's certificate qualified as an intangible eligible for fifteen-year amortization" (2001). The IRS concluded in FSA 200137023 that a company's certificate authorizing production was a Section 197 intangible, but that more factual development was necessary to determine the tax treatment of the taxpayer's costs in this regard. (95 Journal of Taxation 312.)

"No current deduction for property purchase to cancel lease" (2001). In a case of first impression, a taxpayer who purchased a ship to cancel an underlying lease could not allocate any of the payment to the lease termination, according to the Tax Court in

Union Carbide Foreign Sales Corp. (2000). (66 Practical Tax Strategies 56.)

"Section 179 speeds up deductions for equipment purchases" (2001). Section 179(a) allows taxpayers to elect to expense part or all of the cost of certain property used in a trade or business in the year the property is placed in service. In addition, the remaining basis of the property may be depreciated beginning with the year the property is placed in service. This produces larger deductions (and accelerated tax savings) than if the property were depreciated under the normal MACRS guidelines.

First, the author discusses the rules pertaining to the Section 179 deduction, including provisions regarding the property qualifying for the Section 179 election, qualifying taxpayers, the annual ceiling on the expense that may be deducted, the taxable income limit, the maximum expense limit for married taxpayers, making the election, revoking the election, and recapture of the expense deduction. A Section 179 deduction may be claimed by only certain types of taxpayers and with respect to only certain types of property. The taxpayer must be either an individual, C corporation, S corporation, or partnership; the property must be depreciable, tangible, personal (not realty), and used in the taxpayer's trade or business.

Further, the following limitations apply to the expense deduction: (1) the taxpayer's annual Section 179 deduction cannot exceed the maximum annual deduction limitation ($24,000 for 2001); (2) the annual deduction limitation is reduced dollar for dollar for purchases of qualifying property exceeding $200,000; and (3) the deduction allowed for a tax year cannot exceed the taxable income from the active conduct of all the taxpayer's trade or business activities. Any deduction not allowed because of this limitation, may be carried over indefinitely and used when the taxpayer has sufficient taxable income.

Then, the author addresses the selection of the property to expense. To maximize the tax deduction in the year of election, if the taxpayer has property with different MACRS recovery periods, the taxpayer should elect to expense the cost of the property with the longest useful life. This will allow the taxpayer to take larger depreciation deductions for property for which the Section 179 expense election is not made.

Finally, the author explores a variety of other factors to be considered when determining whether to claim a Section 179 deduction for a purchase, including the amount of taxable income, depreciation on the property, and the use of pass-through entities. (S.C. Colburn, 66 Practical Tax Strategies 361.)

"Specific rules apply for opting out of MACRS" (2001). The Tax Court held in *New Gaming Systems, Inc.* (2001) that a taxpayer had failed to properly opt out of the modified accelerated cost recovery system (MACRS), so it could not claim quicker depreciation deductions. (67 Practical Tax Strategies 364.)

"Tax Court requires capitalization of payment for relief of a burdensome lease" (2001). The Tax Court decision in *Union Carbide Foreign Sales Corp.* (2000) illustrates a refinement of the typical situation that arises when a taxpayer acquires more than one asset in a single transaction. In general, if a taxpayer acquires the assets of a business, the consideration paid must be allocated among the various assets; some will be depreciable, some amortizable, and others will be ineligible for cost recovery until sold. If the taxpayer acquires improved real estate, the consideration must be allocated between the nondepreciable land and the depreciable improvements.

What the taxpayer in *Union Carbide* acquired was a vessel that it had been leasing, and it attempted to allocate the purchase price between depreciable basis for the ship and a deduction for a lease cancellation (as a cost of doing business). The IRS argued, however, that the entire amount paid was for the vessel. The taxpayer failed to convince the Tax Court otherwise. (D.L. Surkin, 95 Journal of Taxation 298.)

DISABLED INDIVIDUALS

"Dentist's camera did not qualify for disabled access credit" (2001). A dentist could not claim a disabled access credit for an intraoral camera system that helped him to more efficiently treat hearing-impaired patients, according to the Tax Court in *Fan* (2001). (67 Practical Tax Strategies 180.)

"Tax strategies to assist the disabled and their families" (2001). The Americans With Disabilities Act, along with employer accommodations made to retain qualified employees in a tight labor market, increase the number of disabled individuals who are members of the working public. Also, longer life expectancies increase the ranks of the disabled. Tax laws dealing with disabilities or handicaps touch every element of the tax computation—from gross income to tax credits. Some types of income likely to be received by the disabled are even exempt from tax.

First, the authors discuss gross income and adjusted gross income (AGI). Individuals with disabilities receive a variety of cash benefits from numerous sources. Some of these cash receipts are totally exempt from taxation, others are partially included in gross income, while another group of benefits is fully included in gross income.

Individuals with disabilities are not treated any differently for tax purposes when it comes to deductions for AGI (i.e., above-the-line deductions). One of the deductions that may be worth looking into is the write-off allowed for payments to a medical savings account (MSA). Employees of small businesses and self-employed individuals are allowed to make tax-deductible contributions to MSAs and withdraw the money tax-free when necessary to handle the costs of medical care that is routine and preventive. If the money in the MSA is not spent by the end of the year, the taxpayer is given a choice of having the funds remain in the account or rolled into an IRA. In either case, the activity is tax-free.

Special dependency exemption and itemized deduction rules apply to some individuals who are disabled and for those who support or care for those individuals.

Then, the authors address impairment-related work expenses, medical expenses, tax credits, withholding and FICA payments, filing status, and failure to file a timely tax return.

Finally, the authors consider tax planning. A disabled individual or those who are responsible for this person can make choices that alter the amount and timing of taxes. The presence of flexibility in how certain items are incurred or treated allows for tax planning. Some payments (e.g., nursing care for a dependent child) can be classified as dependent care or medical expenses. Depending on the specifics (e.g., marginal tax rate, level of AGI, and other expenditures), taxpayer classification of the disbursements can play an important role in determining the ultimate tax liability.

The presence of general and specific statutory limits on itemized deductions and medical expenses provides a planning opportunity. Accelerating or deferring payments for deductible medical costs can influence not only the amount of tax but also when it will be paid. (K. Milani & A. Milani, 66 Practical Tax Strategies 97.)

DISCHARGE OF DEBT

(*See* Bankruptcy; Cancellation of Indebtedness)

DISCLAIMERS

"Disclaimer-based estate planning—a question of suitability" (2001). H.M. Zaritsky, 28 Estate Planning 400. (*Digested under* Estate Planning, page 44.)

"Net gift disclaimer of divided marital trusts allowed" (2001). The IRS has concluded in Letter Ruling 200137022, involving a community property taxpayer, that a surviving spouse's disclaimer of a residuary trust and one of three severed marital trusts was a net gift, that the disclaimer did not result in a gift of the other severed marital trusts, and that her retained income interests in the other severed trusts would not be valued at zero under Section 2702. (95 Journal of Taxation 378.)

"The Uniform Disclaimer of Property Interests Act: opportunities and pitfalls" (2001). A.J. Hirsch, 28 Estate Planning 571. (*Digested under* Estate Planning, page 50.)

DISTRIBUTIONS

(*See* Dividends and Distributions; Partners and Partnerships; Pension and Profit-Sharing Plans; Trusts and Trust Taxation)

DIVIDENDS AND DISTRIBUTIONS

(*See also* Reorganizations)

"Dividend alternatives free up more cash for company owners" (2001). Owners of closely held C corporations are better off receiving corporate earnings in various forms other than dividends.

Since a dividend is nondeductible to the corporation and taxable as ordinary income to the shareholder, dividend alternatives ideally are deductible by the corporation or excluded from the gross income of the shareholder (and sometimes both). If a tax is paid, it may be deferred or qualify for capital gains rates. An eye must also be kept on the accumulated earnings tax in Section 531 and the personal holding company tax in Section 541, the sole purpose of which is to enforce "double taxation" by encouraging the payment of dividends currently.

After providing background on corporations and choice of entity, the author considers dividend alternatives. According to the author, closely held C corporations should pay more attention to current fringe benefits and deferred compensation, and de-emphasize loans. Owners of closely held C corporations should also consider whether they would be better off making the S election and avoid "double taxation" entirely, although doing so prevents them from benefiting from the lower corporate tax rates for earnings that are not distributed. (R. Auster, 67 Practical Tax Strategies 353.)

"Formula-based compensation included disguised dividend" (2001). 67 Practical Tax Strategies 126. (*Digested under* Compensation for Personal Services, page 26.)

"Loans to sub followed by dividends to parent disregarded for lack of economic substance" (2001). FSA 200050013 concludes that a transaction designed to lower the tax liability of a subsidiary corporation through dividend payments to a parent corporation should be disregarded for tax purposes. (94 Journal of Taxation 185.)

"Parent stock transferred by subsidiary to parent's employees is a dividend" (2001). A subsidiary's transfer of parent stock to the parent's employees was a dividend distribution, not a capital contribution followed by a retransfer under Regulation § 1.83-6(d), according to FSA 200117020. (95 Journal of Taxation 54.)

"Payment under noncompetition agreement was disguised dividend" (2001). Most of the amount an acquiring corporation paid directly to the acquired company's owner-employee for a noncompetition agreement was really a payment to the company followed by a dividend distribution, according to the Tax Court in *Bemidji Distributing Co.* (2001). (67 Practical Tax Strategies 363.)

"Regulations extend liability-assumption rules to corporate distributions" (2001). The IRS has issued temporary and final regulations that apply rules relating to the manner in which a liability is treated as assumed to distributions of property under Section 301. Under Section 301(b)(2), when determining the taxation of a property distribution made by a corporation to a shareholder with respect to its stock, the distribution is reduced (but not below zero) by any liability assumed by the shareholder in connection with the distribution and any liability the property was subject to immediately before and after the distribution. (66 Practical Tax Strategies 127.)

"Shareholder-employees' compensation included disguised dividends" (2001). 67 Practical Tax Strategies 54. (*Digested under* Compensation for Personal Services, page 27.)

"Use audit guide to structure advances as tax-free loans" (2001). The IRS has recently issued a new audit guide addressing loans to shareholders as part of its ongoing approach to auditing—the Market Segment Specialization Program (MSSP). The MSSP is an integral part of the kinder, gentler image the IRS is trying to cultivate. The fundamental objectives of the MSSP are to increase voluntary taxpayer compliance and to help IRS examiners perform audits more efficiently and effectively by providing technical tax and compliance guidelines for specific industries, classes of taxpayers, or issues. The audit guide, *Market Segment Specialization Program Audit Technique Guide on Shareholder Loans*, relates to the specific issue of loans to shareholders rather than to a specific industry or market segment.

After providing background, the authors discuss key factors considered by the examiner. Altogether, the audit guide presents the twelve key factors from case law that examiners should consider in deciding whether advances are distributions or bona fide loans.

The audit guide directs the examiner to first consider whether an advance to a shareholder is a bona fide loan. The basis for this determination should be the intent of the parties involved at the time of the disbursement. Intent may be difficult to determine several years after the transaction has occurred. However, case law developed through the years provides some objective factors that should resolve some of the ambiguity and lead to a proper determination. Courts have consistently looked beyond the form of a transaction ("loan") to determine its true substance. Characterization of a disbursement as a "note receivable" on the corporate books does not by itself substantiate the intent of the parties. Neither is the testimony of the parties as to intent determinative on its own.

Some additional factors must be considered for S corporations that make advances to shareholders. In addition to the twelve key factors, the agent must consider whether the shareholder was reasonably compensated. If not, a reclassification of all or part of the advances as wages subject to employment taxes may be necessary. If any advances in excess of what is deemed to be reasonable compensation are determined not to be bona fide loans, the taxability of those distributions must be assessed.

The taxability of these excess distributions depends on whether the S corporation has previous C corporation earnings and profits (E&P). If not, the distribution is taxable as capital gain to the extent it exceeds the shareholder's stock basis. If there is prior C corporation E&P, the S corporation's accumulated adjustments account (AAA) must be examined to determine whether it exceeds the distribution. If the AAA exceeds the distribution amount, none of the distribution is taxable as an ordinary dividend. If the AAA is less than the distribution, the excess is taxable as an ordinary dividend to the extent of E&P.

Finally, the authors turn to additional issues, applicable federal rates, exceptions to Section 7872, computations, and interest issues on market-rate loans. (K.B. Friske & D.P. Smith, 67 Practical Tax Strategies 156.)

DIVISIVE REORGANIZATIONS

(*See* Reorganizations)

DIVORCE AND SEPARATION

(*See* Husband and Wife—Divorce and Separation)

E

EARNINGS AND PROFITS

(*See* Dividends and Distributions)

EDUCATION EXPENSES

"College funding tool offers estate planning advantage" (2001). Section 529 authorizes qualified state tuition (QST) programs. A QST program is one established by a state or agency that does either of the following: (1) allows an individual to purchase tuition credits or certificates at a discount for a designated beneficiary, who is then entitled to a waiver of payment of qualified higher education expenses (prepaid tuition plans) or (2) permits an individual to make contributions to an account to meet a designated beneficiary's qualified higher educational expenses (college savings account plans).

Qualified higher educational expenses include tuition, fees, books, supplies, and equipment required for enrollment or attendance. In the case of an individual who is an eligible student, expenses also include reasonable costs for the designated beneficiary's room and board. An eligible student is a student who satisfies the requirements of section 484(a)(1) of the Higher Education Act of 1965 and is carrying at least one half the normal full-time work load for the course of study.

First, the authors discuss plans as a college funding tool. As of September 2001, all fifty states and the District of Columbia have implemented QST programs or have pending programs. College savings account programs have been implemented or are pending in thirty states, four states have prepaid tuition programs, and sixteen states and the District of Columbia have both types of programs.

A common misconception about these plans is that an individual can invest in only his or her own state's plan. In reality, an individual can purchase any state's plan, subject to the residency limitations of several states.

A savings plan allows the contributor to save money in a special college savings account on the beneficiary's behalf. Account owners are not permitted to direct the investment of the funds in their account. The state determines the investment options for these plans, which usually consist of mutual funds with preset stock and bond allocations that are automatically adjusted based on the child's age. The asset allocations shift over the years from more stable investments to more liquid investments as the child approaches college age. Some state plans offer a variable rate of return, and others offer a maximum rate of return.

In comparison with prepaid tuition plan accounts that are considered assets of the student, college savings plan accounts are considered assets of the account owner. A beneficiary is, therefore, more likely to qualify for financial aid.

Then, the authors consider another benefit of QST programs, the SAGE Scholars Program. Under this program, more than 140 private colleges nationwide guarantee "Tuition Reward" scholarships or tuition discounts to students based on the amount saved in their savings plans.

Finally, the authors explore estate tax consequences. (J.R. Pozzuolo & L.M. Kaplan, 67 Practical Tax Strategies 340.)

"Educational incentives can be coordinated for greater tax savings" (2001). With the passage of the Economic Growth and Tax Relief Reconciliation Act of 2001 (EG-TRRA), six different educational incentives are available to taxpayers: (1) amounts paid by the employer under qualified educational assistance programs; (2) scholarship exclusions; (3) Hope Scholarship Credit and Lifetime Learning credit; (4) qualified state tuition programs (QSTPs); (5) education

IRAs (now known as Coverdall Educational Savings Accounts); and (6) qualified tuition and related expense deductions.

These different incentives may have a differential impact in that they can affect the student's return, the return of the student's parents, or both. Also, some of these are subject to phase-out (e.g., Hope/Lifetime Learning credit and education deductions) and others are not. (M.E. Reid & P.J. Harmelink, 67 Practical Tax Strategies 272.)

"Education at golf academy was not deductible by golf instructor" (2001). A course of study at a golf academy that led to an associate degree qualified a golf instructor for new trades or businesses, so the tuition was not deductible, according to the Tax Court in *Fields* (2001). (66 Practical Tax Strategies 312.)

"EGTRRA adds new tax benefits to planning for higher education expenses under Section 529" (2001). Congress continues to expand tax-favored education benefits, and significant liberalization of the rules governing Section 529 plans makes them much more attractive to taxpayers. The rules are complicated and substantial, however, as one would expect where the scheme involves donors, account owners, beneficiaries, state-run and private plans, as well as various issues of public policy, and implicates the federal income, gift, estate, and generation-skipping transfer taxes.

First, the author discusses the types of plans, who may participate, federal requirements, and tax treatment. There are two types of Section 529 plans, tuition credit programs and savings account programs.

Federal law does not limit who may participate in a Section 529 plan as a contributor, account owner, or designated beneficiary. There are no income limitations, and the participants are not required to have any relationship or even to know each other. The only restriction is that the designated beneficiary must be an individual.

There has been some debate over whether a trustee may invest trust assets in a Section 529 plan if distributions from the plan would be permissible under the terms of

the trust. No federal provision prohibits a trust from acting as an account owner.

While the restrictions imposed on Section 529 plans have been eased by the 2001 Act, they continue to be significant and require close attention. One basic limitation is that assets in Section 529 plans may not be used as security for any loan. In addition, federal tax issues with respect to Section 529 plans arise in connection with both income and transfer taxes.

Then, the author addresses creditor protection. It is generally accepted that the assets in a Section 529 plan may be attached by the creditors of the account owner, but not those of the designated beneficiary. Some states are considering legislation to bar creditors of account owners from attaching the Section 529 plan assets.

Finally, the author turns to planning considerations and issues regarding Section 529 plans that remain unclear. (K.M. Stockmal, 95 Journal of Taxation 238.)

"New law expands tax breaks for paying education costs" (2001). The Economic Growth and Tax Relief Reconciliation Act of 2001 (EGTRRA) contains many provisions that help taxpayers meet educational expenses for themselves and their families. The Act accomplishes this help by both enhancing existing provisions and adding new ones to the tax law. These new provisions, of primary benefit to individual taxpayers, include: (1) a higher education expenses deduction; (2) improved education IRAs; (3) enhanced student loan deductions; and (4) improved Section 529 plans.

First, the authors discuss the higher education expenses deduction. For tax years before 2002, individual taxpayers normally cannot deduct education and training expenses of the taxpayer or dependents. Certain education expenses relating to the taxpayer's business or employment, however, are deductible. For employees, the deduction is a miscellaneous itemized deduction that is deductible only if it (and other miscellaneous itemized deductions) exceeds 2 percent of the taxpayer's adjusted gross income (AGI).

For tax years after 2001, and before 2006, new Section 222(a) allows a taxpayer an above-the-line deduction for qualified tuition and related expenses incurred by a taxpayer during the tax year. The expenses must be incurred in connection with enrollment at an institution of higher education during the tax year. The deduction will be allowed, however, for qualified expenses paid during a tax year if those expenses are in connection with an academic term beginning during the tax year or during the first three months of the next tax year.

Then, the authors consider the use of education IRAs, enhanced student loan deductions, and the expanded scope of Section 529 plans. (G.E. Whittenburg, R.G. Bunn & C.F. Venable, 67 Practical Tax Strategies 79.)

"Qualified state tuition programs: more favorable after 2001 Tax Act" (2001). Congress established qualified state tuition programs (QSTPs) in the Small Business Job Protection Act of 1996. On August 24, 1998, the IRS issued proposed regulations to help taxpayers understand the statute. Presently, most of the states have adopted, or are developing, a QSTP.

First, the author discusses the types of plans and their tax advantages. QSTPs differ from state to state, but there are two basic types of programs, according to Section 529(b)(1)(A): a prepaid educational arrangement (PEA) and an educational savings account (ESA). The primary tax benefits of QSTPs are: (1) A QSTP is exempt from income tax, so that the income earned on the contributions grows tax-free. (2) Gifts by a donor can qualify for the annual gift tax exclusion plus the generation skipping tax exclusion, even though (a) the donor retains the right to decide when and by whom the funds are received (i.e., a donor can change beneficiaries) and (b) the donor can reacquire the funds at any time, although subject to a penalty.

Then, the author considers operation of a QSTP. Section 529 imposes a number of requirements for a QSTP to operate. Initially, there must be an account owner.

Finally, the author addresses income tax consequences, estate and gift tax aspects, tax-free rollovers, penalties, drawbacks, comparison of QSTPs to other plans, and comparison of PEAs and ESAs. (M. Schlesinger, 28 Estate Planning 412.)

"Study up on financing a child's college education" (2001). With college costs increasing each year, parents are continually seeking ways to position themselves to finance a college education for each of their children.

First, the authors survey possible sources of monies with which to fund educational expenses. The alternatives include parent's savings, investments in child's name, prepaid tuition programs, education IRAs, scholarships, loans, gifts, tax program incentives, Hope scholarship, Lifetime Learning credit, and employer-sponsored education assistance. Then, the authors summarize their recommendations. (A.A. Neidermeyer & P.E. Neidermeyer, 66 Practical Tax Strategies 12.)

EMINENT DOMAIN

(*See* Losses)

EMPLOYEES

(*See* Business Expenses; Compensation for Personal Services; Deferred Compensation; Fringe Benefits; Pension and Profit-Sharing Plans)

EMPLOYEES' STOCK OPTIONS

(*See* Stock Options)

EMPLOYEE STOCK OWNERSHIP PLANS

(*See* Pension and Profit-Sharing Plans—Employee Stock Ownership Plans (ESOPs))

ENTERTAINMENT EXPENSES

(*See* Business Expenses—Travel and Entertainment)

ERISA

(*See* Pension and Profit-Sharing Plans)

ESOPs

(*See* Pension and Profit-Sharing Plans—Employee Stock Ownership Plans (ESOPs))

ESTATE PLANNING

(*See also* Estates and Estate Tax; Gifts and Gift Tax; Marital Deduction; Trusts and Trust Taxation; Valuation of Property)

"Administration of a business interest held by an estate or trust" (2001). Even with proper planning, administering estates and trusts that hold minority interests in closely held businesses presents special challenges for any fiduciary.

After providing background on the advantages and disadvantages of minority ownership, the authors discuss the importance of obtaining information and the valuation of closely held business interests, including use of the asset-based or "cost" approach, the income approach, and the market approach. Knowledge is power, and to the extent that the fiduciary can gather reliable information about the closely held business, he will be better prepared to properly value and administer an interest in that business, as well as attempt to sell it if appropriate.

In general, a professional, qualified appraiser should be hired. Of course, there are exceptions to the rule, such as when the value of an estate's interest in a closely held business may not be sufficient to warrant a professional appraisal. In those circumstances, a fiduciary may be compelled to calculate his own valuations as a pragmatic and cost-effective solution when assets of relatively low value are involved.

Then, the authors consider administration of closely held business interests, including sale or other disposition. (M.S. Bekerman & S.S. Kirkpatrick, 28 Estate Planning 536.)

"An A-to-Z 'to do' list following EGTRRA" (2001). The Economic Growth and Tax Relief Reconciliation Act of 2001 (EGTRRA or the 2001 Tax Act) is an extraordinarily challenging piece of legislation. In the estate planning area, its quixotic repeal of the estate tax for just one year (2010), its retention of the gift tax with an exemption equivalent frozen at $1 million, and its federal disruption of state death tax regimes are a few of its most conspicuous oddities. By consensus, EGTRRA remains one of the most perplexing pieces of legislation of all time, and the proper strategy for coping with its phased-in effects over the next ten years remains, for many, an unsolved riddle.

Recognizing that Title 5 of EGTRRA addresses many more subjects than just the delayed repeal of the estate tax, the article's A-to-Z "to do" list is designed to put some possible responses to the 2001 Tax Act roughly in order of priority. (R.D. Aucutt, 28 Estate Planning 606.)

"Avoiding the attribution rules in redemptions by estates and trusts" (2001). R.W. Harris, 28 Estate Planning 317. (*Digested under* Redemptions, page 173.)

"Carryover basis: planning and drafting issues" (2001). Although it will require further congressional action to make repeal permanent, the Economic Growth and Tax Relief Reconciliation Act of 2001 (the 2001 Tax Act) phases in repeal of the federal estate tax, with complete repeal to be effective in the year 2010. If complete repeal actually materializes, there is a significant "quid pro quo" extracted from taxpayers. The current rules that permit a basis step-up at death are also repealed. Probably, the primary rationale for the current step-up rules is that it would be unfair to impose a double tax on an heir—first an estate tax, and then a capital gains tax when the heir sells the asset. Consistent with that rationale, when the estate tax is fully repealed in 2010, new carryover basis rules also will become effective.

Notwithstanding the significant uncertainty as to whether repeal will really happen, and the fact that even if it does, the new carryover basis rules do not apply until 2010, it is not too soon to begin planning for carryover basis. Particularly for irrevocable trusts and testamentary documents that may have to operate under a carryover basis regime, there are many issues to consider. The challenge for estate planners is to design estate plans that work well, regardless of the fate of carryover basis.

After providing an overview of the carryover basis rules, the author discusses planning and drafting. For many individuals, even if proper planning is done, it can be anticipated that there will be significant appreciation that cannot be protected from capital gains taxes because the appreciation will far exceed the increases available. This means that planning devices that minimize the impact of capital gains taxes will take on increased importance in the future.

These strategies will include taking full advantage of charitable planning opportunities, such as charitable remainder trusts, charitable lead trusts, and flexible trusts that allow income to be paid out to charity and deducted at the trust level, pursuant to Section 642(c). Other planning devices that reduce the impact of the capital gains tax and currently are employed will take on greater importance. These techniques include the use of variable life insurance, tax-deferred annuities, exchange funds, derivative products such as collars and forward sale contracts, and undoubtedly new products that will be developed by the financial services industries. (D.R. Hodgman, 28 Estate Planning 611.)

"Charitable estate planning with retirement benefits" (2001). S.J. Schlesinger & D.L. Mark, 28 Estate Planning 390. (*Digested under* Charitable Contributions, page 20.)

"College funding tool offers estate planning advantage" (2001). J.R. Pozzuolo & L.M. Kaplan, 67 Practical Tax Strategies 340. (*Digested under* Education Expenses, page 39.)

"Corporate buy-sell agreements as estate and business planning tools" (2001). Buy-sell agreements are an essential estate and business planning tool for owners of closely held corporations. A buy-sell agreement can provide a market for the corporate stock, assure continuity of management, provide estate liquidity, and establish a prearranged means of resolving otherwise potentially contentious valuation and succession issues.

First, the authors discuss restrictions in buy-sell agreements and the events that typically activate buy-sell provisions. A buy-sell agreement may contain a variety of restrictions on the transferability of stock, provided that the restriction is not absolute or unreasonable. The most typical restriction on transferability of stock is to limit the transfer to certain classes of persons, such as members of a family who are working in the business. This is usually combined—in the case of a lifetime buy-out to other than the permitted persons—with a first option or right of first refusal to the corporation, the other shareholders, or some combination of both. These permit the remaining shareholders to decide if the proposed purchaser is a person they want as a fellow shareholder.

The buy-sell agreement typically provides that such events as death, disability, termination of employment, desire of a shareholder to sell stock, divorce, and bankruptcy will give rise to the option, right of first refusal, or mandatory obligation to buy and sell.

Then, the authors consider the purchase price. Establishing the purchase price is one of the most critical provisions of a buy-sell agreement. Too often, a valuation (or method of determining valuation) is selected that yields an inappropriate (or even unworkable) price when finally used. If the agreement provides for a purchase price that is revalued by the IRS for estate tax purposes, the selling shareholder's estate could be liable for estate tax based on the IRS revaluation, although the estate has received only the value based on the provision in the buy-sell agreement. This could result in an unanticipated shift in the beneficial enjoyment of the estate.

Finally, the author addresses methods of funding and payment, entity purchase agreements (corporate redemptions), cross-purchase buy-sell agreements, hybrid buy-sell agreements, estate tax valuation, S corporations, and ethics. (M.H. Zuckerman & J.G. Grall, 28 Estate Planning 599.)

"Creating an amicable estate plan for the decedent's children and the second spouse" (2001). Specific strategies that minimize areas of potential friction can unite a decedent's children from a prior marriage and the surviving spouse, foster cooperation between the parties, and generate tax savings, and only the government will be the loser.

First, the author provides background on the problem of creating an estate plan for the decedent's children and the second spouse. The estate planner's primary objective in second marriage situations should be to create an estate plan that provides the least possible opportunity for conflict between the spouse and the decedent's children, and to find and develop opportunities for all parties to benefit financially. In this respect, it is essential that the estate planner examine the areas of potential conflict and either take steps to lessen the possibility for such conflict or turn these areas into situations in which both sides achieve financial benefits. In this regard, it is the marital trust where most of the opportunities lie.

Then, the author explores strategies involving use of an independent trustee, recognition of the second spouse's assets, giving the children something up front, guarantees for the spouse, waiving the state's prudent investor statute and giving the trustee the authority to invest completely in growth stocks, making gifts from the marital trust, providing for a testamentary power of appointment, and marital trust stub income. (P.B. Tiernan, 94 Journal of Taxation 98.)

"Disclaimer-based estate planning—a question of suitability" (2001). The Economic Growth and Tax Relief Reconciliation Act of 2001 is likely to spur the interest of estate planners in disclaimer-based estate planning, because it creates a rapidly changing set of rules that may make it difficult to design an estate plan that will continue to achieve the desired results. (H.M. Zaritsky, 28 Estate Planning 400.)

"Estate planning benefits of deferred like-kind exchanges of real estate" (2001). M. Kove & J.M. Kosakow, 28 Estate Planning 372. (*Digested under* Like-Kind Exchanges, page 121.)

"Estate planning changes in the 2001 Tax Act—more than you can count" (2001). The Economic Growth and Tax Relief Reconciliation Act of 2001 (EGTRRA or the 2001 Act) is projected to represent the largest single tax reduction legislation enacted since the Economic Recovery Tax Act of 1981.

First, the authors discuss provisions of the 2001 Act concerning reduction in rates, increases in exemptions, retention of the gift tax, the state death tax exemption phaseout, the qualified family-owned business interest rule repeal, conservation easements, qualified domestic trusts, deferral of payment of estate tax, qualified prepaid tuition programs, generation-skipping transfer (GST) tax rules, and modified carryover basis in 2010. The massive changes to the wealth transfer tax system include a return to separate treatment for the gift tax, a series of rate and exemption changes for the estate and generation-skipping transfer taxes, and institution of a new modified carryover basis regime—all capped by total repeal of the estate and GST taxes but only for one year.

Then, the authors consider planning. The 2001 Act, in a general sense, presents three major areas that need to be covered in planning: (1) lifetime gifts and other transfers (including the acquisition and maintenance of life insurance); (2) drafting for estate and GST tax efficient transmission at death; and (3) drafting and lifetime transfers with respect to a carryover basis system. Planning, including drafting, needs to cover three possible situations: (1) the phase-in period of higher estate and GST exemptions and lower rates; (2) any period of repeal of estate and GST taxes and a carryover basis income tax system; and (3) the reversion to the current tax system. (J.G. Blattmachr & L.Y. Detzel, 95 Journal of Taxation 74.)

"Estate planning for procrastinators: those who wait until the last minute" (2001). Even for clients who plan at the last minute, numerous strategies can yield substantial tax savings. This first part of a two-part article analyzes such techniques as gift-tax-free gifts, split ownership of property, and family limited partnerships.

First, the authors discuss ascertaining the client's current situation. One of the first steps that should be taken in advising the client is to review any relevant documents that already are in place, in order to determine the client's current dispositive scheme (if any) and to recommend a course of action.

Second, the authors consider the three-year rule and the reduced incentive for using deathbed gifts to deplete the estate. Often, the first wealth transfer consideration that comes to mind when one thinks of a client who has only a short time to live is the three-year rule of Section 2035. Although this rule is an important consideration and one that will affect many planning recommendations, it actually is quite limited in scope.

Third, the authors consider tax-free gifts. Gifts that qualify for the $10,000 per donee gift tax annual exclusion under Section 2503(b) do not come within the three-year rule, and allow the client to transfer assets during life completely tax-free. Moreover, annual exclusion gifts are generally exempt from generation-skipping transfer tax.

Then, the authors discuss estate reduction by paying the client's debts and obligations. One means for a client to reduce his or her estate is to pay off any outstanding obligations. While taking a deduction for outstanding debts of a decedent under Section 2053 has the same effect, there sometimes are issues of enforceability that may be difficult to resolve after death.

Finally, the authors turn to split ownership of property and the use of family limited partnerships at the last minute. (S.T. Plybon & J.R. Robinson, 28 Estate Planning 422.)

"Estate planning remains crucial despite estate tax 'repeal'" (2001). The Economic Growth and Tax Relief Reconciliation Act of 2001 (EGTRRA) made significant changes in many areas of the Code. One far-reaching change is the "repeal" of the estate tax. Although repeal of the estate tax is a central part of EGTRRA, unusual effective date provisions make the relief long in coming, of short duration, and likely to be amended.

First, the author discusses the ten-year duration. Section 313 of the Congressional Budget Act of 1974 (known as the Byrd rule) provides that any tax cut that is not "paid for" by permanent spending cuts will sunset after ten years unless at least sixty senators vote to waive the Byrd rule at the time the tax cut is enacted. Since EGTRRA is not being paid for by permanent spending cuts but rather by "future surpluses," the Byrd rule applies to this legislation.

Although sixty-two senators voted for EGTRRA, the Republican leadership could garner no more than fifty-three votes in support of waiving the Byrd rule. This means that the estate tax will be repealed effective January 1, 2010, but will be reinstated at 55 percent with only a $1 million unified credit effective January 1, 2011. Accordingly, as written, the repeal of the estate tax will last for only one year.

Next, the author addresses carryover basis. A person may actually be better off dying (if this is not an oxymoron) in 2009 rather than 2010 if he or she has no spouse and has an estate of between $1.3 million and $3.5 million.

Then, the author considers whether the repeal will be extended. The likelihood of EGTRRA being reinstated in its entirety in 2011 is extremely remote.

Finally, the author discusses lifetime gifts and the state death tax credit. (D. Weiss, 67 Practical Tax Strategies 68.)

"Estate planning strategies for clients who wait until the last minute" (2001). In this second part of a two-part article on last-minute planning, the authors explore strategies that depend on the client's condition or on survival of a specified term, as well as income tax issues and planning with retirement benefits.

First, the authors discuss strategies, including private annuity arrangements, charitable lead trusts, and sales of remainder interests, that depend on the client's condition and the use of the IRS tables to leverage value. There are several wealth transfer strategies that can be extremely effective if the client is not so ill that he or she cannot use the IRS tables to value a temporal interest. Under Regulation § 25.7520-1, unless the donor is "terminally ill" (defined as having an incurable illness or other deteriorating physical condition and a 50 percent or greater chance of dying within one year), the donor must use the IRS approved tables to value gifts of annuities, life interests, term interests, remainders, and reversions.

Thus, if the client is not "terminally ill," a substantial savings can be obtained if the client does not live to the life expectancy set forth in the mandated tables, because the interest retained will have been overvalued (and the interest transferred correspondingly undervalued). However, one should exercise caution in this area. If it were determined that the donor was in fact "terminally ill" at the time of the transfer, unintended and even disastrous tax consequences could follow.

Then, the authors address strategies, involving the use of grantor retained annuity trusts (GRATs), short-tem qualified personal residence trusts (QPRTs), and irrevocable life insurance trusts (ILITs), that depend on the client's surviving a given term. In general, and not surprisingly, any strategy that relies on the donor's surviving for a certain period to be effective is not recommended for the client who is not expected to survive the period in question. On the other hand, the strategies discussed present appealing opportunities to transfer potentially significant amounts of wealth at a relatively low cost, and so should not be dismissed out of hand.

Finally, the authors turn to estate enhancement/equalization and spousal transfers, income tax considerations, and planning with employee benefits and IRAs. (S.T. Plybon & J.R. Robinson, 28 Estate Planning 486.)

"Estate planning under 2001 Tax Act presents new challenges" (2001). The Economic Growth and Tax Relief Reconciliation Act of 2001 (the Act), which phases out and repeals the estate tax and the generation-skipping transfer tax, creates a great deal of uncertainty for advisors and their clients.

First, the author provides an overview of the effect of the Act and its sunset provision. Although estate planners must take into account the possibility of permanent repeal, assuming that it will occur is dangerous. Planners instead should play with the cards Congress has dealt. For example, clients with estates larger than the largest exemption amounts in effect before repeal should plan as if these new higher exemptions will take effect, but estate plans will have to be monitored more closely than ever for new legislative developments. In the last quarter-century (and perhaps longer), no nine-year period has gone by in which Congress did not make significant changes to the transfer tax provisions of the Code. There is no reason to believe the next nine years will be any different.

Then, the author addresses the key features of the Act, and planning issues arising in its aftermath. (J.K. Eisen, 28 Estate Planning 515.)

"Estate tax repeal does not end the need to plan" (2001). The Economic Growth and Tax Relief Reconciliation Act of 2001 (EG-TRRA) fulfills many Republican campaign promises. The legislation enhances retirement plan provisions and reduces the marriage penalty, lowers income and estate and gift tax rates, and eventually repeals the estate and generation-skipping transfer (GST) taxes.

But none of these tax reductions is fully implemented for years because the scheduled $1.35 trillion cost of the tax reductions precludes immediate implementation. In order to comply with the Congressional Budget Act, Congress instead enacted elaborate phase-in provisions that spread the costs over ten years and cause the provisions to sunset on December 31, 2010. Between 2002 and 2009, estate and GST taxes will gradually be reduced by a phased-in combination of lower rates and increased exemptions (i.e., increases in the "applicable credit amount," formerly referred to as the unified credit). Full repeal, however, does not occur until the year 2010 and lasts only one year.

Unless a future Congress acts to continue repeal, the present day transfer tax system will be reinstated after 2010. But whether all of the scheduled estate tax and GST rate reductions and repeal will ever see the light of day depends on the continued existence of projected budget surpluses. In the transition period before 2010, income tax rate reduction, retirement plan enhancements, marriage-penalty relief, and increases in the child tax credit are also scheduled to be phased-in. If budgetary surpluses fail to materialize, it is unclear whether scheduled rate reductions and repeal will be permitted to take effect.

First, the author discusses transfer taxes. During the transition period from 2002 through 2009, definitions of what assets are part of the gross estate and provisions for marital and charitable deductions are largely unchanged by EGTRRA. The gross estate includes not only all property the decedent owns outright at death, but also any transferred property in which the decedent retained an interest, certain joint interests, annuities, and some life insurance proceeds. The gross estate is reduced by deductions permitted for certain expenses and debts, by the marital deduction for qualified transfers to the surviving spouse, and by the charitable deduction.

Each individual receives an applicable credit amount (sometimes referred to as the unified credit), which effectively exempts small and moderate-sized estates from estate and gift taxation. In 2001, the exemption equivalent amount is $675,000 and it was scheduled to rise to $1 million in 2006. Even under current law, it is estimated that only 2 percent of all decedents have taxable estates.

Because most estates do not pay transfer tax, the income tax basis of property received from a decedent is more important for most taxpayers than the estate tax. Under current law, the basis of property received from a decedent steps up (or steps down) to fair market value at the date of death or the alternate valuation date. Under EGTRRA, the FMV basis step-up will continue until 2009 and will be replaced for 2010 only by a modified carryover basis provision, discussed in the article. In 2011, the current law system with a $1 million unified credit and FMV basis step up is scheduled to be reinstated, unless a subsequent Congress provides otherwise.

Then, the author addresses the phaseout and repeal, as well as planning for changes in the applicable exclusion. During the transition period, the size of estates exempt from tax will gradually increase to $3.5 million per person. Thus, with proper planning in which each spouse has at least $3.5 million in assets, a married couple could pass $7 million to family members free of estate tax if they both die in 2009.

Finally, the author turns to the retention of the gift tax, the basis of inherited property, reporting requirements, the state death tax credit, additional provisions, retirement asset planning, charitable transfers, and nontax estate planning considerations. (C. Kertz, 67 Practical Tax Strategies 136.)

"Exercising powers of appointment—a simple task or tricky business?" (2001). This article offers practical suggestions for correctly exercising a power of appointment, including expressing a clear intent to exercise the power, satisfying any conditions of the exercise, and properly exercising a power in favor of a trust. A power of appointment is a power to dispose of property. The terms of the grant of the power usually dictate the manner and extent to which it may be exercised by the powerholder.

After providing background on the exercise of powers, the author offers guidelines for exercise, including exercise in favor of a trust and exercise by a legal representative. Most advisors focus so much on the tax ramifications of powers of appointment that

47

they often lose sight of the many administrative and property law issues involved, including the proper exercise of a power. It might be wise to re-examine the nontax issues, so that, together with the tax issues, practitioners will be able to creatively and correctly make use of the many planning opportunities available with powers of appointment. (A.A. Bove, Jr., 28 Estate Planning 277.)

"Family business planning that accomplishes the owner's goals" (2001). The key to effective estate planning for a family business depends on whether the owner wants the business to be liquidated, sold, or continued by the family. This article analyzes the ramifications of each alternative.

First, the authors discuss estate liquidity. It is not unusual for the business to be the most valuable asset in the owner's estate. At the owner's death, the executor will need cash—perhaps a substantial amount of cash—to pay debts, taxes, probate fees, appraiser's fees, and a variety of miscellaneous expenses. The executor may have many assets, but very little cash. Yet, the bills must be paid. Where does the executor get the cash? Convert assets into cash? What if the key asset is the business? Does the executor sacrifice the business to raise cash to pay the taxes? Even if the executor does resort to a sale, can he or she get anything close to full value for the business?

Neither the problem of owner succession nor that of estate liquidity need present an insurmountable obstacle. Both of these difficulties can be avoided with planning and, possibly, some well-arranged life insurance.

Next, the authors discuss liquidating the business. There are situations when liquidation is the only appropriate path, particularly in the case of a single-owner business engaged in a highly specialized or technical activity. Insurance on the owner's life may be used to offset the inevitable loss upon liquidation at death.

Then, the authors address selling the business. If an executor can sell the firm, the family will generally receive an amount closer to the going concern value for the deceased owner's business interest. The family ends up with cash and is relieved of the risks and burdens of managing a business.

Finally, the authors consider family continuation. There are two basic approaches to handling the problems associated with transferring ownership of a business to one family member, while providing for the needs of the estate and its beneficiaries. One approach may be called the "equalization method," and the other, the "buy-sell alternative."

The key motivation in the equalization method is to achieve mathematical equality of the share of the estate passing to each beneficiary. Under the buy-sell approach, the parent and the child who is active in the business enter into a legally binding agreement, similar to any buy-sell agreement between unrelated parties. (D.A. Hjorth & J.P. Connelly, 28 Estate Planning 503.)

"Making estate planning fun (again?)" (2001). Attorneys frequently say that the practice of estate planning has become burdensome and, quite simply, no fun. They complain about the difficulty of keeping up with constantly changing laws and techniques, meeting deadlines, and obtaining fair compensation for their work. They often remain deeply interested in the subject matter, but frustrated with the practice of estate planning.

Certainly, estate planning is not a practice well-suited for everyone. It involves a complex array of tax and nontax laws, and the tax laws, in particular, change almost constantly. Estate planning is, therefore, best suited for attorneys who find an intellectual challenge appealing. Those who prefer the interplay between opposing counsel or between counsel and judges to the quieter pursuits of problem solving and educating clients, will usually enjoy other areas of law more than they will enjoy estate planning.

Still, for those attorneys who are temperamentally and intellectually well-suited to estate planning, there are several things that can be done to make practice more fun—allow enough time for the work, keep up with changes in the law, and charge enough for the work. (H.M. Zaritsky, 28 Estate Planning 248.)

"New U.S. tax act—dramatic consequences for estate, gift, GST regime in the foreign context" (2001). P. Marcovici, T. Lewis, M.J. Michaels, V.A. Dalmas & C. Hsieh-Kammerlander, 12 Journal of International Taxation, No. 9, 10. (*Digested under* Estates and Estate Tax—In General, page 51.)

"On-line fee-based services for estate planners" (2001). D.H. Kelley, 28 Estate Planning 349. (*Digested under* Computers, page 29.)

"Planned basis freezes and ESOPs after the 2001 Tax Act" (2001). S. Etkind, 28 Estate Planning 592. (*Digested under* Pension and Profit-Sharing Plans—Employee Stock Ownership Plans (ESOPs), page 159.)

"Planning for use of the TPT credit yields significant tax savings" (2001). D.L. Herrmann, 28 Estate Planning 478. (*Digested under* Estates and Estate Tax—In General, page 52.)

"Powers of appointment: more (taxwise) than meets the eye" (2001). Powers of appointment can build extensive flexibility into an estate plan. But practitioners using powers of appointment must carefully analyze the somewhat complicated tax ramifications in order to use powers most effectively.

First, the author discusses retained powers—both general and special. When a person makes a transfer, whether in trust or otherwise, and reserves the power to recover the property (as through the exercise of a general power), he has not—in the eyes of the tax law—relinquished dominion and control over the property. Thus, he has made no completed taxable gift of the property. Because the donor has not made a completed gift, the income and losses relating to the property will pass through to the donor of the power.

On the donor's death, if he continues to hold the power, the full value of the property subject to the power will be included in the donor's estate, but not under the Code section governing powers of appointment.

Rather, the property is included under the Code sections relating to retained control over a transfer.

When a special power of appointment is created through a reserved power by the donor, it is not treated as a power of appointment under Section 2041 but rather as a retained power under Section 2036 or Section 2038 for estate tax purposes. As with the retained general power, the donor has not made a completed gift. Accordingly, the income and losses relating to the property subject to the power will pass through to the donor/powerholder, because he continues to be regarded as the owner of the property for tax purposes.

Interestingly, the only Code section specifically stating that a transfer that is subject to the transferor's retained power to control beneficial enjoyment will cause the income or losses on that property to be passed through to the powerholder, deals with a transfer to a trust (under the so-called grantor trust rules). Nevertheless, it would be naive to assume based on this Code section that the concept and tax result apply only to transfers to trusts and would not apply to nontrust transfers (e.g., a power reserved in a deed). If that were so, it would permit a donor who made a transfer with a reserved power to temporarily and repeatedly shift taxable income among an unlimited number of recipients without ever making a completed gift.

Then, the author addresses general powers of appointment granted to another, special powers of appointment granted to another, joint powers, and hybrid powers. (A.A. Bove, Jr., 28 Estate Planning 496.)

"Pre-immigration planning: income, gift, estate, and GST tax strategies" (2001). M.A. Aaronson, 28 Estate Planning 196. (*Digested under* Foreign Corporations, Persons, and Partnerships, page 61.)

"Proper Medicaid planning may permit keeping the home in the family" (2001). This article explores strategies for keeping an individual's home in the family when an application for Medicaid is anticipated. These strategies include safe-harbor transfers of the home and transfers with a reserved life estate.

First, the author discusses long-term care (LTC) insurance. For persons who do not have sufficient LTC insurance, Medicaid transfer restrictions can adversely affect the home of an elder who does not wish to give up any current control. The risk of making a transfer that allows a return of the asset to the original transferor is that the law will change retroactively and eliminate the efficacy of the transfer. This result has occurred twice in the trust area.

Next, the author considers transfers to revocable trusts. Although a home is normally considered an exempt asset for Medicaid purposes, the transfer of a home to a revocable trust can be worse than taking no action at all, because any asset in a revocable trust (including a home) is treated as a countable asset that must be sold and its proceeds spent. In addition, a transfer to others from a revocable trust would be subject to a five-year lookback period, but a transfer from the client directly would be subject to only a three-year lookback period.

Then, the author addresses safe-harbor transfers, including permissible transfers to the spouse and permissible transfers involving other family members. The first and most commonly used safe harbor is a transfer of the home to the person's spouse. The second safe harbor is a transfer of the home to a transferor's child who is blind, disabled, or under age 21. The third safe harbor is a transfer of the home to a sibling who has an equity interest in the home and who resided there for at least one year prior to the transferor's institutionalization. The fourth safe harbor is a transfer of the home to a transferor's child who resided in the home for at least two years prior to the institutionalization and provided care that allowed the parent to remain at home.

Unless one of the safe harbors is used, the lawyer should consider inserting a life estate and a special power of appointment into the deed or transferring the home to an irrevocable grantor trust to begin the running of the Medicaid disqualification period with a minimum of loss of control on the part of the transferor.

Finally, the author turns to other transfers that may be safe, transfers that cause disqualification periods, transfers with reserved or retained life estates, transfers with special powers of appointment, and other transfers. (B.E. Barreira, 28 Estate Planning 177.)

"Statutory freeze partnerships: a useful estate planning technique" (2001). A.K. Long, III, 28 Estate Planning 59. (*Digested under* Partners and Partnerships—In General, page 143.)

"The Uniform Disclaimer of Property Interests Act: opportunities and pitfalls" (2001). The Uniform Disclaimer of Property Interests Act (UDPIA) includes elements that expand opportunities for postmortem estate planning. At the same time, the Act is not free of glitches and ambiguities. If its dubious features do not receive the attention of state legislators, courts will inherit the task of ironing out UDPIA's wrinkles.

After providing background on disclaimers, the author discusses formalities and time limit requirements under UDPIA. A disclaimer under UDPIA—like many previous disclaimer statutes—must be executed in writing, signed by the beneficiary (no witnesses are required), and delivered. The person to whom delivery must be made depends on the sort of gratuitous transfer at issue, as detailed in the Act.

Under UDPIA for the first time, a disclaimer can also be recorded and delivered electronically over the Internet. Electronic transmission of a disclaimer is not currently allowed under the Code, however. Consequently, a disclaimer transmitted in this manner, although valid under UDPIA, will not constitute a tax-qualified disclaimer. For purposes of federal taxation, the disclaimer will be treated as a subsequent gratuitous transfer by the disclaiming beneficiary (or disclaimant).

Although most previous disclaimer statutes have set a deadline for disclaiming, UDPIA does not. As long as the beneficiary declines to take delivery of the inheritance, she can continue to hold open the decision of whether to accept or disclaim it. Still, a disclaimer will not be tax-qualified unless it is delivered within nine months of the testator's death, or by the beneficiary's twenty-first birthday, whichever occurs later.

Then, the author addresses standing to disclaim, disclaimable property, creditors' claims, present interests, future interests, and mistakes. (A.J. Hirsch, 28 Estate Planning 571.)

ESTATES AND ESTATE TAX

(*See also* Disclaimers; Estate Planning; Marital Deduction; Valuation of Property)

In General

"Congress repeals estate tax—for a while" (2001). On May 23, 2001, Congress passed the Economic Growth and Tax Reconciliation Act of 2001. The new law does not address the changes in the tax rules on charitable giving. It does repeal the estate tax, but only for the estates of decedents dying in 2010. (13 Taxation of Exempts 48.)

"Estate planning remains crucial despite estate tax 'repeal'" (2001). D. Weiss, 67 Practical Tax Strategies 68. (*Digested under* Estate Planning, page 45.)

"Estate tax deduction not altered by post-death events, rules Tenth Circuit" (2001). Post-death events cannot be considered when valuing a deduction for unpaid income taxes taken on an estate tax return, ruled the Tenth Circuit in *Estate of McMorris* (2001). (28 Estate Planning 325.)

"Estate tax repeal does not end the need to plan" (2001). C. Kertz, 67 Practical Tax Strategies 136. (*Digested under* Estate Planning, page 46.)

"IRS proposes to allow automatic extension of the estate tax return filing date" (2001). The IRS has issued proposed regulations that would make the granting of a six-month extension of the time for filing the federal estate tax return (Form 706) automatic, and would remove the requirement that the executor provide reasonable grounds for such an extension. Executors should, however, be careful when they take advantage of this change, to avoid penalties for failure to pay estate taxes in a timely fashion. (H.M. Zaritsky, 28 Estate Planning 48.)

"New U.S. tax act—dramatic consequences for estate, gift, GST regime in the foreign context" (2001). Although the Economic Growth and Tax Relief Reconciliation Act of 2001 primarily benefits U.S. citizens and residents, it also contains dramatic changes affecting the U.S. estate, gift, and generation-skipping transfer (GST) taxes that are equally significant for U.S. citizens and non-U.S. persons who invest in the United States or have U.S. family members.

After reviewing current law, the authors provide an overview of the changes. The changes in the Act can be divided into five segments: (1) estate tax changes; (2) GST tax changes; (3) gift tax changes; (4) basis step-up issues; and (5) new reporting requirements.

Estate tax changes include increases in the applicable exemption from the federal wealth transfer tax and a reduction in the maximum marginal estate tax rate.

Effective January 1, 2002, the GST tax exemption equals the exemption from wealth transfer taxes discussed in the article, and the maximum rate of the tax equals the rates for the estate tax discussed in the article. The GST tax is scheduled to be repealed in the year 2010. Absent congressional influence, the tax reverts to the 55 percent maximum rate in 2011 with an exemption of U.S. $1 million indexed for inflation.

The gift tax continues in its present form, with the estate tax rates applying to the gift tax until 2010. An exemption of U.S. $1 million applies after 2001. In 2010, the gift tax continues, with the rate equaling the then highest marginal income tax rate (which is scheduled to decline to 35 percent), even though the estate tax has been repealed.

Once the estate tax is repealed on January 1, 2010, the current basis step-up at death that occurs in certain circumstances will be repealed and replaced with a modified carryover basis.

On January 1, 2010, when the modified carryover basis rules become effective, some transfers at death and by gift must be reported.

Then, the authors discuss the effect of the changes. For many non-U.S. families that have U.S. citizens or residents in the younger generations, the new rules can have very negative tax results absent careful advanced planning. Existing ''inbound'' grantor trusts will need special attention, as will a variety of other holding structures commonly employed by international families. (P. Marcovici, T. Lewis, M.J. Michaels, V.A. Dalmas & C. Hsieh-Kammerlander, 12 Journal of International Taxation, No. 9, 10.)

''Planning for use of the TPT credit yields significant tax savings'' (2001). Section 2013 allows a credit against the federal estate tax due on one estate for all or part of the federal estate tax paid by another estate. More specifically, the credit for tax on prior transfers (the TPT credit) is allowed against the federal estate tax imposed on a present decedent's estate (the ''transferee-decedent'') for federal estate tax paid on the transfer of property to the transferee-decedent from a transferor (the ''transferor-decedent'') who died within ten years before, or within two years after, the transferee-decedent.

To claim the TPT credit, there is no requirement that the transferred property be identified in the estate of the transferee-decedent or that the property be in existence at the time of such decedent's death. The TPT credit is allowed if the property transferred to the transferee-decedent was subject to federal estate tax in the estate of the transferor-decedent and the transferor-decedent died within the prescribed period. This fact is significant because it allows the TPT credit to be claimed in the transferee-dece-

dent's estate even though the property is not subject to tax in such estate.

After providing background, the author discusses the valuation of property for purposes of determining the TPT credit. For this purpose, the value of the property transferred is the value of the property at which it was included in the transferor-decedent's gross estate for federal estate tax purposes, less: (1) any lien or encumbrance thereon that was assumed by or imposed on the transferee-decedent at the time of acquisition; (2) the death taxes that were payable out of the transferred property or that the transferee-decedent might have been required to pay; and (3) any marital deduction that was allowed on the transfer to the decedent.

Then, the author addresses the calculation of the TPT credit, including limitations and the percentage reduction. The TPT credit available to the transferee-decedent's estate is calculated by incorporating certain limitations and a percentage reduction based on the time that has elapsed between the transferor-decedent's death and the transferee-decedent's death.

Finally, the author considers planning to use the TPT credit. Numerous strategies may be implemented to take advantage of the TPT credit. Because of the sizable benefit that may be obtained from claiming the credit, these strategies should be considered before and after the death of all individuals. For spouses in particular, the closeness of their ages, similarity of testamentary wishes, and the fact that the TPT credit may be claimed for property that is not included in the surviving spouse's taxable estate make such strategies especially relevant when planning or administering their estates. (D.L. Herrmann, 28 Estate Planning 478.)

''Post-death certainties do not count in valuing estate'' (2001). 67 Practical Tax Strategies 240. (*Digested under* Valuation of Property—In General, page 264.)

''Post-death events not considered in valuing deduction'' (2001). 66 Practical Tax Strategies 293. (*Digested under* Valuation of Property—In General, page 264.)

"Rental real estate gets installment payment break" (2001). According to Letter Ruling 200114005, interests the decedent owned in residential rental units count as closely held business interests for purposes of Section 6166. Therefore, estate tax attributable to these interests may be paid in installments. (66 Practical Tax Strategies 380.)

"Sometimes less is more: the estate tax tradeoffs involved in the family business elections" (2001). In the last twenty-five years, Congress has added several provisions to the Code that are designed to minimize the effects of federal transfer taxes on family businesses. These include Section 2032A (special-use valuation for certain farm and other family-owned business real property), Section 2057 (estate tax deduction for certain qualified family-owned business interests, or QFOBI), and Section 6166 (deferral and installment payment of estate taxes for certain family-owned businesses).

After providing a brief overview of the statutes, the authors discuss reducing the Section 2032A election. As of this writing, Congress is considering either gradual repeal or significant revisions to the estate tax. In the interim, Congress could consider a legislative fix for the potential effects of a Section 2032A election on the qualification tests for Sections 2057 and 6166. Until this happens, tax professionals should be aware of the tax-saving potential of electing less than the Section 2032A maximum reduction in estate tax values if such an action preserves qualification for Sections 2057 and 6166. Simple algebraic and spreadsheet techniques can aid in determining the optimum Section 2032A election for these purposes. (J.O. Everett, N.B. Nichols, D.B. Davidson & J.L. Lonnes, 94 Journal of Taxation 338.)

"Subsequent litigation cannot alter amount of claim deducted" (2001). In *Estate of O'Neal* (2001) (a case of first impression for the Eleventh Circuit), the court ruled that post-death events cannot be considered when valuing a claim deducted on a federal estate tax return. (28 Estate Planning 548.)

"Use of property after partial disposition not a retained life estate" (2001). In a lengthy opinion, the Tax Court held in *Estate of Wineman* (2000) that a decedent's continued use of a residence and surrounding land after she had given a 24 percent interest in the property to her children was not a retained life estate in the children's share of the property. (28 Estate Planning 30.)

Gross Estate

"Gifts given under power of attorney included in estate" (2001). Pre-death transfers of a decedent's property that were made under a general power of attorney for no consideration were revocable under state law and includable in the decedent's gross estate under Section 2038(a)(1), according to the Tax Court in *Estate of Gaynor* (2001). (67 Practical Tax Strategies 241.)

"Use of property after making gift kept it in estate" (2001). A condominium that the decedent transferred, during her lifetime, to an irrevocable trust for the benefit of her grandchildren was included in her estate because she continued to live there rent free up until her death, according to the Tax Court in *Estate of Trotter* (2001). (67 Practical Tax Strategies 304.)

Income Tax

"Calculation of deduction for income in respect of decedent" (2001). A Kentucky federal district court held in *Estate of Cherry* (2001) that the income tax deduction for the estate tax attributable to income in respect of a decedent (IRD) is computed by first calculating the estate tax on the entire amount (including the marital share), and then beginning the recomputation by removing the IRD before proceeding in the customary fashion (including a recomputation of the marital share). (66 Practical Tax Strategies 299.)

"Court agrees with IRS in calculating Section 691(c) deduction" (2001). According to a Kentucky federal district court in *Estate of Cherry* (2001), the income tax deduction under Section 691(c) is determined by first calculating the estate tax on the entire estate (including the ordinary consideration of the marital share) and then making the recomputation by removing the income in respect of a decedent before proceeding in the customary fashion (including therein a recomputation of the marital share). (28 Estate Planning 327.)

"Deduction offsets 'double tax' on inherited income" (2001). Conflict over calculating the income tax deduction for estate tax paid in connection with income in respect of a decedent (IRD) has arisen again. IRD is included in the gross estate of the decedent and, therefore, subject to the estate tax. Section 691(a), however, also requires IRD to be included in gross income in the year it is received by the beneficiary. To avoid excessive taxation on IRD items, Section 691(c) provides a deduction in the year that IRD is received. The amount of this deduction is the source of major controversy between the IRS and taxpayers.

After providing statutory background, the authors discuss case law, including the Tax Court decisions in *Chastain* (1972) and *Estate of Kincaid* (1985), and the Kentucky federal district court decision in *Estate of Cherry* (2001). The correct calculation of the income tax deduction for estate tax attributable to IRD can be difficult in situations where the estate tax is affected by a charitable deduction or marital deduction. Each of the situations could have been clarified considerably by designating in the will who was to receive the IRD items. If the qualified charitable beneficiary received the IRD items (not being subject to income tax), there would be no subsequent income tax due on the collection of the IRD items. Of course, there would be no Section 691(c) deduction either, since the assets flowing to the charity would not be subject to estate tax.

Chastain seems to stand for the proposition that in the event IRD items do not flow to the charity, the Section 691(c) deduction is preserved for the recipients. Similarly, in the marital deduction context, the situation is clarified by clearly indicating which beneficiary is to receive IRD items. If the surviving spouse is to receive the IRD items, no Section 691(c) deduction is allowed, as the items would not be subject to estate tax (*Cherry* analysis). If a non-spouse receives the IRD items, the Section 691(c) deduction is preserved (*Kincaid* analysis). The key to the Section 691(c) deduction calculation and to avoiding costly litigation is preplanned designation of the beneficiary for IRD items. (C.J. Langstraat & A.M. Cagle, 67 Practical Tax Strategies 86.)

EVASION OF TAX

(*See* Interest and Penalties)

EXCHANGES, TAX-FREE

(*See* Like-Kind Exchanges; Reorganizations)

EXEMPT ORGANIZATIONS

(*See* Tax-Exempt Organizations)

EXPENSES

(*See* Business Expenses)

EXTENSIONS OF TIME

(*See* Assessment and Collection; Procedure)

F

FAILURE TO FILE

(*See* Interest and Penalties)

FAILURE TO PAY TAX

(*See* Interest and Penalties)

FAIR MARKET VALUE

(*See* Valuation of Property)

FARMING

"Unearth 'farmer' status and harvest beneficial tax treatment" (2001). Farmers are entitled to a variety of tax advantages, but the definition of who Is a farmer varies among the relevant tax provisions. Specifically, the Code makes it easier for farmers to do the following: (1) accelerate expenses; (2) avoid estimated taxes; (3) use unique accounting methods; (4) circumvent the uniform capitalization rules; (5) use income averaging; (6) elect methods that defer or accelerate income recognition; and (7) reduce the value of farmland or timber for estate tax purposes.

Naturally, these rules make the definitions of "farming" and "farmer" important to those taxpayers that could potentially qualify for these provisions.

After providing background on the relevant statutory provisions, the authors address administrative and judicial interpretations. Even though the Code and administrative interpretations provide a basis for defining what farming is and who qualifies as a farmer, the sources are still too general to provide guidance in all practical situations.

For this reason, the practitioner must look to judicial decisions that attempt to interpret congressional intent with regard to these definitions. However, courts have demonstrated a lack of consistency because of the lack of a general definition for "farmer."

The judiciary and the IRS are faced with the problem of separating the activities of a taxpayer for classification as a farmer. That is, is the activity engaged in for profit or for a hobby? After this classification is completed, the issue of various overlapping Code sections is inserted to further cloud the problem. (T.D. Englebrecht & A. Moore, 67 Practical Tax Strategies 166.)

FIDUCIARIES

(*See* Pension and Profit-Sharing Plans; Trusts and Trust Taxation)

FINES AND PENALTIES

(*See* Interest and Penalties)

FOOD AND LODGING

(*See* Business Expenses)

FOREIGN CORPORATIONS, PERSONS, AND PARTNERSHIPS

(*See also* Foreign Tax Credit; International Taxation)

"Are certain persons treated as residents of a treaty country liable to tax in such country?" (2001). In Revenue Ruling 2000-59, the IRS addresses three situations for purposes of determining whether a person (a corporation in situations 1 and 2 and a trust in situation 3) is "liable to tax" in a treaty country and thus eligible for treaty benefits as a resident of the treaty country. (3 Business Entities, No. 1, 60.)

"Case of first impression: acquiror had to include subpart F income of voting/grantor trust" (2001). The Tax Court held in *Textron Inc.* (2001), a case of first impression, that a corporation that transferred its stock in a controlled foreign corporation (CFC) to a voting trust did not have to include the CFC's subpart F income in its income because it did not own the stock after the transfer. However, the corporation had to recognize the trust's subpart F income derived from the acquired corporation because the trust was classified as a grantor trust owned by the corporation. (12 Journal of International Taxation, No. 11, 3.)

"CFC restructuring and disposition—how international provisions alter the general rules" (2001). This article highlights some of the more important issues that the domestic corporate shareholder of a controlled foreign corporation (CFC) faces in CFC restructurings and dispositions by using several typical transactions. Specifically, the discussion examines the following types of restructurings and dispositions involving a CFC: (1) a foreign-to-foreign Section 368(a)(1)(C) reorganization ("C" reorganization); (2) a foreign-to-foreign triangular "C" reorganization; (3) an inbound "C" reorganization; (4) a foreign-to-foreign Section 368(a)(1)(B) reorganization ("B" reorganization); (5) a Section 355 distribution of the stock of a CFC; (6) a CFC's sale of all of its assets followed by a Section 332 liquidation into its domestic parent; and (7) a sale of the CFC stock. (J.M. Calianno & B.J. Gregoire, 12 Journal of International Taxation, No. 10, 34.)

"Credit advanced to foreign subsidiary for inventory purchases was equity, not debt" (2001). In FSA 200133013, the IRS reviewed the factors applicable to the determination of whether an interest represented debt or equity, and concluded that a domestic corporation's accounts receivable from its foreign subsidiary were equity and not debt from the time they originated. Thus, the taxpayer could not take a foreign currency loss on the exchange of debt for equity. (95 Journal of Taxation 312.)

"Extraterritorial exclusion replaces FSC regime: mirror rules, broader spectrum" (2001). The Foreign Sales Corporation (FSC) Repeal and Extraterritorial Income Exclusion Act of 2000 (the Act) may increase U.S. competitiveness far beyond the prior regime and is unlikely to pass muster with the European Union (EU).

First, the author discusses the expanded list of beneficiaries. The Act provides benefits comparable to the FSC regime, but a broader spectrum of taxpayers are eligible. Thus, the FSC program's forced repeal and its replacement with the extraterritorial exclusion may have the effect of increasing U.S. competitiveness.

Then, the author addresses extraterritorial exclusion. The Act's intent is to exclude a specified portion of extraterritorial income, the income attributable to foreign trading gross receipts (FTGR). Under Sections 114(c) and (d), business deductions and foreign tax credits attributable to excluded income are disallowed. However, Section 943(d) allows a foreign tax credit for foreign withholding taxes imposed on qualifying foreign trade income (QFTI) if computed under either the FTGR or foreign trade income (FTI) methods. Foreign corporations operating in jurisdictions with significant foreign income taxes might forgo the election to be treated as domestic corporations, since the loss of foreign tax credits might more than offset any extraterritorial benefit.

Section 114(b) clarifies that only a portion of extraterritorial income is excludable, namely QFTI. For a given transaction, Section 941(a) defines QFTI as the gross income that, if excluded, would reduce taxable income by one of the following: (1) 30 percent of foreign sale and leasing income (FSLI) (FSLI method); (2) 1.2 percent of FTGR not to exceed 30 percent of FTI

(FTGR method); or (3) 15 percent of FTI (FTI method).

Finally, the author considers source implications. As under the prior FSC provisions, Section 943(c) limits the foreign-source income on a transaction from which the taxpayer reaps an extraterritorial exclusion benefit. This "haircut rule" applies only to benefits calculated under the FTI and FTGR methods. (E.R. Larkins, 12 Journal of International Taxation, No. 5, 22.)

"Foreign corporation's overpayment interest accrued from prescribed filing date" (2001). The Court of Federal Claims, in *Overseas Thread Industries, Ltd.* (2000), held that interest on overpayments made by a foreign corporation that was not engaged in trade or business in the U.S. accrued on the last day prescribed for filing a tax return rather than the date that the corporation actually filed the return. (12 Journal of International Taxation, No. 3, 6.)

"Foreign entities: proposed regulations under check-the-box rules" (2001). Proposed regulations provide that a business entity wholly owned by a foreign government is a per se corporation and cannot elect to be treated as a disregarded entity. (3 Business Entities, No. 2, 56.)

"FSC repeal legislation enacted: EU challenge underway" (2001). The U.S. House of Representatives on November 14, 2000, approved by a vote of 316-72 a Senate-amended version of H.R. 4986, the FSC Repeal And Extraterritorial Income Exclusion Act of 2000. President Clinton signed the bill into law on November 15, 2000. The legislation is the U.S. response to a World Trade Organization (WTO) ruling that the U.S. foreign sales corporation (FSC) regime constitutes a prohibited export subsidy. The European Union (EU) challenged the FSC rules in the WTO and prevailed not only in the initial determination by a WTO dispute settlement panel, but in a WTO appellate body affirmation of the panel's decision as well. It remains to be seen whether an "out of court" settlement may eventually be reached before the WTO panel or appellate body completes work on the issue. (D. Benson & L. Garrett-Nelson, 12 Journal of International Taxation, No. 2, 33.)

"Guidance on tax attributes in Section 367(b) exchanges will make planning easier" (2001). In an ambitious attempt to synthesize the post-1986 foreign tax credit regime and the corporate tax provisions, the IRS has issued new proposed regulations addressing the carryover of tax attributes, such as earnings and profit (E&P) and foreign taxes, in transactions described in Section 367(b). The proposed regulations cover three major categories of such transactions: (1) inbound asset reorganizations or liquidations; (2) combinations of two or more foreign corporations in a Section 381 transaction; and (3) foreign divisive transactions. The new rules are proposed to apply to Section 367(b) exchanges that occur on or after thirty days after final regulations are published in the Federal Register.

First, the authors discuss repatriation of foreign corporate assets. The new proposed regulations address the carryover of net operating loss (NOL) and capital loss carryovers, and E&P (or deficit in E&P) that is not included in income as an "all earnings and profits amount." Generally, these tax attributes do not carry over from a foreign acquired corporation to a domestic acquiring corporation (and, as a result, are eliminated) unless they are effectively connected to a U.S. trade or business (or, in the case of a relevant U.S. income tax treaty, are attributable to a permanent establishment).

Then, the authors consider carryovers in certain foreign-to-foreign nonrecognition transactions. Proposed Regulation § 1.367 (b)-7 applies to an acquisition by a foreign corporation (foreign acquiring corporation) of the assets of another foreign corporation (foreign target corporation) in a transaction described in Section 381 (foreign 381 transaction). Foreign 381 transactions include foreign-to-foreign C, D, or F reorganizations and foreign-to-foreign Section 332 liquidations. The proposed regulation provides guidance as to the manner and extent to which E&P, deficits, and foreign income taxes of the foreign acquiring corporation

57

and foreign target corporation carry over to the foreign surviving corporation. Generally, non–previously taxed E&P and related foreign income taxes of the foreign acquiring corporation and the foreign target corporation carry over to the foreign surviving corporation and retain their character.

Finally, the authors turn to allocations in certain foreign corporate separations, the special rules for F reorganizations and similar transactions, notice, and changes to Regulation § 1.367(b)-5. (V.A. Gosain, V.R. Kraay & S. Goldstein, 94 Journal of Taxation 242.)

"International aspects of Section 355 transactions" (2001). Normal Section 355 nonrecognition may be modified or overridden by other Code provisions, including Sections 897, 367(b), and 367(e), when foreign persons are involved.

First, the author provides background on Sections 897, 367(b), and 367(e)(1). In some instances, a foreign distributing corporation (Distributing) will be distributing stock of a domestic controlled corporation (Controlled) that has substantial real estate holdings in a Section 355 transaction. Consequently, if Controlled is a United States Real Property Holding Corporation (USRPHC), such a distribution would fall within the ambit of Section 897. Additionally, Distributing (as opposed to Controlled) may be a USRPHC in a Section 355 distribution. Therefore, this distribution would also be subject to Section 897, so general understanding of Section 897 is necessary to determine when and how it applies in the context of a Section 355 transaction.

Section 367(b) and the regulations thereunder apply to Section 355 transactions that involve foreign corporations by dividing them into three categories that include distributions in which: (1) Distributing is a domestic corporation and Controlled is a controlled foreign corporation (CFC); (2) Distributing is a CFC and the distribution is pro rata; and (3) Distributing is a CFC and the distribution is non-pro rata.

As a general proposition, Section 367(b) is designed to preserve the potential application of Section 1248, which converts certain U.S. shareholders' gain on the sale or exchange of stock in a CFC into dividend income.

A domestic Distributing's otherwise nonrecognition distribution to a foreign distributee under Section 355 potentially becomes taxable to Distributing via Section 367(e)(1).

Then, the author addresses the application of Sections 897, 367(b), and 367(e), using eight examples. (J.M. Calianno, 12 Journal of International Taxation, No. 1, 12.)

"IRS guidance on FSC replacement regime" (2001). Revenue Procedure 2001-37 provides guidance on elections made under the Foreign Sales Corporation (FSC) Repeal and Extraterritorial Income Exclusion Act of 2000, which generally repealed the foreign sales corporation provisions (Sections 921 through 927) for transactions entered into after September 30, 2000, and amended the definition of "gross income" to exclude certain extraterritorial income. However, the Act also provided a transition rule for FSCs in existence on September 30, 2000, whereby the FSC provisions remain applicable to FSC transactions for a limited period. (12 Journal of International Taxation, No. 9, 5.)

"IRS OKs tabular schedules for FSC reporting" (2001). The IRS has announced that foreign sales corporations (FSCs) may use tabular schedules as an alternative format to report transactions that generate foreign trading gross receipts for 1999 and prior tax years (Notice 2000-49). (12 Journal of International Taxation, No. 1, 4.)

"New Section 367(b) proposed regulations— has Treasury's fear of tax-attribute trafficking resulted in compliance-proof rules? (Part 1)" (2001). The Section 367(b) proposed regulations provide guidance in an area that has long forced taxpayers to piece together reasonable positions and draw analogies, but unless they are simplified considerably, even well-meaning taxpayers (and IRS agents) may be unable to apply them properly.

The proposed regulations deal with three different types of nonrecognition transactions: (1) inbound asset transactions (C, D, or F reorganizations and Section 332 liquidations involving a transfer of assets from a foreign corporation to a domestic corporation); (2) foreign-to-foreign asset transactions (C, D, or F reorganizations and Section 332 liquidations involving a transfer of assets from one foreign corporation to another foreign corporation); and (3) Section 355 transactions (where either the distributing or the controlled corporation (or both) is foreign). Each type raises its own issues and is subject to its own special rules. Part 1 of this article addresses the foreign-to-foreign transactions.

After providing background on the proposed regulations, the authors discuss foreign-to-foreign asset transactions. The most significant part of the regulations covers the carryover of tax attributes from one foreign corporation to another foreign corporation in an asset transaction described in Section 381. In this context, the most important tax attributes are the earnings and profits (E&P) history and the associated foreign income taxes of the transferor corporation, because they govern the calculation of deemed-paid foreign tax credits and foreign tax credit basket characterization when such E&P is distributed, or deemed distributed, to a U.S. shareholder. The proposed regulations contain several rules relating to these attributes, in an effort to further the policies underlying the foreign tax credit provisions.

These rules take into account not only the Tax Reform Act of 1986 changes to the foreign tax credit provisions but also the Taxpayer Relief Act of 1997 changes, in particular, the long-awaited demise of the "10/50" basket. Under Sections 902 (d)(2)(E) and 902(d)(4), dividends paid by a "noncontrolled Section 902 corporation" (a.k.a. "10/50 company") out of E&P generated after 2002 will be entitled to the same "look-through" treatment that dividends from a "controlled foreign corporation" (CFC) have long enjoyed under Section 904(d)(3). In other words, the character of such dividends for purposes of the foreign tax credit limitation rules of Section 904(d) generally will be the same as that of the income earned by the foreign corporation

itself. Accordingly, the proposed regulations introduce a new term ("look-through corporations") to cover all foreign corporations that may pay dividends subject to look-through treatment, whether CFCs or 10/50 companies after 2002 (Proposed Regulation § 1.367(b)-2(l)(9)). By contrast, 10/50 companies paying dividends before 2003, for which no look-through treatment is available, are called "non-look-through 10/50 corporations" (Proposed Regulation § 1.367(b)-2(l)(10)).

Given the different treatment of these two types of corporations for foreign tax credit purposes, the proposed regulations provide different rules for transactions in which the "foreign surviving corporation" (FS) is one or the other. They also provide a third set of rules, for transactions in which FS is less than 10 percent U.S.-owned.

If FS is a "look-through corporation," its E&P history is divided into three parts under the proposed regulations: (1) "look-through pool"; (2) "non-look-through pool"; and (3) pre-pooling annual layers. After the transaction, distributions from FS are drawn first from its look-through pool, second from the non-look-through pool, and third from the pre-pooling annual layers using an annual last-in, first-out (LIFO) method (Proposed Regulation § 1.367(b)-7(c)(1)).

If FS is a non-look-through corporation immediately after the transaction, its E&P history is divided into two parts: (1) the non-look-through pool and (2) the pre-pooling annual layers. After the transaction, distributions from FS are drawn first from the non-look-through pool, and second from the pre-pooling annual layers using an annual LIFO method (Proposed Regulation § 1.367(b)-7(c)(2)).

The proposed regulations also provide seven special rules that, for the most part, are not dependent on the post-transaction status of FS. Some are administrative, while others represent important anti-abuse rules.

The hovering deficit rules of the proposed regulations clearly would apply in the context of actual dividend distributions. Whether they also would apply in the context of Section 1248 or Section 367(b)

59

deemed dividends is much less clear. This uncertainty is exacerbated by various flaws in the current Section 1248 rules. (B.T. Bress, T.F. Anson & C.A. Dubert, 12 Journal of International Taxation, No. 6, 4.)

"New Section 367(b) proposed regulations (Part 2)" (2001). When corporations undertake certain types of nonrecognition transactions, such as Section 368 asset reorganizations, Section 332 liquidations, or Section 355 transactions, some or all of their tax history generally carries over to other corporations. In proposed regulations issued under Section 367(b) on November 15, 2000, the IRS has addressed the carryover of tax attributes to or from foreign corporations as a result of such transactions, taking into account the special issues that arise when foreign corporations are involved.

The proposed regulations deal with three different types of transactions: (1) inbound asset transactions (C, D, or F reorganizations, and Section 332 liquidations involving a transfer of assets from a foreign corporation to a domestic corporation); (2) foreign-to-foreign asset transactions (C, D, or F reorganizations, and Section 332 liquidations involving a transfer of assets from one foreign corporation to another); and (3) Section 355 transactions (where either the distributing or the controlled corporation, or both, is foreign). Each type raises its own issues and is subject to its own special rules. Part 1 of this article addressed the foreign-to-foreign asset transactions. This part addresses the inbound asset transactions and the Section 355 transactions.

First, the authors discuss inbound asset transactions. In the context of inbound asset transactions of the type described previously, the most important tax attributes are the earnings and profits (E&P), loss carryovers, and basis in assets of the foreign corporation. The proposed regulations provide rules dealing with the first two, but do not address the third.

Then, the authors address Section 355 transactions. The Section 367(b) proposed regulations modify the rules of Section 312(h) when either Distributing or Controlled, or both, is foreign. They provide: (1)

general rules that override the normal rules of Section 312(h) whenever a foreign corporation is involved in a Section 355 transaction and (2) special rules for each of the possible combinations: (a) domestic Distributing/foreign Controlled; (b) foreign Distributing/domestic Controlled; and (c) foreign Distributing/foreign Controlled.

Finally, the authors address reporting requirements. To enable the IRS to keep track of the movement of tax attributes in the Section 355 transactions and in the foreign-to-foreign transactions described in Part 1 of this article, the proposed regulations add such transactions to the list of those that taxpayers must report under Section 367(b). (B.T.N. Bress, T.F. Anson & C.A. Dubert, 12 Journal of International Taxation, No. 7, 18.)

"No interest-netting allowed in computing DISC/FSC income" (2001). The Fifth Circuit in *Dresser Industries, Inc.* (2001) affirmed a district court decision and held that Regulation § 1.861-8(e) did not permit a taxpayer to first offset interest income against interest expense and then apportion only the "net" interest expense between its domestic international sales corporation/foreign sales corporation (DISC/FSC) activities and its non-DISC/FSC activities in computing combined taxable income attributable to qualified export receipts or foreign trading gross receipts. (12 Journal of International Taxation, No. 5, 4.)

"Opportunities for the foreign investor in U.S. real estate—if planning comes first" (2001). M. Hirschfeld & S. Grossman, 94 Journal of Taxation 36. (*Digested under* Real Estate, page 172.)

"Planning for foreign corporations using partnerships to take the plunge into U.S. markets" (2001). For a combination of practical reasons, it is likely that a foreign business seeking to expand into the United States will become a partner with an existing U.S. business. A thorough understanding of the tax consequences of owning a U.S. partnership interest and the various permutations involved—permanent establishment, effectively connected income, branch-level taxation, withholding—is required before any decisions are made.

First, the authors discuss income tax regimes. A foreign corporation can be subject to income tax on its U.S.-source income under two separate tax regimes: (1) the graduated income tax rates applicable to domestic taxpayers on its net income effectively connected with a U.S. trade or business (Section 882(a)) and (2) a 30 percent withholding tax (which may be reduced by treaty) on the gross amount of its U.S. source fixed or determinable, annual or periodic (FDAP) income (Section 881(a)).

Next, the authors consider branch-level taxes. In addition to being subject to U.S. income tax, a foreign corporation is subject to the branch profits tax and the excess branch interest tax when the foreign corporation is a partner in a U.S. partnership that is engaged in a U.S. trade or business.

Then, the authors address interest allocation. A foreign corporation engaged in a U.S. trade or business is required to allocate or apportion its worldwide interest expense to its income effectively connected with the U.S. trade or business.

Finally, the author discusses investments in U.S. realty, withholding tax, and partnership formation and sale. (P.C. Lau & S.L. Soltis, 94 Journal of Taxation 105.)

"Planning for U.S. beneficiaries of foreign trusts under recent regulations" (2001). S.D. Harrington, 28 Estate Planning 258. (*Digested under* Trusts and Trust Taxation, page 251.)

"Pre-immigration planning: income, gift, estate, and GST tax strategies" (2001). Advisors must be aware of the many ramifications—especially tax effects—of country-to-country moves for their clients. For various reasons, most immigration moves have been to the United States. Therefore, pre-move U.S. tax planning is important for the immigrant. To provide that service, an advisor needs an understanding of U.S. income, gift, estate, and generation-skipping transfer (GST) taxation of nonresident aliens (NRAs).

This article provides a summary of these rules. However, due to their complexity, reference to official sources (e.g., statutes, regulations, cases) or consultation with a tax expert in this area is strongly recommended.

First, the author discusses income tax. U.S. citizens and residents generally are taxed on worldwide income. NRAs are taxed only on U.S.-source income. U.S. citizenship generally is obtained either by birth in the U.S. or by naturalization. The definition of "resident" for U.S. income tax purposes is mechanical for the most part. An alien who meets the substantial presence test or the permanent residence test for a year is deemed a U.S. resident for that year.

Next, the author considers source of income rules. NRAs typically are taxable only on U.S.-source income.

Then, the author addresses trusts. For investment, political, and/or other reasons, an NRA may have established a trust in the U.S. and transferred property to it. Trust income is taxable pursuant to the usual grantor or regular trust rules. Each NRA grantor or beneficiary generally is subject to tax only on his allocable share of the trust's U.S.-source income. In contrast, the U.S. resident trust, as well as a U.S. grantor and/or beneficiary, are taxable on their allocable share of all the trust's income.

If a U.S. person transferred property to a foreign trust, such trust generally is treated as a grantor trust for any year that the trust has a U.S. beneficiary.

The rules for trusts as they relate to NRAs are extremely complex. Accordingly, a practitioner should ascertain whether an immigrant client has established any trusts (U.S. or foreign) and, if so, determine the tax consequences of U.S. residency and implement planning for total tax minimization. An NRA who becomes a U.S. resident also should consider planning before making any outbound transfers (i.e., out of the United States).

Finally, the author turns to transfer taxes, including gift tax, estate tax, and generation-skipping tax. (M.A. Aaronson, 28 Estate Planning 196.)

61

"Putting tiered entities into a foreign holding company structure using check-the-box" (2001). P. Grube, 94 Journal of Taxation 5. (*Digested under* Reorganizations, page 178.)

"*Seagate*: Tax Court holds restricted stock gains are subpart F income" (2001). The Tax Court, in *Seagate Technology, Inc.* (2000), addressed the issue of whether gain recognized by a controlled foreign corporation (CFC) on the sale of restricted stock qualified for the trade-or-business exception to subpart F income. The stock had been received as consideration for assets used in the CFC's trade or business and was sold shortly after the restrictions lapsed.

First, the authors discuss subpart F. Subpart F requires U.S. shareholders who own stock directly or indirectly in a CFC to include in their gross income certain undistributed earnings of the CFC (Section 951(a)).

Then, the authors address *Seagate*. The Tax Court rejected the petitioner's argument that the relation-back doctrine applied to characterize the stock gain in accordance with the gain from the prior sale by the CFC of its business assets. Accordingly, the stock gain was held to be subpart F income.

While *Seagate* holds that the stock gain was subpart F income, the opinion indicates that gains from otherwise passive assets under certain circumstances may qualify for the trade-or-business exception. (L.D. Yoder & R.L. Waimon, 12 Journal of International Taxation, No. 4, 40.)

"Section 332 liquidations with foreign corporations: Always consider Section 367" (2001). The normal rules relating to Section 332 liquidations involving domestic corporations may be modified or overridden if either the parent or subsidiary (or both) is a foreign corporation. Sections 367(b) and 367(e) and the regulations thereunder provide special rules that address international concerns relating to Section 332 liquidations involving foreign corporations. These rules may require gain recognition (or permit nonrecognition if certain requirements are satisfied) by a domestic or foreign liquidating subsidiary, income inclusion by a domestic parent, restrictions on the carryover of certain tax attributes, or a modification of the typical treatment of tax attributes.

This article examines how Sections 367(b) and 367(e) and their principal policy considerations apply to Section 332 liquidations by illustrating how these sections may apply to specific types of liquidations—inbound, outbound, and foreign-to-foreign.

First, the author discusses inbound liquidation, where a foreign corporation (FC) liquidates into a domestic corporation (DC). Section 367(b) governs corporate restructurings involving certain nonrecognition provisions (such as Section 332) with respect to which the status of a foreign corporation as a "corporation" is necessary for nonrecognition treatment. As a general premise, Section 367(b) respects a foreign corporation as a corporation except to the extent provided in the regulations. The impetus of Section 367(b) is to prevent the U.S. tax avoidance that can arise when the subchapter C provisions of the Code apply to transactions involving foreign corporations. Since the subchapter C provisions often do not adequately address cross-border aspects of U.S. taxation, Section 367(b) fills the void by causing certain inclusions into income, basis adjustments to assets and to stock and securities, and adjustments to tax attributes. One of the transactions specifically addressed by Section 367(b) is an inbound Section 332 liquidation, in which a principal policy consideration of Section 367(b) is the proper taxation at the shareholder level of previously deferred earnings and profits (E&P).

With respect to requiring proper taxation at the shareholder level, Section 367(b) accomplishes this result by taxing the unrepatriated earnings accumulated during the domestic parent's (direct or indirect) holding period of the foreign liquidating corporation, thus ensuring that (1) a tax deferral is not converted into a forgiveness of tax via Section 332 and (2) the Section 381 carryover basis reflects an after-tax amount.

Pursuant to Regulation § 1.367(b)-3, the domestic parent must include in income as a deemed dividend its "all-E&P amount" with respect to its foreign subsidiary when the foreign subsidiary liquidates.

Then, the author discusses outbound liquidation, where DC liquidates into FC. Section 367(e)(2) and the regulations thereunder set forth rules that permit nonrecognition when the appreciated assets remain subject to the U.S. taxing jurisdiction. Section 367(e)(2) provides that "In the case of any liquidation to which Section 332 applies, except as provided in regulations, subsection (a) and (b)(1) of Section 337 shall not apply where the 80-percent distributee (as defined in Section 337(c)) is a foreign corporation."

Therefore, Section 367(e)(2) generally overrides the normal nonrecognition treatment provided by Section 337(a) and treats the distributing corporation's transfer of assets to its foreign parent as a taxable transaction, except as provided in regulations.

Regulation § 1.367(e)-2(b)(1) reiterates the general rule that a domestic liquidating corporation recognizes gain or loss on a distribution of property to its foreign parent in a Section 332 liquidation.

Finally, the author discusses foreign-to-foreign liquidations, where FC liquidates into its foreign parent (FP). When a foreign subsidiary liquidates into its foreign parent in a Section 332 liquidation, the general rule under Section 367(e) is that the foreign liquidating corporation does not recognize any gain or loss and the foreign parent takes a carryover basis in the assets distributed in the liquidation (Regulation §§ 1.367(e)-2(c)(1) and 1.367(e)-2(c)(3)(i)). However, there are two exceptions to this general nonrecognition rule along with a general anti-abuse rule that may require gain recognition. Also, the IRS has issued proposed regulations addressing the carryover of certain attributes in foreign-to-foreign liquidations.

The two exceptions to the general nonrecognition rule relate to (1) qualifying property and (2) property that formerly was used by the foreign liquidating corporation in a U.S. trade or business. (J.M. Calianno, 12 Journal of International Taxation, No. 6, 36.)

"Squeezing the last drop from the FSC regime" (2001). Final regulations set deadlines for foreign sales corporations (FSCs) deciding to redetermine their grouping strategies. Though the FSC Repeal and Extraterritorial Income Exclusion Act of 2000 (the Act) precludes new FSC elections after September 30, 2000, the final regulations provide tax-saving opportunities for two reasons. First, FSCs terminated because of the Act still have open tax years in which grouping redeterminations can reduce tax liabilities. Second, the Act does not compel FSCs existing on September 30, 2000, to terminate immediately. Under a short-term transitional rule, FSCs can continue applying the FSC provisions to transactions occurring before 2002. Also, a long-term transitional rule permits U.S. exporters to apply the FSC rules to transactions that preexisting and legally binding contracts cover between FSCs (or their related suppliers) and unrelated parties.

This article examines the final regulations and the deadlines for grouping redeterminations under the FSC regime. For this purpose, "grouping redeterminations" involve three decisions that occur after the U.S. exporter files its tax return for a given year: (1) grouping transactions not originally combined; (2) grouping transactions differently than originally combined; and (3) unbundling transactions initially grouped. The rules significantly restrict the time for choosing the optimal approach.

Although the final regulations' time constraints apply specifically to FSC transactions, they may foreshadow future regulations dealing with grouping redeterminations under the extraterritorial exclusion. Many exporters that did not qualify for FSC benefits will qualify for the extraterritorial exclusion. Thus, U.S. exporters should review and upgrade their systems for electronically capturing financial transactions and creating necessary data files so that they will be able to group transactions efficiently and optimally. (E.R. Larkins, 12 Journal of International Taxation, No. 8, 20.)

"Tax year of partnership with foreign partners" (2001). Proposed regulations were issued regarding the tax year of a partnership that has foreign partners. (3 Business Entities, No. 2, 52.)

"The extraterritorial income exclusion enhances the tax benefits once sought from FSCs" (2001). The FSC Repeal and Extraterritorial Income Exclusion Act of 2000, effective for transactions after September 30, 2000, generally replaces the foreign sales corporation (FSC) export tax incentive with an exclusion for "extraterritorial income" (EI), subject to generous transition relief for existing FSCs.

The repeal of the FSC provisions was prompted by a decision of the World Trade Organization (WTO) that the FSC regime was an export contingent subsidy and thus, prohibited under WTO Agreements. Although U.S. officials have expressed optimism that the EI legislation will be accepted by the WTO, the legislation has already been challenged, and the prognosis for its acceptance seems doubtful. Nevertheless, until its possible repeal, the EI exclusion will prove beneficial to many U.S. taxpayers.

After providing historical background on domestic international sales corporations (DISCs) and FSCs, the authors address the EI regime and "qualifying foreign trade income" (QFTI). The heart of the new EI regime is Section 114, which excludes from gross income EI that is QFTI. The exclusion is applicable to any taxpayer and pass-through entity.

Then, the authors compare the EI regime to the FSC regime. The EI regime is simpler than FSC inasmuch as: (1) a taxpayer need not form a special foreign entity to benefit from the EI regime; (2) no intercompany agreements need to be made; (3) no special election has to be timely made to qualify for benefits; and (4) there are no foreign management requirements. The EI applies directly to the U.S. taxpayer, and a taxpayer has to affirmatively choose not to claim the EI exclusion.

Finally, the authors discuss the effective dates and WTO prospects. (A.S. Lederman & B. Hirsh, 94 Journal of Taxation 174.)

"The new extraterritorial income exclusion for S corporations" (2001). The extraterritorial income exclusion mechanism is a fundamental change in the taxation of exporting activities. Under the new tax regime, no separate special purpose domestic or foreign corporation is needed to claim the tax benefits.

The Foreign Sales Corporation (FSC) Repeal and Extraterritorial Income Exclusion Act of 2000 provides that no corporation can elect to be an FSC after September 30, 2000, and an FSC will cease to be an FSC if it generates no foreign trade income for five consecutive years beginning after December 31, 2001. In place of the FSC regime, the new law provides rules that exclude certain extraterritorial income from gross income. Although the FSC provisions are repealed, a transition period is provided for existing FSCs and binding contractual agreements.

After discussing the repeal of the FSC provisions, the authors address the new extraterritorial income exclusion. Under the new law, extraterritorial income that is qualifying foreign trade income is eligible for exclusion from gross income for U.S. income tax purposes. The potential income exclusion is applicable to individuals and corporations, as well as for individual and corporate alternative minimum tax purposes. Because the income exclusion is a means of avoiding double taxation, no foreign tax credit is allowed for income taxes paid or accrued with respect to the excluded income. In addition, expenses that are allocable to the excluded income cannot be deducted.

The amount of the income exclusion is called qualifying foreign trade income. It is the amount of gross income that, if excluded, would reduce the taxable income of a transaction involving a "qualifying foreign trade property" by the greatest of: (1) 1.2 percent of "foreign trading gross receipts" derived from the transaction but not to exceed 30 percent of "foreign trade income" derived from the transaction; (2) 15 percent of "foreign trade income;" or (3) 30 percent of "foreign sale and leasing income" derived from the transaction. A taxpayer can choose any one of the three amounts for any given transaction. If the foreign trading gross receipts method is used for a transaction, the taxpayer, or any related person, cannot have additional qualifying foreign trade income from any other transaction involving the same property.

Then, the authors address S corporation application. The new law does not address how S corporations should claim and report qualifying foreign trade income. Presumably, an S corporation tentatively claims the income exclusion pursuant to Section 1363(c), but shows the excluded income and related expenses separately pursuant to Sections 1363(b) and 1366(a)(1)(A). Individual shareholders should then determine if they can claim the excluded income under the $5 million exception. New Section 942(c) provides that the $5 million threshold for not requiring foreign economic processes is applied at both the entity and shareholder levels.

It is also unclear if individual shareholders can elect not to claim the income exclusion by treating gross receipts from one or more transactions as not being foreign trading gross receipts under new Section 942(a)(3). (S. Soltis & P.C. Lau, 3 Business Entities, No. 2, 40.)

FOREIGN TAX CREDIT

"Cash element of contribution/dividend transaction ignored as attempt to create foreign tax credit" (2001). In FSA 200135020, the IRS concluded that a parent was not eligible for a foreign income tax credit for a dividend received from its foreign subsidiary because the dividend qualified as a nontaxable stock dividend under both a circular-cash-flow analysis and the step-transaction doctrine. (95 Journal of Taxation 379.)

"Foreign tax credit limitation final regulations under Sections 864(e) and 904(d), proposed regulations under Sections 902 and 904" (2001). The IRS issued final regulations on December 29, 2000, under Sections 864(e)(5) and 864(e)(6) relating to the allocation and apportionment of affiliated group interest and other expense allocation and apportionment for alternative minimum tax (AMT) purposes, and under Section 904(d), notably with respect to distributions by controlled foreign corporations (CFCs) that are not eligible for look-through treatment under Section 904(d)(3) and Regulation § 1.904-5. These rules generally finalize provisions that had been proposed in 1992. They also amend certain provisions of the final regulations issued in 1992 under Section 904.

In a separate document issued on the same day, the IRS released proposed regulations under Sections 902 and 904, notably with respect to the cessation of post-1986 Section 902 pooling when a foreign corporation no longer has a "qualifying shareholder." This article reviews these provisions and the potpourri of others in the final and proposed regulations. (A. Fischl, L. Greenwald & N. Suit, 12 Journal of International Taxation, No. 10, 16.)

"Foreign tax credit planning for S corporations" (2001). With the globalization of business, S corporations have increased their international operations; an S corporation can operate overseas by simply making export sales directly to foreign customers. As a company's foreign activities become more extensive and complex, it may need to maintain a foreign presence with personnel and assets situated abroad.

First, the authors discuss choice of foreign entity. An S corporation, generally, should consider obtaining flow-through treatment for any foreign operation that will be subject to significant foreign income tax. Flow-through treatment is also desirable for any operation that would generate subpart F income if it were operated as a foreign corporation. Subpart F income is income that is immediately taxable to the S corporation's shareholders even though it is not repatriated. Subpart F income is generally passive income and income earned outside its country of incorporation by a controlled foreign corporation from certain transactions involving related parties.

65

A foreign corporation may be the preferred structure if it is anticipated that the income of the foreign operation is subject to no or low foreign tax and is not subpart F income. Use of a foreign corporation allows an S corporation's shareholders to defer U.S. income tax on untaxed or low-taxed foreign income. The benefit of tax deferral may outweigh the loss of the foreign tax credit.

Then, the authors address the foreign tax credit and planning strategies. Probably the most important foreign tax planning issue for an S corporation is utilization of the foreign tax credit by its shareholders. A U.S. taxpayer is taxed on its worldwide income. To prevent double taxation of income earned overseas ("foreign source income"), a U.S. taxpayer is allowed to credit foreign income taxes against its U.S. tax liability.

In planning and structuring its foreign operations, an S corporation must have a thorough understanding of foreign tax credits and the effect of the selected foreign structure on the use of foreign tax credits. Careful analysis and planning are essential to optimize the benefit of foreign tax credits and minimize the overall U.S. and foreign taxes for the S corporation and its shareholders. (S. Soltis & P.C. Lau, 3 Business Entities, No. 3, 36.)

"FTC election period runs from credit year, not carryover year" (2001). According to the Tax Court in *Chrysler Corp.* (2001), the ten-year period within which a taxpayer may elect to take a foreign tax credit (FTC) rather than deduct the foreign taxes begins to run on the due date of the return for the year in which the taxpayer elects the credit, and not from the year to which the credit is carried over. (12 Journal of International Taxation, No. 9, 7.)

"Necessary elements of creditable foreign tax not met by U.K. tax on appreciation in privatized utilities" (2001). In FSA 200112011, a windfall tax imposed on privatized U.K. utilities was found not to satisfy the requirements for a creditable tax under Sections 901 and 903. (94 Journal of Taxation 374.)

FOUNDATIONS

(*See* Tax-Exempt Organizations—Private Foundations)

FRAUD

(*See* Interest and Penalties)

FRINGE BENEFITS

(*See also* Business Expenses; Compensation for Personal Services; Deferred Compensation; Pension and Profit-Sharing Plans)

"Cafeteria plan regulations expand mid-year election menu" (2001). Final regulations expand the list of situations in which participants can change their cafeteria plan elections, but give plan administrators no discretion in handling other circumstances.

After providing background, the author discusses the new rules. In 2000, the IRS issued final and proposed regulations dealing with mid-year cafeteria plan elections. In 2001, the IRS modified both the final and proposed regulations, further liberalizing (and clarifying) the regulations with respect to those circumstances under which an employee could change his or her cafeteria plan election with respect to accident and health coverage, group-term life insurance coverage, dependent care assistance, and adoption assistance.

While the regulations are certainly welcome in their expansion of the circumstances in which participants will be allowed to change their elections, the regulations are disappointing in that they are an exclusive list. There is no discretion for a plan administrator to address circumstances not within the four corners of the regulations. (B. Salkin, 66 Practical Tax Strategies 211.)

"Cafeteria plan rules for mid-year election changes—final regulations at last" (2001). Over the last year, the IRS has made significant progress toward finalizing the guidance required to interpret Section 125. In particular, the IRS recently completed the issuance of final regulations relating to the circumstances under which an employee is permitted to make a mid-year election change under a cafeteria plan (an "election change"). Issued in two installments—TD 8878 (the "2000 regulations") and TD 8921 (the "2001 Regulations")—these rules are the first final regulations under Section 125 and clarify and expand on the earlier proposed and temporary regulations.

After providing background on cafeteria plans, the rationale for safe-harbor status, and prior guidance, the authors discuss the 2000 regulations. The 2000 regulations address only election changes relating to accident or health coverage and group-term life insurance coverage. Pursuant to the 2000 regulations, an election change may be made if, under the relevant facts and circumstances, an event in one of the following categories has occurred: (1) a change-in-status event; (2) a special enrollment event; (3) the entry of certain judgments, decrees, or orders; (4) entitlement to Medicare or Medicaid; or (5) the Family and Medical Leave Act of 1993 (FMLA).

Then, the authors consider the 2001 regulations. The substance of the 2001 regulations had been previewed in a set of proposed regulations issued at the same time as the 2000 final regulations. While the 2000 final regulations generally represent the gradual refinement of longstanding proposed rules regarding when an employee may be permitted to make election changes, the 2001 regulations deal with several issues about which cafeteria plan guidance had heretofore been largely silent, i.e., whether an employee can be permitted to make an election change if the benefit plan coverage provided or potentially available to the employee changes during the year or if the cost of such coverage goes up or down.

The 2001 regulations extend the right to make election changes based on changes in cost or in coverage to most qualified benefits, except a health flexible spending account (FSA). In addition, they make some technical changes to the 2000 final regula-

tions. Finally, the authors address effective dates and amendments. (K. Anderson, M.G. Roshkoff & P.J. Schneider, 94 Journal of Taxation 344.)

"COBRA regulations are complete at last as IRS finally fills in the blanks" (2001). The 2001 final regulations under the Consolidated Omnibus Budget Reconciliation Act of 1985 (OBRA) generally cover matters first addressed in the 1987 proposed regulations and about which the IRS, having changed its thinking, sought further public comment prior to finalizing these rules. These matters include the definition of "small employer," the determination of the number of group plans an employer maintains, the interaction between the Family and Medical Leave Act (FMLA) and COBRA, the effect of mergers and acquisitions on COBRA obligations, the extension of the maximum COBRA coverage period on account of disability, the application of COBRA to flexible spending arrangements, and employer withdrawals from multi-employer plans. The 2001 final regulations also clarify certain provisions that were part of the 1999 final regulations. (P.J. Schneider, 95 Journal of Taxation 285.)

"Final regulations clarify qualified transportation fringe benefit rules" (2001). The IRS has issued final regulations that provide guidance, in question and answer format, to employers that furnish qualified transportation fringe benefits to employees. (66 Practical Tax Strategies 175.)

"How small is de minimis for fringe benefit exclusion?" (2001). Nonmonetary recognition awards having a fair market value of $100 do not qualify as de minimis fringe benefits, according to a legal memorandum from the IRS Office of Assistant Chief Counsel (ILM 200108042). (66 Practical Tax Strategies 254.)

"Mass transit commuting exclusion has mass appeal" (2001). The following benefits can be offered on a pretax basis through a commuter expense reimbursement plan: (1) transit passes (i.e., a pass, token, voucher, or similar item that entitles an individual to use mass transit); (2) van-pooling (i.e., transportation provided by an employer in a vehicle that seats at least six, excluding the driver); and (3) qualified parking (i.e., parking on or near the employer's business premises, or at a location from which the employee commutes to work). Section 132(f)(2) places limits on the amounts that employees can receive pre-tax for these benefits.

After discussing the mass transit commuting exclusion, the author provides an illustration of its advantages. The advantages of commuter expense reimbursement plans for employees are the savings of income, Social Security, and Medicare taxes, and in some states the state and local taxes. (T.A. Cardello, 67 Practical Tax Strategies 349.)

"Vacation pay in asset and deemed asset sales: a half-baked trap for the unwary" (2001). The Tax Court held in *Schmidt Baking Co.* (1996) that an accrual-method corporation was entitled to a deduction for vacation (and severance) pay in the year of accrual where, in order to guarantee the funding and payment of the vacation pay obligation, the corporation purchased an irrevocable letter of credit in favor of its employees within two and a half months after the end of its tax year. However, in 1998, Congress enacted Section 404(a)(11), which effectively overturned this result by requiring that the vacation or severance pay actually be received in the pocket by employees within two and a half months after the end of the year of accrual in order for the payor to receive the deduction in that year.

In addition to the obvious disadvantages of this statutory rule for normal on-going business operations, it may pose a substantial hardship in asset sales and deemed asset sales under Section 338 by restricting or precluding the employer-seller's deduction for accrued vacation pay attributable to the year of sale—particularly when the employer ceases to exist (or is treated as such) prior to actual payment of the vacation pay liability. Thus, Section 404(a)(11) provides a potential trap for unwary employers who do not fully appreciate its impact or adequately pre-plan the treatment of vacation pay in accordance with its strict requirements.

After providing background on the vacation pay deduction, *Schmidt*, and Section 404(a)(11), the authors address the vacation pay obligation in the context of an actual or deemed asset sale. If an accrual-method corporation sells (or is deemed to sell) its assets under Section 338 or Section 338(h)(10), and makes a cash payment to its employees in the amount of their earned vacation pay prior to the sale and within the two-and-a-half-month window, if applicable (i.e., with no deferred compensation element), the company will be entitled to deduct its vacation pay under its normal accrual method of accounting. Furthermore, where the accrual-method employer sells its assets but retains the accrued vacation pay obligation and thereafter pays such obligation to its employees (or ex-employees) in cash within two and a half months after its ensuing year-end, the company is once again entitled to deduct the vacation pay in the prior year under its normal method of accounting. Obviously, such treatment presupposes that the selling corporation is still in existence and has not liquidated until after payment of the vacation pay obligation and that the vacation pay meets the actually paid within two-and-a-half months requirement under the Section 404 regulations, and is thus not treated as deferred compensation.

Rather than paying the vacation pay obligation directly, the employer could establish an escrow arrangement to pay the obligation. The deduction will be allowed for the prior year of accrual to the extent actual payment is made to employees within two and a half months after the employer's year-end.

Where a corporation sells its assets and is immediately liquidated, or is treated as liquidated in accordance with deemed asset sale treatment pursuant to an election under Section 338 (or Section 338(h)(10)), and the transferor (or deemed transferor) does not pay (or make arrangements for payment of) the vacation pay obligation within two and a half months after the seller's year-end, the vacation pay deduction will not be available for the seller's final tax return and will be lost to the seller (since the seller will not be in existence at the time the vacation pay is actually paid and included in the gross income of employees).

Then, the authors discuss the deemed actual payment argument, the seller's vacation pay liabilities in the hands of the purchaser, inclusion of the vacation pay liability in the seller's amount realized, potential solutions or mitigating measures, and pass-through entities. (R.W. Harris & B.J. Verhoeven, 3 Business Entities, No. 6, 22.)

FUEL CREDITS

"Waiver needed to obtain fuel credits" (2001). The Tax Court, in an unpublished opinion, held in *Crop Care Applicators, Inc.* (2001) that an agricultural chemical application company was not entitled to fuel credits under Section 34, since it had not obtained prior customer waivers. (66 Practical Tax Strategies 290.)

G

GENERATION-SKIPPING TRANSFER TAX

"Estate tax repeal does not end the need to plan" (2001). C. Kertz, 67 Practical Tax Strategies 136. (*Digested under* Estate Planning, page 46.)

"Final regulations approve certain changes in grandfathered GST trusts" (2001). J.B. O'Grady & J.S. Stringer, 28 Estate Planning 526. (*Digested under* Trusts and Trust Taxation, page 248.)

"Generation-skipping transfer tax planning after the 2001 Act: mostly good news" (2001). Among the useful changes made by the Economic Growth and Tax Relief Reconciliation Act of 2001 (EGTRRA or the 2001 Act) are an expansion of the automatic generation-skipping transfer (GST) exemption allocation rule, a new rule permitting trusts to be severed, a direction for relief with respect to making or electing out of allocations, a new rule directing that a GST allocation is effective if there has been substantial compliance, a limited provision allowing for retroactive allocations, and a clarification of the valuation rules used to determine a trust's inclusion ratio.

First, the authors discuss rates, exemptions, and repeal. EGTRRA is best known to estate planners for its provisions that lead to the one-year repeal of the estate and GST taxes. The 2001 Act's pattern of gradual tax reduction, one-year repeal, and restoration of these taxes in 2011 is so bizarre that these provisions in their current form probably will never be fully effective. Changes could occur over the next several years before the effective dates of any significant portion of the legislation. As a result, EGTRRA is not likely to have the simplifying impact on estate planning that one would expect repeal legislation to have.

Then, the authors address the fix-up provisions. EGTRRA makes significant changes to the GST tax rules intended to reduce the likelihood that taxpayers will be harmed by inadvertent failures to allocate GST exemption and other traps found within the complex rules relating to the GST tax. Like the rest of the 2001 Act, these changes are scheduled to vanish in 2011. Unlike the repeal portions of EGTRRA, however, the fix-up provisions are relatively noncontroversial and almost revenue neutral.

There are six principal fix-ups: (1) an expansion of the automatic GST exemption allocation rule; (2) a new rule permitting trust severances; (3) a direction to Treasury to grant extensions of time to allocate or to elect out of allocation of GST exemption in appropriate circumstances; (4) a new rule directing that a GST exemption allocation is effective, if there has been substantial compliance with the rules for making an allocation; (5) a new rule permitting retroactive allocation of GST exemption in limited instances; and (6) a clarification of the valuation rules that are used to determine a trust's inclusion ratio. (C.A. Harrington, C.S. McCaffrey, L.L. Plaine & P.H. Schneider, 95 Journal of Taxation 143.)

"New U.S. tax act—dramatic consequences for estate, gift, GST regime in the foreign context" (2001). P. Marcovici, T. Lewis, M.J. Michaels, V.A. Dalmas & C. Hsieh-Kammerlander, 12 Journal of International Taxation, No. 9, 10. (*Digested under* Estates and Estate Tax—In General, page 51.)

"Structure generation-skipping gifts for tax savings" (2001). The generation-skipping transfer (GST) tax is being repealed for only 2010, but with proper planning, transfers initiated in other years can be classified for tax purposes as having been made in that year.

First, the author discusses preparing for 2010 terminations and distributions. Direct skips are not the only taxable GSTs. The GST tax (and GST tax repeal) also applies to "taxable distributions" and "taxable terminations.'' There is a critical difference between the direct skip and these other types of GSTs. A direct skip is a one-step transaction; that is, the gift or bequest occurs simultaneously with the GST.

Taxable distributions and taxable terminations are the result of two-step transactions. The first step is a transfer to a trust that has at least one beneficiary who is only one generation below the transferor. This beneficiary is the "nonskip person," typically a child of the transferor. The second step is where the trust, or a distribution from it, no longer has any such nonskip person as a beneficiary. That is the point where some or all of the trust assets pass from the children's generation to the grandchildren's generation. Although we might refer to the trust as a "generation-skipping trust," the taxable "generation-skipping transfer" will not have occurred until this second step.

There is a delay between the original gift or bequest to the generation-skipping trust, and the subsequent taxable GST. It is this delay that creates the planning opportunity. The delay means that a taxpayer can do the first step now (in a testamentary document or in an irrevocable inter vivos transfer), which will mature into a GST in 2010 when such transfers are not subject to GST tax.

Next, the author considers strategies for dealing with the dilemma created by delay GSTs. A grandparent is not going to want to give a child a general power of appointment over a nonexempt trust, because that eliminates completely the opportunity to make major gifts in 2010 free of both gift and GST taxes. On the other hand, if the child does not have a general power of appointment and dies before 2010, that could be a taxable termination, subject to the GST tax at the highest estate tax rate. Although this will not be a detriment to a child whose estate is already in the highest estate tax bracket, it could greatly increase taxes where the child's estate is not in the highest bracket.

There are different possible ways of addressing this dilemma. None of these alternatives is perfect, but they all may be considered:

(1) Instead of creating one nonexempt trust, the grandparent could create two nonexempt trusts and give the child a general power of appointment in only one of them. The amount going into the trust over which the child would have a general power of appointment could be either (a) an amount calculated to take advantage of the lower estate tax brackets that the child's estate might be eligible for or (b) a core amount that is unlikely to be transferred to the child's children during his or her lifetime (i.e., the amount the child may need for living expenses).

(2) The grandparent could give the child a nongeneral power of appointment in the nonexempt trust, and could give someone other than the child the power to appoint trust property to the child. If there was a change in the child's health so that it appeared he or she would not be alive by the year 2010, a portion of the trust could be distributed outright to the child. This way it would be included in the child's gross estate and not subject to GST taxes at his or her death.

(3) The grandparent could name other beneficiaries of the trust besides the child. These would be other nonskip beneficiaries (i.e., beneficiaries at the child's generational level), such as the grandparent's other children or a child's spouse. If the child dies before 2010 but another nonskip beneficiary is still alive, the child's death would not create a taxable termination at that time.

Then, the author addresses preparation for post-2010 terminations and distributions. One of the cruel twists of the new law is that in 2010, when there is no GST tax, there is also apparently no GST exemption.

Finally, the author turns to practical issues in GSTs and the impact of other GST rules, including allocation rules. (M.A. Goldberg, 67 Practical Tax Strategies 196.)

"Tips for preparing generation-skipping transfer tax returns" (2001). The preparation of generation-skipping transfer (GST) tax returns involves not only calculating the value of generation-skipping transfers and the appropriate tax, but also allocating GST exemption. Once made, an allocation is irrevocable, except that an allocation made on a second, timely filed return can supersede a previous allocation if the second allocation clearly states that it modifies the first. In addition, automatic allocation rules take effect if no election is made prior to nine months after the date of the transferor's death (or the date his estate tax return is due, whether or not a return is required), or if the election is not timely filed.

After providing background on GST tax, the authors discuss Form 709. All taxable gifts are reported on Schedule A of Form 709. Direct skips are reported in Part 2 of Schedule A, and all other gifts are reported in Part 1. Direct skips include outright gifts to a skip person and gifts to a trust deemed to be a skip person (if all the current interests in the trust are held by skip persons).

Then, the authors consider Form 706. Transfers subject to GST tax taking effect on the transferor's death are reported on Form 706, the estate tax return. Each transfer is reported on the appropriate schedule (i.e., Schedules A through I) of Form 706 for estate tax purposes and again on Schedules R and R-1. Finally, the authors address Form 706-GS(D-1), Form 706-GS(D), Form 706-GS(T), and other forms. (D.R. Thornburg & C.A. Lowenhaupt, 28 Estate Planning 208.)

GIFTS AND GIFT TAX

(*See also* Estate Planning; Estates and Estate Tax; Marital Deduction)

"Adequate disclosure: its impact on gift tax return strategies" (2001). Final regulations on the valuation of prior gifts for purposes of determining estate and gift tax liability and the period of limitations for assessing and collecting gift tax were issued on December 3, 1999. The regulations were designed to reflect changes to the Code made by the Taxpayer Relief Act of 1997 and the IRS Restructuring and Reform Act of 1998 (the Acts).

First, the author discusses statutory changes. Section 6501(c)(9) was amended to provide that the three-year gift tax statute of limitations does not commence running unless and until the gift is adequately disclosed on a gift tax return. This change is effective for gifts made in calendar years ending after August 5, 1997. The Acts also made conforming changes to Sections 2001 and 2504.

A new paragraph (f) was added to Section 2001 precluding revaluation for estate tax purposes with respect to gifts adequately disclosed on a gift tax return for which the statute of limitations has run. This change overrules the Tax Court decision in *Estate of Smith* (1990) and the other cases discussed in this article. This change is effective for gifts made after August 5, 1997.

Section 2504(c) was amended to drop the requirement that a current gift tax must be paid to achieve finality of valuation for gift tax purposes. The statute is amended to extend finality to gifts with respect to which the time has expired for assessment of tax under Section 6501. This amendment is also effective for gifts made after August 5, 1997.

Next, the author addresses changes to prior law regarding time for assessing gift tax, revaluation of a prior gift for purposes of determining gift tax on a subsequent gift, revaluation of prior gifts for estate tax purposes, and Chapter 14 exceptions.

Then, the author considers requirements for adequate disclosure. Regulation § 301.6501(c)-1(f)(2), following the statutory language of Section 6501(c)(9), provides that a transfer will be considered adequately disclosed only if it is reported in a manner adequate to apprise the IRS of the nature of the gift and the basis for the value so reported. Regulation § 301.6501(c)-1(f)(2) contains a list of information that, if submitted, will be considered adequate disclosure.

Finally, the author discusses miscellaneous points covered by the final regulations, the improvements made by the final regulations regarding assurance that the burden of adequate disclosure has been met, generation-skipping tax planning, and gift tax return strategies. (M.D. Mulligan, 28 Estate Planning 3.)

"Annual exclusion denied for reciprocal gifts" (2001). In *Estate of Schuler* (2000), the IRS denied the annual exclusions claimed by the decedent—and then by his estate—for significant transfers of closely held stock to members of his brother's family. Because his brother had made similar transfers to members of the decedent's family, the Tax Court held that this was a reciprocal transaction designed to pass additional property to the decedent's family free of gift tax. The result was an increase in the amount of adjusted taxable gifts listed on the decedent's estate tax return. (28 Estate Planning 225.)

"Choose gifts that get the most attractive tax package" (2001). Tax planning for gifts involves more than just the annual exclusion, as the type of gift given can have income tax—as well as transfer tax—implications.

First, the authors discuss the unlimited exclusion pursuant to Section 2503(e). Section 2503(e) provides unlimited exclusions for gifts of the following: (1) the cost of medical services made directly to a health care provider and (2) tuition paid directly to an educational institution.

Next, the authors address income/ appreciation shifting, basis considerations, and selecting the property to give (including the advantages and disadvantages of giving cash, securities, personal property, various types of receivables, real property, life insurance, jointly held property, and gift loans). The ideal property to give as a gift is property that has a very high appreciation potential but a low gift tax value, produces a substantial current income flow that will be shifted to a lower-income donee, and will be held indefinitely by the donee so that a possible basis step-up is of little concern.

In reality, few individuals have such perfect gift property in their possession. Consequently, selection of an appropriate asset to give becomes one of working within the constraints introduced by the individual's actual asset mix and personal preferences. Trade-offs occur between appreciation potential and basis step-up opportunities.

Then, the authors consider the transfer of investment opportunities. If a client is aware of an investment that has excellent appreciation potential, instead of consummating the transaction oneself, the client could direct family members to make the investment. If necessary, sufficient cash or other property can be given to these family members (making full use of available annual exclusions) so that they can make the purchase. If the investment opportunity involves an operating business, bringing family members in as shareholders or partners from the inception of the activity can produce long-run transfer tax savings.

Finally, the authors turn to disclosure requirements. Regulation § 301.6501(c)-(1)(f) defines "adequate disclosure" for gift tax purposes. The regulation encompasses all types of property gifts. (P.J. Streer & C.D. Strobel, 66 Practical Tax Strategies 165.)

"Defined value gifts: Does IRS have it all wrong?" (2001). L.P. Hood, Jr., 28 Estate Planning 582. (*Digested under* Valuation of Property—In General, page 262.)

"Gift giving allowed under power of attorney" (2001). Gifts made pursuant to a general power of attorney were held to be valid gifts, according to the Tax Court's decision in *Estate of Pruitt* (2000). (28 Estate Planning 123.)

"Gift incomplete if check paid after donor's death" (2001). The relation-back doctrine, which treats a gift as complete when the check is given rather than when it is paid, does not apply to gifts to noncharitable donees, ruled the Second Circuit in *Rosano* (2001). (28 Estate Planning 445.)

"Gifts given under power of attorney included in estate" (2001). 67 Practical Tax Strategies 241. (*Digested under* Estates and Estate Tax—Gross Estate, page 53.)

"Gifts made under power of attorney were void" (2001). The Federal Circuit affirmed the Court of Federal Claims in *Estate of Swanson* (2001), holding that gifts made on a decedent's behalf under a power of attorney were void and includable in the decedent's gross estate. (67 Practical Tax Strategies 122.)

"Indirect gifts failed to multiply gift tax exclusion" (2001). Recent cases apply the substance-over-form doctrine to prevent taxpayers from expanding their excludable gifts by making transfers to multiple persons that ultimately benefit a single person.

Section 2501 imposes a tax on the transfer of property by gift. The tax applies "whether the gift is direct or indirect and whether the property is real or personal, tangible or intangible." The tax is imposed on a calendar-year basis, and some exceptions apply (e.g., transfers for educational expenses or medical expenses). Section 2503, however, provides an exclusion for the first $10,000 of gifts to each recipient. This exclusion is sometimes viewed as a loophole to avoid gift tax. Some taxpayers try to escape paying the gift tax by making their gift giving look like they have made direct transfers of $10,000 to several recipients. These transfers, however, are really indirect transfers totaling more than $10,000 to an intended recipient, structured in an effort to avoid gift tax.

After providing statutory background, the authors discuss case law. Many courts have held that if the transfers are direct in form but not in substance, the taxpayer is liable for the gift tax that would have resulted had the transfers truly been direct.

Then, the authors address planning. As demonstrated in the cases discussed in this article, desired gift tax results are at risk when subsequent transfers are made from collateral donees to donees more closely related to the donor. The tax planner who suggests the use of multiple donees to maximize use of the annual exclusions (or has a client who suggests this strategy) needs to educate the client on the potential for disallowance of exclusions. (C.J. Langstraat & A.M. Cagle, 66 Practical Tax Strategies 227.)

"Net gift disclaimer of divided marital trusts allowed" (2001). 95 Journal of Taxation 378. (*Digested under* Disclaimers, page 36.)

"New U.S. tax act—dramatic consequences for estate, gift, GST regime in the foreign context" (2001). P. Marcovici, T. Lewis, M.J. Michaels, V.A. Dalmas & C. Hsieh-Kammerlander, 12 Journal of International Taxation, No. 9, 10. (*Digested under* Estates and Estate Tax—In General, page 51.)

"No annual exclusion for indirect gifts, rules Tax Court" (2001). A decedent's yearly gifts of stock in the family funeral home to the wives of her sons and grandson, were determined by the Tax Court in *Estate of Bies* (2000) to be indirect gifts from the decedent to her sons and grandson since, each year, the women immediately transferred their shares to their husbands. Other actions taken by the decedent, her sons, and grandson indicated that the decedent's ultimate intent was for the company to be owned by the three men. (28 Estate Planning 223.)

"No extra annual exclusions for reciprocal gifts" (2001). The Eighth Circuit has affirmed the Tax Court in *Sather* (2001), holding that the transfers of stock by three brothers and their wives to their nieces and nephews were reciprocal transfers made in exchange for identical transfers from the nieces' and nephews' parents to the donor's own children. Therefore, each donor was entitled to a gift tax exclusion only for gifts to his or her own children. (67 Practical Tax Strategies 120.)

"Reciprocal trust doctrine was applied to gifts" (2001). In *Sather* (2001), the Eighth Circuit held that transfers of stock by brothers to their nieces and nephews were reciprocal transfers and would be disallowed for gift tax purposes. (28 Estate Planning 553.)

"Spousal interests in GRATs not exempt from gift tax" (2001). The Seventh Circuit has affirmed the Tax Court in *Cook* (2001), holding that the spousal interests created in their respective grantor retained annuity trusts (GRATs) were not "qualified interests" within the meaning of Section 2702, and therefore were not entitled to exemptions from gift tax liability. (67 Practical Tax Strategies 376.)

"Tax Court appears to misapply the 'passing' rule in _Shepherd_" (2001). Federal estate and gift taxes are not imposed on the value held by the decedent or donor transferor or on the value received by the transferee, but rather on what "passes" from transferor to transferee. At issue in _Estate of Stinson_ (7th Cir. 2000) was the gift tax consequences of an individual's forgiveness of indebtedness owed to her by a corporation owned by her children and grandchildren. It appears that the _Stinson_ court did not correctly apply the passing rule to the facts of that case. The author believes the same criticism can be made of all but one of the Tax Court opinions in _Shepherd_ (2000).

After reviewing the authorities illustrating the passing rule, the author addresses the decisions made in _Stinson_ and _Shepherd_. In _Stinson_, the court ruled that the value of the gift was the amount forgiven, not the resulting increase in the value of the stock of the corporation after marketability and minority interest discounts. The court concluded that the amount of the forgiveness was the value that passed from the taxpayer, observing that the existence of other ways of valuing the gift from the point of view of the donees was not controlling.

Shepherd, like _Stinson_, involved the transfer of assets to an existing entity in which persons other than the transferor had substantial ownership interests. After a partnership was formed, the donor executed two deeds transferring real estate into the partnership. The partnership showed the donor as a 50 percent owner and each of the donor's two sons as 25 percent owners. In the Tax Court, the IRS argued that the transfer, in essence, constituted a gift by the taxpayer of an undivided 50 percent interest in the land to his two sons. The taxpayer contended that the gifts represented gifts of minority interests in the partnership. The parties agreed that the appropriate discount would be 33.5 percent if the taxpayer's position was correct.

The majority opinion was written by Judge Thornton and joined in by ten other judges. The majority rejected the contention that the gift was of an enhanced partnership interest, and held that the taxpayer made

indirect gifts to each of his two sons of an undivided 25 percent interest in the land. The majority allowed a 15 percent discount for the undivided interest in the land.

Then, the author suggests planning steps to avoid the problems illustrated by _Stinson_ and _Shepherd_. (M.D. Mulligan, 28 Estate Planning 368.)

"Tax Court disallows use of SCIN" (2001). In _Estate of Costanza_ (2001), the Tax Court held that absent an affirmative showing that there existed a real expectation of repayment, a sale of property from a parent to a child using a self-canceling installment note (SCIN) will not qualify as a bona fide transaction to avoid estate tax. To the extent that any property transferred from the decedent to his son exceeded the consideration actually paid by the son, such amount constituted a gift under Section 2512(b). (28 Estate Planning 551.)

"Transfer in exchange for self-canceling installment note was part gift" (2001). The Tax Court has held in _Estate of Costanza_ (2001) that a father's transfer of two properties to his son in exchange for a self-canceling installment note (SCIN) was a gift to the extent that it exceeded the consideration actually paid. (67 Practical Tax Strategies 121.)

"Transfer of assets to family partnership was not a taxable gift" (2001). In _Estate of Strangi_ (2000), the Tax Court held that the family limited partnership (FLP) to which the decedent had transferred numerous personal assets (including securities, real estate, and insurance policies) in return for a 99 percent partnership interest was valid under Texas law and would not be disregarded for estate tax purposes. The court further ruled that the IRS could not disregard the partnership under Section 2703(a) because the IRS failed to timely argue the economic substance doctrine under Section 2036(a).

In addition, the transfer of assets to the family partnership was not a gift because the decedent maintained a continuing interest in the partnership and his contributions were reflected in his capital account. Finally, the court found that the valuation of the decedent's partnership interest should be higher than what the estate claimed on its estate tax return (due to a lower discount being allowed), because the family partnership and its corporate general partner were inextricably linked and functionally inseparable. (28 Estate Planning 118.)

GROSS ESTATE

(*See* Estates and Estate Tax—Gross Estate)

GROSS INCOME

"Attorney's contingent fee included in client's income" (2001). The Seventh Circuit has affirmed the Tax Court in *Kenseth* (2001), holding that the part of the proceeds from a settlement paid directly to the taxpayer's attorney under a contingent fee contract were includable in the taxpayer's income. (67 Practical Tax Strategies 311.)

"Transfer of punitive damages to charity does not avoid all tax" (2001). 66 Practical Tax Strategies 250. (*Digested under* Trusts and Trust Taxation, page 256.)

H

HOLDING COMPANIES

(*See* Affiliated Corporations)

HOME

(*See* Business Expenses; Personal Residence)

HOME OFFICE EXPENSE

(*See* Business Expenses)

HUSBAND AND WIFE

Divorce and Separation

"Divorce can permit division of CRUT without adverse tax consequences" (2001). 95 Journal of Taxation 117. (*Digested under* Trusts and Trust Taxation, page 248.)

"Later settlement of a claim was transfer incident to divorce" (2001). The Fourth Circuit affirmed a Tax Court decision in *Young* (2001) holding that the transfer of land from a husband to his former wife was a transfer incident to divorce for purposes of the Section 1041 nonrecognition of gain rules. (66 Practical Tax Strategies 249.)

"Overpayment credited to couple's estimated tax allocated according to separate liability or by agreement (2001). The amount of a couple's joint overpayment in one year that was credited to the following year's estimat-ed tax should be allocated in proportion to their separate tax liabilities unless an agreement between the couple to the contrary can be shown, according to ILM 200130036. (95 Journal of Taxation 250.)

"Regulations clarify tax on divorce-related stock redemption" (2001). Proposed regulations add certainty that tax will be due, and by which spouse, when a corporation redeems stock on behalf of a spouse or former spouse. In addition to providing a flexible means for a couple to choose who will owe the tax, the proposed regulations are also designed to prevent whipsaw situations in which each spouse separately asserts that the other should recognize the gain. (67 Practical Tax Strategies 254.)

"Regulations clarify tax on stock redemptions incident to divorce" (2001). The IRS issued proposed regulations on stock redemptions incurred incident to a divorce. These proposed regulations are designed to remove inconsistencies caused by simultaneously applying the "on behalf of" standard of Temporary Regulation § 1.1041-1T(c), Q&A-9 ("Q&A-9") to one spouse, while applying the "primary and unconditional obligation" standard of *Wall* (4th Cir. 1947) to the other. They are designed to prevent whipsaw against the government, where both parties to a divorce-related stock redemption avoid paying tax on the transfer of stock to the corporation.

When the proposed regulations are made final, they will provide a consistent standard for determining the tax consequences of divorce-related stock redemptions. The primary and unconditional obligation standard will be used to determine the tax consequences of both spouses. Under Proposed Regulation § 1.1041-2(c), the parties will be able to make an election to ensure that the transaction is treated as a constructive distribution to the nontransferor spouse. (T.R. Koski, 67 Practical Tax Strategies 282.)

"State statute does not revoke beneficiary designation after divorce" (2001). S.N. Gary, 28 Estate Planning 376. (*Digested under* Pension and Profit-Sharing Plans—In General, page 155.)

"What benefits ex-spouse is not always alimony" (2001). Two recent Tax Court cases explore whether various types of payments are deductible by the payor spouse as alimony. In *Zinsmeister* (2000), the Tax Court disallowed deductions for payments made on a second mortgage for a house the former wife lived in. The nondeductible payments in *Berry* (2000) were for the former wife's attorney's fees. (66 Practical Tax Strategies 119.)

Innocent Spouse

"Has the innocent spouse become the over-protected spouse? Reflections on recent cases" (2001). Reform of the innocent spouse provisions was seen as appropriate and necessary, as the complicated and highly technical system that had been in place for more than a quarter-century was perceived as placing too many burdens on truly innocent spouses. The onslaught of claims for relief under the new provisions, however, and the IRS's cautious approach to interpreting the rules—especially in the initial cases that have been litigated—may obscure the potential for unfairness toward the "noninnocent" spouse.

First, the author discusses the new provisions. In 1998, Section 6015 replaced Section 6013(e). The new law provides expanded relief from joint and several liability on a joint return, principally as follows:

(1) Section 6015(b) refers to "erroneous items," rather than specifying income, deductions, credits, and basis. It relaxes the requirements for obtaining relief and makes partial relief available on a proportionate basis.

(2) Section 6015(c) provides for an election for separate liability with respect to a deficiency relating to a joint return. The electing individual may be divorced, separated, or no longer living with the other spouse. A successful election will relieve a spouse from liability attributable to the other spouse.

(3) Section 6015(f) authorizes the IRS to grant equitable relief from liability where relief is not available under Sections 6015(b) and 6015(c) and, taking into account all the facts and circumstances, it is inequitable to hold the spouse liable for any portion of the unpaid tax or deficiency.

Then, the author addresses recent cases. Section 6015(e) provides for Tax Court review of a taxpayer's claim for relief. Among the cases discussed is the Tax Court decision in *Corson* (2000). Here, the IRS had contended that a spouse had no right to challenge its decision to grant relief to the other spouse. The IRS relied on the Ninth Circuit decision in *Estate of Ravetti* (1994). The basic reason, as stated by the Ninth Circuit in Ravetti, was that a "taxpayer generally has no standing to challenge the tax liability determination of another taxpayer ... [and] therefore lacks standing to challenge the 'innocent spouse' relief granted to his or her spouse."

The Tax Court in *Corson* recognized that prior law would have blocked the husband's objections to the settlement. It found, however, that the 1998 Act demanded a different result. New Section 6015(e)(4) demonstrated, as the husband argued, "a congressional intent that the nonelecting spouse become a 'full player' in the process of determining innocent spouse relief, such that each of three parties now has rights to fully litigate such issues." (R.H. Feldman, 94 Journal of Taxation 51.)

"How 'ignorant' must innocent spouse be for tax relief?" (2001). Even under newly expanded innocent spouse rules, a taxpayer's ignorance of the taxability of income does not offer protection if there was knowledge of the transaction giving rise to the omitted income.

First, the author provides background on the types of relief available. Effective for any tax liability arising after July 22, 1998, and any unpaid tax liability that arose before July 23, 1998, Section 6015 provides for three types of relief: (1) innocent spouse relief under Section 6015(b); (2) separation of liability under Section 6015(c); and (3) equitable relief under Section 6015(f).

Then, the author addresses the Tax Court decision in *Cheshire* (2000). In *Cheshire*, the Tax Court denied innocent spouse relief to an ex-spouse who knew her husband received a retirement distribution that was not included on their joint income tax return, even though she reasonably believed her ex-husband's assertion that he had consulted with an accountant and was advised that the portion of the distribution used to pay off the mortgage on their home was not taxable. The Tax Court denied relief under Section 6015(b) because the spouse seeking relief had actual knowledge of the transaction giving rise to the omitted income. In a divided opinion, the Tax Court also denied separation of liability relief under Section 6015(c). The majority held that the taxpayer's ignorance of the fact that the retirement distribution was incorrectly reported on the return was irrelevant. The Tax Court did, however, grant relief from the accuracy-related penalty under Section 6015(f). (T.R. Koski, 66 Practical Tax Strategies 4.)

"Innocent spouse relief granted for tax on inherited IRA" (2001). A husband was entitled to innocent spouse relief from liability for a deficiency determined with respect to his wife's receipt of IRA distributions from her father's estate, in *Braden*, a 2001 Tax Court memorandum case. (66 Practical Tax Strategies 301.)

"Mental abuse may be duress for innocent spouse relief" (2001). A bankruptcy court in Florida held in *Hinckley* (2000) that a taxpayer may be awarded innocent spouse relief if, due to mental abuse, she signed a return with a known omission of income. (66 Practical Tax Strategies 108.)

"Proposed regulations clarify 'innocent spouse' relief requirements" (2001). Ever since the innocent spouse relief rules were expanded by the enactment of Section 6015 in 1998, questions have arisen regarding their application. The proposed regulations offer some guidance. (66 Practical Tax Strategies 245.)

"State tax implications of the new federal innocent spouse rules" (2001). L.M. Johnson & B. Clements, 10 Journal of Multistate Taxation and Incentives, No. 10, 4. (*Digested under* State Taxes—In General, page 204.)

"Successful requests for innocent spouse relief" (2001). The Tax Court determined in *King* (2001) that a loss had been denied from an activity found not to have been entered into for profit. Innocent spouse relief came in the form of the separate liability election in Section 6015(c). In *Kling* (2001), the Tax Court found that income had been unreported. The innocent spouse qualified for complete relief from joint and several liability under Section 6015(b)(1). In SCA 200112001, an earned income tax credit was disallowed after unreported income was uncovered. Section 6015(b) relief was found to apply. (66 Practical Tax Strategies 375.)

"What is 'actual knowledge' for innocent spouse relief?"(2001). The Tax Court in *Martin* (2000) held that knowledge of a source of income without knowing the amount of such income is not "actual knowledge" necessary for the IRS to deny innocent spouse relief. (66 Practical Tax Strategies 44.)

I

INCOME

(*See* Gross Income)

INCOME IN RESPECT OF DECEDENTS

(*See* Estates and Estate Tax—Income Tax)

INCOME TAX RETURN PREPARERS

(*See* Tax Practice and Practitioners)

INCORPORATION

"Nonrecognition on incorporation of subsidiary denied for lack of nontax business purpose" (2001). Transfers to a corporation did not qualify for Section 351 treatment because of a lack of business purpose, according to FSA 200125001. (95 Journal of Taxation 313.)

"Personal liability on transferred debt did not prevent gain recognition" (2001). Shareholders in an incorporated family farm had to recognize gain on the transfer of assets to the corporation under Section 357 to the extent that the liabilities that were assumed plus the liabilities to which the property was subject exceeded the total of the adjusted basis of the property that was transferred to the corporation, according to the Tax Court in *Seggerman Farms Inc.* (2001). (67 Practical Tax Strategies 62.)

INDEBTEDNESS

(*See* Cancellation of Indebtedness; Interest Paid)

INDIVIDUAL RETIREMENT ACCOUNTS

(*See* Pension and Profit-Sharing Plans—Individual Retirement Accounts (IRAs))

INHERITANCE TAXES

(*See* Estates and Estate Tax)

INNOCENT SPOUSE

(*See* Husband and Wife—Innocent Spouse)

INSTALLMENT SALES

(*See* Accounting Methods—Installment Sales)

INSURANCE AND INSURANCE COMPANIES

"Aggressive viatical settlement transactions: gambling on human lives" (2001). Aggressive viatical settlements, known as wet-ink transactions, arguably appear to be illegal and invalid. Although the law is not entirely clear, it is possible that the assignment of the policy may be void.

First, the authors discuss changes in the viatical industry and the creation of the wet-ink transaction. Viatical companies have moved farther down the slippery slope, with their entry into the realm of wet-ink transactions, which are arguably the most obvious cases of fraud in the industry. In these extreme cases, viatical companies are recruiting all types of people (old and young, sick and healthy) to purchase life insurance policies solely for resale. The transaction is fraught with misconduct at all angles. The insured receives a lump-sum payoff equal to a percentage of the face amount of the policy (in most cases, up to 3.5 percent) and will sometimes make misleading statements regarding health status in applying for the policy. The insurance agent and/or viatical company receive (or split) the commission for formulating the transaction, and the investor seeks to cash in on the proceeds via a premature, unforeseen death of the insured.

Then, the authors address the questionable legality of such transactions, the effect of finding the wet-ink viatical illegal, insurance company reactions, the need for regulatory guidance, and advice for investors. It appears that wet-ink transactions are scams, lacking in validity as well as legality. The Supreme Court has held this position for over a century, declaring that life insurance polices purchased solely for resale to a third party are mere wagering contracts that are against public policy, and will be held invalid. Recently, insurance providers have recognized this problem and imposed restrictions on such transactions. In addition, viatical industry regulators have finally caught on and are working to resolve this issue. (J.A. Baskies & B.J. Samuels, 28 Estate Planning 76.)

"An HMO wins the insurance battle, but will HMOs lose the war?" (2001). G.M. Griffith, 12 Journal of Taxation of Exempt Organizations 145. (*Digested under* Tax-Exempt Organizations—Hospitals and Other Health Care Organizations, page 236.)

"Dealing with EGTRRA's impact on an insurance professional's practice" (2001). The Economic Growth and Tax Relief Rec-

onciliation Act of 2001 (EGTRRA) was signed into law on June 7, 2001. Regardless of how absurd, frivolous, or irresponsible it was to enact a law that has a built-in 365-day estate tax repeal and that may or may not return hundreds of sections of law to where they were almost a decade prior to its automatic expiration date (assuring both confusion and uncertainty), it is law. Those who advise about life insurance matters need to learn it, and understand its implications and how to deal with it.

First, the authors discuss what life insurance advisors and agents should be doing. The authors' advice includes: re-positioning, planning to plan ahead, training your mindset to expect change, remembering not to be totally driven by tax planning, doing a better job of interviewing clients, building more flexibility into plan design, reviewing everything, creating a new and improved policy suitability guideline, and communicating more often and more selectively.

Then, the authors consider advising clients and additional guidance for practitioners. Success as a life insurance advisor is directly related to the ability to help others see, as well as solve, their problems. Although the new law has solved some problems and some people's problems, it has created and compounded problems for others. Many people are confused, misinformed, or under-informed. They are seeking sound, objective, and practical advice about life insurance and how it legitimately fits into their estate plan. These problems are opportunities for those planners, advisors, and agents who are willing to learn and realistically and creatively deal with change. (S.R. Leimberg & A.E. Gibbons, 28 Estate Planning 403.)

"Extracting hidden value from unwanted life insurance policies" (2001). For a life insurance policy to have life settlement potential, the insured must have a life expectancy of twelve years or less and a negative change in health. It is difficult for many to understand why one would drop/sell a life insurance policy at that time. It would appear that this is the time when the insured and his advisors acknowledge that their earlier decision to buy life insurance was well-founded. But this reasoning may be shortsighted.

Insureds let life insurance policies lapse for as many reasons as they bought the policies in the first place. When peoples' needs and circumstances change because of retirement, marriage, changes in health, or fluctuations in estate size, they may decide that the insurance they originally purchased is no longer necessary.

Suppose that clients are reviewing their estate planning for the second or third time in their lives. They are older and wealthier. Assume that earlier planning encompassed insurance on the husband's life owned by an irrevocable life insurance trust (ILIT). Now, the clients believe that survivorship insurance (i.e., a life insurance policy that pays at the second death) would be more cost-efficient. When they buy second-to-die coverage, they often surrender the existing life insurance. The proceeds are sometimes used to help pay for the new second-to-die policy.

With second-to-die insurance, as long as one of the lives is healthy, it makes no difference if the other life is not. When one client is rated or uninsurable, chances are that his/her existing life insurance is a salable asset. Advisors should apprise their clients of this possibility.

After providing background, the authors discuss income replacement, business situations (group-term life insurance, key-person insurance, creditor insurance, buy-sell agreements, and nonqualified deferred compensation), divorce, mergers and acquisitions, additional issues, the three-year rule, and discount planning.

Then, the authors address tax treatment. The proceeds of a true viatical settlement—when the insured is expected to die within twenty-four months—are not usually subject to federal income tax. If the policy owner is someone other than the insured, however, and that person has an insurable interest in the insured because the insured is an employee, officer, or director, or because the insured has a financial interest in the trade or business of that person, proceeds will be taxed in the same manner as a life settle-

ment. The tax treatment of a life settlement is very favorable.

Finally, the authors turn to underwriting requirements. To underwrite a life settlement, one needs: (1) an application; (2) a copy of the policy; (3) an "in force" illustration assuming a zero cash surrender value at 95; (4) the most recent annual policy statement; (5) executed medical authorization forms; (6) medical records; and (7) family medical history. (M.P. Greenberg & J.E. Mayer, 28 Estate Planning 434.)

"Insurer's payment to state on conversion to for-profit status deductible under origin of claim doctrine" (2001). According to TAM 200126008, a required payment to the state made by a not-for-profit mutual insurance company on its conversion to a for-profit stock company was currently deductible under Section 162, under the origin of the claim doctrine. (95 Journal of Taxation 183.)

"IRS revamps taxation of split-dollar arrangements" (2001). The IRS, in Notice 2001-10, has issued interim rules regarding the tax treatment of split-dollar arrangements. (66 Practical Tax Strategies 173.)

"IRS, reversing course, issues new interim guidance for split-dollar life insurance" (2001). In Notice 2001-10, the IRS—after decades of silence—announced a new interpretation of how to tax split-dollar life insurance. The Notice "clarifies" the prior revenue rulings on split-dollar plans and, pending further action, provides taxpayers with "interim" guidelines to follow. The guidelines introduce an entirely new approach to split-dollar plans, and in the process reverse an income tax position that has been followed for over thirty-five years. While the Notice focuses primarily on the income tax treatment of "equity" split-dollar plans used by employers, it also applies to corporate shareholders and arrangements involving gifts.

After providing background, the authors discuss Notice 2001-10, TAM 9604001, and the new IRS approach. In a ground-breaking development, Notice 2001-10 applies either

Section 83 or Section 7872 to employer payments under equity plans. Recognizing, however, that employer payments have not been taxed this way, the IRS gives taxpayers a choice of characterizing employer payments as loans (subject to Section 7872), nonloans (subject to Section 83), or as payments of compensation (subject to Section 61).

In the nonloan characterization, equity split-dollar will now be taxed under Section 83, but the theory of TAM 9604001—that the "earnings increments" are taxable—will not be applied, at least for now. The Notice never mentions the TAM but it does appear to give some legitimacy to its analysis. Any change to this treatment will be applied prospectively. Thus, for the time being, the final word on the TAM has been postponed. Additionally, although the economic benefit theory is retained, the Notice makes several major changes to the term rates used to value the life insurance protection.

Although the Notice does clarify some things, it raises a number of unresolved issues and questions while adding more complexity to an already complicated subject. Most important, since plans are not now being grandfathered, immediate attention must be paid to existing as well as pending split-dollar arrangements.

Then, the authors address split-dollar methods and the interim guidance. The Notice provides that employer payments under equity split-dollar will be taxed under either Section 83 or Section 7872. The IRS's premise is that in an equity plan, the employer is either making loans to enable an employee to acquire a policy interest or is acquiring the interest for itself and providing economic benefits to the employee. In the event, however, that an employer pays premiums but does not acquire an ownership interest, the Notice states that the payments will be treated as compensation to the employee.

If a plan can qualify for loan treatment, it will be taxed under Section 7872; if it cannot be treated as a loan, it will be taxed under Section 83.

Finally, the authors consider post-notice strategies and split-dollar variations. Overall

taxpayers are in pretty much the same position they were in before the Notice, except that now policy rollouts in equity plans may be taxable under Section 83. The new guidance will have an impact on variations such as reverse split-dollar, private split-dollar, and some of the split-dollar conversion techniques. (A.T. Brisendine & F.T. Scudere, 94 Journal of Taxation 294.)

"IRS ruling taxes plan as both split-dollar and interest-free loan" (2001). On October 6, 2000, the IRS released Field Service Advice (FSA) 200040001. The IRS ruled that a split-dollar plan created in conjunction with the sale of a medical practice would be taxed as a split-dollar arrangement under Revenue Ruling 64-328 to the participating employees and as an interest-free loan under Section 7872 to the selling corporation. (A.R. Kingan, 28 Estate Planning 19.)

"Key issues to consider when drafting life insurance trusts" (2001). S.V. Grassi, Jr., 28 Estate Planning 217. (*Digested under* Trusts and Trust Taxation, page 250.)

"Life insurer's proration method for calculating dividends-received deduction approved" (2001). In TAM 200038008, the IRS ruled that a life insurer's proration methodology for separate accounts is appropriate for determining both the insurer's and the policyholders' share of a dividends-received deduction. The ruling holds that a proration methodology set forth in prior law for separate accounts, with adjustments to reflect changes made by the Deficit Reduction Act of 1984, is an appropriate method for determining the company's and the policyholders' share of the deduction. (94 Journal of Taxation 58.)

"Notice 2001-10 will have dramatic effects on split-dollar arrangements" (2001). Notice 2001-10 will render conventional split-dollar arrangements far more appealing than ever before, by reducing the amount of taxable income to the employee from the P.S. 58 table amounts to the Table 2001 amounts. In addition, Notice 2001-10 indicates that the employee must be taxed on any economic benefit provided under a split-dollar agreement.

First, the authors discuss income taxation of split-dollar arrangements generally. The income tax treatment of split-dollar life insurance arrangements was generally set forth in Revenue Rulings 64-328 and 66-110, both of which are reviewed in Notice 2001-10. These rulings described arrangements between employer and employee where benefits were split contractually under either a collateral assignment or endorsement method.

Next, the authors consider valuation of pure term benefit. Notice 2001-10 explains that the IRS realizes that the present rule, that the taxpayer may value the pure term benefit under a conventional split-dollar arrangement by the lower of the P.S. 58 rate or the actual rate charged by the insurer for one-year term coverage available to all standard rates, produces an inaccurate and unjustifiable result. With Notice 2001-10, the IRS revokes Revenue Ruling 55-747 and substitutes new Table 2001, by which taxpayers may value the current life insurance protection provided under split-dollar arrangements and qualified retirement plans. Table 2001 uses much lower values, based on the more recent mortality experience reflected in the tables under Section 79(c), relating to the valuation of group-term life insurance coverage.

Then, the authors address equity split-dollar arrangements. Notice 2001-10 establishes six specific rules by which the IRS will determine whether an equity split-dollar arrangement should be taxed as a loan or as current compensation income.

Finally, the authors evaluate the IRS position, provide planning strategy, and discuss the IRS request for public comment. (H.M. Zaritsky & S.R. Leimberg, 28 Estate Planning 99.)

"Typical life insurance planning mistakes and some suggested solutions" (2001). This article analyzes a number of frequently occurring life insurance planning mistakes and offers some suggestions to either avoid or mitigate the effect of each potential mistake.

First, the authors discuss the three-corner life insurance policy transaction—different owner, insured, and beneficiary. Any time an insurance policy has three different parties involved as owner, insured, and beneficiary, there is the potential for an inadvertent gift at the insured's death. The problem can be solved by being sure that if the policy owner is not the insured, the policy owner is always the policy beneficiary.

Next, the authors address the two-party entity-related life insurance problem—the entity as an owner of the policy and an individual as the beneficiary (not split-dollar). Assuming the policy is not structured under a split-dollar arrangement, if an entity owns a policy on the life of an individual (whether an employee, a shareholder, or an independent contractor such as a director), the entity must be the beneficiary of the policy, or there will be inadvertent, adverse income tax consequences to the insured or to the beneficiary.

Then, the authors consider successor owners, designation of a minor child as beneficiary, undocumented employee benefit life insurance transactions, the three-year transfer rule, "controlling" shareholder split-dollar arrangements, "funding" a non-qualified deferred compensation plan for both ERISA and tax purposes, the transfer for value rule, implementing insured-owned reverse split-dollar arrangements, establishing split-dollar arrangements, partnership (or limited liability company) key person coverage, loans, and S corporations. (L. Brody & L.A. Althauser, 28 Estate Planning 51.)

"Using life insurance and annuities for asset protection" (2001). Depending on state law, annuities and life insurance may be exempt from creditors' claims.

First, the author discusses insurance. "Insurance" is usually defined by reference to applicable state law. This is true even for income tax purposes. A major income tax benefit of insurance is that it can accumulate income tax-free and proceeds are not subject to income tax.

Exemptions from creditors' claims vary from state to state, but for the most part are minor and often protect only the insurance element of the contract. This can be a valuable right if the insured later becomes uninsurable. Moreover, protection varies depending on whether the debtor is the insured or a beneficiary. Among the states that have generous exemptions are Florida, Hawaii, and, under some circumstances Louisiana. Some states also extend spendthrift protection for a beneficiary's interest in a policy.

Other methods can be used to protect life insurance. These methods frequently correspond to the estate planning goal of excluding the proceeds of life insurance from the insured's estate for death tax purposes. One method is to have the policy owned directly by the heirs. Another common estate planning device for life insurance is the irrevocable life insurance trust (ILIT).

Then, the author addresses annuities, private annuities, the exhaustion regulations, and the strategy of combining a private annuity and insurance. The benefit of a private annuity can be enhanced through its use with a foreign variable life insurance policy. Use of a life insurance policy can shield income derived from the proceeds of the sale of property transferred by the annuitant. In general, a foreign life insurance policy is purchased, usually by an ILIT. The policy can make a variety of investments, including forming an entity, such as a corporation. In the private annuity/foreign life insurance policy scenario, the policy would form and fund a corporation, which in turn enters into the private annuity arrangement with the annuitant, i.e., the annuitant transfers property to the corporation in exchange for an unsecured promise to pay the annuity. (P. Spero, 28 Estate Planning 12.)

INTERCOMPANY TRANSACTIONS

(*See* Affiliated Corporations; Allocations Among Related Taxpayers)

INTEREST AND PENALTIES

(*See also* Assessment and Collection; Procedure; Tax Practice and Practitioners)

"Business owner not liable for payroll tax penalty" (2001). A bankruptcy court, in *Nutt* (2001), disallowed the IRS's claim in a Chapter 11 case for amounts owed by the owner of a corporation for an unpaid penalty assessed for failure to pay over trust fund taxes. (67 Practical Tax Strategies 380.)

"Claimed reliance on accountant did not avoid penalties" (2001). The Tax Court held in *Bowen* (2001) that the taxpayers did not reasonably rely on their accountant/return preparer in order to avoid the Section 6662 accuracy-related penalty, but held that the taxpayers' petition for redetermination was not frivolous or groundless for Section 6673 penalty purposes. (66 Practical Tax Strategies 242.)

"Embezzlement not reasonable cause for not filing" (2001). A Pennsylvania federal district court magistrate judge recommended granting summary judgment in favor of the IRS in *Classic Printing* (2001). The judge found that, as a matter of law, the court lacked subject matter jurisdiction on three of the quarters in which the taxpayer failed to file refund claims and also found that the taxpayer did not, as a matter of law, have reasonable cause to abate the assessed penalties for failure to file and pay tax and for the failure to deposit. (66 Practical Tax Strategies 289.)

"Final determination withstands taxpayer's challenge" (2001). A Florida federal district court held in *Konkel* (2000) that the IRS did not abuse its discretion in issuing a notice of final determination and a notice of intent to levy the Section 6672 trust fund recovery penalty. (66 Practical Tax Strategies 47.)

"Financial difficulties may be reasonable cause" (2001). The Ninth Circuit held in *Van Camp & Bennion* (2001) that a corporation's financial difficulties may be reasonable cause to excuse or abate the underpayment of tax penalty. (67 Practical Tax Strategies 109.)

"Interest is refunded until due date not credit date" (2001). 67 Practical Tax Strategies 244. (*Digested under* Procedure—Refunds, page 166.)

"No statute of limitations on penalty for failing to register a tax shelter" (2001). 94 Journal of Taxation 375. (*Digested under* Assessment and Collection—Statute of Limitations, page 8.)

"Updated IRS guidance on disclosures that avoid penalties" (2001). Revenue Procedure 2001-11 updates Revenue Procedure 99-41, which identifies circumstances where the disclosure on a taxpayer's return of a position with respect to an item is adequate to reduce the understatement of income tax under Section 6662(d) (substantial understatement aspect of the accuracy-related penalty), and avoid the preparer penalty under Section 6694(a) (understatements due to unrealistic positions). (12 Journal of International Taxation, No. 2, 4.)

INTEREST PAID

(*See also* Business Expenses; Interest and Penalties; Passive Loss Rules; Real Estate)

"Corporation may use tax book value to apportion interest expense" (2001). In Letter Ruling 200102041, the IRS ruled that a corporation may change to the tax book value method of asset valuation for apportioning its interest expense. (94 Journal of Taxation 252.)

INTERNATIONAL TAXATION

(*See also* Foreign Corporations, Persons, and Partnerships; Foreign Tax Credit)

In General

"A platform for international e-commerce tax rules" (2001). "Physical presence" is and probably will remain the key concept in determining whether source-based tax liability is triggered in the context of e-commerce—with or without the protection of a bilateral double tax treaty.

First, the author discusses the Organization for Economic Cooperation and Development (OECD) model treaty. The OECD model treaty is the commonly accepted standard for double tax treaties. Under the OECD model treaty, business profits of a nonresident company may be taxed only if they are attributed to a permanent establishment (PE) that the company maintains in the taxing country.

Then, the author considers U.S. taxation. U.S. domestic tax law does not use the PE concept. Absent a double tax treaty, the U.S. taxes foreign corporations if their income falls into either one of the following two basic categories: (1) U.S.-source income or (2) income effectively connected with a U.S. trade or business (ECI). (W.L. Andrews III, 12 Journal of International Taxation, No. 1, 44.)

"A platform for international e-commerce tax rules (Part 2): What should the new rules look like?" (2001). Part 1 of this article observed that existing tax rules—however inadequate—must be used as sieves through which e-commerce fact scenarios are sifted, and the author proposed a foundation on which e-commerce taxation can be built. This concluding installment covers the rules in Germany, the U.K., Canada, and Australia, and provides an analysis of what new rules should look like. (W.L. Andrews III, 12 Journal of International Taxation, No. 8, 10.)

"Applying Section 482 to third-party lease-strips—has the IRS overreached?" (2001). The IRS has taken an aggressive position in applying Section 482 to "lease-stripping" transactions, an approach that has the potential to expand the reach of Section 482 to several new areas. Section 482 grants the IRS authority to make income adjustments to require arm's-length dealings between related parties. What is unusual about the IRS's application of Section 482 is that the parties to these lease-strip transactions are not related, and the IRS admits it. Instead, the IRS advances that the parties are acting with a common design to avoid taxation.

First, the authors discuss the essentials of a typical lease-strip. While lease-stripping transactions typically involve numerous parties and produce complex schematics when diagramed, in substance they all use the same technique to produce tax savings. That is, the underlying transaction seeks to separate (or strip out) income from a leased tangible asset and thereafter allocate that

income to the party not subject to tax, and provide a high basis asset to one who can either take advantage of the depreciation deduction or net operating losses.

Then, the authors address the application of Section 482. While several issues exist as to the application of Section 482 to lease-stripping transactions, the biggest hurdle is whether the statute even applies because of the lack of common ownership and control.

The IRS's proposed application of the common plan theory to lease-stripping transactions appears to be quite aggressive. It raises several questions as to whether this theory could or will be applied to other types of transactions. (M.M. Levey & W.S. Garofalo, 12 Journal of International Taxation, No. 12, 12.)

" 'Benefits and burdens' approach used to determine where sales to foreign customers occurred" (2001). Sales of inventory property by a domestic corporation ("USCo") to non-U.S. customers took place outside the United States, according to FSA 200052002. Thus, USCo earned foreign-source income on the sales under Section 863. (94 Journal of Taxation 185.)

"Environmental tax shifts are multiplying" (2001). The shifts in Western Europe have been small, and compromises have often been made in the fine print. Worldwide, moreover, environmental taxes generate barely 3 percent of all tax revenue, mainly through motor fuel levies. Yet studies suggest that energy taxes will need to climb far above current levels to address problems such as global climate change—enough to generate perhaps 15 percent of all government revenues. If taxes do eventually shift that far—and worldwide—the small shifts of the past decade in Western Europe will be seen as the halting beginnings of a sweeping historical trend.

After providing background on pollution taxes, the author discusses the use of revenues from environmental taxes to cut conventional taxes on income, wages, profits, sales, trade, and built property. (D.M.

Roodman, 12 Journal of International Taxation, No. 3, 40.)

"Extraterritorial exclusion replaces FSC regime: mirror rules, broader spectrum" (2001). E.R. Larkins, 12 Journal of International Taxation, No. 5, 22. (*Digested under* Foreign Corporations, Persons, and Partnerships, page 56.)

"Foreign trade zones offer a variety of tax and other benefits" (2001). Foreign trade zones (FTZs) are designated geographical areas that, for purposes of customs and tariff laws, are treated as being outside of the United States. The use of FTZs enables firms engaged in the import or export of foreign goods or the remanufacture of foreign-made goods to realize substantial tax and duty benefits. In addition to examining some of these benefits, this article reviews the procedures to be followed in order to establish and begin using an FTZ.

FTZs may be established as either "general purpose zones" (GPZs) or "subzones." All FTZs originate with the Foreign Trade Zone Board, which is part of the U.S. Department of Commerce. GPZs must be located within sixty miles (or ninety minutes driving time) from the outer limits of a U.S. Customs port of entry. Subzones are specialized FTZs established for a single user and may be located anywhere in the United States, subject to certain oversight conditions. This flexibility in subzone location can eliminate the start-up costs associated with relocating to an already established GPZ. As discussed in detail in the article, companies often include, as part of their application for a subzone, written approval from various local entities, which may be paramount to the FTZ Board's ultimate approval.

Given the wide variety of activities that can occur in an FTZ, firms using FTZs can obtain many significant benefits, including deferral of customs duties, lower tariffs, elimination of time-consuming drawback applications, quota leveraging, and exemption from state and local property taxation for imported goods held in an FTZ and for goods produced in the United States and held

in an FTZ for export. Goods held within an FTZ also may be exhibited by a firm without first having to pay import duties or meet customs requirements, which may attract more buyers.

States generally provide their own personal property tax exemptions for inventory held in a qualifying FTZ. Because applications for subzones require some coordination with local taxing jurisdictions, in order to be approved by local taxing authorities a firm may agree to pay all or a portion of the inventory taxes despite the availability of an exemption. Still, the advantages of operating in an FTZ are so substantial that firms have been willing to forgo state inventory tax relief just to realize those benefits. The situation is especially germane to the granting of subzone status, because approval by the locality can be critical to the federal FTZ Board in deciding whether to approve a site.

The local office of the U.S. Customs Service has oversight responsibilities for activating GPZs previously designated by the FTZ Board. The article describes the process by which a GPZ attains active status. Firms that wish to use a subzone must first apply to the FTZ Board in Washington, D.C. This process involves the submission of a great deal of additional data, including detailed information on certain economic factors listed in the article, such as overall employment impact, extent of value-added activity, extent of foreign competition in relevant products, and other information relating to public interest and net economic impact considerations.

FTZ users are subject to fees and various reporting and other compliance requirements. They must maintain inventory controls and records and be subject to spot checks and audits by customs officials. However, given the right circumstances (e.g., a company engaged in international activity that maintains a high level of inventory), the use of FTZs can result in tremendous operating cost savings. A basic understanding of the scope of those benefits and the procedures by which FTZs are used is the first step toward realizing these savings. (S.P. Weitzner & G. Marques, 11 Journal of

Multistate Taxation and Incentives, No. 8, 20.)

"How to gain a competitive advantage with customs planning" (2001). Increasingly, the strength of the U.S. dollar, the burgeoning e-commerce market, and the ever-growing competition in the international marketplace have resulted in more U.S. companies entering markets in the European Union (EU) and having to deal with EU customs regulations. This increased exposure highlights the significant cost that customs duties can represent when doing business in the EU. It also points to the need for customs planning that achieves bottom-line cash savings, reduces the risk of exposure to penalties, and facilitates prompt customs clearance so that there are no unnecessary delays in getting the product to market.

After providing background on customs planning and determining customs duties, the author discusses suspense arrangements. Once the duty rate applicable to imported goods and the customs value have been established, the availability of any suspense arrangements may be investigated. These enable goods to be imported into the EU without the payment of customs duties, or with the payment postponed in order to obtain significant cashflow advantages. In some instances, the relief of duties is extended to include value-added tax (VAT). (F. Van der Wielen, 12 Journal of International Taxation, No. 4, 6.)

"If you send it, tax will come: how the Section 863 proposed regulations could affect the telecommunications industry" (2001). Proposed regulations that the IRS issued on January 17, 2001, under Sections 863(d) and 863(e), address the characterization and source of income from space and ocean activities, and international communications activities, respectively.

After providing background on source rules, the authors address communications, space, and ocean income. Because of the absence of double taxation, Congress has expressed concern about allowing cross-crediting against U.S. tax on income that is unlikely to be taxed by any foreign country.

Because it believed that income from space or ocean activity was unlikely to be taxed by any foreign country, Congress decided to prevent cross-crediting against the U.S. tax on this income by enacting Section 863(d) to generally treat this income as 100 percent U.S.-source income when derived by a U.S. person. However, Congress believed that a portion of income from communications activity was more likely to be subjected to foreign tax and, accordingly, enacted Section 863(e) to generally treat income from international communications activity as 50 percent U.S. source and 50 percent foreign source when derived by a U.S. person.

In addition, Congress was concerned that (1) U.S. corporations might conduct activities through foreign corporations to defer U.S. tax and to alter the foreign tax credit (FTC) consequences of the source rules for U.S. persons and (2) foreign corporations might avoid U.S. tax on income from business activities conducted in the United States. To deal with these concerns, Congress granted Treasury the authority to issue regulations to create exceptions to the general statutory rules

Then, the authors consider the impact of the proposed regulations—including the character, source, and other tax consequences of space and ocean income, communications income, and communications income involving space and ocean activity, followed by treaty considerations. The proposed regulations on source and characterization of income from space and ocean activities and communications activities, if finalized in their current form, would have a dramatic impact on the taxation of the telecommunications and other related industries. The requirement that taxpayers establish the two points between which they are paid to transmit communications will force many domestic and foreign companies to change the way they transact and account for communications activities.

The overlap between space and ocean activity and communications activity as described in the proposed regulations—in a world where a growing percentage of communications are transmitted via satellites or undersea fiber optic cables—effectively expands the scope of subpart F income and creates adverse FTC consequences. Because the proposed regulations will have the effect of converting certain income from foreign source to U.S. source, foreign corporations and foreign partners in joint ventures could incur U.S. tax for the first time. (D. Nosler, W.T. Rudd, M. Lebovitz & S. Bates, 12 Journal of International Taxation, No. 5, 8.)

"Importing and exporting basis and other tax attributes: do we need a new system?" **(2001).** The treatment of basis and other tax attributes when assets enter or leave U.S. taxing jurisdiction is an issue that pervades the rules relating to cross-border transactions. The purpose of this article is mainly descriptive and only incidentally prescriptive: to set out and analyze the confused state of the law in this area, to lay bare the many discontinuities, to question the legitimacy of some of the policy objectives that have been offered up to justify this or that exception— all with a view to advancing the issue of whether we need a new system and perhaps specifying the criteria that any new system should satisfy, but without making premature judgments about the specific contours of what the law should be.

First, the author discusses the current law regarding basis importation and exportation, including abuse of the current law and the impact of Sections 367 and 877. Basis and other tax attributes can be imported into or exported from United States taxing jurisdiction in essentially two ways. One way is for the asset with which the tax attributes are associated to move physically into or out of U.S. taxing jurisdiction without changing ownership. A simple example is a foreign corporation's movement of equipment formerly used offshore to a U.S. trade or business.

The other way in which a tax attribute can become subject to or leave U.S. taxing jurisdiction is through the change in status of the person that has the attribute, whether the person remains the same or transfers the attribute through a disposition of assets to a new "owner" of the attribute with a status different from that of the first owner.

There are several observations to be made about the consequences of the general rules. The principles that the import or export of an asset does not change basis, that gain or loss is not recognized until it is realized, and that the Code's nonrecognition rules with respect to realized gains and losses apply to asset importation and exportation, combine in various ways to result in the recognition of gain or loss that accrued while the asset was totally outside U.S. taxing jurisdiction and—less often because of elaborate anti-abuse rules—the nonrecognition of gain or loss that accrued while the asset was within U.S. taxing jurisdiction. This stands in sharp contrast to the Code's and the IRS's treatment of other tax attributes.

In its treatment of both export and import transactions, probably the most significant statutory exception to the no-adjustment, no-taxation rule is Section 367. In addition, Section 877 provides an exception to the no-adjustment, no-taxation rule.

Then, the author considers the Clinton Administration's proposals. (P.M. Daub, 12 Journal of International Taxation, No. 11, 16.)

"International aspects of Section 355 transactions" **(2001).** J.M. Calianno, 12 Journal of International Taxation, No. 1, 12. (*Digested under* Foreign Corporations, Persons, and Partnerships, page 58.)

"IRS updates list of countries granting exemptions for international operation of ships and aircraft" **(2001).** Revenue Ruling 2001-48 provides an updated list of countries that grant U.S. persons equivalent exemptions from tax for various categories of income from the international operation of ships and aircraft to assist foreign persons who derive income from these operations in determining whether the income is exempt from U.S. taxation under Section 872(b) or Section 883(a). (12 Journal of International Taxation, No. 12, 4.)

"New U.S. tax act—dramatic consequences for estate, gift, GST regime in the foreign context" **(2001).** P. Marcovici, T. Lewis,

93

M.J. Michaels, V.A. Dalmas & C. Hsieh-Kammerlander, 12 Journal of International Taxation, No. 9, 10. (*Digested under* Estates and Estate Tax—In General, page 51.)

"OECD revises commentary on e-business and permanent establishments" (2001). The Organization for Economic Cooperation and Development (OECD) announced on January 9, 2001, that a broad consensus had finally been reached between its thirty member states on the application of the current definition of "permanent establishment" to web sites and servers. At the same time, it released amendments to the Commentary to the 1997 OECD Model Tax Convention. The changes bring some much-needed clarity but also some unwelcome hurdles to those doing business electronically. Despite the consensus, there were a few dissenting voices. (M. Perkins, 12 Journal of International Taxation, No. 4, 50.)

"Opportunities for the foreign investor in U.S. real estate—if planning comes first" (2001). M. Hirschfeld & S. Grossman, 94 Journal of Taxation 36. (*Digested under* Real Estate, page 172.)

"Proposed regulations on treatment of payments by domestic reverse hybrid entities" (2001). On February 26, 2001, proposed regulations were issued under Section 894 relating to the eligibility for treaty benefits of items of income paid by a domestic reverse hybrid entity. (3 Business Entities, No. 4, 57.)

"Second annual APA report: more filings, shorter completion time" (2001). The IRS has released its second annual report on advance pricing agreements (APAs) and the APA program, as required by the Ticket to Work and Work Incentives Improvement Act of 1999. The report covers the structure and activities of the APA program in calendar year 2000. (12 Journal of International Taxation, No. 7, 4.)

"Stepping up the pressure on tax havens—Part 1" (2001). Part 1 of this article covers the major developments up to the Organization for Economic Cooperation and Develop-ment's (OECD's) issuance, on November 24, 2000, of the Framework for a Collective Memorandum of Understanding on Eliminating Harmful Tax Practices.

After providing background on tax evasion on cross-border interest income, the author discusses OECD recommendations issued in 1997, the 1998 OECD report on tax havens, and implementation of the report. The OECD has proposed changes in potentially harmful preferential tax regimes in OECD member states, and in the operation of tax havens (both offshore and onshore) in member and nonmember states.

The OECD issued two recommendations in 1997 intended to combat tax evasion in the international context: (1) the Recommendation on the Use of Tax Identification Numbers in an International Context ("TIN Recommendation") and (2) the Recommendation on the Use of the Revised Standard OECD Magnetic Format for Automatic Exchange of Information ("Magnetic Format Recommendation").

In 1998, the Committee on Fiscal Affairs of the OECD issued a report, "Harmful Tax Competition: An Emerging Global Issue" ("the 1998 Report"), which the OECD Council approved on April 9, 1998, with significant abstentions from Luxembourg and Switzerland.

Tax evasion in the international context is a financial law issue with global implications, and resolution of this problem, as detailed in the 1998 Report, requires standardized rules and multilateral regulatory cooperation.

Next, the author addresses the European Union (EU) agreement on information exchange. The EU has agreed to exchange information about cross-border interest payments within the EU, that is, interest originating in one member state paid to individual residents of another member state. The Directive would enter into force in 2003, after a unanimous vote by EU member states in late 2002.

Then, the author considers the IRS proposal on reporting interest earned by nonresident aliens. On January 16, 2001, the IRS issued proposed regulations, evidencing a major change in U.S. government policy, that would require banks within the United States to report annually to the IRS on Form 1042-S all interest earned by nonresident alien individuals on bank deposits within the United States not effectively connected with a U.S. trade or business.

Finally, the author turns to the OECD's June 2000 report and the OECD announcement that six tax havens have agreed to implement reforms. The OECD's June 2000 Report summarizes the results of the work of the Forum on Harmful Tax Practices.

On June 19, 2000, the OECD announced that six jurisdictions (Bermuda, the Cayman Islands, Cyprus, Malta, Mauritius, and San Marino) had agreed, each by an advance-commitment letter, to implement reforms. (D.E. Spencer, 12 Journal of International Taxation, No. 4, 26.)

"Stepping up the pressure on tax havens— Part 2" (2001). Part 1 of this article covered the major developments in combating international tax evasion up to the Organization for Economic Cooperation and Development's (OECD's) issuance on November 24, 2000, of the Framework for a Collective Memorandum of Understanding on Eliminating Harmful Tax Practices (''November 2000 Framework''). The concluding part of this article picks up with the November 2000 Framework, including a comparison with the European Union (EU) Directive on exchange of information; covers recent initiatives in Brazil and Mexico; and winds up with a discussion of efforts to develop standardized rules for various global financial issues. (D.E. Spencer, 12 Journal of International Taxation, No. 5, 36.)

"Targeting international money laundering (Part 2)" (2001). The first article of this series discussed financial-transaction money laundering and international money laundering, both prohibited by 18 U.S.C. section 1956, and suggested that the international money-laundering provisions of 18 U.S.C. section 1956(a)(2) would provide the broadest vehicle to prosecute offshore activity. This no longer appears to be true. Instead, the financial-transaction money-laundering statute, and the use of creative prosecutorial approaches in connection thereto, have come to the fore. (I.M. Comisky & M.D. Lee, 12 Journal of International Taxation, No. 9, 18.)

"The Customs/IRS intersection on transfer pricing" (2001). Until Ruling No. 546979 (August 30, 2000), issued by the Customs Service, expressed reliance on the process of a bilateral advance pricing agreement (APA) approved by the IRS, it appeared that the two agencies charged with collecting tax revenues on international sales transactions had seldom conferred. Ruling No. 546979 breaks new ground, opening up the possibility of future coordinated administrative action by the agencies. This article reviews the ruling and speculates about how it could be applied in the future. (M.K. Neville, Jr. & S.D. Harris, 12 Journal of International Taxation, No. 9, 28.)

"The extraterritorial income exclusion enhances the tax benefits once sought from FSCs" (2001). A.S. Lederman & B. Hirsh, 94 Journal of Taxation 174. (*Digested under* Foreign Corporations, Persons, and Partnerships, page 64.)

"The paradox of tax havens: consequences of the subjective approach" (2001). The author suggests a model anti-tax-haven approach in line with the taxpayer's perspective on tax havens rather than the tax authorities' perspective.

First, the author discusses the traditional objective approach and the perspective of the tax authorities. Under this approach, a country or territory is considered a tax haven only if it has been so designated by tax authorities or legislation. This approach has produced two variations: the ''designated jurisdiction approach'' and the ''transactional approach.'' Under the first approach, which is actually a strict objective approach, a tax haven is where legislation or the tax authorities say it is. There is no exception, unless it is provided by law. Under the second variation, which is a moderate objective approach, a tax haven is also where legislation or the tax authorities say it is, but the nature and purpose of the transaction is considered.

Then, the author reconsiders the tax haven concept, using the subjective approach. The subjective nature of a tax haven is a haven from the perspective of the taxpayer who is deciding which country or territory will effectively constitute a good haven to avoid or evade the tax treatment of his home country or country of tax liability. As a consequence of the subjective approach to tax havens, the question changes from which country is a tax haven for which taxpayer to which country is susceptible of being a tax haven for which taxpayer.

Finally, the author addresses anti-tax haven model legislation. The best way to effectively combat what a taxpayer subjectively considers a tax haven is to follow the same logic as the taxpayer, and draft regulations or legislation in accordance with the subjective approach. The model proposed in this article is a generic version that can be adapted to each particular country's situation. (J.M. Ngoy, 12 Journal of International Taxation, No. 1, 34.)

"The war against corruption goes international" (2001). The Foreign Corrupt Practices Act of 1977 (FCPA) makes it a criminal offense for U.S. companies and foreign companies subject to U.S. law to pay bribes to foreign government officials.

On November 21, 1997, twenty-nine members of the Organization for Economic Cooperation and Development (OECD) and five nonmember signatories adopted the OECD Convention on Combating Bribery of Foreign Public Officials in International Business Transactions (OECD Convention), which is intended to eliminate corruption as an accepted practice. The OECD Convention has itself spawned major changes to the FCPA. Among other changes, the reach of the Act now extends to any U.S. national anywhere in the world.

Although the FCPA has the potential to erode U.S. commercial competitiveness, an international effort to combat corruption on a worldwide scale became inevitable, and several victories have been achieved. They include: (1) the Inter-American Convention Against Corruption signed by the Organization of American States on March 29, 1996;

(2) the International Chamber of Commerce's new rules against corruption; (3) the World Bank's strategy to battle bribery; (4) the International Monetary Fund (IMF) policy of denying loans to countries where corruption is rampant; and, most recently, (5) the OECD Convention to combat bribery.

After providing background on the FCPA, its perceived disadvantages, and the international effort to combat corruption, the authors provide an overview of the FCPA's provisions. The FCPA consists of two substantive parts: (1) accounting requirements and (2) bribery prohibitions. Under the accounting requirements, public companies must keep accurate accounts and put in place strict accounting controls aimed at uncovering and deterring corruption. Under the bribery prohibitions, U.S. companies, citizens, and residents are forbidden from making illicit payments to foreign officials to procure a commercial benefit.

Then, the authors consider corrupt practices under the FCPA. For a business or commercial entity to be liable under the FCPA, it must be any "issuer" or "domestic concern"—a test that is easily satisfied. However, the question of its foreign subsidiaries is far more uncertain.

Finally, the authors address multinational efforts against corruption. (S.E. Vecchi & K.C. Chua, 12 Journal of International Taxation, No. 3, 8.)

"U.S. tax and Customs consequences of dealing with a related foreign supplier (Part 1)" (2001). For many years, IRS and Customs officials fought separately, sometimes ineffectively,' to establish arm's-length valuations in related-party import transactions. However, legislative action and agency cooperation have now created an environment in which the IRS and Customs can attack improper import valuations as a unified force within the Treasury Department. With the enactment of Section 1059A, the addition of Section 6103(l)(14), and the Mutual Assistance Agreement, the IRS and Customs now appear adequately armed to launch a coordinated challenge when importers claim a tax basis that exceeds the declared Customs value.

First, the authors discuss Section 1059A. Under Section 1059A, importers generally are barred from taking a cost or inventory basis (tax basis) in property acquired from a related person that exceeds the value of the property as declared for Customs valuation purposes.

Then, the authors address Section 6103(l)(14) and the Mutual Assistance Agreement executed by the IRS and Customs with a view toward promoting interagency communication and cooperation. Section 6103(l)(14) provides for information-sharing between the IRS and Customs with respect to return information.

As the IRS and Customs personnel communicate and cooperate more frequently, the likelihood increases that valuation discrepancies will be discovered by either or both agencies. Because importers are often permitted, under the Customs rules, to value merchandise for duty assessment at an amount that is lower than the amount appropriately determined for tax purposes, the importer has essentially the same burden of proof whether examined by Customs or the IRS. In a Customs audit, the importer must be able to establish that any amounts excluded from the purchase price in computing dutiable value were proper exclusions. Similarly, from a tax perspective, if the value reported for Customs purposes is lower than the basis reported for income tax purposes, the importer must be able to satisfy the IRS that the difference between the two valuations is attributable to items that were properly excluded for Customs purposes.

Since it is more likely that an importer dealing with a related foreign supplier will be subject to an IRS audit, in a case where there are differing valuations, the IRS may communicate with Customs for assistance under the Mutual Assistance Agreement to determine whether such difference is attributable to properly excluded items in arriving at dutiable value. Conversely, if Customs should determine, as a result of an audit, that certain costs were improperly excluded, it may, in the spirit of the Mutual Assistance Agreement, advise the IRS that a reduction in the tax basis of the imported merchandise may be appropriate. (D.I. Meyer & W.D.

Outman II, 12 Journal of International Taxation, No. 11, 30.)

"Will U.S. standardization erode key flexibility in APAs?" (2001). The U.S. advance pricing agreement (APA) process is designed to produce a formal agreement between the taxpayer and the IRS on three basic issues: (1) the factual nature of the intercompany transactions to which the APA applies; (2) an appropriate transfer pricing methodology (TPM) to apply to those transactions; and (3) the expected arm's-length range of results from application of the TPM to the transactions. The taxpayer has the option of seeking a unilateral, bilateral, or multilateral APA. A unilateral APA involves solely an agreement between the taxpayer and the IRS. If a treaty country is involved, the IRS encourages the taxpayer to seek a mutual agreement with the foreign competent authority under the applicable tax treaty.

In addition to the agreement between the taxpayer and the IRS, the U.S. competent authority will also attempt to reach a mutual agreement with the competent authorities of the treaty partners. The APA process contemplates full coordination between the competent authorities on all subsequent administrative matters.

After providing an overview of the APA process, the author discusses the steps in the APA process, including the prefiling conference, APA submission, evaluation and negotiation, the agreement, and monitoring and administration (the annual report, future exams, renewal, and disclosure).

Then, the author considers strategic issues in deciding to seek an APA. Before initiating the APA process, the taxpayer, in concert with its outside advisors, should conduct a cost-benefit analysis to determine whether an APA is the most cost-effective way to proceed.

Finally, the author addresses new developments in the U.S. and global APA processes. New U.S. developments include the early-referral program and small business taxpayer APA program. Many global tax authorities have established either formal or informal APA programs. Many countries follow the Organization for Economic Cooperation and Development (OECD) transfer pricing guidelines, or have used the guidelines as the basis for developing their own more specific legislation. (R.E. Ackerman, 12 Journal of International Taxation, No. 2, 12.)

"You ought to be in pictures—the sequel: an update of worldwide incentives for film and video production" (2001). Many nations around the world continue to support their local film and television production industries through subsidies and various tax and other incentive programs. These benefits often can be obtained by nonresident production companies, sometimes through co-production ventures with local entities. This article, an update of a three-part series offered in 1999 and 2000, examines some new or revised business and tax incentives for film and video production from around the world. As illustrated in the article, however, changes frequently occur with regard to applicable rules. Therefore, the information presented should be used as a guide, and the most-current, specific rules should be studied before entering into particular transactions.

Taxpayers residing in Australia are provided a deduction for the capital investment in an "eligible film" that is also an "Australian film," one that has significant Australian content. The Australian Film Finance Corporation (FFC) is a federal government agency that serves as a source of funds for the nation's film production industry, providing grants to subsidize the financing of "qualifying Australian films." The Australian Film Commission, another government agency, offers additional assistance in project development and media.

Canada has a thriving film and television production industry and possesses a unique blend of cultural diversity, natural beauty, good exchange rates, abundant technical resources, and low production costs. Ontario offers a tax credit for computer animation and special effects and a television production services tax credit based on certain qualifying labor expenses. Various other Canadian assistance programs are described, including the Canadian Television Fund, Alberta Film Development program, the Newfoundland and Labrador Film Development Corporation, Enterprise Prince Edward Island, and the Yukon Film Location Incentive Program.

In recent years, Ireland has established itself as a favored location for both domestic and international film productions. Ireland's Finance Act of 2000 extended the expiration date to 2005 of a significant tax deduction for corporate and individual investors in film. To qualify, a film production must be certified as including maximum Irish content and must involve a qualifying company that may include one incorporated or resident outside of Ireland provided it carries on a trade or business through an Irish branch or agency.

Under Netherlands tax law, limited partnerships that share in the production cost and gain from films may qualify for several tax benefits that apply only to entrepreneurs. The article discusses benefits and limitations of these partnership provisions.

In 1999 Puerto Rico passed the Film Industry Development Act (the Film Act), intended to promote the local film industry and related activities, create incentives for private investment and attract foreign capital, and create an infrastructure to support development of the film industry in Puerto Rico. Projects that are granted a license under the Film Act receive various tax exemptions and rate benefits for a ten-year period. In addition, investors in a film project receive a tax credit for disbursements paid to Puerto Rico residents.

The United Kingdom has long been a popular location for both film and television production, due in part to its first-rate studio, laboratory, and post-production facilities. Under new rules effective in 2000, accelerated tax depreciation writeoffs have been extended and more liberal criteria for qualification as a British film were established. A new governmental body, the Film Council, was launched in May 2000 to consolidate and manage U.K. governmental funding as a whole, with renewed national commitments to supporting "high quality innovative and commercially attractive screenplays."

Many states in the United States also offer a variety of business and tax incentives for film production carried on within their borders. These benefits range from credits against income tax to exemptions from sales and use tax on certain purchases associated with the production of film. Accompanying the article is a list of useful contact information for various state and local film commissions. The author points out that the film industry also has its own language. Explanations of some of the unique terminology is presented in a two-page glossary of accounting and technical terminology. (J.M. Tolin, N. Adler, J.A. Jedrlinic, M.T. Masuda & M.F. Mullen, 11 Journal of Multistate Taxation and Incentives, No. 3, 20.)

Argentina

"Leasing: Argentina finally approves a law that's up to world standards" (2001). For years, international and local financial institutions have complained about the tax and procedural inequalities of regulations that hindered leasing activities in Argentina (Law 24.441). A new law (25.248) has now been approved that solves these problems and provides tax benefits for real estate transactions. It revokes the particular provisions of Law 24.441 relating to leasing and Decrees 627/96 and 873/97, which regulated the tax impact of that law. (C.E. Alfaro, 12 Journal of International Taxation, No. 1, 56.)

"The tax consequences and opportunities relating to domestic and foreign partnerships in Argentina" (2001). For legal and cultural reasons the use of partnerships is not widespread in Argentina. Tax considerations play an important role in encouraging or discouraging their use. However, the use of partnerships can present Argentine and U.S. tax planning opportunities as well as tax burdens. Because the term ''partnership'' has a variety of meanings in Spanish and lacks an equivalent term, it is necessary at the outset to define its scope. In this article, when the authors refer to a partnership, they are referring to a contractual agreement between two or more persons entered into in order to share profits (or losses) combined with the intention to act as partners (affecto societatis) while recognizing the other partners (intuitue personae). A distinctive feature of Argentine law is that in a partnership at least one partner must not enjoy limited liability; i.e., does not limit its responsibility to the amount it contributed to the partnership.

First, the authors briefly describe the legal features of the main types of business organizations that operate in Argentina, including partnerships. Then, the authors discuss the income tax treatment of these entities and analyze the tax issues that arise from the use of Argentine partnerships, focusing on questions related to foreign investment and income taxation, and describe the tax treatment of investments made by Argentine investors through foreign partnerships.

The use of partnerships is not widespread in Argentina for both legal and commercial reasons. When they are used it is often because of the benefits provided by Argentine tax law, such as timing advantages, and for non-Argentine tax law reasons, such as achieving the benefits of a flow-through entity in the United States. In order to reduce their tax advantages under Argentine law, Argentine limited liability companies (SRLs) and certain Argentine partnerships are now treated as capital companies for income tax purposes in a relatively recent Argentine statutory tax reform, and as such are taxable as separate taxpayers. But some entities are still considered to be reporting entities. The use of reporting entities can provide tax advantages but sometimes reporting companies pose legal and commercial problems because of their limited use in the marketplace. The use of reporting entities by foreign principals in Argentina may make it impossible for them to offset income with losses.

Investment in foreign partnerships by Argentine residents can be disadvantageous in terms of timing compared with investment in foreign corporations. For Argentine tax purposes, foreign partnerships, unlike domestic partnerships, are treated as flow-through entities. In any case, the taxation in

99

Argentina of Argentine residents who invest in foreign partnerships is far from clear.

Finally, the authors consider tax treaties. With respect to tax treaties, under the most recent reports related to the Organization for Economic Cooperation and Development (OECD) Model Treaty, in cases other than partnerships that are now treated as taxable entities, Argentine partners, rather than Argentine partnerships, are entitled to claim the tax treaty benefits. (G. Gotlib & W.C. Keininger, 3 Business Entities, No. 4, 40.)

Australia

"Australian tax reform in 2001 federal budget, thin cap legislation" (2001). On May 22, 2001, the Australian government released the 2001 federal budget, which confirmed the start date of several important previously announced tax measures and outlined proposed amendments to the draft thin capitalization and debt/equity test legislation. (12 Journal of International Taxation, No. 10, 5.)

"Australia proposes new thin cap rules" (2001). On February 21, 2001, the Australian government released for public comment exposure draft legislation covering proposed changes to the thin capitalization rules, removal of the debt-creation rules, and some general provisions for determining whether a security is to be classified as debt or equity for Australian tax purposes. (12 Journal of International Taxation, No. 7, 9.)

"Australia's new thin cap rules: moving the debt/equity borderline" (2001). The Australian government released for public comment on February 21, 2001, exposure draft legislation entitled "The New Business Tax System (Thin Capitalization and Other Measures) Bill 2001" (draft bill), which introduces changes to the thin capitalization regime as recommended by the Ralph Review of Business Taxation. The draft bill broadly adopts the previously announced recommendations, but with some significant changes.

The thin capitalization regime aims to limit the tax deductibility of interest and other debt expenses resulting from a disproportionate application of debt funding to the Australian operations of international entities both foreign and domestically owned. The draft bill also seeks to define more generally "debt" and "equity" for tax purposes. This will in turn determine whether the return to the investor will be treated as a distribution or as a deductible expense across a range of provisions within the income tax law.

First, the author discusses the debt/equity distinction. As well as amending the thin capitalization regime, the draft bill provides some fundamental changes to the debt/equity distinctions for tax purposes. There is a move toward an economic-substance approach and away from a form approach.

Then, the author considers the new interest withholding tax exemption. Interest paid on debentures issued after June 30, 2001, by nonresident companies operating in Australia through permanent establishments will be exempt from interest withholding tax.

Finally, the author addresses who the new thin cap rules will affect, how interest deductibility limits will be determined, which debt will be taken into account, debt creation rules to be repealed, calculation of the safe-harbor test, when the new rules apply, required preparation, and how Australia compares with its major trading partners. (D. Lockie, 12 Journal of International Taxation, No. 5, 30.)

Barbados

"China-Barbados treaty ratified" (2001). 12 Journal of International Taxation, No. 7, 12. (*Digested under* International Taxation—China, page 105.)

Belgium

"A guide to European holding companies—Part 2: Belgium, the Netherlands, and Spain" (2001). The authors continue their series on how intelligent use of a European holding company can eliminate or reduce foreign withholding taxes.

First, the authors discuss Belgium. Requirements have changed for using the Belgian participation exemption for intercompany dividends and capital gains realized on shares as a result of the 1997 Belgium budget and the ruling by the European Union (EU) Court of Justice in *Denkavit* (1996). Belgium does not provide a privileged tax regime for holding activities. However, a Belgian company that is subject to Belgian corporate income tax (CIT) or a Belgian branch of a foreign company is eligible, under appropriate circumstances, for benefits of the Belgian participation exemption, which provides a favorable tax regime for dividends and capital gains on shares.

Then, the authors address the Netherlands. The main benefits of the Dutch holding company remain accessible to an extensive tax treaty network, the Dutch tax ruling practice, and the transparency of its holding regime.

Finally, the authors consider Spain. Spain offers a substantial advantage vis-à-vis other attractive European holding company locations as dividends distributed by the Spanish holding company to non-Spanish resident shareholders are exempt from the Spanish withholding tax on dividends. (S.C. Ruchelman, E. Van Asbeck, G. Canalejo, W. Heyvaert, M.T. McGowan & S. Neidhardt, 12 Journal of International Taxation, No. 1, 22.)

Brazil

"Brazil reduces royalty withholding rate" (2001). After increasing the withholding tax on certain outbound royalty payments to 25 percent, the Brazilian government reviewed its position with respect to its overall technology and development policies, and decided to cut the tax rate back to 15 percent. The recently created Extraordinary Contribution for Economic Intervention (CIDE) was maintained on outbound royalty payments related to technology, know-how, and industrial property in general. (12 Journal of International Taxation, No. 7, 10.)

Canada

"Canada's revised FIE rules: stay cautious" (2001). Canada released revised draft foreign investment entity (FIE) legislation on August 2, 2001 (the Revised Rules), which replace, and address many of the fundamental concerns arising from, the draft FIE rules that were released on June 22, 2000.

First, the author addresses the purpose of the Revised Rules, the definition of "FIE," the carrying value of investment property, the look-through rules, and the principal-business exception. The purpose of the Revised Rules remains unchanged—to prevent tax avoidance by taxpayers that directly or indirectly invest in or otherwise transfer property to FIEs. Subject to various exceptions discussed in the article, the Revised Rules apply to taxpayers (including controlled foreign affiliates) that hold participating interests in an FIE. When applicable, the Revised Rules continue to add an amount in computing the taxpayer's income (or the controlled foreign affiliate's foreign accrual property income (FAPI)) under either the accrual method (based on the FIE's underlying income) or the mark-to-market method (based on changes in value at least annually during the holding period).

"FIE" is generally defined as a nonresident corporation or trust, or a fund, joint venture, organization, or syndicate existing and governed under the laws of a country other than Canada unless: (1) the carrying value of the entity's investment property at the end of its tax year is not more than 50 percent of the carrying value of all the entity's property at that time or (2) the entity's principal business is not an investment business. In determining whether an entity is an FIE, all exchangeable or convertible participating interests are deemed to have been exchanged for, or converted into, participating interests of the entity immediately before the particular time, and are otherwise deemed not to exist at the particular time.

The "carrying value" of an entity's property continues to be generally determined as the amount at which its property would be valued on its balance sheet if prepared under Canadian generally accepted accounting principles (GAAP) or under substantially similar accounting principles. However, a taxpayer may now make an election to value the property of the entity at fair market value, rather than at book value. This election could allow an entity to avoid FIE status if it has significant assets on its balance sheet that are not investment property that have a high fair market value and relatively low book value (such as certain internally developed intellectual property).

The Revised Rules continue to include a look-through provision that applies in determining whether an entity is an FIE.

Even if more than 50 percent of the carrying value of all of an entity's property is investment property, the entity will not be an FIE if its principal business is not an investment business.

Then, the author discusses other exemptions from the Revised Rules, the use of the accrual method, the use of the mark-to-market method, avoidance of double taxation, tracked interests, and foreign insurance policies.

Finally, the author considers problems with the Revised Rules. Although the Revised Rules rectify many of the anomalies in the prior draft FIE rules, increased equity has come at the expense of increased complexity. The Revised Rules have ballooned to approximately forty-seven pages of draft legislation. This complexity makes the Revised Rules difficult to understand and interpret, and various anomalies remain. As a result, it is hard to discern clear tax policy objectives and to reconcile the FIE rules with other provisions in the Income Tax Act (Canada) that impact cross-border transactions. Consequently, the Revised Rules may continue to negatively affect the Canadian tax consequences of certain cross-border investments. The Revised Rules, when finalized, will generally apply to tax years commencing after 2001. (P. Marley, 12 Journal of International Taxation, No. 12, 28.)

"Canadian court offers hope for cleaning up errors: record the taxpayer's intention" (2001). Some basic fears are endemic to tax planning. In particular, there may be some tax provision lurking out there that one has failed to take into account, or a client may have failed to communicate all of the necessary facts relevant to determining Canadian tax liability. Also, there is the possibility that the other professional advisors involved in a particular transaction have miscommunicated facts or simply erred in offering advice, potentially occasioning a lot of subsequent finger-pointing in the event of a tax meltdown.

First, the author discusses the Ontario Court of Appeal decision in *Juliar* (2000)—which offers a ray of hope for beleaguered planners in the Canadian context. The message of the case is this: as long as an effort is made to ensure that, in the course of planning, there is a clear evidentiary path demonstrating that the intention of a plan was not to result in Canadian tax, one may still be able to clean up errors after the fact without undue cost and hardship. Bad planning, misunderstanding, or poor communication need not necessarily undermine any particular plan or give rise to a successful claim for professional negligence.

Then, the author analyzes the decision. From its reasons in *Juliar*, the court's view seems clear—its ability to provide relief by way of rectification depended on unequivocal proof that the taxpayers intended the transaction to be one giving rise to no immediate tax consequences whatsoever. (S.L. Van Der Hout, 12 Journal of International Taxation, No. 2, 26.)

"Canadian Economic Statement proposes significant tax cuts" (2001). The Economic Statement delivered by the Honorable Paul Martin, the Minister of Finance, on October 18, 2000, amounted to a mini-budget that was soon followed by the calling of a general election by the government. The Economic Statement delivers good news to Canadian individuals and corporations by proposing or confirming modest income tax rate reductions, including a reduction of the capital gains inclusion rate. Several additional proposals include two of considerable interest in the cross-border context.

First, the author discusses corporate income tax reductions. The Economic Statement sets out a schedule for federal corporate income tax reductions, essentially specifying the timetable proposed in the 2000 Federal Budget.

Then, the author addresses personal income tax measures and capital gains tax reduction. (A.H. Kingissepp, 12 Journal of International Taxation, No. 2, 34.)

"*Canadian Pacific v. The Queen*: *Shell Canada* revisited under GAAR" (2001). This article discusses one of the most recent and important general anti-avoidance rule (GAAR) cases, the Tax Court of Canada's decision in *Canadian Pacific Ltd. v. The Queen* (2000). In *Canadian Pacific*, the central issue was the deductibility of interest payments, pursuant to paragraph 20(1)(c) of the Act, on soft currency loans made by the taxpayer. The facts in *Canadian Pacific* were substantially the same as those in *The Queen v. Shell Canada Limited* (1999), a case decided by the Supreme Court of Canada.

The taxpayers in both cases entered into a series of transactions that combined soft-currency (sometimes referred to as weak-currency) loans and foreign exchange forward contracts. The net result of the transactions, subject to the GAAR issue, was to increase the amounts that were currently deductible by the taxpayer during the term of the loans, and to generate a foreign exchange gain (treated as a capital gain) for the taxpayer on repayment of the loan. In *Shell*, the Supreme Court decided in favor of the taxpayer and found that, under the circumstances, the four requirements for the deductibility of interest under paragraph 20(1)(c) were met.

Shell confirms the principle that the legal form must prevail over the economic substance of a transaction. However, unlike in *Canadian Pacific*, the transactions considered in *Shell* were entered into before the enactment of GAAR in 1988. As a result, the Supreme Court in *Shell* did not address the GAAR issues that the Canada Customs and Revenue Agency (CCRA) otherwise might have raised with respect to these types of transactions. *Canadian Pacific* is therefore a very significant case because the court addressed the same facts as in *Shell* but in the GAAR context.

After providing background on the GAAR and *Canadian Pacific*, the author discusses the reasoning of the Tax Court in *Canadian Pacific*. The Tax Court's decision is not at all surprising in light of the Supreme Court's comments about soft-currency loans in *Shell*. It is expected that these comments will also make it very difficult for the Crown to succeed in its pending appeal of the Tax Court decision in *Canadian Pacific* to the Federal Court of Appeal. It is hoped that the appellate court will clarify that GAAR is to be analyzed based on the legal rights and obligations of the parties, as opposed to the economic substance of the transaction. (A.H. Kingissepp, 12 Journal of International Taxation, No. 7, 42.)

"Supreme Court of Canada further clarifies partnership taxation" (2001). There is no definition of "partnership" (or "partner") in the Income Tax Act (Canada) (ITA). Subdivision j of Division B in Part I of the ITA speaks to the taxation of partnerships and their members, but generally presupposes the existence or cessation of a partnership. Thus, in construing the provisions of the ITA applicable to partnerships, the pertinence of private law concepts to the scheme of the ITA is of particular prominence.

This issue has been highlighted by the position recently taken and subsequently revised by the Canada Customs and Revenue Agency (CCRA) in respect of the status of an entity formed under the Delaware Revised Uniform Partnership Act as a partnership for purposes of the ITA. Two recent decisions of the Supreme Court of Canada released concurrently, *Backman* (2001) and *Spire Freezers Ltd.* (2001), further elucidate principles relevant to the intersection of the ITA and partnership law.

At issue in *Backman* and *Spire Freezers* was the validity of partnerships for purposes of the ITA. Despite the similarity of the facts, there were key distinctions, as evidenced by the differing dispositions of the cases reached by the Supreme Court. In *Spire Freezers*, the court held that a valid

103

partnership existed, but reached the opposite conclusion in *Backman*. (J.A. Colden, 12 Journal of International Taxation, No. 8, 38.)

"Transfer pricing in Canada—an update" (2001). The transfer pricing audit environment in Canada is becoming more and more aggressive and Canada, like many other countries, has reacted by putting in place formal standards in response to those of its nearest neighbor, the United States.

First, the author provides an overview of Canadian transfer pricing law. Canadian tax law with regard to transfer pricing is very brief and there are no detailed regulations embodied in the law as there are, for example, in the U.S. Section 247 of Canada's Income Tax Act (the Act) became effective for tax years beginning after 1997, replacing briefer and less specific older legislation. Under Section 247, the Canada Customs and Revenue Agency (CCRA) may adjust the pricing between non-arm's-length parties where the terms or conditions differ from those at which arm's-length parties in similar circumstances would transact.

The Organization for Economic Cooperation and Development (OECD) guidelines are not embodied in the law. Rather, the Act specifies that when a taxpayer and a nonresident person with whom the taxpayer is not dealing at arm's length participate in a transaction or a series of transactions and the terms or conditions differ from those that would have been made had the parties been dealing at arm's length, the terms or conditions can be adjusted to those that would have been made had the parties been dealing at arm's length.

Under subsection 251(1) of the Act, related parties are automatically deemed not to deal with one another at arm's length. Further, it is a question of fact whether unrelated persons deal with each other at arm's length.

Then, the author addresses administrative guidelines. Canada has very broad administrative guidelines on transfer pricing. A good part of these are found in Information Circular 87-2R (the Circular), which was finally released in September 1999 and outlines the CCRA's proposed administrative approach to Canada's new transfer pricing rules. While the Circular does not have the force of law, it provides guidance to taxpayers (and assessors) with respect to the application of the transfer pricing rules set out in the Act and is one of the key documents in understanding the CCRA's intent in interpreting the law. The CCRA has announced that it plans to supplement the Circular with a memoranda series expanding on specific topic areas.

Finally, the author considers transfer pricing differences between countries, CCRA's transfer pricing auditing process, changes to the annual information return, and CCRA's support of advance pricing agreements. (D. Bale, 12 Journal of International Taxation, No. 2, 6.)

"Update on Delaware partnerships in Canada: CCRA reversal" (2001). On November 28, 2000, the Canada Customs and Revenue Agency (CCRA) issued a technical interpretation reversing the preliminary view it had taken in July 2000. In that technical interpretation, the CCRA acknowledged that the characterization of an entity formed under foreign partnership legislation must be determined by fully analyzing the attributes of the entity and comparing them to the attributes of a Canadian partnership and a Canadian corporation.

After fully analyzing the attributes of an entity formed under the Delaware Revised Uniform Partnership Act (DRUPA), the CCRA concluded that its attributes more closely resembled those of a Canadian general partnership under Canadian common law and, as such, an entity governed by DRUPA would be treated as a partnership for Canadian income tax purposes. In addition, the CCRA indicated that the existence of a separate legal entity clause in the foreign partnership legislation would not, in and by itself, preclude an arrangement from being considered as a partnership for Canadian income tax purposes.

After discussing the CCRA reversal, the author considers the lack of a bright-line test and the potential uncertainty for other foreign entities. The CCRA's revised view on DRUPA partnerships potentially creates some uncertainty for purposes of characterizing other foreign entities as corporations for Canadian income tax purposes. (P. Marley, 12 Journal of International Taxation, No. 2, 39.)

"U.S.-Canada treaty does not prohibit application of FTC limitation" (2001). For purposes of computing a taxpayer's foreign tax credit (FTC) limitation, the 1980 U.S.-Canada income tax treaty does not prohibit the U.S. from applying its law to allocate a portion of the taxpayer's aggregate interest expense to its gross income attributable to permanent establishments maintained in Canada and to dividends received from a Canadian corporation, even though the interest expense is not deductible for Canadian tax purposes, according to TAM 200134007. (12 Journal of International Taxation, No. 12, 8.)

Chile

"Chile enacts anti-evasion tax reform bill" (2001). Chile's anti-evasion tax legislation was published in the Official Gazette on June 19, 2001, with most of its provisions becoming effective on that date. (12 Journal of International Taxation, No. 11, 9.)

"Chile's Finance Ministry proposes reforms to capital markets; key foreign exchange controls lifted" (2001). During April 2001, Chile's Finance Ministry announced several proposed reforms, many of which must be carried-out through the enactment of a new law, designed to modernize and stimulate the country's capital markets. In conjunction with this reform, Chile's Central Bank announced that it was eliminating a majority of the foreign exchange restrictions imposed on investments. (12 Journal of International Taxation, No. 11, 11.)

China

"China-Barbados treaty ratified" (2001). The tax treaty negotiated between China and Barbados, ratified on October 27, 2000, contains some favorable provisions and creates an opportunity for international investors to use Barbados as a jurisdiction for investment into China. (12 Journal of International Taxation, No. 7, 12.)

"Despite treaties, China's lower withholding rate is important for foreign enterprises" (2001). Interest, rent, royalties, and other China-source income of foreign enterprises is subject to withholding tax in the People's Republic of China (China), unless the income is attributable to a permanent establishment of the foreign enterprise in China. This is part of the foreign enterprise/foreign investment enterprise tax system, which taxes income of a permanent establishment of a foreign enterprise in China, income of a foreign investment enterprise in China, or income from other China sources.

The withholding tax rate, set forth in 1991 tax legislation, was 20 percent on the gross amount. The State Council of China decided in November 2000 that, retroactive to January 1, 2000, the withholding tax rate will be reduced from 20 percent to 10 percent. (S. Stricker-Kellerer, 12 Journal of International Taxation, No. 5, 45.)

"Moving under one roof: consolidating foreign-invested businesses in China" (2001). Existing regulatory restrictions compel foreign investors in China to use discrete legal entities, such as equity joint ventures, cooperative joint ventures, or wholly foreign-owned subsidiaries (collectively referred to as foreign invested enterprises (FIEs)) to undertake business operations in China sector by sector or project by project.

FIEs use various consolidation models. This article examines some of the more popular consolidation vehicles used by multinational corporations in China.

First, the author discusses mergers. In a merger, two or more FIEs are merged into one FIE, either by absorption (one of the predecessor FIEs becomes the surviving entity) or establishment (an entirely new FIE is formed from the merger of predecessor FIEs).

Next, the author considers joint stock companies (JSCs). A JSC can be formed by

105

the merger of two or more FIEs, with the investors in the predecessor FIEs holding shares in the JSC.

Then, the author addresses Chinese holding companies. Under this arrangement, a Chinese holding company (CHC) is formed, with the predecessor FIEs acquired as subsidiaries of the CHC in exchange for shares in the CHC.

Finally, the author turns to asset acquisitions. An asset acquisition occurs when one FIE purchases the businesses of other FIEs. (R. Chang, 12 Journal of International Taxation, No. 10, 47.)

"Questions remain for foreign enterprises with licensing arrangements in China" (2001). Foreign enterprises licensing manufacturing technology to Chinese licensees or providing technical services have faced uncertainties over the last few years with respect to whether and how their income from services and royalties will be taxed in the People's Republic of China (PRC). Their main concern has not been about the foreign enterprise income tax levied in the PRC since 1991—under this regime, royalties and service fees are subject to a 20 percent withholding tax, reduced to 10 percent under most treaties for the avoidance of double taxation signed by the PRC.

Beyond the treaty provisions, Chinese domestic regulations provide for a further reduction (below the 10 percent level) or even a full exemption from the enterprise income tax under specific circumstances, depending primarily on the technology to be advanced and granted under preferential terms. No explicit guidelines have been established for these criteria, but in practice most foreign enterprises do not expect a reduction below the 10 percent treaty level. (S. Stricker-Kellerer, 12 Journal of International Taxation, No. 4, 56.)

"Taxation of foreign professional service firms in China" (2001). Foreign consulting companies doing business in China generally choose various forms of activities. These include providing services: (1) outside of China to Chinese customers or to foreign customers relating to things Chinese; (2) through traveling consultants, their own representative offices, or foreign investment subsidiaries; or (3) through contractual arrangements with other companies, representative offices, or individuals in China. All of these structures need to be categorized under the Chinese tax system, distinguishing between: (1) domestic enterprises subject to taxation of their worldwide income; (2) foreign enterprises subject to taxation on the income attributable to a permanent establishment in China; and (3) foreign enterprises subject to withholding tax on other China-source income.

Once subject to taxes, two kinds of taxes are primarily relevant: (1) business tax (a kind of turnover tax) with a rate of 5 percent on gross income and (2) foreign and foreign investment enterprise income tax with either a 10 percent withholding tax on gross China-source income or a 33 percent profit tax on profits attributable to a permanent establishment or domestic enterprise (with some reductions in tax rates depending on location and business sector).

Based on this system, the State Taxation Administration of the People's Republic of China issued Notice No. 82 (2000) on May 12, 2000, which deals primarily with (1) general principles of income allocation for professional service firms providing services both inside and outside of China and (2) certain apportionment rules. (S. Stricker-Kellerer, 12 Journal of International Taxation, No. 9, 39.)

"What does China's entry into the WTO mean for investors?" (2001). There seems to be no doubt that China will make major changes to its tax system on its admission into the World Trade Organization (WTO). In particular, it will adopt a unified income tax regime for domestic and foreign businesses.

First, the author discusses the impact on the Chinese income tax system. Adjustments to tax incentives have already been made and more are expected in the process. For example, in 2000 China promulgated measures to encourage the development of the software and integrated circuit industries. Another trend is the extension of tax incentives to both domestic and foreign businesses. In addition, China has extended some tax incentives geographically. Most of the incentives, as originally designed, were granted to stimulate economic growth in the coastal region. Some of these incentives have been extended to inland areas.

Then, the author addresses value-added tax (VAT). China will change its VAT regime to make it more compatible with international practices. Measures in this respect include adoption of a consumption-type VAT and possibly expansion of its coverage. Introduction of a consumption-type VAT would be good news for investors, as they would be entitled to input credit for VAT paid on capital goods. Investors in service industries would likely experience changes in their tax burden with the expansion of VAT coverage.

Finally, the author considers property taxes. China is expected to combine the two separate property tax systems currently in force. Such changes would not have any major impact on investors. (T.H. Wang, 12 Journal of International Taxation, No. 8, 4.)

Colombia

"Colombia enacts tax reform" (2001). On December 29, 2000, the Colombian Congress enacted changes to Colombian law affecting value-added tax (VAT), customs duties, income tax, and other taxes. (12 Journal of International Taxation, No. 7, 13.)

Denmark

"Special expat tax rate in Denmark will attract experts of all kinds" (2001). The purpose of the Danish expat tax rate is to offer a flat-rate income tax, currently 25 percent, to researchers and high-earning employees recruited abroad and employed by Danish employers for a period of up to three years. The arrangement will allow Denmark to attract experts of all kinds, who would otherwise be discouraged by the high income tax rate.

After providing background on the expat scheme, the author discusses timing issues. Only employees and researchers who become fully liable to pay tax in Denmark may opt for the scheme. They must take up the position immediately after the date on which they become fully liable for income tax (in practice, one month after taking up residence in Denmark) for a maximum period of thirty-six months. There are no specific requirements as to the nature of the job (for example, athletes can make use of the rules).

Then, the author addresses additional requirements, high-earning employees, researchers, basis of taxation, new employment, and additional taxation. (A.M. Ottosen, 12 Journal of International Taxation, No. 3, 43.)

European Union

"Changes in LAN-itude: duty refunds now available for computer peripheral exports" (2001). One of the long-term goals of the international trading system is to foster free trade. That goal may be thwarted if members of the World Trade Organization (WTO) classify products in ways that place them in categories not eligible for reduced or duty-free treatment. The European Union (EU) did just that for certain computer peripheral products but, in a far-reaching court decision, the EU action has been struck down.

Since January 2000, exporters of these products to the EU have been able to count on duty-free treatment for their exports, but they can now file for duty refunds on some earlier shipments, which could prove to be quite significant. This article looks into the history of the EU's role in imposing duties on computer peripherals and the changes that have recently been made to those duties allowing exporters to apply for the refunds. (M.K. Neville, Jr. & F. Van Der Wielen, 12 Journal of International Taxation, No. 10, 50.)

"FSC repeal legislation enacted: EU challenge underway" (2001). D. Benson & L. Garrett-Nelson, 12 Journal of International

Taxation, No. 2, 33. (*Digested under* Foreign Corporations, Persons, and Partnerships, page 57.)

"Harmonizing VAT in the EU—the Commission's new strategy" (2001). When Frits Bolkestein became the European Union's (EU's) new Commissioner for Taxation and the Internal Market in September 1999, he acknowledged that value-added tax (VAT) is an area where legislative action is required to realize the objective of a fully functioning internal market.

First, the author discusses the new VAT strategy and each of its four objectives in detail. The new strategy is built around four main objectives: (1) simplification; (2) modernization; (3) more uniform application of existing provisions; and (4) reinforced administrative cooperation.

Simplification and modernization and a more uniform application of the VAT rules formed two of the three pillars of the 1996 Programme for the Single Market (the third pillar being the change to the definitive system). Indeed, the 1996 Programme lists the following main barriers to a true single market: extreme complexity; that several of the provisions of the EU Sixth VAT Directive are out of date and not adapted to current commercial practices; and differences in the application of VAT rules between member states.

Reinforced administrative cooperation is an obvious fourth objective. Under the current system, deliveries are exempt (zero-rated) when sent from one member state to another, thus creating important flows of untaxed goods within the EU. Also, there are an increasing number of transactions in which the customer (recipient of the delivery) is liable to pay the tax. Exchange of information and mutual assistance with assessment, auditing, and collection between member states, are therefore vital requirements to improve the adherence to the current system by businesses.

Then, the author analyzes the Bolkestein strategy. The question is whether the four above objectives can be met without a fundamental change in the VAT system. Bolkestein's decision to (temporarily) drop the ambition to rewrite the VAT rules can be seen as giving up on one of the fundamental objectives of the Treaty of Rome—to "establish, within the framework of an economic union, a common market within which there is healthy competition and whose characteristics are similar to those of a domestic market." (A. Murrath, 12 Journal of International Taxation, No. 2, 20.)

France

"Another mixed-bag French Finance Bill" (2001). The French Finance Bill for 2001 introduces several crucial new measures regarding taxation of French and foreign corporations, as well as individuals. Some significant provisions demonstrate the legislature's intent to simplify and decrease the corporate and individual tax burden (e.g., reduction in the global corporate income tax rate as well as the individual income tax progressive rates). However, other measures stiffen the tax burden on corporations (e.g., changes in the application of the participation exemption regime, reduction of the *avoir fiscal* granted to nonindividual taxpayers). This article addresses only the main features of the Finance Bill adopted by Parliament on December 20, 2000.

First, the authors discuss the corporate income tax rate reductions pursuant to the Finance Bill for 2001. Next, the authors address the reduction of the *avoir fiscal*. Under the Finance Bill for 2001, the *avoir fiscal* is decreased to 25 percent for tax credits used during the 2001 tax year, and to 15 percent for those that will be used during the 2002 tax year. As under the Finance Bills for 1999 and 2000, only corporations not benefiting from the French participation exemption regime are subject to this reduction.

Then, the authors consider the modification of the participation exemption regime. Companies that benefit from the French participation exemption regime are exempted from corporate income tax on 95 percent of the gross amount of the dividend received. Currently, this specific tax regime applies to companies owning stock representing either:

(1) at least 10 percent of the stock-equity of a subsidiary or (2) FRF 150 million in the stock-equity of the subsidiary.

Pursuant to the Finance Bill for 2001, to benefit from the French participation exemption regime, a company must now hold at least 5 percent of the stock-equity of a subsidiary. The FRF 150 million threshold is repealed. This percentage is computed at the time that the dividend is paid.

Finally, the authors discuss extension of the scope of long-term capital gain, reduction of accelerated depreciation coefficients, modification of the *societe de capital risque* tax regime, modification of the wage tax computation basis, lower individual income tax rates, subsidies for investments in overseas French possessions or territories, and inheritance tax due when transferring stock or interest in an operating company owned through a shareholders agreement. (P. Bayle & M. Vaslin, 12 Journal of International Taxation, No. 3, 14.)

"U.S. and France agree on Social Security taxation; refunds may be available" (2001). The IRS announced in Notice 2001-41 that the U.S. and French Competent Authorities have reached an agreement on the tax treatment of contributions to, and distributions from, the French Social Security regime. The agreement clarifies the application of Article 18 (Pensions) of the 1994 U.S.-France income tax treaty. (12 Journal of International Taxation, No. 9, 7.)

Germany

"How does Germany's recent tax reform affect the investment funds market?" (2001). The Upper House of the German Parliament agreed to the "Tax-Drop-Down-Law" on July 14, 2000. The Mutual Funds Act basically did not change but minor modifications to the corporate and income tax laws will significantly affect investments in funds. Although the press reported about unjustified disadvantages for foreign funds, no changes have been made to the Foreign Investment Law so far. This article discusses whether the German Tax Reform Act changes the market radically and is particularly relevant for American investors in German funds and American funds engaged in the German market. (B. Heller & M. Hammer, 12 Journal of International Taxation, No. 7, 58.)

"Still more German tax reforms" (2001). The German Tax Reform Act, which became effective as of January 1, 2001, generally represents the return to a classic corporate tax system and contains a substantial reduction in tax rates, as well as the introduction of a national participation exemption for dividends and capital gains on the sale of shares for corporations. The tax reductions are financed primarily through reduced spending but also through an increase in indirect taxes. However, taxpayers also must face prolongations of the depreciation periods and a tightening of the thin capitalization rules.

The German Parliament has asked the federal government to issue a white paper with regard to further changes in the German tax law, which are designed to make Germany an attractive foreign investment country. The main areas of further change are the tax treatment of (1) reorganizations; (2) affiliated companies; and (3) foreign investments.

A commission of experts has discussed suggestions for further changes in the German tax law and on April 19, 2001, the German Ministry of Finance (MOF) finally issued its report on the discussion results. The report both answers remaining questions with regard to the rules already effective and offers an overview of planned changes. While there is some uncertainty, these changes are considered likely in the near future. The German administration may even decide on the first changes in 2001. (J. Menger & I. Kahl, 12 Journal of International Taxation, No. 10, 26.)

Hong Kong

"Hong Kong issues long-awaited guidance on taxation of stock options" (2001). The Hong Kong Inland Revenue Department (IRD) has finally published the long-awaited

109

Practice Note (Departmental Interpretation and Practice Note No. 38 (DIPN 38)), which at least makes clear to taxpayers, in general terms, the IRD's position on the tax treatment of options. However, it also leaves a few questions unanswered.

First, the authors discuss the key guidelines in DIPN 38, which can be summarized as follows. The IRD reconfirms its previous stance that gains from exercising rights to options having a Hong Kong source will continue to be taxable even after the individual has left Hong Kong. Also, as a practical measure, IRD offers the taxpayer an opportunity to report a notional gain based on the fair market value of the shares as of the day before the date of submission of the final return.

Taxability will depend on whether (1) the right was granted in respect of a Hong Kong or non–Hong Kong employment; (2) the right was granted conditionally or unconditionally; and (3) the services were performed in Hong Kong at the date of grant or during the "vesting period."

Then, the authors address taxability of options, source-based liability, taxable gain computation, tax compliance, tracking systems, and reporting the full amount of gain. (S. McGrath & A. Shih, 12 Journal of International Taxation, No. 10, 54.)

"Taxation of e-commerce in Hong Kong" (2001). The Hong Kong Inland Revenue Department (IRD) has issued new Departmental Interpretation and Practice Note (DIPN) No. 39 on "Profits Tax Treatment of Electronic Commerce." DIPN 39 is for the information and guidance of taxpayers and their authorized representatives and does not have binding force or affect a person's right of objection or appeal to the Commissioner of IRD, the Board of Review, or the courts.

The key points covered by DIPN 39 include: (1) the presence of a server generally would not amount to the carrying on of a business in Hong Kong; (2) "agent" for Hong Kong tax purposes does not include a "server" or an Internet service provider who merely operates a server under a web site hosting arrangement; (3) the IRD would examine all facets of a taxpayer's e-com-

merce operations in Hong Kong to determine whether the taxpayer carried on a business in Hong Kong and whether its e-commerce profits are derived from Hong Kong; and (4) for purposes of withholding tax on royalties, the IRD will distinguish payments for products or services and payments for the use of or right to use copyright materials. The latter will be subject to withholding tax. (S. McGrath, 12 Journal of International Taxation, No. 12, 42.)

India

"India cuts taxes, introduces transfer pricing legislation" (2001). The Indian Finance Minister presented the budget in Parliament on February 28, 2001, introducing transfer pricing legislation, reducing tax rates on individuals and domestic companies, and originating or modifying other provisions that U.S. and other foreign investors should consider. (12 Journal of International Taxation, No. 7, 13.)

Indonesia

"Netherlands-Indonesia tax treaty still applies" (2001). 12 Journal of International Taxation, No. 7, 15. (*Digested under* International Taxation—Netherlands, page 113.)

Italy

"Draft 2001 Italian corporate and tax reform unveiled" (2001). On June 28, 2001, the Italian government issued draft legislation that would considerably affect the tax features of Italian structures and that anticipates abolishment of the local tax in a medium-term plan to have only one major tax at a 33 percent rate. (12 Journal of International Taxation, No. 10, 7.)

"Italian CFC rules and subpart F compared" (2001). The aims of Italian and U.S. controlled foreign corporation (CFC) provisions are similar—to avoid deferral of income tax on earnings of foreign entities controlled by domestic shareholders and discourage use of companies in low-tax jurisdictions—but the regimes differ in several significant aspects.

First, the author compares Italian and U.S. CFC law. While the Italian and the U.S. CFC provisions have similar objectives, they apply different approaches. Both regimes assume that not all of the income of all controlled foreign entities will be subject to anti-deferral rules. While the U.S. approach is to tax all CFCs wherever organized but only on income derived from certain types of transactions, the Italian approach is to tax only some foreign entities—i.e., those located in tax havens—but on all of their income.

The Italian CFC law appears to be considerably simpler than its subpart F counterpart. The difference in relative complexity might be explained by the fundamental differences in the conceptual approaches that the two countries take in regard to the taxation of foreign income. The U.S. tax system attempts to subject income of U.S. individuals and corporations from the investment of capital abroad to the same level of tax as income from capital invested at home. To create that effect (''capital export neutrality''), while at the same time allowing a limited possibility for deferral (but not exemption) on certain targeted categories of active foreign income, the U.S. legislation must apply a highly complex set of rules.

Unlike the U.S. system, the Italian tax system does not seek to equalize taxes on foreign- and domestic-source income. Rather, it allows substantial corporate-level exemptions for foreign dividends, provided they are not derived from a company located in a tax haven. Thus, under the Italian approach, abusive conduct requiring corrective measures is not indicated just because foreign income may be subject to relatively low taxes. The only real abuse, under the Italian system, is the use of tax havens to shield income from any significant tax anywhere. Thus, the corrective measure to combat that abuse can be framed as a relatively simple measure that targets all income flowing through designated tax havens.

Then, the author addresses European Union (EU) application questions. One of the principal issues is the extent to which Italy's CFC rules will apply to low-tax jurisdictions that are EU members. (A. Silvestri, 12 Journal of International Taxation, No. 12, 20.)

''2001 Italian budget lowers corporate tax, enhances tools to reduce tax burden'' (2001). The 2001 Italian budget law reduces the Italian corporate income tax from 37 percent to 36 percent starting from year 2001, and to 35 percent from year 2003 for calendar-year companies. (12 Journal of International Taxation, No. 7, 15.)

Mexico

''Mexican tax reform—compliance, anti-avoidance, and economics'' (2001). Mexican tax reform measures for 2001 focus on three core areas: (1) promoting voluntary compliance with tax obligations; (2) ensuring that the tax law is aligned with the economic climate; and (3) combating tax avoidance and evasion. The law passed and was published in the Official Gazette on December 31, 2000.

First, the authors discuss income tax changes. The reduced withholding tax rate (4.9 percent) on interest paid by Mexican residents to nonresident financial institutions expired on December 31, 2000. The 2001 reforms provide for a general withholding tax of 10 percent.

The 4.9 percent rate continues to apply, however, to interest paid on debt bonds by Mexican residents to nonresidents that are located in a country that has concluded or is negotiating a tax treaty with Mexico (the latter countries include Ecuador, Greece, Indonesia, Luxembourg, Poland, Portugal, Romania, and Venezuela). The 4.9 percent also applies to gains from the sale of publicly issued debt bonds, although when the effective beneficiary of more than 5 percent of the interest from the placing of these bonds is a related party of the issuer, the withholding tax for residents in a nontreaty country is increased to 40 percent.

111

Then, the authors address changes in regard to value-added tax (VAT) and the Federal Fiscal Code. (R. Suarez & L. Coronado, 12 Journal of International Taxation, No. 4, 36.)

"Partial Mexican withholding refund possible on dividends to U.S. companies" (2001). In certain circumstances, Mexican companies that distribute dividends to companies resident in the United States may be in a position to receive a partial refund of taxes withheld on those dividends. In terms of the provisions of Mexico's Income Tax Law (the Law), beginning January 1, 1999, corporate entities that distribute dividends to residents abroad are required to withhold the income tax payable, and calculate it in conformity with the procedure for such purposes in the Law. Companies that distribute dividends to residents abroad and that calculate the tax in conformity with the Law actually withhold 7.6925 percent of the total amount distributed. (12 Journal of International Taxation, No. 10, 8.)

Netherlands

"A guide to European holding companies—Part 2: Belgium, the Netherlands, and Spain" (2001). S.C. Ruchelman, E. Van Asbeck, G. Canalejo, W. Heyvaert, M.T. McGowan & S. Neidhardt, 12 Journal of International Taxation, No. 1, 22. (*Digested under* International Taxation—Belgium, page 100.)

"Despite capital tax rate reductions, Netherlands focuses on exemptions" (2001). When structuring an investment in the Netherlands, the Dutch capital tax should be taken into account. As one of the last European Union (EU) countries, the Netherlands still levies capital tax on each contribution of capital divided into shares of Dutch-resident entities. The determination of an entity's residency for capital tax purposes is in principle based on the "all facts and circumstances" test as described in the General Tax Act. According to Dutch case law, an entity's place of effective management and control

seems to be the most relevant factor for this test. However, an entity effectively managed and controlled outside the EU, but having its statutory seat in the Netherlands (e.g., a Dutch BV or NV), is deemed to be a resident of the Netherlands for capital tax purposes. In addition, capital tax is levied on entities that transfer their place of effective management and control to the Netherlands, unless such entity was previously a resident of another EU member state.

The authors discuss the available capital tax exemptions. The Legal Transactions Tax Act provides for, among others, the following capital tax exemptions: share-for-share merger exemption, business merger exemption, internal reorganization exemption, and demerger exemption.

The Dutch Under-Minister of Finance has published his policy regarding certain aspects of capital tax exemptions. The policy is discussed in this article. (M. Molenaars & E. Bongers, 12 Journal of International Taxation, No. 9, 42.)

"Netherlands announces policy objectives for conduit companies" (2001). The Under-Minister of Finance informed the Dutch Lower House on March 20, 2001, of his policy objectives with respect to the tax aspects of the business establishment climate. The objectives concern entities with no or barely any real presence in the Netherlands that are used mainly as "conduit" companies for interest or royalty payments within the group. Two measures announced by the Under-Minister are notable.

The first measure provides that no advance ruling will be granted for a proposed "conduit" transaction unless a minimum relationship with the Netherlands exists. The second measure provides that when an entity runs no (or hardly any) risk with respect to the receipt and payment of interest or royalties within the group, the granting of an advance ruling will be subject to an additional condition. The ruling will be granted only if the requester agrees to the spontaneous exchange of information with the source country (i.e., without a previous request by a foreign authority). (M. Molenaars & E. Bongers, 12 Journal of International Taxation, No. 7, 61.)

"Netherlands-Indonesia tax treaty still applies" (2001). The Dutch Ministry of Finance published a Decree on January 8, 2001, in which it confirmed that the Netherlands and Indonesia will apply the tax treaty that was terminated by Indonesia in 2000, as if it were still effective during calendar year 2001. (12 Journal of International Taxation, No. 7, 15.)

"Proposed amendments to Dutch fiscal unity regime revisited" (2001). The long expected amendments to the proposal of law to amend the fiscal unity rules in the Netherlands were published on June 1, 2001. (12 Journal of International Taxation, No. 11, 13.)

"Proposed changes to Dutch fiscal unity regime affect existing BV1/BV2 structures" (2001). On June 1, 2001, the State Secretary sent to Parliament a ministerial memorandum of amendments (MMoA) to a bill to amend the Dutch fiscal unity (group taxation) regime. In general, the MMoA benefits taxpayers by introducing various simplifications and improvements to the original bill. However, the amended bill contains a provision intended to curb the use of BV1/BV2 structures. A BV is a private limited liability company. (12 Journal of International Taxation, No. 10, 9.)

"Report recommends changes to Netherlands' corporate tax regime" (2001). The Dutch International Corporate Income Tax Study Group released its long-expected report on June 11, 2001, on the desirability and feasibility of changing the Dutch corporate income tax burden. An important factor in this report is the competitive position of the Netherlands, with its attractive business establishment climate within and outside the European Union (EU).

The report recommends changing the corporate income tax rate, abolishing the capital tax, and amending the participation exemption regime. It also addresses dividend stripping, hybrid loans, anti-abuse provisions in the Corporate Income Tax Act, and depreciation of Dutch real estate and purchased goodwill. (M. Molenaars & E. Bongers, 12 Journal of International Taxation, No. 10, 58.)

"The Netherlands: 2000 tax wrap-up" (2001). The highlight of 2000 in Dutch tax was the enactment of the Dutch Personal Income Tax Act 2001. The first proposals for the Act, which were presented in 1999, made it clear that the rules would be based on completely new principles (from "source system" to "schedular system"). During 1999 and 2000, more and more rules were proposed, and in 2000, the changes and discussions proceeded at such a fast pace that it was almost impossible to keep up with the status of the proposed rules. As a result of the introduction of the Personal Income Tax Act 2001, changes were also introduced to the Corporate Income Tax Act 1969 and several other tax acts.

First, the authors discuss corporate income tax. In connection with the Corporate Income Tax Act 1969, important changes were made in regard to excess dividend distributions, rules against trade in loss companies, written-down receivables, and the Secretary of Finance's intention to appoint a corporate income tax study group

Then, the authors address employee stock options. On June 26, 1998, new rules entered into force with regard to the taxation of employee stock options. Under these rules, the taxable benefit of an employee stock option consists of two elements: the intrinsic value and the expectation value. Under the former rules, the option would become taxable at the moment that it became unconditional (i.e., as soon as all restrictions connected to exercising the option were fulfilled). Under the new rules, effective December 28, 2000, employees have the opportunity to determine the taxable moment as either when the stock option becomes unconditional or when it is exercised. This possibility, however, refers only to the taxation of the expectation value. The taxation of the intrinsic value can be postponed only from the moment of receiving a conditional option until the moment that the option becomes unconditional.

Finally, the authors consider capital tax, revenue rulings and decrees, double taxation, the European Union Code of Conduct, new tax treaties, the fiscal unity regime, interest payments on hybrid loans, the participation exemption, the Personal Income Tax Act 2001, and the taxation of cross-border employment. (H.B. Doornbosch & S. Berings, 12 Journal of International Taxation, No. 8, 30.)

Portugal

"Portugal introduces comprehensive transfer pricing rules" (2001). Within the scope of tax reform on direct taxation, Portugal has enacted for the first time a set of extensive rules dealing with transfer pricing. (12 Journal of International Taxation, No. 7, 15.)

Puerto Rico

"Prospects improve for use of R&D credit in Puerto Rico" (2001). In September 2000, the IRS issued a new version of Form 5735 (Possessions Corporation Tax Credit (Under Sections 936 and 30A)), which a possessions corporation must attach to its return in order to compute its allowable credit. Under the interpretation of the amended double-counting prohibition in Section 280C(c)(1) that is expressed in the instructions to Form 5735, a possessions corporation that has elected the percentage limitation method will not lose any part of this credit if it undertakes qualified research activities in Puerto Rico. (R.S. Griggs, 12 Journal of International Taxation, No. 7, 57.)

"Puerto Rico seeks new tax incentives to compensate for loss of Section 936" (2001). Bills have been introduced in both houses of Congress at the behest of the Puerto Rico government to amend the Internal Revenue Code so as to provide new tax benefits to compensate for the 1996 phase-out of Section 936.

First, the author discusses the proposed amendments to Sections 951, 956, and 245. The proposed amendments have three elements: (1) they would not change the provisions of existing law under which the remaining "grandfathered" benefits of Sections 936 and 30A will expire at the end of the tax year beginning in 2005; (2) they would amend Sections 951, 956, and 245 to allow a controlled foreign corporation (CFC) to make a 90 percent tax-free investment in "U.S. property," or to distribute an 85 percent tax-free dividend to its U.S. parent or other U.S. corporate shareholders, out of its earnings from a manufacturing business in Puerto Rico; and (3) they would provide existing Section 936 corporations with a limited safe-harbor rule for the transfer of manufacturing intangibles to CFCs.

Then, the author addresses the coordination of the proposed amendments. (R.S. Griggs, 12 Journal of International Taxation, No. 11, 41.)

Russia

"Russia's tax system overhaul includes clearer VAT rules" (2001). As part of an ongoing overhaul of the Russian tax system, the second part of the new Tax Code will become effective from January 1, 2001. This introduces fundamental changes for several taxes, including value-added tax (VAT). The changes are generally welcome, in that the notoriously unclear and business-unfriendly Russian VAT system will become a lot more transparent. However, there are still a number of question marks over the drafting of certain parts of the new law. (12 Journal of International Taxation, No. 1, 8.)

Singapore

"Exchange of information in Singapore's tax treaties" (2001). Globalization has made it more important than ever for national tax administrations to be able to access offshore taxpayer information, including offshore bank records. The Organization for Economic Cooperation and Development (OECD) observed that unduly restrictive banking secrecy laws not only cause a loss of revenue to governments but also impede international tax cooperation. More recently, the OECD recommended that the application of bank secrecy rules to tax matters be limited and that bilateral and multilateral intergovernmental cooperation for tax enforcement and collection be enhanced.

Singapore's tax treaties are generally based on the OECD model tax treaty. The strict banking laws in Singapore, the current practice of Singapore's tax authorities on the exchange of information, and a host of financial tax incentives are clearly consistent with Singapore's goal of becoming a world-class financial center. On the other hand, the successful conclusion of a full U.S.-Singapore treaty will enhance the substantial trade and investment presence that the United States has in Singapore. It will also benefit Singapore residents venturing into, or already in, the huge U.S. market. (T.H. Teck, 12 Journal of International Taxation, No. 7, 50.)

Spain

"A guide to European holding companies— Part 2: Belgium, the Netherlands, and Spain" (2001). S.C. Ruchelman, E. Van Asbeck, G. Canalejo, W. Heyvaert, M.T. McGowan & S. Neidhardt, 12 Journal of International Taxation, No. 1, 22. (*Digested under* International Taxation—Belgium, page 100.)

Sweden

"Swedish governmental committee proposes major tax changes" (2001). A governmental committee presented a tax proposal for major changes in Swedish corporate taxation on February 15, 2001, implying an abolition of capital gains taxation on shares held for business purposes, and new controlled foreign corporation legislation. (12 Journal of International Taxation, No. 7, 16.)

United Kingdom

"A guide to European holding companies— Part 3: United Kingdom" (2001). This third and last part of a series on European holding companies focuses on several special features of the U.K. rules on foreign tax credits for dividend withholding tax and defenses to controlled foreign corporation (CFC) assessment.

First, the authors discuss the U.K. corporate tax rate, and taxation of domestic, foreign-source dividends from a U.K.-resident holding company. Companies resident in the U.K. pay corporation tax at 30 percent on their worldwide income and gains. A U.K.-resident company that is not a financial dealer is not subject to corporation tax on dividends and other income "distributions" received from another U.K.-resident company. Foreign-source dividends are subject to corporation tax, but this is usually reduced by U.K. double-taxation relief in the form of foreign tax credits. The U.K. will generally grant a foreign tax credit for foreign dividend withholding tax that is otherwise irrecoverable. Until March 31, 2001, "excess" foreign tax credits were automatically lost and could not be carried forward or backward.

Next, the authors address Finance Act 2000 (FA 2000) and changes to U.K. foreign tax credit rules. Several significant changes to the U.K. foreign tax credit rules were enacted in FA 2000. These proposals have a major and somewhat adverse impact on the U.K. as a location for an international holding company, especially when that U.K.-resident holding company itself indirectly owns various non-U.K.-resident operating companies via a Dutch "mixer" company. The most significant changes proposed in FA 2000 did not take effect until March 31, 2001.

The principal proposed changes enacted in Finance Act 2000 are: (1) to remove the potential for "mixing" outside the U.K. high-taxed and low-taxed non-U.K. income, prior to repatriation to the U.K. and (2) an alternative regime for "onshore mixing," together with carryback (up to three years)

115

and unlimited carryforward of certain unused U.K. foreign tax credits.

Then, the authors consider treatment of dividends paid from the U.K. to the United States. The Finance Act 1998 abolished the advance corporation tax (ACT), effective April 6, 1999. The prepayment function that ACT served was replaced for large companies by the new requirement to account for corporation tax quarterly.

Finally, the authors discuss the U.K. tax treaty network, capital gains/losses on disposal of operating company shares, cross-border interest payments, anti-deferral regimes related to controlled foreign corporations, capital tax on formation and transfer of securities, substance requirements, other issues involved in setting up a U.K. holding company, and combining benefits of Dutch and U.K. holding companies. (S.C. Ruchelman, E. Van Asbeck, W. Heyvaert, M.T. McGowan & S. Neidhardt, 12 Journal of International Taxation, No. 3, 20.)

"Preelection U.K. budget—major business tax reforms deferred" (2001). The Finance Bill resulting from the 2001 U.K. budget was the shortest for some time and relatively uncontroversial, with many of the new measures having been announced in advance.

First, the authors discuss company taxation. The major company taxation provisions include further changes to the double taxation relief (DTR) regime that caused so much controversy in 2000.

Then, the authors consider environmental measures. These include enhanced capital allowances and new aggregates and climate-change levies.

Finally, the authors address other measures, including the availability of a new type of business entity, the limited liability partnership (LLP). An LLP is a separate corporate entity and the liability of members is limited. However, for U.K. income tax, corporation tax, and capital gains tax purposes, it is treated as a transparent entity, with members taxed as if they were partners carrying on a business in partnership. (K. Howlett & C. Sylvester, 12 Journal of International Taxation, No. 8, 24.)

"2001 U.K. budget announced" (2001). The U.K. budget, announced on March 7, 2001, focused on personal tax concessions for families and the lower-paid in order to pave the way for a general election later in the year. (12 Journal of International Taxation, No. 7, 17.)

"U.K. act—*Hoechst* and *Metallgesellschaft*: The Inland Revenue's position" (2001). The European Court of Justice ruled in 2001 that it was discriminatory for the U.K. to deny a German parent company with a U.K. subsidiary the right to make a group income election. The Inland Revenue is now making known its position on the impact of the case. Not surprisingly, it is stating that the decision applies only to U.K. companies paying dividends to an immediate parent company resident in a European Economic Area country, and only when the treaty between that country and the U.K. did not provide a tax credit refund. (12 Journal of International Taxation, No. 11, 14.)

Vietnam

"New U.S.-Vietnam agreement removes major trade obstacles" (2001). Minister Vu Khoan and Trade Representative Charlene Barshefsky signed a bilateral trade agreement (the BTA) between Vietnam and the United States on July 13, 2000.

First, the author discusses the scope of the BTA. The BTA addresses four primary areas: (1) trade in goods; (2) protection of intellectual property rights; (3) trade in services; and (4) investment.

Then, the author outlines changes that the BTA is expected to bring about regarding trade in goods between the United States and Vietnam. Trade in services, intellectual property rights, and investment are outside the scope of the article.

The BTA, the first of its kind for Vietnam, creates a framework for the United States and Vietnam to remove all remaining major obstacles to normalization of their economic relations, which both American and Vietnamese businesses have long been awaiting. The BTA requires Vietnam to make many structural reforms, which cannot be effected overnight, and there will surely be a transition period as each country feels its way before circumstances become desirable and effective. However, significant and positive changes are ahead and, once ratified, the BTA can be expected to create a strong foundation for a new and mutually beneficial direction for both countries. (V.H. Duyen, 12 Journal of International Taxation, No. 3, 34.)

Virgin Islands

"Tax incentives in the U.S. Virgin Islands improve under amended industrial development program" (2001). Although synonymous with sandy beaches, fine resorts, great shopping, and golf, to the business community the U.S. Virgin Islands (USVI) have earned a reputation for attractive incentives that can result in higher business profits. For nearly thirty years, the USVI have had a generous economic incentives law in place to develop and expand business in the territory. Act 6390, which became law on February 1, 2001, made substantial changes to the prevailing incentives program.

While the USVI income tax is tied closely to the Internal Revenue Code, the USVI imposes and administers its own local tax regime that includes gross receipts taxes, excise taxes, real property taxes, and customs duties. Under the incentives program, a maximum 90 percent reduction of the corporate income tax results in an effective tax rate of 3 percent to 4 percent. There is an additional 90 percent exemption from individual income tax liability for USVI residents on dividends or partnership distributions they receive from beneficiary businesses. The incentives law provides beneficiary businesses a 100 percent exemption from the USVI gross receipts tax, similar exemptions from real property and excise taxes, and a reduction in the normal customs duty imposed on imported goods.

Act 6390 seeks to improve on the original incentives law, first by preserving the existing tax relief. In addition, the new Act expands and clarifies the definition of "qualifying business" (where the original law was vague), with added attention now given to high-tech industries, and it extends the renewal benefit periods. The law also doubles the minimum investment requirement and lays the groundwork for establishment of various penalties against noncompliant firms.

In a significant change from the prior law, Act 6390 has created four categories of potential beneficiary businesses, and imposes application and compliance fees based on the particular category under which an enterprise is classified. Under the new scheme, the list of qualifying industries is far more specific than under the previous statute, with added attention now given to high-tech industries, such as telecommunications and health care, and various services businesses not limited to but including investment managers and advisers, research and development, business and management consultants, software developers, e-commerce businesses, international public relations firms, international trading and distribution, and any other businesses serving clients located outside the Virgin Islands.

The amended law now also specifically includes entities that are limited liability companies or trusts, and also permits foreign (non-U.S.) corporations to apply for and receive benefits as well. This component of the amendment seems to signal the territory's desire to develop into a bona fide international business center. Another significant change concerns the stricter procurement rules under the new statute requiring beneficiaries to purchase goods and services from Virgin Islands resident individuals or firms that have been officially licensed to do business in the territory for at least one year prior to the vendor's transaction.

While tax incentives influence many business decisions, such benefits are rarely the *only* reason companies expand or move their operations to a given location. The USVI offers a business-friendly environment, with the security and stability of the U.S. government, little concern about currency issues, and access to U.S. courts. Investors also may seek various business advantages the mainland does not offer, such as relaxed immigration rules and shipping regulations, a skilled workforce, well-developed telecommunications systems, and prime rental space at bargain rates.

Given the more comprehensive provisions of Act 6390, the USVI sends a strong message to the international business community regarding its desire to attract large-scale business for the mutual benefit of its investors and its people. (M.A. Opper & B.W. McIntosh, 11 Journal of Multistate Taxation and Incentives, No. 8, 6.)

INVOLUNTARY CONVERSIONS

(*See* Losses)

J

JEOPARDY ASSESSMENTS

(*See* Assessment and Collection)

JOINT RETURNS

(*See* Husband and Wife)

JUDICIAL PROCEEDINGS

(*See* Procedure)

L

LAND

(*See* Real Estate)

LIFE INSURANCE

(*See* Fringe Benefits; Insurance and Insurance Companies)

LIKE-KIND EXCHANGES

"Changing position, IRS allows reverse like-kind exchange safe harbor" (2001). Reverse like-kind exchanges can qualify for safe-harbor gain nonrecognition under Section 1031, according to Revenue Procedure 2000-37. (12 Journal of International Taxation, No. 1, 6.)

"Estate planning benefits of deferred like-kind exchanges of real estate" (2001). The IRS has issued Revenue Procedure 2000-37, which provides a new safe harbor that may be used to qualify a reverse like-kind exchange of real estate as a tax-deferred exchange under Section 1031.

After providing background on the benefits of like-kind exchanges, the authors discuss structuring deferred like-kind exchanges, including deferred exchange safe harbors. In 1991, the IRS issued final regulations on deferred exchanges, which contained four deferred exchange safe harbors. The purpose of the safe harbors is to avoid a situation where the taxpayer would be deemed to be in constructive receipt of the sale proceeds before the replacement property is received. If the taxpayer is in constructive receipt, the exchange does not qualify for deferral of gain under Section 1031.

For example, one popular safe harbor is the use of a qualified intermediary. Under Regulation § 1.1031(k)-1(g)(4), the qualified intermediary is not deemed to be the transferor's agent. Accordingly, the qualified intermediary may receive the sale proceeds and continue to hold those proceeds and use them to acquire the replacement property without fear that the transaction will not qualify as a like-kind exchange.

Then, the authors address the reverse-Starker exchange. Unfortunately, the 1991 regulations do not apply to exchanges in which the replacement property is acquired before the relinquished property is transferred. This reverse like-kind exchange is also known as a reverse-Starker exchange after the case that resulted in the adoption of the original Section 1031 regulations. The new reverse-Starker safe harbor described in Revenue Procedure 2000-37 is designed to cover such situations.

Finally, the authors consider qualified exchange accommodation arrangement requirements, as set forth in Revenue Procedure 2000-37, and permissible agreements. (M. Kove & J.M. Kosakow, 28 Estate Planning 372.)

"Exchange accommodation titleholder and deferred Section 1031 exchanges" (2001). A common problem with deferred exchanges under Section 1031 is finding a replacement property. Deferred exchanges are much easier if the taxpayer can manufacture his own replacement property. Typically, this involves finding an accommodation party to acquire replacement property land, build improvements, and to exchange the replacement property with the taxpayer.

An important problem with such a transaction is the risk that the accommodation party will be treated as the agent of the taxpayer. There often is little economic reality to the accommodation party's ownership of the replacement property. The IRS has promulgated Revenue Procedure 2000-37 (the revenue procedure), which lays down some rules in this area.

The accommodation party, in the words of the revenue procedure, is an "exchange accommodation titleholder." An exchange accommodation titleholder, which can be a partnership, a limited liability company (LLC), or a corporation, is a rather extraordinary entity under the tax law. Its ownership of assets would normally be disregarded under general tax principles. Nevertheless, the revenue procedure respects the exchange accommodation titleholder's ownership of replacement property if certain requirements are satisfied. An exchange accommodation titleholder may be considered an extraordinary entity, since the tax law treats it as the tax owner of property where there may be practically no substance to such ownership.

After addressing the problem of finding a replacement property, the author discusses the safe harbor. The IRS will not challenge: (1) the qualification of property as either "replacement property" or "relinquished property" for purposes of Section 1031 and the regulations thereunder or (2) the treatment of the exchange accommodation titleholder as the beneficial owner of the property for federal income tax purposes if the property is held in a qualified exchange administration agreement (QEAA). The arrangement must be documented in accordance with the requirements of the revenue procedure in order to qualify for the safe harbor.

Next, the author considers new terms. The revenue procedure introduces three new terms into the exchange lexicon: (1) "exchange accommodation titleholder"; (2) "qualified indicia of ownership"; and (3) "qualified exchange accommodation arrangements."

Then, the author considers the intention to exchange. The taxpayer must have a bona fide intent that the property held by the exchange accommodation titleholder represents either the replacement property or the relinquished property in an exchange that is intended to qualify for nonrecognition of gain or loss under Section 1031.

Finally, the author turns to drafting a QEAA, treatment of property for other purposes, recasting payments, burdens and benefits of ownership, and what happens if there is no exchange. (T.F. Cuff, 3 Business Entities, No. 1, 40.)

"New safe harbor promotes reverse exchanges" (2001). Revenue Procedure 2000-37 offers guidance for taxpayers to engage in like-kind exchanges in which they receive replacement property before transferring the property being relinquished.

First, the author discusses the provisions of Revenue Procedure 2000-37. The procedure consists of three parts: (1) safe harbor; (2) nine requirements; and (3) several allowed agreements.

The Revenue Procedure 2000-37 safe harbor is found in section 4.01 of the procedure. If either the replacement property or the relinquished property is held in a qualified exchange accommodation arrangement (QEAA), the IRS will treat the exchange accommodation titleholder (EAT) as the beneficial owner of the property so held. The effect of this rule is that the IRS will ignore factors often used by courts in determining who owns property and treat the EAT as the owner of the property. To obtain this treatment, however, the property must be held in a QEAA. Property is treated as being held in a QEAA if all of the requirements listed in the procedure are met.

Depending on how one counts, section 4.02 of the procedure lists nine requirements that must be satisfied for the property to be treated as held in a QEAA.

The true benefit of Revenue Procedure 2000-37 is found in its section 4.03, which states that the IRS will allow taxpayers to enter into several agreements with an EAT without affecting the safe harbor.

Tax practitioners can be very creative in structuring exchanges that fall squarely within the various like-kind exchange safe harbors that are now available. With all of these opportunities, taxpayers should be made aware any time they consider disposing of property or acquiring new property that they may be able to obtain like-kind exchange treatment if they plan to acquire or dispose of other property within six months from the time the planned transaction occurs. (B.T. Borden, 66 Practical Tax Strategies 68.)

LIMITATIONS, STATUTE OF

(*See* Assessment and Collection—Statute of Limitations)

LIMITED LIABILITY COMPANIES

"Assessment in single-member LLC's name is valid against owner" (2001). The IRS concluded, in FSA 200114006, that an employment tax assessment erroneously made in the name and employer identification number of a single-member limited liability company (LLC) was valid against the company's sole owner. (67 Practical Tax Strategies 182.)

"Assessments made against disregarded entity are valid against the entity's sole owner" (2001). Two substantially similar field service advice memoranda (FSAs 200114006 and 200105045) both concluded that employment tax assessments made in the name and employer identification number of a single member LLC are valid assessments against the company's sole owner. (3 Business Entities, No. 4, 57.)

"Drafting partnership and LLC agreements: Part 1" (2001). T.F. Cuff, 3 Business Entities, No. 3, 22. (*Digested under* Partners and Partnerships—In General, page 136.)

"Drafting partnership and LLC agreements: Part 2" (2001). T.F. Cuff, 3 Business Entities, No. 4, 26. (*Digested under* Partners and Partnerships—In General, page 136.)

"Drafting partnership and LLC agreements: Part 3" (2001). T.F. Cuff, 3 Business Entities, No. 5, 38. (*Digested under* Partners and Partnerships—In General, page 137.)

"Drafting partnership and LLC agreements: Part 4" (2001). T.F. Cuff, 3 Business Entities, No. 6, 12. (*Digested under* Partners and Partnerships—In General, page 138.)

"IRS offers arguments for attacking family LLC" (2001). FSA 200049003 explores various grounds for attacking the validity of a family limited liability company (FLLC) as a means for reducing the transfer tax value of assets. (66 Practical Tax Strategies 113.)

"LLC employees may participate in consolidated group's ESOP" (2001). 95 Journal of Taxation 54. (*Digested under* Pension and Profit-Sharing Plans—Employee Stock Ownership Plans (ESOPs), page 159.)

"Member of LLC treated as general partner for purposes of passive activity rules" (2001). In *Gregg* (2000), an Oregon federal district court held that a member of a limited liabiltiy company (LLC) should be treated as a general partner for purposes of the passive activity rules. (3 Business Entities, No. 2, 53.)

"Separate exemption applications not needed for single-member LLCs owned by exempt support organization" (2001). In Letter Ruling 200134025, the IRS has ruled that an exempt organization may form single-member limited liability companies (LLCs) to hold property without having to have each of the single-member LLCs file Form 1023 ("Application for Recognition of Exemption Under Section 501(c)(3) of the Internal Revenue Code"). (95 Journal of Taxation 248.)

"State tax treatment of LLCs and RLLPs: update for 2001" (2001). B.P. Ely & P.C. Bond, 11 Journal of Multistate Taxation and Incentives, No. 2, 26; B.P. Ely & C.R. Grissom, 3 Business Entities, No. 4, 14. (*Digested under* State Taxes—In General, page 205.)

"Tax considerations in choice of entity decision" (2001). M.A. McNulty, 3 Business Entities, No. 5, 16. (*Digested under* S Corporations, page 192.)

"The evolving use of limited liability companies by tax-exempt organizations" (2001). The limited liability company (LLC) form, and the ability to freely elect it, can solve organizational problems for exempt organizations, but raise attribution problems if an entity is "disregarded."

After providing background on LLCs, the author discusses the impact of entity classification on tax-exempt organizations. Unless an election is made to the contrary, a single-member entity owned by a tax-exempt organization is treated as a branch or division of the exempt organization. All items of income, loss, deduction, and credit are reported on the parent organization's tax return as though the activities were conducted by the parent directly. An election can be made to classify the wholly owned entity as an association if the above result could jeopardize the tax-exempt status of the parent organization.

Then, the author considers disregarded entities of exempt organizations. Focusing on a single-member LLC of a Section 501(c)(3) organization, there appears to be no per se requirement that a disregarded entity's organizing documents must meet the organization test. The IRS takes the position, however, that nothing in the disregarded entity's organizing documents should prohibit the entity from operating exclusively for exempt purposes. Further, if the organizing documents do not satisfy the organizational test, the past and planned activities of the LLC will be closely scrutinized by the examining agent or determination specialist to ensure that the entire entity (including the disregarded entity) complies with the operational test.

Finally, the author addresses unrelated business income issues, S corporation planning using LLCs, use of LLCs for real estate holdings, state and local tax, qualification for exempt status, and using LLCs as joint venture entities. (R.W. Friz, 13 Taxation of Exempts 112.)

"The tax consequences of accepting charitable contributions through a single-member LLC" (2001). The IRS has yet to take a public position on the question of whether the donor will receive a charitable contribution deduction if the donor makes a gift to a limited liability company (LLC) whose sole member is a charitable organization described in Section 170(c)(1) and recognized as exempt from tax under Section 501(c)(3). However, the IRS has announced that it intends to publish guidance answering this question by June 30, 2002, which will be the end of the period covered by the most recent Treasury/IRS business plan. Based on the regulations and other statements the IRS has made about the tax treatment of single-member LLCs—in particular, LLCs of which a charity is the single member—there is a sound basis for concluding that the donor should receive the same deduction when contributing real estate, or any other property, to a charity's single-member LLC as to the charity itself.

After providing background on LLCs, the author discusses the deductibility of a gift to an LLC. To be deductible as a charitable contribution under Section 170, a contribution or gift must be "to or for the use of" one of a short list of eligible donees. A gift to a single-member LLC of which a Section 501(c)(3) charity is the sole member should be considered a gift "to" the charity for purposes of Section 170. (C.E. Livingston, 13 Taxation of Exempts 107.)

LIMITED PARTNERSHIPS

(*See* Partners and Partnerships)

LIQUIDATIONS

"Checking-the-box constitutes plan of liquidation" (2001). The IRS issued proposed regulations clarifying that a "check-the-box" election by a subsidiary corporation to convert to a partnership or disregarded entity is treated as an adoption of a plan of liquidation for purposes of Section 332. (3 Business Entities, No. 2, 56.)

"Letter ruling applies basis adjustment rules to S corporation shareholders receiving liquidating distributions over more than one tax year" (2001). 3 Business Entities, No. 3, 59. (*Digested under* S Corporations, page 187.)

"Section 332 liquidations with foreign corporations: Always consider Section 367" (2001). J.M. Calianno, 12 Journal of International Taxation, No. 6, 36. (*Digested under* Foreign Corporations, Persons, and Partnerships, page 62.)

"When service corporations liquidate as part of a change in form of entity—the problem of goodwill" (2001). The IRS has often had issues with professionals doing business in corporate form. A particular problem for taxpayers seeking to abandon that form in favor of modern pass-through entities offering limited liability is whether there will be goodwill, requiring gain recognition on the liquidation of the preexisting corporation. Case law demonstrates that careful attention to details can ensure a favorable outcome.

First, the author provides background on the concept of goodwill and the applicable law. Section 197(c)(1) allows goodwill that has been acquired by the taxpayer in order to be used in a trade or business or activity engaged in for profit to be amortized over fifteen years. Amortizable goodwill is Section 1231 property. Section 197(c)(2) treats self-created goodwill—which is not amortizable—as meeting the criteria for a capital asset under Section 1221 providing it is not created in connection with a transaction or series of transactions involving the acquisition of assets constituting a trade or business.

Then, the author considers case law. Taxpayers who want to liquidate their corporations and avoid gain recognition on goodwill have the best opportunity for success if they can show that the services they perform for the corporation are personal in nature and are the reason for the corporation's success. If, however, the corporation has a covenant not to compete with the individual that will limit the individual's ability to take corporate clients with him, then the value may well be with the corporation and not the individual. In closely held corporations that depend on the services of their owners, there is unlikely to be a covenant. But if those corporations have covenants with key employees that forbid them from competing, then it is the corporation that is likely to be held to have the value and not the individual.

One of the key factors to be considered is whether the corporate business is being continued by its corporate owners or is being sold to another party. The court decisions indicate that where the business is being sold for an amount in excess of the value of its tangible assets, goodwill will be present. Thus, a corporation that is liquidated and its business sold for an amount in excess of the value of its tangible assets will most likely be found to have goodwill at liquidation. In cases where the former corporate business was operated as a partnership or sole proprietorship following liquidation by its former owners, there is a greater likelihood that no goodwill will be found because the argument can be made that the real value is with the individual performing the services, not the corporation that was the recipient of those services. (J.C. Zimmerman, 95 Journal of Taxation 110.)

LOSSES

(*See also* Capital Gains and Losses; Net Operating Loss; Passive Loss Rules)

"Closing facility does not trigger loss deduction" (2001). A taxpayer cannot claim a loss deduction in the year it closes down a facility that it does not sell until a later year, according to FSA 200141026. (67 Practical Tax Strategies 362.)

"Gambler loses out on tax treatment for losses" (2001). The Tax Court, in an unpublished summary opinion, *Erbs* (2001), held that a taxpayer was not engaged in the trade or business of gambling and, therefore, his gambling losses were deductible as an itemized deduction rather than as a trade or business expense. (67 Practical Tax Strategies 186.)

LUMP-SUM DISTRIBUTIONS

(*See* Pension and Profit-Sharing Plans—Distributions)

M

MARITAL DEDUCTION

(*See also* Estate Planning; Estates and Estate Tax; Gifts and Gift Tax; Trusts and Trust Taxation; Valuation of Property)

"Marital deduction disallowed for potential increased annuity payments" (2001). In *Estate of Sansone* (2001), a California federal district court held that the part of a marital trust that provided for an increase in annual payments to a surviving spouse if inflation occurred was a defeasible interest and was not deductible under Section 2056(b). (28 Estate Planning 443.)

"Marital deduction reduced by spouse's contribution to trust for children" (2001). In measuring the amount that passes to a surviving spouse for purposes of the estate tax marital deduction, reductions may need to be made for payments the surviving spouse makes in connection with the bequest, as shown in TAM 200131001. (67 Practical Tax Strategies 191.)

"Mortgage reduces marital deduction for joint property" (2001). The IRS explains, in TAM 200104008, how estate tax returns should report mortgaged property owned by the decedent and spouse as tenants by the entirety. (66 Practical Tax Strategies 233.)

"No marital deduction for assets passing under settlement agreement" (2001). Assets that passed to a surviving spouse pursuant to two settlement agreements were not eligible for the marital deduction, a New Jersey federal district court ruled in *Estate of Mergott* (2000). (28 Estate Planning 121.)

"No marital deduction for property acquired in settlement of annuity" (2001). In *Davies* (2000), a Maine federal district court held that payments received by a surviving spouse in recognition of her annuity rights in trust and in settlement of her elective share claims did not qualify for the marital deduc-

tion under Section 2056. According to the court, property acquired via settlement and property surrendered were indistinguishable, and did not qualify for the marital deduction. (28 Estate Planning 228.)

MARITAL TRANSFERS

(*See* Husband and Wife; Marital Deduction)

MARRIED TAXPAYERS

(*See* Husband and Wife; Marital Deduction)

MEDICAL EXPENSES

(*See also* Fringe Benefits)

"Medical deduction allowed for payments made in prior years" (2001). According to a Minnesota federal district court in *Zipkin* (2000), the taxpayer was able to deduct construction payments made in prior years for a specially designed home as medical expenses. (66 Practical Tax Strategies 118.)

MORTGAGES

(*See* Interest Paid; Personal Residence; Real Estate)

MUTUAL FUNDS AND SIMILAR INVESTMENTS

"Fresh alternative to mutual funds offers tax benefit" (2001). Exchange-traded funds

(ETFs) combine the investment diversification and professional management of mutual funds with the greater ability to defer tax offered by direct stock ownership.

After providing background on ETFs, the authors discuss the tax treatment of ETFs, including long-term capital gain, in-kind redemption, and actual tax savings. Both ETFs and mutual funds issue securities that represent a set of portfolios. Both offer diversification in portfolio composition and convenience of transaction. Mutual funds, however, do not have creation/redemption for physical shares, and units cannot be traded in the secondary market, whereas ETFs can. This leads to significant differences between them. Mutual fund shareholders dispose of their investment only by means of redemption for cash. This may force the mutual fund managers to sell the underlying securities. That sale of securities leads to the realization of capital gains, which may have tax consequences for all shareholders in that mutual fund. This is a serious disadvantage of mutual funds.

On the other hand, ETF shareholders can dispose of their investment by redeeming the ETF creation units for physical stocks or by selling their shares for cash in the secondary market. Neither action would force the ETF manager to sell the securities, so no capital gains are realized by the fund or the other ETF shareholders. Therefore, ETFs are more tax-efficient than the mutual funds.

Further, ETF shareholders can buy or sell their shares anytime during trading hours, while mutual fund shareholders can trade only at the end of the trading day. As a consequence, ETF shareholders can more actively manage their investment. Moreover, ETF shares are traded through broker-dealers. There is no need for transfer agents to track the stock ownership. As a result, ETF management fees are far less than mutual fund fees.

When ETF shareholders request redemption, it is not a taxable event on the part of the ETFs because securities are distributed—an in-kind redemption. Nevertheless, the ETF shareholders requesting the redemption may owe tax because the redemption is a disposition of investment; and it is not a like-kind exchange. (A.S. Meziani & J.G.S. Yang, 67 Practical Tax Strategies 100.)

"Tax differences offset bond and stock fund similarities" (2001). Many considerations should be weighed before committing new funds to a high-yield corporate bond fund (or high-yield corporate bonds) or a stock fund (or stocks). The differences are more critical when the investment is going to be held in a portfolio outside of a qualified retirement plan because of the preferential tax treatment given to long-term capital gains in contrast with interest income. Unlike government bonds, high-yield corporate bonds fluctuate in a similar pattern as do the stocks of the issuers of high-yield bonds. In contrast, government bonds often trade in an opposite direction because when the economy is in a recession, or when the stock market is experiencing a lot of turmoil, investors flee to the government bond market as a safe haven.

Thus, investing in high-yield corporate bond funds may not be a good way to diversify an investment portfolio that already has a large allocation to stock funds.

First, the author discusses timely investment. Over the last year before this article was published, most of the major stock indexes declined substantially. Investors are very weary and are deciding if they should shift funds from their stock mutual funds to bond funds. With the large and recent interest rate cuts by the Federal Reserve Board, Treasury bonds have surged in price—resulting in much lower yields. Because high-yield bonds are more sensitive to the economy and corporate profits, yields have remained relatively high. Investors who are jittery about the stock market may want to sell their stock mutual funds and direct the proceeds into high-yield corporate bond funds.

Then, the author considers taxes. An investment in a typical stock fund can be expected to produce long-term capital gains along with dividend income. The proportion of long-term capital gains and dividend income varies depending on the objective of the fund. An aggressive growth fund is more likely to produce a very large portion of long-term capital gains relative to dividend income. In contrast, a growth and income fund would normally produce approximately equal amounts of long-term capital gains and dividend income. On the other hand, a high-yield corporate bond fund is generally going to produce large dividend distributions (from interest income) and only modest long-term capital gains. The tax advantage of long-term capital gains is that they are generally taxed at no more than 20 percent.

Finally, the author addresses the present value of money, estate planning, impact on itemized deductions, mortgage interest deductions, state income taxes, and allocation to fixed income investments. (P.R. Fink, 66 Practical Tax Strategies 282.)

N

NEGLIGENCE

(*See* Interest and Penalties)

NET OPERATING LOSS

"Applying Section 382 to loss corporation affiliates of exempt organizations" (2001). R.J. Mason, M.V. Rountree & H.A. Levenson, 12 Journal of Taxation of Exempt Organizations 139. (*Digested under* Tax-Exempt Organizations—Hospitals and Other Health Care Organizations, page 237.)

"Dual consolidated loss rules applied to bar use of foreign NOLs" (2001). In FSA 200101007, the IRS concluded that the parent of a domestic consolidated group could not offset the net operating losses (NOLs) incurred from foreign activities, under the dual consolidated loss rules of Section 1503(d). (94 Journal of Taxation 186.)

"Section 381 limitation on NOL carryovers also applies to AMT NOL carryover" (2001). According to TAM 200044003, the limitation on the use of net operating loss (NOL) carryovers under Section 381 (c)(1)(B) for certain corporate acquisitions applies to the computation of an alternative tax NOL carryover deduction. (94 Journal of Taxation 118.)

"Supreme Court takes a favorable approach to specified liability losses on consolidated returns" (2001). In *United Dominion Industries, Inc.* (2001), the Supreme Court was faced with determining how to compute the loss eligible for a ten-year carryback in the context of a consolidated group, and concluded that the single-entity approach embodied in the consolidated return regulations should be used. *United Dominion* involved the application of the special liability loss (SLL) rules in the context of consolidated returns. Some of the members of the consolidated group had other net taxable income greater than their product liability losses. Thus, on a separate-return basis these members had taxable income, while the consolidated group had a net operating loss (NOL).

Under Section 172(b)(1)(C), an SLL can be carried back ten years. The types of losses eligible for this treatment are listed in Section 172(f) and include "product liability losses" as well as certain other types of losses. Under Section 172(f)(2), however, the SLL cannot exceed the NOL for the year.

After providing background, the author discusses the issue in *United Dominion* in view of the consolidated return regulations. The issue in *United Dominion* was whether under the consolidated return regulations the members of a consolidated group could be treated as a single entity for purposes of the SLL carryback rules. The statute authorizing consolidated returns does not provide any guidance on this issue.

Then, the author addresses the resolution of the split in the circuits on the issue in *United Dominion* and the significance of the decision. The decision resolved a narrow issue that some observers might say was not worthy of the Court's attention. The primary question that remains is whether the IRS should amend the consolidated return regulations to apply the separate-entity approach to the SLL. The answer should be no; there is no reason to think that the consolidated group should be viewed as a collection of separate entities for this particular purpose, while the single-entity theory prevails in other situations for all of the reasons provided by Congress and the IRS.

The decision should have implications in other situations in which special rules apply, such as the bad debt losses of commercial banks and life insurance companies. Perhaps most important, the case does publicize the possibility of the ten-year carryback. (W.E. Seago, 95 Journal of Taxation 175.)

NONPROFIT ORGANIZATIONS

(*See* Tax-Exempt Organizations)

NONRESIDENT ALIENS

(*See* Foreign Corporations, Persons, and Partnerships)

NOTICE OF DEFICIENCY

(*See* Assessment and Collection—Notice of Deficiency)

O

OPERATING LOSSES

(*See* Net Operating Loss)

OVERPAYMENT OF TAX

(*See* Procedure—Refunds)

P

PARENT CORPORATION

(*See* Affiliated Corporations)

PARTNERS AND PARTNERSHIPS

(*See also* Accounting Methods; Limited Liability Companies; Passive Loss Rules; S Corporations; Tax Shelters)

In General

"Creative transactional planning using the partnership merger and division regulations" (2001). The final partnership merger and division regulations, which are generally effective for transactions occurring after January 3, 2001, not only provide helpful guidance but in some instances also create planning opportunities that were not previously available. Transactional planning techniques using the new regulations include the following:

(1) Under Regulation § 1.708-1(c) (the merger regulations), the tax-free division of assets among partners who together control multiple partnerships can be accomplished in circumstances where the partnership "anti-mixing bowl" rules of Sections 704(c)(1)(B) and 737(a) otherwise would trigger taxation.

(2) The merger regulations also facilitate umbrella partnership real estate investment trust (UPREIT) operating partnership (OP) unit transactions where some of the partners in the partnership transferring the property want cash, others want OP units,

and the "substantiality" rules of Regulation § 1.704-1(b)(2)(iii) present an obstacle.

(3) Under Regulation § 1.708-1(d) (the division regulations), various structures can be used to engage in a partnership spinoff of certain assets prior to the admission of a new partner.

First, the authors discuss the merger regulations. The merger regulations generally provide that the form of a partnership merger accomplished under laws of the applicable jurisdiction will be respected for federal income tax purposes if the partnership undertakes the transaction in one of two prescribed forms, either the "assets-up" form or the "assets-over" form.

Then, the authors address the new division regulations. Although the division regulations clarify in some respects the determination of which partnership in a division transaction is considered to be a continuation of the prior partnership, they do not make any fundamental changes in that determination.

The central function of the division regulations is to specify when the state law form chosen for the division will be respected for federal income tax purposes, and when it will be recast into a different form for federal income tax purposes. Whether the state law form of the division is respected for federal income tax purposes can have a critical effect on the subsequent application of certain other important rules of subchapter K, such as the anti-mixing bowl rules of Sections 704(c)(1)(B) and 737.

Like the prior guidance under Section 708(b)(2)(B), new Regulation § 1.708-1 (d)(1) provides that on the division of a partnership, one or more resulting partnerships will be treated as a continuation of the prior partnership if the members of the resulting partnership or partnerships had an interest of more than 50 percent in the capital and profits of the prior partnership.

Finally, the authors consider planning strategies. The merger and division regulations afford practitioners new opportunities to structure partnership transactions in a manner that comports with both the business and tax objectives of the partners. (B.D. Rubin & A.M. Whiteway, 95 Journal of Taxation 133.)

"Dealing with the contribution of property to a partnership—Part 2" (2001). Part 1 of this article, dealing with allocations of contributed partnership property, provided an overview of the economic effect requirement under Section 704(b) and the relationship of that section to Section 704(c). Part 2 deals with Section 704(c)(1)(A) and depreciable property, disguised sales, and contributions of encumbered and unencumbered property to a partnership.

First, the author discusses Section 704(c)(1)(A) and depreciable property. If property contributed to a partnership (704(c)(1)(A) property) is depreciable, the regulations establish a rule that substitutes a loss of depreciation deductions in lieu of recognition of precontribution unrealized appreciation.

Then, the author addresses the rules governing disguised sales in the context of partnerships and offers suggestions for avoiding a disguised sale characterization. A disguised sale within the meaning of Section 707(a)(2)(B) consists of a contribution of property or services to a partnership by a partner and a distribution of cash or other property by the partnership to that partner or some other partner under circumstances that indicate that the contribution and distribution should be characterized as constituting a single, integrated transaction.

Not all transfers of property from a partnership followed by a distribution to the contributing partner are taxed as sales under Section 707(a)(2)(B). Before the transaction is treated as a sale, the two transfers, when viewed together, must properly be characterized as a sale of property under Section 707(a)(2)(B)(iii). What Section 707(a)(2)(B) leaves open, unfortunately, is determining when two transfers are properly viewed together as a sale.

Finally, the author addresses contributions of unencumbered property and encum-

bered property. (H.E. Abrams, 3 Business Entities, No. 1, 18.)

"Drafting partnership and LLC agreements: Part 1" (2001). This is the first of a series of articles on the author's personal perspective for drafting venture agreements for partnerships and limited liability companies (LLCs).

No excellence of a form agreement will substitute for thought, experience, and careful lawyering. Drafting a venture agreement is one of the most difficult drafting challenges an attorney will face. This results from the flexibility of the venture relationship and the different challenges that may be encountered by the venture in the future.

A short agreement may leave issues unresolved. These agreements may turn out to be the most complex and the most difficult to interpret when the venture confronts issues not dealt with adequately by the agreement. A difficult task for the drafter is to balance economic considerations against the need for detail and anticipation of future events.

After reviewing drafting principles and the provisions in a venture agreement, the author explores a paradigm to illustrate considerations in drafting concerning basic venturer information, jurisdiction, definitions, purposes of the venture, powers of the venture, term of the venture, venturers' interests (rights and terms, classes of interests), and warranties and representations. It is useful to consider venture agreements in the context of a specific example. In the paradigm, a number of individuals are interested in forming Thrush, LLC. Thrush is organized to undertake a wide range of activities—certain terrorist activities, commerce in confidential information, commerce in firearms, direct sales of pharmaceuticals, offering various forms of entertainment and gaming (including certain activities operated through street vendors), operating a financial laundry to cleanse money, and reproducing and marketing facsimiles of Federal Reserve notes. Thrush's activities will be conducted by an international network of agents. (T.F. Cuff, 3 Business Entities, No. 3, 22.)

"Drafting partnership and LLC agreements: Part 2" (2001). Part 1 of this article dealing with drafting partnership and limited liability company (LLC) agreements laid out some drafting principles that have worked well for the author over the years and discussed certain venture agreement provisions, including basic venturer information, the governing jurisdiction, definitions, purposes, powers, the term of the venture, classes of interests, and warranties and representations, and used as a paradigm, Thrush, LLC, a venture that was organized to undertake a wide range of activities conducted by an international network of agents. This Part 2 of the article picks up where Part 1 left off.

First, the author discusses initial or additional capital contributions. There are typically three possible sources of capital for a venture—the venturers themselves, lenders, or venture operations. Capital contribution provisions can be as complex as a purchase and sale agreement.

Then, the author addresses defaults in capital contributions. The venture agreement should address the possibility of default. Matters are friendlier among the principals if this contingency is addressed when the venture is being organized than when a venturer defaults on an obligation to make an additional capital contribution and his fellow venturers are confronted with the need for a remedy.

Many provisions are available to deal with capital contribution defaults. One respected adviser suggests that you should always provide for a buy out or forfeiture of the interest of a defaulting venturer rather than permit him to continue as a venturer with a reduced interest. Other advisors disagree with this suggestion and have a wide variety of other remedies for dealing with capital contribution defaults, including: (1) reduction in the interest of the defaulting venturer; (2) permitting the other venturers to make a deemed loan to the defaulting venturer, with the funds then treated as a capital contribution to the venture; (3) loss of management or voting rights; (4) suit for specific performance of the obligation to

contribute; and (5) forfeiture of the interest of the defaulting venturer.

Finally, the author considers cash-flow distributions, allocations of nonrecourse liabilities, Section 754 elections, accounting methods, and transfers of interests. (T.F. Cuff, 3 Business Entities, No. 4, 26.)

"Drafting partnership and LLC agreements: Part 3" (2001). This third article in a series reviews the author's personal perspective on putting together venture agreements for partnerships and limited liability companies (LLCs).

First, the author discusses rights of first negotiation or first refusal. A venturer who is permitted to sell his venture interest may be permitted to sell that interest only after complying with a right of first refusal or a right of first negotiation, either of which may be held by the venture or the other venturers. A right of first refusal requires a venturer who intends to sell his venture interest to first find a buyer and negotiate a sale agreement with that buyer. Before he can sell his interest, however, he must offer the venture interest either to the venture or to the other venturers on the negotiated terms of the purchase agreement—or perhaps on terms specified in the venture agreement.

The right of first negotiation is an alternative to the right of first refusal. There is a range of terms for the right of first negotiation. Some rights of first negotiation merely provide a period during which the selling venturer must negotiate in good faith with the other venturers to seek to reach terms for the sale of the offered interest to the other venturers.

Next, the author considers buy-sell provisions. The drafter of a venture agreement needs to consider providing an exit strategy for a venturer wishing to wind up his participation in the venture. A standard solution to this problem is to include a buy-sell provision in the venture agreement.

Then, the author addresses mandatory purchase provisions. There may be events that will require the automatic repurchase of a venturer's interest. Typical events are the death or permanent incapacity of an individual venturer or the bankruptcy of a venturer.

The venture agreement should clearly set forth mandatory repurchase events.

Finally, the author discusses management and meetings. No excellence of drafting will eliminate or anticipate all management disputes. The best that can be done is to delineate who has the authority to do what and how disagreements among the venturers are to be resolved.

Most venture agreements have some provision for at least an annual meeting of venturers and special meetings on an as-needed basis. (T.F. Cuff, 3 Business Entities, No. 5, 38.)

"Drafting partnership and LLC agreements: Part 4" (2001). This is the fourth article in a series in which the author recounts his personal perspective on drafting joint venture agreements for partnerships and limited liability companies (LLCs).

First, the author discusses meetings of the venturers. Venture agreements may provide for an annual meeting and special meetings on an as-needed basis. A venture agreement should specify the time and place of annual meetings, what constitutes a quorum (perhaps 51 percent) for voting, and the procedure for special meetings, including who may call meetings, notice requirements, and whether special meetings can consider matters other than those set forth in the notice.

Then, the author considers budgets and business plans. The annual budget process may be the most important annual management event. A venture agreement should specify the requirements for the budget or even include a sample or first-year budget, which may be a simple annual budget, or a complex budget broken down by quarters or months. The budget may have a few or many line items.

Typically, the manager will prepare the budget and submit it to the venturers for approval. The venture agreement should specify a due date for the manager to send the budget to the other venturers. The venturers then usually have a specified period to accept or object to it. The venture agreement should specify what is the standard of venturer approval of the budget.

Disagreements over the budget ideally will be resolved quickly. The venture agreement should provide for what happens if there is an extended disagreement over the budget. It may provide that the manager will continue to operate the business under the last approved budget until a new budget is approved. Pending approval of the new budget, the old budget may be escalated by a specified cost of living index, or provide that specified items may be adjusted (e.g., the line item for property taxes will automatically adjust to permit payment of current property taxes). The first year's budget often is consented to by the parties signing the agreement.

Finally, the author addresses economic reports, standard of care, standard of discretion, indemnification, preparation and filing of tax returns, dispute resolution, withdrawal and expulsion, liquidation procedures, covenants not to compete, admission of new venturers, financial audit, tax audit, lock-in with respect to contributed property, attorneys and accountants, and miscellaneous provisions. (T.F. Cuff, 3 Business Entities, No. 6, 12.)

"Final regulations apply Regulation § 1.1502-34 stock aggregation rules to Section 732(f)" (2001). The IRS issued final regulations (Regulation § 1.732-3) to clarify that Regulation § 1.1502-34 applies for purposes of Section 732(f). (3 Business Entities, No. 6, 35.)

"Final regulations on partnership mergers and divisions" (2001). 3 Business Entities, No. 2, 51. (*Digested under* Reorganizations, page 176.)

"Final regulations under Section 708 on partnership mergers and divisions" (2001). The IRS adopted final regulations governing the tax consequences of partnership mergers and divisions, effective for partnership merger or division transactions occurring on or after January 4, 2001. Partnerships that had previously undertaken transactions within the scope of the new regulations may elect to apply the final regulations to such transactions if they occurred on or after January 11,

2000, which was the publication date of the proposed regulations.

The final regulations, which were issued under Section 708 (the ''Section 708 regulations''), provide guidance on the form of a partnership merger or division that the IRS will respect. Failure to structure a partnership merger or division in a manner that is consistent with the forms prescribed by Regulation § 1.708-1 may result in reclassification of the merger or division by the IRS, with tax basis and holding period ramifications to the partners. Moreover, if the substance of the transaction more closely resembles a sale or exchange of either a partnership interest or a partnership property, taxes could be imposed.

The Section 708 regulations generally follow the guidance provided by the proposed regulations and are certainly an improvement over prior rules and regulations for which the IRS should be commended. One potentially troublesome aspect of the final regulations is that the IRS did not elect to define the terms ''merger'' or ''division'' with respect to transactions involving partnerships. The lack of such definitions could result in practical difficulties with respect to attempting to structure a partnership merger or division.

First, the authors discuss partnership mergers. In general, the final Section 708 regulations follow the form of the proposed regulations in providing that the form of a partnership merger or division, if accomplished under the laws of the applicable jurisdiction, will be respected as long as the partnership undertakes the steps through one of the two forms prescribed by the regulations.

Then, the authors address partnership divisions. If, in a partnership division, a ''prior partnership'' transfers certain assets and liabilities to a ''resulting partnership'' in exchange for interests in the resulting partnership, and immediately thereafter, the prior partnership distributes its interests in the resulting partnership to the partners who are designated to receive the interests in the resulting partnership, a partnership division has occurred by utilizing the assets-over form. (See Regulation § 1.708-1(d)(3)(i).)

Alternatively, in a partnership division, the prior partnership may distribute certain assets and liabilities to some or all of its partners who then contribute the assets and liabilities to a resulting partnership in exchange for interests in the resulting partnership. In the latter case, a partnership division has occurred in the assets-up form. (See Regulation § 1.708-1(d)(3)(ii).)

As with partnership mergers, the default rule for partnership divisions is the assets-over form. (See Regulation § 1.708-1(d)(3)(i).) Under the Section 708 regulations, when a partnership divides into two or more partnerships under applicable jurisdictional law and undertakes a division using a form other than the assets-up form, the transaction is characterized for tax purposes under the assets-over form.

Finally, the authors turn to tax return treatment. In general, the final Section 708 regulations follow the guidance provided by the proposed regulations with respect to the tax return filing consequences of partnership mergers and divisions to merging or consolidating partnerships. (W.H. Caudill & C.J. Lallo, 3 Business Entities, No. 5, 6.)

''Investment plan is partnership despite lack of state-law entity'' (2001). In Letter Ruling 200131008, a joint investment arrangement between an investment bank and its employees was found to be a partnership for federal tax purposes, notwithstanding that no state-law entity was created. (95 Journal of Taxation 248.)

''IRS seeks comments on disguised sales of partnership interests'' (2001). In Notice 2001-64, the IRS announced that it was considering issuing long-awaited proposed regulations under Section 707(a)(2)(B) relating to disguised sales of partnership interests. When the IRS issued final regulations effective April 1991 regarding Section 707(a)(2), Regulation § 1.707-7 was reserved for rules on disguised sales of partnership interests. (3 Business Entities, No. 6, 35.)

''Medical billing arrangement between clinic and exempt health system is not a part-

nership'' **(2001).** 95 Journal of Taxation 376. (*Digested under* Tax-Exempt Organizations—Hospitals and Other Health Care Organizations, page 237.)

"Offer in compromise denied for partner's share of partnership's taxes" (2001). The IRS may not accept an offer-in-compromise submitted by a general partner, in her individual capacity, to compromise her share of the outstanding employment tax obligations of the partnership, according to ILM 200127009. (95 Journal of Taxation 252.)

"Partnership interest transfers under the holding period final regulations: opportunities and traps remain" (2001). TD 8902 (2000) adopts final regulations relating to a partner's determination of the holding period of the partnership interest when portions of the interest are acquired at different times. Regulation § 1.1223-3 adopts the IRS's approach originally set forth in Proposed Regulation § 1.1223-3 and generally provides that the holding period of a partnership interest will be divided if a partner acquires portions of an interest at different times or if an interest is acquired in a single transaction that gives rise to different holding periods under Section 1223.

The IRS's multiple-holding-period approach still differs markedly from the methods currently used by most practitioners. As a result, and as previously predicted, Regulation § 1.1223-3 may provide opportunities for some partners who dispose of all or a portion of their partnership interests, and may ensnare others. The final regulation applies to transfers of partnership interests (and distributions of property from a partnership) that occur after September 20, 2000.

First, the author discusses holding period issues. The regulations' principal rule on holding periods, as stated in Regulation § 1.1223-3(b), is that the portion of a partnership interest to which a holding period relates is determined by using a fraction, the numerator of which is the fair market value (FMV) of the portion of the partnership interest received in the transaction to which the holding period relates, and the denominator of which is the FMV of the entire

partnership interest (determined immediately after the transaction). Examples in the final regulations indicate this rule has the virtue of (relative) administrative simplicity, in comparison to tracing the partnership's use of the proceeds of a particular contribution of cash (or other property). The regulations, however, absolutely foreclose the use of tracing to establish that a later contribution creates no new (short-term) asset, but rather may be attributable to an earlier contribution (or merely supplies current operating funds) and, thus, the holding period arguably still should be long-term.

Then, the author considers examples illustrating the treatment of interests issued solely for cash and interests not issued for cash—and explores the planning opportunities arising under the final regulations. Through the use of several examples, the author identifies numerous available approaches to (and the corresponding consequences of) the determination of a partner's holding periods for interests in a partnership. The author also explores many nuances arising under the IRS's position as reflected in Regulation § 1.1223-3 for determining holding periods.

Inherent in the IRS position is that a partner often will have multiple holding periods for the interest. In some situations, this is mandated by statute, e.g., for sales of partnership interests where the partnership owns capital and noncapital assets contributed by a partner or the partnership holds collectibles, Section 1202 stock, or Section 1250 assets that are subject to special tax rates with respect to all or a portion of the gain. (S.I. Banoff, 94 Journal of Taxation 211.)

"Partnership transaction recast under Regulation § 1.701-2(b) anti-abuse rule" (2001). A chief counsel advice (CCA 200128053) concluded that the IRS may use Regulation § 1.701-2(b) to recast a transaction that was structured solely to obtain a stepped-up basis in the partnership's assets under Section 732(b). (3 Business Entities, No. 6, 38.)

"Possible consequences of options to acquire partnership interests" (2001). Unlike the corporate model, which benefits from preferential tax treatment in some aspects and with which practitioners have decades of experience, a grant of options in the partnership context involves a great deal of uncertainty. While the economics of the transaction are clear, the mechanics are much less clear, even in the simplest situations involving noncompensatory options.

After providing a basic example, the authors discuss the grant of the option and the option holding period. The tax treatment of the grant of the option is dealt with in a fairly straightforward manner under the open-transaction doctrine, which has been applied by the courts to options. Specifically, there are no immediate consequences to either the grantor or the grantee on the issuance of the option. In the partnership context, the transaction is held open because of the difficulty in determining whether the premium eventually will be income to the partners on a lapse of the obligation or will be a contribution to capital, along with the strike price, on exercise.

During the period in which the option holder retains the option, a portion of any increase in the value of partnership assets from their value at the time of grant, along with income realized and retained by the partnership, is economically accruing to the holder.

Then, the authors consider the lapse of the option and the exercise of the option. Most of the uncertainty involving options to acquire a partnership interest relates to exercise of the option when the underlying assets have appreciated in value. There are at least three possible ways to view this transaction: (1) treating the exercise as a bargain purchase by the grantee from the issuer (here, the partnership); (2) bifurcating the exercise into two separate transactions—the contribution of the strike price by the grantee coupled with reclassification of the premium as a contribution to capital and a taxable shift of capital equal to the value of the option, the increase in the value of the option accruing as a contingent liability of the partnership; and (3) same as (2), previously, except that the contingent obligation is viewed as that of the partners individually instead of as a

liability of the partnership. (C.S. Armstrong & M.K. Cooper, 94 Journal of Taxation 356.)

"Profits interest substantially nonvested at time of grant treated as received as of date of grant" (2001). Revenue Procedure 2001-43 clarifies the application of Revenue Procedure 93-27 in connection with a grant of a profits interest in a partnership in return for services provided to or for the benefit of the partnership where the profits interest is substantially nonvested (within the meaning of Regulation § 1.83-3(b)) at the date of grant. In Revenue Procedure 93-27, the IRS stated generally that if a person receives a profits interest in a partnership as consideration for the provision of services to or for the benefit of the partnership, the IRS will not treat the receipt of the partnership interest as a taxable event to the partner or the partnership. (3 Business Entities, No. 5, 49.)

"Proposed regulations on basis of corporate partner's interest in partnership" (2001). The IRS has issued proposed regulations relating to special rules for determining the basis of a partner's interest under Section 705. The regulations would prevent inappropriate increases or decreases in the adjusted basis of a corporate partner's interest in a partnership resulting from the partnership's disposition of the corporate partner's stock. (66 Practical Tax Strategies 248.)

"Revenue Procedure 2001-43 and partnership profits interest: try, try again" (2001). Revenue Procedure 2001-43 was designed to answer many of the questions that were raised when the IRS addressed the profits interest issue in Revenue Procedure 93-27.

First, the authors provide background. In Revenue Procedure 93-27, the IRS created a safe harbor in which the receipt of a partnership profits interest (as opposed to a capital interest) in exchange for services provided to or for the benefit of the partnership generally will not be treated as a taxable event for either the partner or the partnership.

141

Then, the authors discuss Revenue Procedure 2001-43. Revenue Procedure 2001-43 attempts to clarify Revenue Procedure 93-27 by providing guidance on the treatment of a grant of a nonvested interest in partnership profits for the provision of services to or for the benefit of the partnership. The IRS intended to clarify Revenue Procedure 93-27 by providing that the determination of whether an interest granted to a service provider is a profits interest is made at the time the interest is granted even if, at that time, the interest is substantially nonvested (within the meaning of Regulation § 1.83-3(b)). Revenue Procedure 2001-43 provides that in certain circumstances the IRS will not treat either the grant of a profits interest or the event that causes the interest to become substantially vested as a taxable event for the partner or the partnership. According to the revenue procedure, taxpayers in such circumstances need not file an election under Section 83(b).

Under the revenue procedure, a service provider will be treated as receiving the interest on the date of its grant despite any restrictions on the interest, provided that (1) the partnership and the service provider treat the service provider as the owner of the partnership interest from the date of its grant and the service provider takes into account the distributive share of partnership income, gain, loss, deduction, and credit associated with that interest in computing his income tax liability for the entire period during which he has the interest; (2) upon the grant of the interest or at the time that the interest becomes substantially vested, neither the partnership nor any of the partners deducts any amount (as wages, compensation, or otherwise) for the fair market value of the interest; and (3) all other conditions of Revenue Procedure 93-27 are satisfied. (D.L. Walton & H.T. Belanger, 3 Business Entities, No. 6, 4.)

"Revenue Procedure 2001-43, Section 83(b), and unvested profits interests—the final facet of *Diamond*?" (2001). In Revenue Procedure 2001-43, the IRS issued long-awaited guidance regarding the tax treatment of service providers who receive unvested or

"restricted" profits interests in partnerships (or limited liability companies (LLCs) or other entities classified as partnerships) in exchange for services. Service providers who meet all the requirements of the procedure may avoid recognition of income on both the receipt and the vesting of the profits interest—even absent a Section 83(b) election. The procedure also clarifies that the partnership and the service provider must treat the service provider as a partner for tax purposes prior to the vesting of the profits interest. Reliance on Revenue Procedure 2001-43 may lead to unanticipated tax consequences for some service providers, however, particularly for those who fail to satisfy all of the procedure's requirements and neglect to make a Section 83(b) election.

First, the authors provide background on partnership interests for services, profits interests under subchapter K, profits interests under Section 83, and unvested profits interests. Prior to issuance of Revenue Procedure 2001-43, there was virtually no guidance—apart from one decided case (the 1987 California federal district court decision in *Kobor*)—on the tax treatment of the issuance and vesting of partnership profits interests. No Code provision, legislative history, regulations, or rulings explicitly dealt with these issues.

Then, the authors address the guidance provided by Revenue Procedure 2001-43 in conjunction with Revenue Procedure 93-27. In Revenue Procedure 2001-43, the IRS responded to the need of practitioners for guidance with respect to nonvested profits interests, but in a way that seems to have left many practitioners less than satisfied. The new procedure, in section 3, clarifies Revenue Procedure 93-27 by providing that the determination of whether an interest granted to a service provider is a profits interest is made at the time the interest is granted, even if the interest is substantially nonvested at that time. Furthermore, if the profits interest granted to a service provider meets the requirements of both revenue procedures (i.e., Revenue Procedure 93-27 and Revenue Procedure 2001-43), the IRS will treat neither the grant of the interest nor the event that causes the interest to vest as a taxable event for the partner or the partnership. Revenue Procedure 2001-43 also states that if the requirements of both revenue procedures are satisfied, the service provider need not file an election under Section 83(b).

To fall within the safe harbor of Revenue Procedure 2001-43, all of the conditions of Revenue Procedure 93-27 must be satisfied. In addition, both the partnership and the service provider must treat the service provider as the owner of the partnership interest from the date of grant, and the service provider must take into account the distributive share of income, gain, loss, deduction, and credit associated with the interest in computing the service provider's income tax liability for the entire period during which the service provider holds the interest. Finally, neither the partnership nor any of the partners may deduct any amount for the fair market value (FMV) of the interest, either on grant or vesting of the interest.

In effect, Revenue Procedure 2001-43 gives the service provider the benefits of a valid Section 83(b) election. Under the procedure, the transaction is treated as if the service provider had made a valid Section 83(b) election when the FMV of the profits interest was zero. Thus, the service provider partner reports no income on grant or vesting, and the partnership claims no deduction. In addition, as would occur with a valid Section 83(b) election, the service provider should be treated as the owner of the interest and her holding period for the interest should begin on the day after the profits interest is transferred. (G.E. Mincey, E.B. Sloan & S.I. Banoff, 95 Journal of Taxation 205.)

"Sale of partnership interest terminated the partnership" (2001). In FSA 200132009, the IRS determined that a sale of a partnership interest to an S corporation by a limited liability company (LLC) owned by the S corporation's sole shareholder and his wife terminated the partnership. (3 Business Entities, No. 6, 37.)

"Sales or exchanges of interests in pass thrus" (2001). The IRS has issued final regulations under Section 1(h) providing guidance on the treatment of gains arising from sales or exchanges of interests in partnerships, S corporations, and trusts.

First, the author discusses statutory capital gains rates. Section 1(h) provides different maximum rates of tax for different types of long-term capital gains.

Then, the author addresses the new rules in detail. The final regulations provide helpful guidance on the treatment of gains arising from sales or exchanges by pass-thru entities with which practitioners need to be familiar. Because Section 1250 capital gains are likely to occur more frequently than collectibles gains, the regulations would have been more helpful if they had included examples that illustrated 1250 capital gains, rather than focusing on collectibles gains. (D.M. O'Leary, 3 Business Entities, No. 1, 34.)

"Special rules for partner in "trader" partnership" (2001). 66 Practical Tax Strategies 308. (*Digested under* Passive Loss Rules, page 152.)

"Statutory freeze partnerships: a useful estate planning technique" (2001). A Section 2701 freeze partnership can potentially reduce appreciation within the taxable estate and in some cases also reduce the present taxable estate.

First, the author explains how a freeze partnership works and compares the freeze partnership to other strategies, including a grantor-retained annuity trust (GRAT), a dynasty trust, and an irrevocable life insurance trust (ILIT). The concept of Section 2701 is relatively simple. It allows the creation of the following equity interests: (1) a preferred interest paying a fixed and certain rate of return, with no participation in equity growth and (2) a common interest that enjoys all income, growth, and appreciation above and beyond the preferred return. The preferred interest is frozen in value, which accounts for the name freeze partnership. However, rather than determining the value of the common interest under the normal willing buyer/willing seller rule, Section 2701 requires that the value of the preferred interest first be determined and then subtracted from the value of the entity as a whole; the result is the value of the common interest, which may be further reduced for minority or similar discounts.

Moreover, in calculating the value of the preferred interest, any preferential rights granted to the preferred interest, which are found not to be mandatory or "qualified" payment rights, are disregarded. This can result in the preferred interest being assigned a zero value if the distributions to be made to the preferred interest holder are optional or noncumulative. As a result, under the subtraction method, if the preferred interest is valued at zero, then the value of the common interest will equal the value of the entire partnership, even though the common interest may represent only a small portion of the equity ownership.

Next, the author discusses eliminating the estate tax in growing estates. The concepts of eliminating estate tax and growing an estate may at first appear mutually exclusive. However, if the growth consists substantially of taxable income, the combination of a freeze partnership and an intentionally defective grantor income trust (IDGIT) to hold the common partnership interest can result in not only freezing the amount of the taxable estate, but actually reducing the taxable estate to as close to zero as the client desires.

Then, the author considers avoiding guaranteed payment treatment under Section 707(c). In order for the freeze partnership to fall within the safe harbor of Section 2701, the payment to the preferred partner must be a "qualified payment right" meeting the requirements of Regulation § 25.2701-2 (b)(6).

Finally, the author provides advice for situations in which investment returns drop below preferred returns. (A.K. Long, III, 28 Estate Planning 59.)

"Tax considerations in choice of entity decision" (2001). M.A. McNulty, 3 Business Entities, No. 5, 16. (*Digested under* S Corporations, page 192.)

"Taxpayer appeals LIFO recapture case involving preconversion contribution to partnership" (2001). The taxpayer has filed an appeal with the Eleventh Circuit of the Tax Court's decision in *Coggin Automotive* (2000). In reaching its decision, the Tax Court used the "aggregate approach" to partnerships to find that a C corporation was considered to own its pro rata share of LIFO inventory held through a partnership and, therefore, was subject to LIFO recapture tax when it converted to S corporation status. (3 Business Entities, No. 4, 56.)

"Taxpayer wins economic substance argument but loses case" (2001). In *Salina Partnership LP* (2000), the Tax Court found that a taxpayer's investment in a partnership had economic substance. However, the Tax Court also held that a short sale by the partnership created a partnership liability, which had disastrous tax consequences for the taxpayer. (3 Business Entities, No. 2, 53.)

"Transactions involving stock of corporate partner" (2001). As promised in Revenue Ruling 99-57, proposed regulations disallow basis adjustments in certain transactions involving the stock of a corporate partner. (3 Business Entities, No. 2, 52.)

"Transfer of a partnership interest at death creates tough issues for the successor" (2001). The death of a partner raises many income tax issues for the deceased partner's successor in interest. These issues relate to the successor's obligation to dispose of the interest as required by the partnership agreement or the successor's right to continue as a partner by stepping into the shoes of the deceased partner. In either event, the successor must determine its initial basis in the interest acquired from the decedent.

The successor also must determine the extent to which a Section 754 election would be beneficial and whether the partnership has, or is willing to make, the election. Finally, the successor should identify any income in respect of a decedent (IRD) represented by the partnership interest, determine when the IRD must be included in gross income, and compute the Section 691(c) deduction to which the successor is entitled.

First, the authors discuss closing the partnership year for a deceased partner. For partnership tax years beginning after 1997, a partnership tax year closes with respect to a partner whose entire interest in the partnership terminates (whether by reason of death, liquidation, or otherwise). As a result, the partnership must determine the items of income, gain, loss, or deduction attributable to the short tax year ending on the date of death. The decedent's distributive share of each item is allocated to his capital account and reported on his final Form 1040. If the partnership distributed cash or property to the partner prior to death, these distributions were charged against the partner's capital account on the date of distribution. Thus, the date-of-death capital account balance includes the decedent's undistributed share of partnership income for the year.

Next, the authors consider the successor's basis. Because the successor acquires its partnership interest from a decedent, the successor's initial tax basis is the fair market value (FMV) at which the interest is included in the deceased partner's gross estate for federal estate tax purposes. If the successor is allocated a share of partnership liabilities under Section 752(a), the basis is increased by this share. Depending on the terms of the partnership agreement, the FMV of a deceased partner's interest is either the interest's liquidation value or the interest's going-concern value.

Then, the authors address IRD. Section 691 defines "IRD" as any item of gross income to which a decedent was entitled at death but which was not included in the decedent's gross income because of the decedent's method of accounting. The right to such unrealized income is an asset included in the decedent's gross estate and subject to estate tax. Nevertheless, the basis in the IRD asset does not step up to FMV when the asset is transferred at death. Instead, the decedent's zero basis in the IRD asset carries over to the person (the decedent's estate or other beneficiary) who acquires the right to receive the income. As a result, such person must include the IRD in gross income for the year in which the IRD is finally realized. A person who must recognize IRD is allowed an income tax deduction (Section 691(c) deduction) for the federal estate tax attributable to the IRD asset.

Finally, the authors explore the sale of a deceased partner's interest and liquidation of the interest. (S.M. Jones & D.M. Maloney, 94 Journal of Taxation 24.)

"Treasury and IRS unveil ambitious business plan for 2001" (2001). On April 26, 2001, Treasury and the IRS released the 2001 Priorities for Tax Regulations and Other Administrative Guidance. This article lists projects in the IRS business plan that are relevant to partnerships and S corporations. (3 Business Entities, No. 4, 55.)

Family Limited Partnerships

"Another family limited partnership case" (2001). The Tax Court issued another decision in a family limited partnership case in *Estate of W.W. Jones II* (2001). Two holdings in this case were especially interesting. First, the Tax Court held that there was no taxable gift when the decedent contributed property to his family limited partnerships because the contributions were reflected in full in the contributing partner's capital account. Second, the Tax Court did not allow any discount for built-in gains in the property when the partnership interest was transferred. (3 Business Entities, No. 4, 53.)

"Avoid tripping on family limited partnership trap" (2001). Transferring a family business from one generation to the next may result in substantial federal estate and gift tax. In some instances, tax payments seriously harm or bankrupt an enterprise. The family limited partnership is a technique often used in this process for shifting future appreciation to heirs and enabling valuation discounts for minority interests and lack of marketability while permitting continued control. The IRS has given warning that it intends to disregard such partnerships in certain transfers of voting stock, however, by returning the stock to a business owner's estate at death under Section 2036(b)

First, the authors discuss Section 2036(b) and illustrate the Section 2036(b) trap using TAM 199938005. In general, Section 2036 applies to people who give away interests or property with strings attached. If the transferor retains the right to possess or enjoy property or to determine who will do so, Section 2036(a) returns it to the former owner's estate at death. According to this rule, a decedent's gross estate includes any property given away if he or she retained for life any of the following: (1) the possession or enjoyment of the property; (2) the right to income from the property; or (3) the right, either alone or with others, to designate who possesses or enjoys the property or the income it generates.

This does not apply to property that the owner actually sells for adequate and full consideration in cash or the equivalent. It does apply to all other transfers, whether made outright to recipients or indirectly through a device such as a trust or limited partnership.

Then, the authors discuss eight principles that should be considered when arranging a family business' succession of ownership in order to avoid the Section 2036(b) trap. In brief, planners should simply recognize a likely trap and guide their clients around it, especially since this area of tax law still is changing and estate planning steps taken today may be judged in light of the law applicable years from now, at a client's death. (J.R. Oliver & C.A. Granstaff, 66 Practical Tax Strategies 268.)

"'Charitable lid' formula used in connection with FLP disregarded" (2001). 95 Journal of Taxation 116. (*Digested under* Charitable Contributions, page 21.)

"Court approves tax savings from family limited partnerships" (2001). In both *Estate of Strangi* (2000) and *Knight* (2000), the Tax Court accepted the validity of family limited partnerships as vehicles for reducing transfer taxes. (66 Practical Tax Strategies 112.)

"Economic substance of family limited partnerships" (2001). Two Tax Court opinions, *Estate of Strangi* (2000) and *Knight* (2000),

make it clear that the Tax Court will take into account business purpose and economic substance in determining whether a family limited partnership will be recognized for federal estate tax purposes. (3 Business Entities, No. 2, 54.)

"Family limited partnerships: the open issues" (2001). By now, word has reached the hinterlands that the Tax Court has rejected most of the IRS's arguments against valuation discounts for interests in family limited partnerships (FLPs). In several cases, the court has established that (1) An FLP may be respected for wealth transfer tax purposes even if it is motivated by tax avoidance and not by business purposes, even if it is formed shortly before the death of a senior family member, and even if it holds only investment assets and conducts no business. (2) Section 2703, requiring that certain types of transfer restrictions be ignored for valuation purposes, has no application to the basic discounts for lack of control or lack of marketability inherent in an FLP interest. (3) Section 2704(b), requiring that certain restrictions on liquidation of an entity be ignored for valuation purposes, has no application to restrictions on a partner's right to have the partnership liquidate his or her partnership interest (as opposed to restrictions imposed on rights to liquidate the entire partnership).

Despite these important taxpayer victories, however, there still is cause for caution when approaching FLPs. This article examines the questions that remain open and that may continue to threaten discount planning.

First, the author discusses appeals. Even the issues on which the taxpayers have completely prevailed in the Tax Court will not finally be resolved until they have been passed on by courts of appeals. Doubtlessly, several of the recent Tax Court decisions will be reviewed, with published opinions to be issued by the appellate courts, and it is entirely possible that some of the rulings in favor of the FLPs could be reversed.

Finally, the author considers issues that remain unresolved involving indirect gifts, Section 2036(a), and quantifying the discounts. (J.A. Bogdanski, 28 Estate Planning 282.)

"Let the donor beware of the charitable family limited partnership" (2001). Charitable family limited partnerships (FLPs) appear to be alive and well in the financial and estate planning community.

First, the author addresses partnership structures. Charitable FLPs have two standard forms, with variations, depending on whether the primary purpose is avoiding income taxes or transfer taxes.

Then, the author addresses tax issues. FLPs are being upheld by the courts, which have accepted the premise that putting a partnership wrapper around assets lowers their fair market value because the donee has only a partnership interest, which interest does not carry control of the assets within the partnership and is not itself marketable. This is true even if the assets within the partnership are marketable assets, including securities. The decisive fact is whether the partnership has substance.

Finally, the author addresses charity and other issues. While a charitable FLP may be structured in a manner that arguably does not violate applicable sections of the Code, it provides substantial donor benefits that may adversely affect the accepting charity. (C.D. Duronio, 12 Journal of Taxation of Exempt Organizations 272.)

"Save transfer taxes with family limited partnerships" (2001). The 2000 Tax Court decisions of *Estate of Strangi* and *Knight* indicate that family limited partnerships (FLPs) continue to be effective estate planning mechanisms. Although in both *Strangi* and *Knight*, the IRS argued that the existence of the FLPs should be disregarded because the FLPs lacked economic substance, the Tax Court found that the existence of FLPs and their associated effect on the net value of the underlying assets are respected for federal transfer tax purposes.

Based on the Tax Court's well-reasoned opinions in *Strangi* and *Knight*, FLPs appear to remain an effective tool for the transfer of wealth at a discount. Such a discount, moreover, can provide significant transfer tax savings. In *Strangi*, the Tax Court used the net asset approach for the valuation of the FLP. This approach applies a minority interest and a marketability discount to the net asset value of an entity. An 8 percent minority interest discount and a 25 percent marketability discount were accepted by the court in *Strangi*, for an aggregate discount of 31 percent from the net asset value of the FLP.

After providing background on the transfer of assets through an FLP, including valuation discounts related to restrictions, the author discusses the holdings in regard to economic substance. Specifically, the Tax Court held that an FLP has sufficient economic substance under the willing buyer/willing seller standard to be respected for federal transfer tax purposes.

Then, the author addresses the issue of whether a gift was made by the decedent on formation of the FLP. According to the Tax Court, a contribution of assets to a pro rata FLP in exchange for a less valuable partnership interest does not result in a taxable gift if the contribution is allocated to the capital account of the transferor.

The author also considers the impact of Chapter 14. The IRS has relied on the valuation rules of Sections 2703 and 2704 of Chapter 14 as a means of negating the valuation discounts associated with the transfer of FLP interests. But according to the Tax Court, an FLP is not disregarded under Section 2703 as a "restriction on the right to sell or use" the underlying assets of the FLP. Section 2704 does not apply to partnership agreements that have liquidation restrictions consistent with state law and that restrict the withdrawal rights of limited partners.

In conclusion, the author notes the impact of Section 2036(a), which provides that the value of the gross estate includes the value of all property interests transferred by the decedent during lifetime (except in the case of a bona fide sale for full and adequate consideration) if the decedent retained for life the possession or enjoyment of the property, or the right to the income from the property. Estate planners should be aware of the potential application of Section 2036(a) to negate the tax benefits associated with the transfer of FLP interests. (P.J. Walsh, 66 Practical Tax Strategies 324.)

147

"Transfer of assets to family partnership was not a taxable gift" (2001). 28 Estate Planning 118. (*Digested under* Gifts and Gift Tax, page 76.)

Partnership Allocations and Distributions

"A lesson in doing it the hard way: on remand, Tax Court finds for taxpayer in *Interhotel*" (2001). By definition, a safe harbor will shield and protect you from storms. For federal income tax purposes, making proper use of a safe harbor can save taxpayers time, money, and effort, as illustrated by the Tax Court decisions in the *Interhotel* saga—*Interhotel Company, Ltd.* (1997) (*Interhotel I*) and *Interhotel II* (2001). The Tax Court's original errors in analyzing the partnership minimum gain provisions, which led to an appeal, reconsideration on remand, and the taxpayer's ultimate victory, would have been avoided had the allocations of income in the partnership agreement complied with the substantial economic effect safe harbors in the regulations.

After reviewing the facts, the author analyzes the decisions in *Interhotel I* and *Interhotel II*. The Tax Court's initial decision in *Interhotel I* was a controversial one. The issue was whether the allocation of income by a partnership to a partner would be sustained. The IRS contended, among other things, that if a partnership agreement did not comply with the substantial economic effect safe harbors in Regulation § 1.704-1(b)(2)(ii), a partner could not take into account the minimum gain inherent in lower-tier partnerships in determining whether an upper-tier partnership had a positive or a negative balance in its capital account. This aspect of the decision was sharply criticized, because it called into question the loss allocations that arise in many tiered partnership arrangements.

Fortunately, the government recognized the error of its ways when the case was appealed to the Ninth Circuit. The justice Department conceded in its brief that the Tax Court's analysis of the rules concerning minimum gain in tiered partnerships was

erroneous, and the Ninth Circuit remanded the case for reconsideration. The IRS did not give up, however, and contested in the Tax Court whether the allocations made by the taxpayer should be respected.

The Tax Court has issued its decision on remand in *Interhotel II*, completely vindicating the taxpayer's position. As a result, the allocations used by the taxpayer were sustained, even though the taxpayer had not complied with the safe harbor set forth in the regulations. Nonetheless, the case illustrates why taxpayers generally should use the safe harbors in Regulation § 1.704-1(b)(2) in drafting the allocation provisions in a partnership or limited liability company (LLC) agreement. (R.M. Lipton, 95 Journal of Taxation 69.)

"Allocation of partnership income made in accordance with partners' interests in partnership" (2001). On remand from the Ninth Circuit, the Tax Court in *Interhotel Company, Ltd.* (2001) held that a special allocation of 100 percent of partnership income earned after June 20, 1991, and allocated to the corporate general partner of the partnership should be respected because the allocation was made in accordance with the partners' interests in the partnership. (3 Business Entities, No. 5, 50.)

"Final regulations issued for partnership allocation of nonrecourse liabilities" (2001). The IRS has issued final regulations relating to the allocation of nonrecourse liabilities by a partnership. The regulations revise tier three of the three-tiered allocation structure contained in the current nonrecourse liability regulations, and also provide guidance regarding the allocation of a single nonrecourse liability secured by multiple properties. (66 Practical Tax Strategies 62.)

"Making the most of the partnership debt allocation rules: IRS modifies third-tier allocations" (2001). Changes to the Section 752 regulations specifically address the manner in which partners share partnership nonrecourse liabilities, and adopt a flexible rule dealing with situations in which multiple partnership assets serve as collateral for a single nonrecourse partnership liability.

The modifications generally follow the proposed regulations, continuing the thought process initiated in Revenue Ruling 95-41. The new rules go further, however, modifying Regulation § 1.752-3(a)(3) to provide that allocations of excess nonrecourse liabilities may be made in accordance with "excess Section 704(c) gain" as well as "excess reverse Section 704(c)" gain. Finally, in response to questions following the issuance of the proposed regulations, the drafters make it clear that the new excess nonrecourse liability allocation methodology may not be used for Section 707 disguised sale purposes.

First, the authors discuss allocating partnership nonrecourse liabilities. Under Regulation § 1.752-1(a)(2), a partnership liability is a nonrecourse liability to the extent that no partner (or person related to a partner) bears the economic risk of loss for that liability under the rules set forth in Regulation § 1.752-2.

Partnership nonrecourse liabilities are allocated among partners based on the three-tier system of Regulation § 1.752-3. Those rules place a priority on ensuring that partners who are allocated deductions or receive distributions financed by partnership nonrecourse liabilities have enough basis in their partnership interests to support such items. The regulations allow a partner contributing debt-encumbered property (or a partner in a partnership that has revalued its property under Section 704(b)) to receive a priority allocation of partnership nonrecourse liabilities to avoid recognizing gain under Section 731(a) caused by a shifting of the liability to other partners in the partnership.

Then, the authors consider Section 704(c) methodologies. Section 704(c)(1)(A) requires that income, gain, loss, and deduction, with respect to property contributed to a partnership by a partner, be shared by the partners so as to take account of the variation between such property's fair market value and tax basis at the time of its contribution. Regulation § 1.704-3(a)(1) states that the allocations must be made using a reasonable method, and identifies three as such: (1) the traditional method in Regulation § 1.704-3(b); (2) the curative method in Regulation § 1.704-3(c); and (3) the remedial method in Regulation § 1.704-3(d).

Finally, the authors address the effect of Revenue Ruling 95-41 and new regulatory modifications. Revenue Ruling 95-41 offered welcome guidance in explaining the three-tier regulatory structure for allocating partnership nonrecourse liabilities in that it acknowledged the possibility of increasing a contributing partner's Tier Three liability allocation to the extent the partner contributed property with excess Section 704(c) built-in gain over Section 704(c) minimum gain. This was particularly important for those searching for a way to allocate nonrecourse liabilities to a contributing partner over and above that partner's Section 704(c) minimum gain share when contributed liabilities were subsequently paid down, collateralized by other partnership property, or as the partners' Tier One liability shares increased. The ruling's statement, however, that such excess is only a "factor" to be given appropriate weight in light of all other items of partnership profit left many wondering what other factors should be considered and how much relative weight should be given to each factor. (J.A. Erickson & R.F. Pillow, 94 Journal of Taxation 261.)

"Permission for securities partnerships to aggregate contributed property for Section 704(c) allocations" (2001). Revenue procedure 2001-36 grants automatic permission for certain securities partnerships to aggregate contributed property for purposes of making Section 704(c) allocations. (3 Business Entities, No. 4, 53.)

"Share of nonrecourse liabilities for purposes of Section 752 and the at-risk rules" (2001). 3 Business Entities, No. 4, 54. (*Digested under* At-Risk Rules, page 8.)

Partnership Audits and Proceedings

"Deficiency notice timely and negligence penalty upheld" (2001). The Tax Court held in *Ruggiero* (2001) that a notice of deficiency issued within one year from the final court decision of a partnership or affected item is timely and that the IRS may assess the additions to tax for negligence or intentional disregard of rules. (67 Practical Tax Strategies 174.)

"Final TEFRA audit and litigation regulations issued as IRS intensifies its focus on partnership audits" (2001). As the entity of choice for new business ventures, tax partnerships are now facing increased scrutiny from a challenged IRS. In this context, the final regulations governing the TEFRA unified procedures acquire even more significance. For the most part, the new rules are helpful, eliminating a tangle of proposed and temporary regulations.

First, the authors discuss the jurisdictional deposit requirement. The changes to the jurisdictional deposit rules found in Regulation § 301.6226(e)-1(a)(1) are the most noteworthy and arguably have the most dramatic impact of all the provisions in the final regulations.

To challenge the IRS's audit determinations contained in a notice of final partnership administrative adjustment (FPAA), a petition may be filed in the Tax Court, the Court of Federal Claims, or in federal district court. Before filing a petition for readjustment in a district court or in the Court of Federal Claims, Section 6226(e) requires that the partner filing the petition make a jurisdictional deposit. The deposit must equal the increase in the tax liability of the petitioning partner that would result if the IRS's adjustments to the partnership items were sustained.

What Section 6226(e) does not provide is a method for calculating the required deposit if the partner bringing suit is itself a pass-through entity, such as a partnership or S corporation, that has no direct tax liability resulting from the adjustments to partnership items. The proposed and temporary regulations were silent on the requirement of a jurisdictional deposit for pass-through partners.

Final Regulation § 301.6226(e)-1(a)(1) requires that the pass-through partner deposit the amount by which the tax liabilities of all

indirect partners holding an indirect interest in the partnership through the pass-through partner would be increased if the IRS's adjustments to the partnership items were sustained.

Then, the authors address the small partnership exception. Excepted from the scope of the TEFRA unified procedures under Section 6231(a)(1)(B) are "small partnerships." The final regulations clarify the application of the small partnership exception to partnerships having partners who are: (1) C corporations; (2) nonresident aliens; or (3) pass-through entities.

Finally, the authors consider passive activity losses as affected items, ownership by husbands and wives, issuance of a second notice of the beginning of an administrative proceeding, elections under Section 6223(e), place for filing an administrative adjustment request, penalties, and consents executed on behalf of limited liability companies. (J.Z. Ackerman & C.P. La Puma, 95 Journal of Taxation 261.)

"IRS issues final regulations on unified partnership audit procedures" (2001). Final regulations relating to the unified partnership audit procedures became effective as of October 4, 2001. (3 Business Entities, No. 6, 34.)

"New tension between entity and aggregate theories of partnership taxation" (2001). In *Rhone-Poulenc Surfactants and Specialties* (2000), a sharply divided Tax Court held that Section 6229 did not provide a separate and exclusive period of limitation for making assessments with respect to partnership items, but was instead an alternate period to the one contained in Section 6501. The court further held that the tolling provision contained in Section 6229(d), which provides that the running of the period under Section 6229(a) is suspended after the IRS issues a final partnership administrative adjustment (FPAA), suspends the general period of limitation contained in Section 6501.

In so holding, the Tax Court appears to have embraced wholeheartedly the aggregate theory of partnership taxation at the expense of the plain language of Section 6229 and

Congress's clear intent to apply the entity theory under the unified partnership audit and litigation procedures enacted as part of the Tax Equity and Fiscal Responsibility Act of 1982 (TEFRA). (M.K. White, 3 Business Entities, No. 3, 14.)

"Notice partner's petition for readjustment dismissed after TMP filed petition" (2001). In *Columbia/St. David's Healthcare System LP* (2001), the Fifth Circuit affirmed the Tax Court's judgment in an unpublished opinion. The Fifth Circuit held that Section 6226(a) precludes any other partner from filing a readjustment petition if the tax matters partner (TMP) files a timely and valid petition within the ninety-day period even if the TMP's petition does not seek to readjust all items listed in the notice of final partnership administrative adjustment (FPAA). (3 Business Entities, No. 6, 37.)

"Parent company's bankruptcy does not convert partnership items of subsidiary to nonpartnership items" (2001). In FSA 200122023, the IRS ruled that the bankruptcy of a parent corporation did not convert partnership items of a subsidiary corporation into nonpartnership items. (3 Business Entities, No. 4, 54.)

"Partners must be individually assessed prior to collection activity" (2001). 66 Practical Tax Strategies 373. (*Digested under* Assessment and Collection—In General, page 6.)

"Partners not entitled to refund based on claim of right to settlement on terms consistent with settlement made with another partner" (2001). *Prochorenko* (2001) is a Federal Circuit case applying the byzantine Tax Equity and Fiscal Responsibility Act of 1982 (TEFRA) partnership provisions to an unusual set of facts. (3 Business Entities, No. 3, 61.)

"Request for prompt assessment made with respect to decedent partner converts partnership items into nonpartnership items" (2001). In *Callaway* (2000), the Second Circuit addressed a Tax Equity and Fiscal Responsibility Act of 1982 (TEFRA) part-

nership provision issue of first impression in the Courts of Appeals. (3 Business Entities, No. 1, 58.)

"Tax assessments against a partnership not binding on partners" (2001). 3 Business Entities, No. 6, 37. (*Digested under* Assessment and Collection—In General, page 6.)

"TEFRA partnership decisions" (2001). This article discusses two decisions, *Rhone-Poulenc Surfactants & Specialties* (3d Cir. 2001) and *Hirschfield* (SDNY 2001), that address the jurisdiction of a court over partnership proceedings. (3 Business Entities, No. 4, 54.)

"True-ups are partnership items subject to special partnership limitations period" (2001). FSA 200125014 comes to grips with whether "true-ups" are subject to the Section 6229 special period of limitations for assessing any tax with respect to partnership items. The FSA concludes that since a true-up involves a computational adjustment to properly reflect the treatment of a partnership item, the assessment period of Section 6229 applies to true-ups. (3 Business Entities, No. 5, 52.)

"Without FPAA, no Tax Court jurisdiction over partnership items used to compute partner's basis in his interest" (2001). In FSA 200112005, the IRS concluded that the Tax Court lacked jurisdiction to adjust partnership items in a deficiency proceeding because the IRS had not already issued a final partnership administrative adjustment (FPAA). (94 Journal of Taxation 376.)

PASSIVE LOSS RULES

"Disposition frees up suspended passive losses despite S election" (2001). 66 Practical Tax Strategies 61. (*Digested under* S Corporations, page 185.)

"Member of LLC treated as general partner for purposes of passive activity rules" (2001). 3 Business Entities, No. 2, 53.

(*Digested under* Limited Liability Companies, page 123.)

"S corporation may deduct suspended PALs incurred while it was a C corporation" (2001). 3 Business Entities, No. 1, 56. (*Digested under* S Corporations, page 188.)

"Self-charged fees cannot offset passive income" (2001). The Fourth Circuit has reversed the Tax Court in *Hillman* (2001), holding that a taxpayer could not offset passive management deductions against related nonpassive management income where neither the Code nor the regulations provided for such tax treatment. (67 Practical Tax Strategies 50.)

"Self-charged management fee not deductible against related nonpassive management fee income" (2001.) In *Hillman* (2001), the Fourth Circuit reversed the Tax Court and held that the plain language of Section 469(a) prohibits the deduction of self-charged management fee expenses against related nonpassive management fee income. (3 Business Entities, No. 4, 52; 3 Business Entities, No. 6, 35.)

"Special rules for partner in "trader" partnership" (2001). A partner in a "trader" partnership may claim as a trade or business expense the Section 162 expenses of the partnership, but must treat his ordinary income or losses as not arising from a passive activity, according to FSA 200111001. (66 Practical Tax Strategies 308.)

"Substantiation can be crucial for exception to passive loss rules" (2001). The taxpayer in *Mowafi* (2001) did not qualify as a real estate professional, so losses he incurred from a rental real estate activity were subject to the passive activity loss rules, according to the Tax Court. The case highlights the need for keeping contemporaneous records to substantiate deductions. (67 Practical Tax Strategies 119.)

"Suspended passive activity losses survive S election" (2001). M.R. Martin & J.E. Tierney, 66 Practical Tax Strategies 273. (*Digested under* S Corporations, page 191.)

PAYMENT OF TAX

(*See* Assessment and Collection)

PENALTIES

(*See* Interest and Penalties; Tax Practice and Practitioners)

PENSION AND PROFIT-SHARING PLANS

(*See also* Compensation for Personal Services; Fringe Benefits)

In General

"Charitable estate planning with retirement benefits" (2001). S.J. Schlesinger & D.L. Mark, 28 Estate Planning 390. (*Digested under* Charitable Contributions, page 20.)

"Excess pension plan assets can be put to various uses" (2001). Section 401(a)(2) specifies that prior to the satisfaction of all liabilities with respect to employees and beneficiaries, no assets or income of a qualified plan may be used for, or diverted to, purposes other than those benefiting employees exclusively. The Code and ERI-

SA, however, expressly permit the sponsor of a defined benefit (DB) pension plan to recover excess assets from the plan on compliance with certain conditions.

If "excess" assets in a terminated DB plan result from "actuarial error," the employer/plan sponsor may receive a reversion of excess assets, after the plan has satisfied all liabilities to participants and beneficiaries. An "actuarial error" exists only when plan assets have been accumulated based on reasonable actuarial assumptions, and total assets exceed the cost of providing accrued benefits for all participants and beneficiaries on the date of plan termination.

Practically speaking, however, a for-profit employer cannot simply terminate its pension plan and receive a reversion of excess assets. This option is foreclosed effectively by Section 4980, which imposes an excise tax of 50 percent of any asset reversion to an employer from a pension plan, in addition to ordinary income tax.

Recent cases have clarified the extent to which an employer can use the excess assets in its pension plan. (M.S. Melbinger & J.M. Hahn, 67 Practical Tax Strategies 204.)

"Free at last—IRS finalizes relief from the qualified plan anti-cutback rule" (2001). Final regulations provide relief from the anti-cutback rule in Section 411(d)(6), particularly as it applies to optional forms of benefit payments under a qualified retirement plan.

First, the author provides background on the anti-cutback rule. Speaking broadly, Section 411(d)(6) protects a number of rights, benefits, and features under a plan (collectively, the "Section 411(d)(6) protected benefits"). These include: (1) accrued benefits themselves; (2) optional forms; (3) early retirement benefits and retirement-type subsidies described in Section 411(d)(6)(B)(i); and (4) certain other rights, benefits, and features under a plan that have value to a participant, such as the defined benefit feature (i.e., the right to have a benefit determined under a definite formula) of a defined benefit plan and the individual account feature of a defined contribution plan.

Then, the author discusses the final regulations. Generally, a Section 411(d)(6) protected benefit that has accrued by the later of the effective date or the adoption date of a plan amendment may not be eliminated or reduced by that plan amendment. In certain instances, however, the final regulations permit all Section 411(d)(6) protected benefits to be eliminated or reduced.

The final regulations provide relief in five different sets of circumstances, affecting optional forms of benefit payments under defined contribution plans, elective transfers of benefits between such plans, elective transfers of distributable benefits between plans, payments in kind, and annuities.

Finally, the author addresses planning opportunities provided by the final regulations. (S.D. Baum, 94 Journal of Taxation 90.)

"Guidance on changes to qualified plan benefits limitations" (2001). Revenue Ruling 2001-51 provides guidance in question-and-answer format relating to the increases in the Section 415 limitations on qualified plan benefits and contributions enacted as part of the Economic Growth and Tax Relief Reconciliation Act of 2001. (67 Practical Tax Strategies 368.)

"Guidance on effective dates for retirement plan rules" (2001). In Notice 2001-56, the IRS provides guidance on applying the effective dates of changes made to the Section 401(a)(17) compensation limit by the Economic Growth and Tax Relief Reconciliation Act of 2001. (67 Practical Tax Strategies 248.)

"IRS sets out to make EGTRRA work, with guidance on catch-up contributions and increased plan limits" (2001). The Economic Growth and Tax Relief Reconciliation Act of 2001 (EGTRRA or the 2001 Act) increased many of the limitations applicable to retirement plans under the Code. For example, EGTRRA increased the limitation in Section 401(a)(17) on the amount of a participant's compensation that a qualified plan may take into account and the limitations in Section 415 on the amount of the contributions that

153

may be allocated or the benefit that may be provided by a qualified plan. The 2001 Act also added Section 414(v) to the Code, under which catch-up contributions may be made under a retirement plan by certain individuals. In effect, these catch-up contributions increase the limitation in Section 402(g) and other Code provisions on the amount of elective deferrals that those individuals may make each year.

Not surprisingly, the increases made by EGTRRA to the limitations in the Code raise certain technical questions. To begin to answer these questions, the IRS has provided a variety of guidance. Notice 2001-56 and Revenue Ruling 2001-51 implement the increases in the limitations of Sections 401(a)(17) and 415. Proposed regulations explain how to apply the catch-up provisions of Section 414(v). (S.D. Baum, 95 Journal of Taxation 336.)

"IRS updates and expands its retirement plan compliance correction program" (2001). In Revenue Procedure 2001-17, the IRS updated and clarified its guidance under the Employee Plans Compliance Resolution System (EPCRS) for correcting defects in qualified plans and Section 403(b) arrangements. The new procedure makes several substantive and a number of procedural changes to EPCRS. The changes in Revenue Procedure 2001-17 reflect a continuing evolution in the IRS's approach to the difficulties faced by plan sponsors and their advisors in complying with the complex rules for retirement plans. The alterations made by this revenue procedure advance that evolution by expanding the programs and clarifying the availability and limitations on the programs.

After providing background on EPCRS, the authors discuss the changes. Under Revenue Procedure 2001-17, several programs have been consolidated, voluntary procedures have been expanded, formal procedures have been established for anonymous submissions, changes have been made to self-correction procedures, and several other expansions have been made.

The changes expand the scope of the programs to permit: (1) group submissions to correct systemic problems affecting more than one plan sponsor; (2) formal anonymous submissions; (3) self-correction and IRS-supervised correction for defects occurring in simplified employee pension plans (SEPs); and (4) correction for employers that were ineligible to sponsor Section 401(k) plans at the time they adopted the plan.

Revenue Procedure 2001-17 also extends the self-correction period and otherwise facilitates correction in the case of certain transfers of plan assets and plan mergers, and adds a new safe-harbor correction for the common problem of permitting employees to participate in a qualified plan before they are eligible. (C.F. Reish, B.L. Ashton & N.J. White, 95 Journal of Taxation 31.)

"New law significantly alters retirement plan landscape" (2001). On June 7, 2001, President Bush signed into law the Economic Growth and Tax Relief Reconciliation Act of 2001 (EGTRRA). A long list of provisions with varying effective dates increase retirement plan benefit and contribution limits and alter a wide range of other plan rules, mainly to the advantage of employees.

First, the author discusses the higher contribution and benefit limits, as well as catch-up contributions. A variety of contribution and benefit caps have been increased by the new law. EGTRRA provides an additional increase in the IRA maximum contribution limit for individuals who had attained age 50 by the end of the tax year of $500 for 2002 through 2005 and $1,000 for 2006 and thereafter. Thus, these individuals will be able to make deductible IRA contributions of up to $3,500 in 2002 through 2004, $4,500 in 2005, $5,000 in 2006 and 2007, and $6,000 in 2008 and thereafter.

Second, the author considers plan loans. Effective with loans made after 2001, permissible borrowers under a tax-qualified plan include sole proprietors, partners owning more than 10 percent of the capital or profits interest in a partnership, and an employee or officer of an S corporation owning more than 5 percent of the outstanding stock of such corporation. The owner of an IRA, however, continues to be prohibited from borrowing from his or her IRA.

Next, the author addresses rollover procedures. Effective for distributions made after 2001, the IRS can waive the sixty-day period within which to effect a rollover to an IRA. A waiver could be granted only if the failure to waive the sixty-day requirement would be against equity or good conscience.

Another provision increases the likelihood of automatic rollovers of qualified plan distributions. Effective for distributions occurring after the Secretary of Labor has issued implementing regulations (which must occur not later than three years after enactment of EGTRRA), a direct rollover must be the default option for involuntary distributions that exceed $1,000 (but are less than $5,000) and are eligible rollover distributions from qualified retirement plans. The distribution must be rolled over automatically to a designated IRA, unless the participant affirmatively elects to have the distribution transferred to a different IRA or a tax-qualified plan or to receive it directly.

Then, the author turns to the impact of the EGTRRA on cash-or-deferred plans, employee contributions, tax-exempt organizations, employee stock ownership plans, distributions, funding, credits, notice for benefit reductions, and miscellaneous changes. Finally, the author provides guidance on conforming plan amendments. (B. Salkin, 67 Practical Tax Strategies 36.)

"Proposed regulations on catch-up contributions" (2001). The IRS has issued proposed regulations on the requirements for retirement plans providing catch-up contributions to individuals age 50 or older under Section 414(v). (67 Practical Tax Strategies 370.)

"State statute does not revoke beneficiary designation after divorce" (2001). The U.S. Supreme Court ruled in *Egelhoff v. Egelhoff ex rel. Breiner* (2001) that ERISA preempts a state revocation- on-divorce statute. As a result, a decedent's ex-spouse received his retirement plan.

After providing background on *Egelhoff*, the author discusses its implica-

tions. *Egelhoff* raises two issues relating to the overlap between state property law rules and retirement plans governed by ERISA. The first is whether ERISA may be used to invalidate other state statutes that affect the disposition of property interests at death. The dissent notes that many slayer statutes (i.e., statutes that deprive a person who kills another of any property interests the slayer would otherwise receive as the result of the deceased person's death) can affect the determination of the beneficiary under ERISA plans. Under the majority's reasoning in *Egelhoff*, slayer statutes—and perhaps other statutes—could be preempted by ERISA. The majority suggests that uniformity among various states' slayer statutes may make preemption unnecessary, but, as the dissent points out, the slayer statutes are not at all uniform.

The second issue raised by the *Egelhoff* decision is that of fairness: What can be done to improve the fairness of the distribution of property at death? The policy behind revocation-on-divorce statutes (that of carrying out a decedent's presumed intent) seems as applicable to retirement plans as to other transfers taking effect at death. In the course of a dissolution proceeding, spouses will agree to—or a court will dictate—an equitable division of the spouses' property. After the divorce, it seems unjust to permit a beneficiary spouse to obtain additional property at the decedent's death, unless the decedent intended that result.

In conclusion, the author states that the question of the distribution of property at death has long been a matter of state law. In this area, it makes sense to permit state legislatures and probate courts to determine the appropriate results. Unless and until Congress enacts an exception to ERISA preemption, state courts—acting in equity—should use the constructive trust doctrine to prevent the unjust enrichment of a former spouse. (S.N. Gary, 28 Estate Planning 376.)

"2001 Act makes many positive changes to tax-favored retirement plans—Part 1" (2001). The Economic Growth and Tax Relief Reconciliation Act of 2001 (EGTRRA or the 2001 Act) generally increases limits

155

on contributions and benefits under tax-favored retirement plans, includes catch-up provisions and other incentives to encourage savings, and repeals or provides relief from many of the restrictions and rules that had applied to tax-favored retirement plans. The first part of this article focuses on the types of plans sponsored by relatively larger employers—defined benefit and defined contribution plans, profit sharing and stock bonus plans, Section 401(k) plans, Section 457 plans, multiemployer plans, and tax-sheltered annuities.

First, the author discusses qualified plans, including the impact of the 2001 Act on contributions and benefits, the compensation limit, profit-sharing and stock bonus plans, elective deferrals, funding limits, other deduction limits for defined benefit plans, nondeductible contributions to defined benefit plans, loans, top-heavy rules, Section 411(d)(6) relief, the cash-out rule, notice requirements, valuation, and user fees.

Then, the author addresses 401(k) plans. Finally, the author turns to SIMPLE plans, ESOPs, multiemployer plans, tax-sheltered annuities, and Section 457 plans.

In conclusion, the author states that although implementation of the new EGTRRA rules may take some time and effort, clearly the changes wrought by Congress for retirement plans, participants, and beneficiaries will have a long-lasting favorable effect. Practitioners will have to ensure that taxpayers take maximum advantage of the increased contribution limits, especially in light of the changes to the estate tax over the next few years. (S.D. Baum, 95 Journal of Taxation 96.)

"2001 Act makes many positive changes to tax-favored retirement plans—Part 2" (2001). The first part of this article discussed the changes made by the Economic Growth and Tax Relief Reconciliation Act of 2001 (EGTRRA or the 2001 Act) to the types of plans sponsored by relatively larger employers—defined benefit and defined contribution plans, profit-sharing and stock bonus plans, Section 401(k) plans, Section 457 plans, multiemployer plans, and tax-sheltered annuities. This part examines the

changes to the various types of individual retirement accounts (IRAs) and the rollover rules, new tax credits, and miscellaneous other changes. Suggestions also are made on how to take advantage of the opportunities presented by the 2001 Act to increase contributions to, or benefits under, tax-favored retirement plans.

First, the author addresses IRAs. Liberalized ceilings on contributions and the addition of the "catch-up" contribution feature for participants at least fifty years of age are perhaps the most visible of the EGTRRA changes to the IRA rules. Like icebergs, however, there is much more below the surface—separate "deemed IRA" accounts and a new "qualified Roth contribution program" in qualified plans, a quadrupling of the contribution limit for education IRAs along with an expanded definition of "qualified education expenses," the general elimination of the need for a "conduit" IRA in a rollover, and much more.

Next, the author discusses education IRAs. Several changes have been made to improve the advantages and availability of education IRAs, effective for tax years beginning after 2001.

Then, the author considers simplified employee pensions (SEPs). EGTRRA's SEP provisions increase elective deferral limits, provide catch-up provisions, increase the compensation limit, increase the contribution limit, and increase the limit on deductible contributions.

Finally, the author turns to the Simple IRA, rollovers, tax exclusions and credits, and other matters. (S.D. Baum, 95 Journal of Taxation 165.)

Coverage and Participation

"Cross-testing final regulations validate new comparability plans" (2001). Most cross-tested defined contribution (DC) plans should be able to satisfy one of the new requirements and continue cross-testing. Most aggregated defined benefit (DB)/DC plans should likewise be able to continue testing on a defined benefit basis.

After providing background, the author discusses combined DB/DC testing and DC plan cross-testing. For plan years after 2001, nondiscrimination testing of combined DB/DC plans based on benefits requires the DB/DC plan to satisfy one of the following: (1) be "primarily defined benefit in character;" (2) consist of broadly available separate plans; or (3) pass a "gateway" test.

Similarly, to cross-test a DC plan in plan years after 2001, the plan must comply with any of the following: (1) provide broadly available allocation rates; (2) have age-based allocation rates based on either a "gradual age or service schedule" or a uniform target benefit allocation; or (3) satisfy a minimum allocation gateway.

Then, the author considers the definition of "compensation," the availability of allocation rates, and the use of transition allocations. (M.S. Melbinger, 67 Practical Tax Strategies 132.)

"Negative elections spur positive retirement plan participation" (2001). In 1998, the IRS issued Revenue Ruling 98-30, formally approving negative election arrangements for the first time. Under Revenue Ruling 98-30, contributions under an automatic enrollment program do not fail to be elective deferrals under the regulations, as long as the employee who is automatically enrolled has the opportunity to make an election not to participate in the plan. The IRS reasoned that the opportunity to elect not to participate in the plan was the equivalent of electing to receive cash, so the definition of "elective deferral" was in fact met. Revenue Ruling 98-30 applied only to newly hired employees, but the authorization for the use of automatic enrollment was extended to existing employees in Revenue Ruling 2000-8 under the same rationale.

The most recent rulings released by the IRS implement the goal of the Treasury and Labor Departments to increase retirement savings by extending the negative election concept to qualified retirement plans and annuity savings programs other than employer-sponsored 401(k) plans. Specifically, the use of negative elections has been approved for use in Section 403(b) annuity plans (for

teachers and employees of tax-exempt organizations) and Section 457 plans (for employees of governmental agencies and tax-exempt organizations.) The extension of the negative election concept to these additional areas has the potential to significantly increase retirement plan savings rates. However, they also raise additional concerns regarding state wage-payment laws.

After providing background on government encouragement of negative election arrangements, the author discusses the advantages. The advantages of using negative elections depend on the type of plan the employer is sponsoring. However, nonhighly compensated employee participation in salary-deferral-type retirement plans tends to rise when automatic enrollment rules (with a negative election option) are in place.

Finally, the author turns to the potential applicability of state payroll withholding laws. (S.J. Arsenault, 67 Practical Tax Strategies 73.)

Distributions

"IRS proposes new, liberalized minimum distribution regulations" (2001). The new proposed regulations on minimum distributions ease many of the previous stringent requirements. The proposed regulations, which provide a simple uniform distribution table, will result in lower required distributions for most individuals.

First, the authors discuss the uniform distribution table. Beginning in 2002, all IRA owners (with one exception) must use a new uniform distribution table (UDT) to calculate minimum required distributions (MRDs). No longer does the IRA owner need to make a distribution election on the required beginning date (RBD), worry about whether to recalculate life expectancy, choose a fixed term, or select the hybrid method. These concepts are now obsolete.

Then, the authors address designated beneficiaries. Under the proposed regulations, the designated beneficiary is determined not on the RBD, but as of the last day of the calendar year following the calendar year of the owner's death. The owner is free

157

to change beneficiaries during his lifetime, whether or not the RBD has occurred. Any person who is a beneficiary as of the date of the owner's death, but is not a beneficiary as of December 31 of the calendar year following the year of death (the applicable date), is not taken into account in determining the designated beneficiary. An IRA account agreement may not, however, allow a person to have the discretion to change an IRA owner's beneficiaries after the IRA owner's death; otherwise, the owner will be treated as not having a designated beneficiary.

Finally, the authors consider post-death distribution rules, trust rules, and additional issues. (R.S. Franklin & R.T. Kleinknecht, 28 Estate Planning 355.)

"Proposed regulations reduce many required minimum distributions" (2001). On January 11, 2001, the IRS, without warning, changed the rules for determining required minimum distributions from IRAs, 401(k)s, 403(b)s, and other qualified plans. The new rules are much simpler and substantially reduce amounts that must be withdrawn each year. Thus, IRAs and qualified plans now offer greater opportunity for accumulating wealth. The article provides a summary of the new rules in question-and-answer form.

Pension plans that make distribution in the form of an annuity and other annuity plans are for the most part not discussed in this article in the interest of simplicity, since the rules for these plans are substantially unchanged. Also (unless otherwise specified), "plan" and "IRA" are used interchangeably in this article, as are "IRA owner," "owner," and "employee" since minimum distribution rules for IRAs and individual account plans are the same.

The new rules, although in the form of proposed regulations, can be relied on in 2001. Proposed minimum distribution regulations were first published in July 1987 and controlled minimum distributions until now. The new proposed regulations are much simpler than the previous rules and should benefit most people. Hopefully, final regulations will allow persons now taking distributions from inherited IRAs to use the new rules and substantially reduce their required

minimum distributions. (H.M. Esterces, 66 Practical Tax Strategies 196.)

"The simpler minimum distribution rules for qualified plans and IRAs under the new proposed regulations" (2001). On January 17, 2001, the IRS published new proposed regulations dealing with the required minimum distribution rules that apply to benefits held in qualified retirement plans and individual retirement accounts.

First, the author provides background. The original proposed regulations were complex and contained many traps for the ill-informed participant or beneficiary. The participant was required to make two irrevocable elections at the required beginning date (RBD). The participant had to: (1) identify the designated beneficiary for purposes of determining the period over which the plan benefit or IRA had to be distributed and (2) elect whether the life expectancy of the participant and, if the spouse was the designated beneficiary, the life expectancy of the participant's spouse, were to be redetermined each year. The original proposed regulations referred to the method of distribution under which life expectancies were redetermined as the recalculation method. The choice had a significant impact on the timing of distributions from that point on, and could result in the distribution of the participant's entire plan benefit or IRA by the end of the year following his or her death.

The new proposed regulations eliminate both elections that were required under the original rules and, for most participants and their beneficiaries, provide for a longer distribution period—and consequently smaller required distributions.

The new proposed regulations do not change the determination of a participant's RBD. The new rules permit a qualified retirement plan to mandate that the RBD for all employees is April 1 after the calendar year in which the employee reaches age 70½, regardless of whether the employee has retired.

Then, the author considers lifetime distributions and the new proposed regulations. The new rules greatly simplify the method of determining the required minimum distributions during a participant's lifetime. Under Proposed Regulation § 1.401(a)(9)-5, Q&A-1(a), while the participant is alive the minimum distribution is determined annually by dividing the "applicable distribution period" into the value of the participant's plan benefits and IRAs as of the valuation date (December 31 in the case of an IRA) in the year preceding the year in which the distribution has to be made. The applicable distribution period generally is determined using the uniform distribution period table in Proposed Regulation § 1.401(a)(9)-5, Q&A-4(a)(2), which is based on the participant's age and the age of an individual ten years younger than the participant in each distribution calendar year.

Finally, the author explores the new rules regarding the participant's death before the RBD, spousal rollovers, the designated beneficiary, the trustee as beneficiary, and effective dates. (L.A. Mezzullo, 94 Journal of Taxation 274.)

Employee Stock Ownership Plans (ESOPs)

"'Anti-abuse' provisions for S corporation ESOPs become law" (2001). An amendment to Sections 409 and 4979(a) under the Economic Growth and Tax Relief Reconciliation Act of 2001 provides that three bad things happen if there is a "nonallocation year" with respect to an employee stock ownership plan (ESOP) maintained by an S corporation. First, the amount allocated in a "prohibited allocation" to an individual who is a "disqualified person" is treated as distributed to such individual (i.e., the value of the prohibited allocation is includable in the gross income of the individual receiving the prohibited allocation). Second, an excise tax is imposed on the S corporation equal to 50 percent of the amount involved in such a prohibited allocation (subject to a special rule in the case of the first nonallocation year). Third, an excise tax is imposed on the S corporation with respect to any "synthetic equity" owned by a disqualified person. (3 Business Entities, No. 4, 49.)

"ESOP's distribution of S corporation stock, followed by rollover to IRA, did not terminate S election where company immediately repurchased its stock" (2001). 3 Business Entities, No. 4, 52. (*Digested under* S Corporations, page 185.)

"LLC employees may participate in consolidated group's ESOP" (2001). In Letter Ruling 200116051, the IRS ruled that limited liability companies (LLCs) disregarded for all tax purposes will be treated as part of the parent corporation's controlled group for employee stock ownership plan (ESOP) purposes. (95 Journal of Taxation 54.)

"Planned basis freezes and ESOPs after the 2001 Tax Act" (2001). For certain business owners, a sale of closely held stock to an employee stock ownership plan (ESOP) can accomplish multiple objectives: (1) a tax-deferred conversion of part or all of the business owner's privately held stock to publicly traded securities; (2) a corporate-level tax deduction for the value of the contributions to the ESOP in order to acquire the privately held shares; (3) the creation of an employee benefit program tied to the financial performance of the company; and (4) the partial or complete exemption from taxation at the closely held company level, if an S election is made.

While the sale to an ESOP does not reduce estate taxes, it creates more liquidity for the business owner—in the form of marketable securities that can easily be sold to pay estate taxes, or to use in other estate planning tools, such as grantor retained annuity trusts (GRATs), or the purchase of additional life insurance. A sale to an ESOP also is an excellent way to partially or completely dispose of an interest in a closely held business.

After exploring the tax as well as nontax benefits of ESOPs, the author focuses on estate planning with S corporation ESOPs. There are several strategies available for those who own shares in a profitable S corporation that has an ESOP. The planning objectives center on how to most efficiently and with the least audit risk, for estate planning purposes, take advantage of the S

159

stock holdings, which: (1) will be generating significant taxable income (if the business is profitable) and (2) possibly will be appreciating more rapidly than if there was not an ESOP shareholder (i.e., the ESOP shareholders will not be requiring current withdrawals of cash to pay income taxes, so more money will be left in the company to reinvest into the business and expand and develop its operations). Two common estate planning tools that should be among the first to be considered are: (1) a "defective" grantor trust and (2) a GRAT.

As a result of the 2001 Tax Act, estate planners will have the desire, and with ESOPs, some ability, to fine-tune the basis of assets that will be retained by the estate. (S. Etkind, 28 Estate Planning 592.)

"Purchase of subsidiary resulted in plan disqualification" (2001). An employee stock ownership plan (ESOP) failed to meet the minimum participation standards of Section 410 after employees in an acquired corporation were aggregated with the taxpayer's own employees, according to the Tax Court in *Beals Bros. Management Corp.* (2001). (67 Practical Tax Strategies 251.)

Individual Retirement Accounts (IRAs)

"Are points on first home worth paying with IRA funds?" (2001). Should the first-time homebuyer withdraw up to $10,000 from a deductible IRA to pay points in order to get a lower interest rate on a mortgage related to the purchase of a first home? The analysis of this question is based on a computer model that considers the choice between: (1) leaving the deductible IRA intact and paying an interest rate that is based on paying no points to the lender or (2) withdrawing an amount not in excess of $10,000 from the deductible IRA and using the distribution to pay points (and income taxes related to the withdrawal) to qualify for a lower annual interest rate on the mortgage.

A computer model was constructed to portray the after-tax wealth accumulation associated with each of those two alternatives. A deductible IRA is a traditional (i.e.,

non-Roth) IRA, the contributions to which were above-the-line deductions for the taxpayer. The entire distribution from a deductible IRA is taxed as ordinary income.

After providing background on points, the authors discuss the results of the computer model. In choosing between taking a mortgage without paying points or "buying down" the interest rates on a mortgage by withdrawing from an IRA to pay the required points and the associated federal income tax on the withdrawal from the IRA, there are many relevant variables. These include: (1) the manner in which the taxpayer's non-IRA investment funds will be taxed (e.g., ordinary income tax, capital gains tax, or no tax); (2) the pretax rate of annual earnings or annual growth that will be realized in both the IRA investment fund and the non-IRA investment funds; (3) the marginal income tax rate applicable to any annual ordinary income earned by non-IRA investment funds; (4) the marginal income tax rate at which the IRA will be taxed when it is liquidated when the taxpayer reaches age $70\frac{1}{2}$; and (5) the relationship between the mortgage interest rate without points and the mortgage interest rate and number of points associated with the mortgage for which there will be a "buy down" of the mortgage interest rate.

Because this study has so many relevant variables, the analysis focused on the interest rate on the "buy down" mortgage that would render the taxpayer indifferent between taking the higher interest rate mortgage without the points or taking the lower interest rate mortgage by making a withdrawal from his or her IRA. The withdrawal from the IRA would be used to pay the points and the tax associated with the IRA withdrawal.

This indifference interest rate permits the reader to evaluate particular offers from mortgage lenders. (S.J. Baxendale & R.M. Walter, 66 Practical Tax Strategies 35.)

"How multigeneration IRA preserves cash flow for children" (2001). A multigeneration IRA is an IRA that makes distributions successively to the IRA owner, then to the IRA owner's spouse, and then to the IRA owner's children. It uses a technique used by the rich to get richer: They simply let the magic of tax-free compounding work for them. Similarly, the multigeneration IRA owner simply defers the receipt of distributions from the IRA as long as possible to permit the maximum tax-free compounding within the IRA wrapper and then, when distributions must begin at age 70½, the IRA owner takes the minimum distributions required by selecting the optimum distribution method. Thus, the IRA owner puts the magic of tax-free compounding to work.

First, the author considers an example that illustrates the plan and provides distribution projections. Then, the author analyzes the results of the projections and addresses planning considerations. The multigeneration IRA works most dramatically where parents can afford to delay IRA distributions to age 70½ and can afford to use the recalculation method to minimize distributions, and where parents wish to provide children with the maximum IRA income stream after their deaths.

If parents cannot afford the maximum delay in distributions and minimization of distributions, the multigeneration IRA can still work, but less dramatically. The parents simply delay beginning distributions as long as is comfortable and, when distributions begin, make whatever larger distributions to themselves that they need. While this will provide reduced benefits for the children, it still will provide multigeneration benefits. (G.J. Robinson, 28 Estate Planning 22.)

"Tax rate predictions affect Roth versus traditional IRA choice" (2001). Which IRA is better from an after-tax investment point of view? Focusing on the ultimate performance measure, the after-tax rate of return on investment, analysis reveals that whether one type of IRA is better than the other depends on an individual's tax rates when funds are invested compared with an individual's tax rates when funds are withdrawn.

After providing background on the different tax rules applicable to traditional and Roth IRAs, the authors consider the general findings of their analysis of the performance of the Roth versus the traditional IRA. The

traditional IRA is the better investment alternative for most individuals because it is most likely that the tax rate at withdrawal will be lower than the tax rate at the time of investment. This conclusion appears to be contrary to the current conventional wisdom. The confusion arises because the nominal account balance will generally be higher in a Roth IRA than a traditional IRA. This occurs because the net investment in a Roth IRA is larger. Focusing on the return per investment dollar, however, the traditional IRA outperforms the Roth IRA for most individuals. (G.W. Kutner, L.D. Doney & J.P. Trebby, 66 Practical Tax Strategies 19.)

Loans

"Elimination of restrictions on plan loans to S corporation shareholders, partners, and sole proprietors" (2001). Prior to the Economic Growth and Tax Reconciliation Act of 2001 (the 2001 Act), one of the few disadvantages of operating a business as an S corporation, a partnership, or a sole proprietorship, as compared to the operation of a business as a C corporation, was the inability of qualified plans to make loans to most S corporation shareholders, partners, and sole proprietors. The 2001 Act levels the playing field by eliminating the provision that treated plan loans to partners, sole proprietors, and more than five percent S corporation shareholders as prohibited transactions. (3 Business Entities, No. 5, 57.)

"Tax-free pension plan loan burst by balloon payment" (2001). According to the Tax Court, the taxpayer, in *Plotkin* (2001), had to treat a pension plan loan as a taxable distribution because the loan terms did not require repayment by means of substantially level payments within five years. (66 Practical Tax Strategies 319.)

PERSONAL EXPENSES

(*See* Business Expenses—Personal Expenses Versus Business Expenses)

PERSONAL RESIDENCE

(*See also* Real Estate)

"Are points on first home worth paying with IRA funds?" (2001). S.J. Baxendale & R.M. Walter, 66 Practical Tax Strategies 35. (*Digested under* Pension and Profit-Sharing Plans—Individual Retirement Accounts (IRAs), page 160.)

"No resulting trust in home maintained by same-sex couple" (2001). The Seventh Circuit in *Scott* (2000) affirmed a ruling by the Tax Court that a resulting trust in a residence was not created in favor of the survivor of a same-sex relationship. (28 Estate Planning 28.)

"Operation of personal residence exclusion rules clarified in new proposed regulations" (2001). New proposed regulations under Section 121 provide guidance to practitioners regarding several issues that needed clarification after the wholesale changes to the statute made by the Taxpayer Relief Act of 1997 and amended by the 1998 IRS Reform Act. The new rules are slated to become effective after they are finalized.

The major topics covered in the proposed regulations include: (1) eligibility for the exclusion; (2) the amount of the exclusion and limitations on that amount; (3) the exemption for those filing joint returns; and (4) other special issues.

First, the authors discuss eligibility. The various elements of eligibility for the Section 121 exclusion include the basic requirements that must be met in order to qualify (i.e., meeting the ownership and use tests), as well as certain special situations that result in exceptions. In addition, the meaning of "used as a principal residence" and the impact of the two-year rule on eligibility are considered.

Next, the authors address the reduced exclusion. Section 121(c) offers relief in the nature of a partial exclusion if an otherwise ineligible taxpayer is selling or exchanging a principal residence because of a change in employment, health reasons, or "unforeseen circumstances." While the statute circum-

scribes the latter term with the commonly employed phrase "to the extent provided in regulations," Proposed Regulation § 1.121-3(a) broadens this by stating that "unforeseen circumstances" will be set forth in several places such as "forms, instructions, or other appropriate guidance including regulations and letter rulings."

Then, the authors consider joint returns. The rules are slightly different for taxpayers filing a joint return.

Finally, the authors explore other special issues. The proposed regulations also cover sales by expatriates, sales of remainder interests, sales of depreciated property, and sales of property that is partially used as a principal residence. (W.R. Simpson & J.L. Morris, 94 Journal of Taxation 165.)

"Proper Medicaid planning may permit keeping the home in the family" (2001). B.E. Barreira, 28 Estate Planning 177. (*Digested under* Estate Planning, page 49.)

"Proposed regulations furnish home-sale exclusion guidance" (2001). On October 6, 2000, the IRS issued proposed regulations for Section 121. The proposed regulations, while not complete in coverage, do provide valuable guidance for taxpayers structuring their transactions.

First, the author discusses the facts-and-circumstances test. Proposed Regulation § 1.121-1(a) contains the general provisions of the law. A taxpayer can exclude gain from the sale or exchange of property, if during the five-year period ending on the date of the sale or exchange, such property has been owned and used by the taxpayer as the taxpayer's principal residence for periods aggregating at least two years. Proposed Regulation § 1.121-1(b) addresses the definition of "principal residence." This section provides that whether or not property is the taxpayer's principal residence, and whether or not property is used by the taxpayer as the taxpayer's principal residence (if a taxpayer uses more than one property as a residence), depends on all the facts and circumstances.

Next, the author considers the "use" requirement and explores the definition of "use" for purposes of the Section 121 exclusion.

Then, the author addresses depreciation adjustments. Proposed Regulation § 1.121-1(d) prevents a taxpayer from using the Section 121 exclusion to shelter gain attributable to certain depreciation deductions. The exclusion does not apply to so much of the gain from the sale or exchange of property as does not exceed the portion of the depreciation adjustments (as defined in Section 1250(b)(3)) attributable to periods after May 6, 1997, in respect to the property. Proposed Regulation § 1.121-1(e) prescribes that the Section 121 exclusion does not apply to the extent that depreciation attributable to periods after May 6, 1997 exceeds gain allocable to the business-use portion of the property.

Finally, the author discusses dollar limitations, the general rule limiting a taxpayer to one sale or exchange every two years, reduced exclusion, property of a deceased spouse, property owned by a spouse or former spouse, cooperative housing corporations, involuntary conversions, out-of-state residence care, sales of remainder interests, expatriates, the election not to have the exclusion apply, and other sources of guidance relevant to the application of Section 121. (M. Schlesinger, 66 Practical Tax Strategies 132.)

"Putting home in trust reduced excludable gain" (2001). Gain on the sale of a taxpayer's principal residence that was put in a trust qualified for the home-sale exclusion only to the extent that the taxpayer was deemed an owner due to a retained "5 or 5 power," according to Letter Ruling 200104005. (66 Practical Tax Strategies 182.)

"Rental deductions are more restrictive at home" (2001). 67 Practical Tax Strategies 184. (*Digested under* Business Expenses—Personal Expenses Versus Business Expenses, page 13.)

"Renting home office to employer can reduce deductions" (2001). 67 Practical Tax Strategies 184. (*Digested under* Business

Expenses—Personal Expenses Versus Business Expenses, page 13.)

"Revocation of favorable Section 121 ruling may have collateral implications" (2001). In Letter Ruling 200004022, a husband and wife were able to claim the exclusion under Section 121(b) for the sale of their principal residence despite the fact that the house had been held in a partnership prior to the sale. In Letter Ruling 200119014, however, the IRS revoked Letter Ruling 200004022 as not being in accord with the current views of the IRS. Nevertheless, the IRS failed to say exactly what its current views are, and how those views might affect other transactions or planning with disregarded entities. (95 Journal of Taxation 118.)

PERSONAL SERVICE CORPORATIONS

(*See* Professional Corporations)

POINTS

(*See* Interest Paid)

POWERS OF APPOINTMENT

(*See* Estate Planning; Estates and Estate Tax)

PREPARATION OF RETURNS

(*See* Tax Practice and Practitioners)

PRIVATE FOUNDATIONS

(*See* Tax-Exempt Organizations—Private Foundations)

PROCEDURE

(*See also* Assessment and Collection; Interest and Penalties; Tax Practice and Practitioners)

In General

"Alternative dispute resolution can beat litigation" (2001). Although still in their infancy, alternative dispute resolution (ADR) programs allow taxpayers to settle some issues with the IRS more expeditiously and with lower professional fees than traditional litigation.

First, the authors discuss ADR activities and options. ADR is considered to have various advantages over litigation. The relative advantage of ADR shrinks, however, as the process assumes more litigation-like characteristics (i.e., more procedural, legal formality). Some ADR processes are unassisted (i.e., the parties settle the matter themselves without outside help). Most of the more-formalized processes, however, are assisted.

Unassisted ADR is a fancy term to describe what we all do daily—negotiate. The disputing parties set a time and place (and possibly an agenda) to discuss a resolution to the dispute with no third-party assistance. An extremely informal form of negotiation would be a conference or lunch meeting set to discuss the particular issue/topic.

Assisted ADR comes in a variety of types. They range in levels of formality and are distinguished between adversarial (those that usually include professionals inhabiting traditional roles inside a "win/lose" environment) and facilitative (those that bring the party's participation to the forefront and include a neutral third party or parties that guide the parties toward their own resolution of the dispute).

Then, the authors address the IRS's perspective, ADR procedures, and mediation and arbitration. The IRS Office of Appeals has offered two forms of ADR on a limited basis since late 1995, mediation and arbitration coupled with early referral of issues. These processes have been expanded over the past few years and have been codified in Section 7123.

The procedures used to move an issue to mediation vary between the Office of Chief Counsel and the Office of Appeals. Since both the taxpayer and the IRS are "getting the feel" in this arena, both the process and the tenor of the proceedings should be expected to change often and be updated frequently as both sides gain experience. (R.S. Mark, R. Desbrow & J.C. Miller, 67 Practical Tax Strategies 227.)

"Appeals may execute closing agreement for certain docketed cases" (2001). A Tennessee federal district court affirmed in *Crowell* (2001) a bankruptcy court's decision that a closing agreement executed by an associate appeals chief is valid, even though related Tax Court cases were pending. (66 Practical Tax Strategies 291.)

"Burden of proof did not shift under Section 7491" (2001). The Tax Court held in *Sykes* (2001) that the burden of proof did not shift to the IRS, since the taxpayers did not first introduce credible evidence with respect to the amount of the taxpayers' cash hoard. (67 Practical Tax Strategies 175.)

"Information statements can now be provided to taxpayers electronically" (2001). Temporary and proposed regulations allow employers and payers to electronically provide taxpayers with copies of their Forms W-2 ("Wage and Tax Statement"), Forms 1098-T ("Tuition Payments Statement"), and Forms 1098-E ("Education Loan Statement"). World Wide Web technology may be used to provide the forms electronically.

After providing background, the author discusses encouragement for electronic filing by the Revenue Reconciliation Act of 1998 (RRA '98). Section 6011(f), added by RRA '98, authorizes the Treasury to encourage the use and to promote the benefits of electronic tax administration programs as they become available.

Then, the author considers the rules and requirements for filing electronically. The temporary and proposed regulations on electronically provided information statements are consistent with congressional policy to increase electronic filings in order to increase compliance and minimize compliance costs. They also incorporate the concerns of government that the statements' recipients will have: (1) the ability to access their statements in a timely manner and (2) the information that they need to make an informed decision as to whether to access their statements electronically. In addition, the temporary and proposed regulations reflect the desires of information statement providers to reduce compliance costs and modernize business practices. (N.J. Foran, 13 Taxation of Exempts 100.)

"IRS memo explains requirements for offer in compromise" (2001). 67 Practical Tax Strategies 182. (*Digested under* Assessment and Collection—In General, page 6.)

"IRS rolls out its new program to resolve ongoing issues before taxpayers file" (2001). Revenue Procedure 2001-22 contains the guidelines for a new and innovative prefiling agreement (PFA) program.

A significant and costly problem for larger business taxpayers arises when the treatment of a particular issue involves multiple years and, often, multiple audits. The new IRS is trying out a program to get these issues resolved before the taxpayer files its next return. A successful pilot project has led to the adoption of a full-fledged program, with IRS estimates that seventy-five taxpayers will be accepted.

After providing background on large-case issue resolution, the author discusses the highlights of Revenue Procedure 2001-22, the Large and Mid-size Business (LMSB) PFA request, and the selection process. Revenue Procedure 2001-22 is de-signed to allow eligible taxpayers to resolve, before filing of the next-year tax return, the tax treatment of an issue likely to be disputed in a post-filing audit. Guidelines are set forth on taxpayer eligibility, suitable and unsuitable issues, PFA request criteria, the IRS screening and processing methodology, steps to follow in examining and resolving the issue, development and execution of the PFA, and other miscellaneous information. The program is available to all taxpayers under the jurisdiction of the LMSB division.

Revenue Procedure 2001-22 contains a list of suitable, unsuitable, and exclusive international issues as guidelines for a taxpayer considering if a particular issue has PFA potential. The potential PFA issue must meet a stern test, in that it must involve either an agreed-on factual determination or application of "settled tax law" as it relates to agreed-on facts between the taxpayer and the IRS.

Section 4 of the procedure lists the specific information required to be included in the PFA request. No format is suggested in the guidelines, other than that the document must be in writing and signed by an authorized party under penalties of perjury. A request in either letter or memorandum form should be acceptable. Section 5 of Revenue Procedure 2001-22 covers the PFA selection process after the PFA request is submitted by the taxpayer. Section 6 of the procedure covers the workflow for PFAs that are accepted into the program.

Then, the author considers the PFA closing agreement. The LMSB PFA document executed between the taxpayer and the IRS is treated as a closing agreement under Section 7121 and must comply with the requirements of Revenue Procedure 68-16.

Finally, the author turns to other issues affecting potential PFA participants, future programs, and the impact of the LMSB PFA program. (D.R. Stubblefield, 94 Journal of Taxation 197.)

"IRS waived signature requirement on joint return" (2001). The Tenth Circuit held, in *Olpin* (2001), that the IRS waived the signature requirement on the taxpayers' joint individual income tax return when it accepted the return, failed to send the return back to the taxpayers for the proper signatures, and used the unsigned return during a bankruptcy proceeding. (66 Practical Tax Strategies 178.)

"Offer in compromise denied for partner's share of partnership's taxes" (2001). 95 Journal of Taxation 252. (*Digested under* Partners and Partnerships—In General, page 140.)

"Prefiling agreement program: expanded and permanent" (2001). The prefiling agreement (PFA) program will be offered permanently and in an expanded format to large and mid-size business taxpayers (Revenue Procedure 2001-22 and IR-2001-9). PFAs allow a taxpayer to request examination of specific issues relating to a tax return before it is filed. (12 Journal of International Taxation, No. 5, 6.)

"Tax Court correct forum for income tax levy appeal" (2001). An Ohio federal district court dismissed a tax levy appeal case in *Geller* (2001) because the Tax Court has jurisdiction over income tax issues and liabilities, and an appeal to a district court is only proper when the Tax Court lacks jurisdiction. (67 Practical Tax Strategies 360.)

Attorney Fees

"IRS was wrong, but no attorney's fees awarded" (2001). A Pennsylvania federal district court held in *Bloom* (2001) that although the IRS was wrong and lost its counterclaim, the taxpayer did not establish all of the requirements necessary to be awarded reasonable litigation costs. (67 Practical Tax Strategies 299.)

"Must exhaust administrative remedies to get attorney's fees" (2001). The Tax Court held in *Jensen* (2000) that the taxpayer must exhaust all administrative remedies in order to be awarded attorney's fees pursuant to Section 7430. (66 Practical Tax Strategies 45.)

"Taxpayer not prevailing party so no litigation costs awarded" (2001). The Fourth Circuit affirmed the Tax Court's decision not to award litigation costs to the taxpayers in *Dang* (2001). (67 Practical Tax Strategies 174.)

Confidentiality and Disclosure of Return Information

"IRS may disclose another taxpayer's return information in a multiple-party transaction" (2001). The IRS may disclose tax return information of buyers of a business pursuant to an interrogatory from the seller, according to ILM 200121007. (95 Journal of Taxation 187.)

"Special agents' good-faith interpretation of law precludes damages" (2001). A Florida federal district court held in *Comyns* (2001) that a special agent's disclosure of the criminal nature of the investigation was not an unlawful disclosure under Section 6103 that permits damages under Section 7431. (67 Practical Tax Strategies 44.)

Refunds

"Employee statement needed for employer to get FICA refund" (2001). FSA 200044001 offers guidance on the type of written statement an employer must receive from employees in order to obtain a refund of overpaid employee and employer FICA tax. (66 Practical Tax Strategies 50.)

"Fuel excise tax credits are not limited by one-claim rule" (2001). The Tax Court, in *FPL Group, Inc.* (2001), adopted a federal court's interpretation of the interplay between Sections 34 and 6427(i) by holding that taxpayers seeking to obtain additional credits for fuel excise taxes for non-highway use are not limited to the one-claim doctrine, which limits refund claims. (66 Practical Tax Strategies 241.)

"Interest is refunded until due date not credit date" (2001). The Court of Federal Claims held in *Marsh & McLennan Cos.*

(2001) that the taxpayer was entitled to interest on its overpayment from the date of the overpayment to only the due date of the return for which the overpayment was credited. (67 Practical Tax Strategies 244.)

"IRS reverses its position on late returns and refund claims: the mailbox rule will apply" (2001). In July and August 2000, the Second and Eighth Circuits issued conflicting opinions in two cases concerning the ability of late-filing taxpayers to claim refunds. New developments have effectively eliminated the conflict between the circuits and provided taxpayers with the certainty, if the facts are supportive, of a favorable outcome.

First, the author provides background on the conflicting opinions. The cases with the coincidental fact patterns were *Weisbart* (2d Cir. 2000) and *Anastasoff* (8th Cir. 2000).

Then, the author addresses the development of the IRS position. Despite the IRS's victory in *Anastasoff*, and despite victories in several lower courts under identical facts, the IRS has now conceded that refunds should be granted under these facts. The IRS issued AOD 2000-09 to formally announce its acquiescence in *Weisbart* and describe the exact nature of the concession. The IRS explained that it will henceforth apply the mailbox rule of Section 7502(a) to refund claims contained in late returns mailed within three years of their due date, and, further, those refund claims will be deemed to have been received on the date of mailing for purposes of Section 6511(b)(2)(A), the three-year look-back rule.

In addition, new Regulation § 301.7502-1(f) specifically states that Section 7502 will apply separately to a refund claim contained within a late return if the postmark is within the three-year period (plus any extensions of time to file) from the date the tax was paid or deemed to have been paid, assuming all other conditions of Section 7502 are satisfied. The new regulation then goes even further, and states that such a return will itself be deemed under Section 7502 to have been filed on the postmark date.

Finally, the author analyzes the IRS position and discusses the effective date for the new rules. (P.N. Jones, 94 Journal of Taxation 81.)

"Mailbox rule exception was not met" (2001). A Georgia federal district court granted a summary judgment in *Cardinal Textile Sales, Inc.* (2001), holding that the taxpayer did not satisfy the necessary requirements to rely on the mailbox rule exception for filing timely refund claims. (67 Practical Tax Strategies 302.)

"Return with error was a valid claim for refund" (2001). An original filed return that contains an invalid Social Security number can be considered a valid refund claim, according to SCA 200108041. (66 Practical Tax Strategies 302.)

"Untimely suit prevents payment versus deposit determination" (2001). A New Jersey federal district court in *Pransky* (2001) held that a bankruptcy petition filed more than two years after the IRS's notice of disallowance was too late to contest the disallowance, but the court had jurisdiction to decide whether a remittance was a deposit or payment of tax for subsequent years. (67 Practical Tax Strategies 46.)

Summonses

"Accountant's documents not covered by privilege" (2001). A Massachusetts federal district court held in *Cavallaro* (2001) that certain documents prepared by accountants were not privileged and thus not protected by the attorney-client privilege. (67 Practical Tax Strategies 358.)

"Summons quashed based on attorney-client privilege" (2001). A California federal district court held in *Segerstrom* (2001) that an IRS summons should be quashed, since it requested information and documents that were protected from disclosure by the attorney-client privilege. (66 Practical Tax Strategies 290.)

Tax Court

"'Mailbox rule' applied despite mailing instructions error" **(2001).** A properly addressed petition sent to the Tax Court using a private delivery service was timely sent and thus timely filed even though it arrived late because the airbill had been completed incorrectly, in *Estate of Cranor* (2001). (66 Practical Tax Strategies 244.)

"Postmark date controls when determining if petition was timely" **(2001).** The Tax Court in *Hendley* (2000) dismissed a petition for lack of jurisdiction when it determined that the taxpayer's petition for redetermination was not timely filed. The postmark date, rather than extrinsic evidence, determines whether the petition was timely filed. (66 Practical Tax Strategies 45.)

"Tax Court properly applied equitable recoupment doctrine" **(2001).** The Ninth Circuit has affirmed the Tax Court in *Estate of Branson* (2001), holding that the Tax Court has the authority to apply the doctrine of equitable recoupment and that the doctrine was properly applied when the court's revaluation of stock resulted in an income tax overpayment by a residuary beneficiary and an estate tax deficiency. (67 Practical Tax Strategies 318.)

PROFESSIONAL CORPORATIONS

"Are amounts paid to shareholder/employees wages or dividend distributions?" **(2001).** 3 Business Entities, No. 5, 55. (*Digested under* Compensation for Personal Services, page 25.)

"Engineering company was not a personal services corporation" **(2001).** A corporation engaged in geotechnical testing and engineering services was not a qualified personal service corporation, according to the Tax Court in *Alron Engineering & Testing Corp.* (2000). Consequently, it was not subject to the 35 percent flat tax rate under Section 11(b)(2). (66 Practical Tax Strategies 126.)

"When service corporations liquidate as part of a change in form of entity—the problem of goodwill" **(2001).** J.C. Zimmerman, 95 Journal of Taxation 110. (*Digested under* Liquidations, page 125.)

PROFIT-SHARING PLANS

(*See* Pension and Profit-Sharing Plans)

Q

QUALIFIED TERMINABLE
INTEREST PROPERTY (QTIP)

(*See* Marital Deduction)

R

REAL ESTATE

(*See also* Capital Gains and Losses; Depreciation and Amortization; Interest Paid; Like-Kind Exchanges; Personal Residence)

"Agreement to name mall after company does not produce impermissible tenant services for REIT" (2001). An agreement by a real estate investment trust (REIT) to name a mall project after a company did not constitute services furnished to a tenant, according to Letter Ruling 200140026. (95 Journal of Taxation 375.)

"Developer could allocate estimate costs to lots sold" (2001). The Tax Court held, in *Hutchinson* (2001), that under the alternative cost method, a real estate developer, in calculating gain on the sale of residential lots, could allocate to the developer's bases in the lots sold estimated construction costs relating to certain common improvements to the development. (66 Practical Tax Strategies 314.)

"Estate planning benefits of deferred like-kind exchanges of real estate" (2001). M. Kove & J.M. Kosakow, 28 Estate Planning 372. (*Digested under* Like-Kind Exchanges, page 121.)

"Federal and state tax consequences of synthetic leasing—multiple benefits, minimal risks" (2001). Tax practitioners who operate in multiple jurisdictions have long made use of transactions that are treated in one manner for one jurisdiction and differently in another jurisdiction. The goal is a structure in which the taxpayer receives the most favorable results possible in each of the jurisdictions involved.

Synthetic leasing is such a structure. Although the transaction is structured and documented in the form of a lease, the benefits and burdens of ownership establish that the lessee, not the lessor, is the owner of the property for tax purposes. The lessor's title ownership of the property is more like a security interest in the property.

To achieve this result, a synthetic lease relies on the fundamental U.S. tax principle that the substance of a transaction and not the form governs the U.S. federal tax consequences. Using a synthetic lease in a context in which another system respects the form, or applies different rules to determine the substance, creates the opportunity for two different persons to be treated as the owner for U.S. tax purposes and for the purposes of the second jurisdiction (or applicable system), respectively. (S.G. Frost & P. Carman, 95 Journal of Taxation 361.)

"Final regulations exclude some construction allowances" (2001). Final regulations explain when lessees can exclude construction allowances received from lessors to construct qualified long-term real property. (66 Practical Tax Strategies 52.)

"Final regulations on Section 467 rental agreements" (2001). The IRS has issued amendments to the regulations under Section 467. The final regulations adopt, without change, the proposed regulations and clarify three amendments to the regulations. (66 Practical Tax Strategies 121.)

"Find the right place for REITs in an investment portfolio" (2001). Real estate investment trusts (REITs) currently possess several favorable investment attributes that should provide investors with important diversification benefits and an attractive total return. While REITs avoid the double taxation problem of C corporations, they are required to distribute to shareholders almost all of their taxable income as dividends in order to retain their REIT status. This distribution requirement may present an impediment to investing in REITs for taxable accounts. Investors may employ strategies, however, to mitigate the adverse impact of a high level of dividend distributions on REIT after-tax return.

After providing background on REITs, including their favorable investment attributes, qualifying for REIT status, and taxation of the REIT shareholder, the author compares retirement and taxable accounts. Because a large portion of a REIT's total return is composed of dividends, most of which are immediately taxable as ordinary income, and because REITs are expected to generate equity-like returns, REITs make ideal candidates for retirement accounts. There are, however, several situations where the investor will want to place a REIT investment in a taxable account:

(1) The investment is not intended to meet retirement needs. Instead, it is intended to meet a shorter-term goal, such as the down payment on a house.

(2) Other investments that are actually less tax efficient than REITs are allocated to retirement plans up to the contribution limits. Examples of investments that might fall into this category are high-yield bonds and equities that are traded with sufficient frequency for capital gains to be short term and, consequently, taxed at ordinary income tax rates.

(3) The retirement plan at work does not offer an opportunity to invest in REITs. (This will very often be the case.) While most investors can always invest in REITs through IRAs, the annual contribution limits for an IRA are rather limited, even after the increased amounts allowed under the Economic Growth and Tax Relief Reconciliation Act of 2001.

(4) The REITs are intended as a source to meet immediate income needs. Since REITs offer a high level of immediate income plus the opportunity for the income stream to increase with inflation, REITs are ideally suited for a retiree who needs to augment his or her other income sources. (R.B. Toolson, 67 Practical Tax Strategies 92.)

"IRS again okays synthetic lease arrangement—not a financing transaction" (2001). In recently released FSA 1998456, the IRS concluded that a synthetic lease between a taxpayer and a special-purpose entity should be treated as a sale-leaseback for tax purposes and not as a financing transaction. (94 Journal of Taxation 56.)

"IRS relies on obsolete revenue rulings in finding accounting method change had no effect on REIT status" (2001). Positive adjustments resulting from a corporation's change in accounting method does not affect its status as a real estate investment trust, according to Letter Ruling 200115023. (95 Journal of Taxation 57.)

"Landlord's lease termination payments to tenant were capital gain" (2001). 94 Journal of Taxation 118. (*Digested under* Capital Gains and Losses, page 18.)

"Lease surrender payment is taxed as capital gain" (2001). The amount a tenant with a below-market rent was paid to surrender lease rights in a premises was capital gain, not ordinary income, according to Letter Ruling 200045019. (66 Practical Tax Strategies 53.)

"Opportunities for the foreign investor in U.S. real estate—if planning comes first" (2001). Congress enacted the Foreign Investment in Real Property Tax Act of 1980 (FIRPTA) to ensure that foreign investors are subject to at least one level of federal income tax when they dispose of U.S. real estate investments. Notwithstanding FIRPTA's simple, clear-cut directive, foreign investors still face a host of planning opportunities and potential problems.

First, the authors discuss the essential considerations that should be understood before any decisions are made to invest in the United States. These considerations include: (1) who is a foreign investor; (2) the activities that rise to the level of a trade or business; (3) the estate and gift tax ramifications of U.S. investments; and (4) the basic tenets of tax liability under FIRPTA and the withholding mechanism that ensures collection of the tax.

Then, the authors explore planning opportunities, including partnership versus REIT investments and possible investment structures. Notwithstanding FIRPTA, planning opportunities still exist for foreign investors seeking to invest in U.S. real estate. Prudent use of secured debt as an alternative investment vehicle can potentially eliminate all U.S. tax exposure. For those seeking equity positions, care in structuring the investment can limit the tax exposure to one level of tax on sale or possibly no tax. The key for any investor is to do the planning before acquiring the U.S. real estate. Once the asset has been acquired, there is far less flexibility to restructure the investment without potentially triggering a tax liability. (M. Hirschfeld & S. Grossman, 94 Journal of Taxation 36.)

"Rental real estate gets installment payment break" (2001). 66 Practical Tax Strategies 380. (*Digested under* Estates and Estate Tax—In General, page 53.)

"State nonconformity to federal legislation could complicate REIT planning" (2001). S.D. Smith, S. Amitay & J.K. Stewart, 3 Business Entities, No. 1, 30. (*Digested under* State Taxes—In General, page 202.)

"Taxpayer must capitalize costs of cleaning up preacquisition contamination" (2001). In Letter Ruling 200108029, the IRS ruled that a taxpayer had to capitalize the costs incurred to clean up land contaminated before the taxpayer purchased it. The IRS further ruled that insurance proceeds related to the cleanup must be treated as a reduction of basis and would be taxable only if the taxpayer's basis in the land was less than zero. (94 Journal of Taxation 316.)

"The real spin on the new spinoff ruling— should corporate-owned real estate be put into REITs?" (2001). On June 4, 2001, the IRS issued Revenue Ruling 2001-29, holding that a real estate investment trust (REIT) could be engaged in an "active trade or business" within the meaning of Section 355(b), and obsoleting Revenue Ruling 73-236, which held to the contrary. After this ruling, a corporation is no longer precluded from spinning off rental real estate into a REIT. While most practitioners were not surprised by the ruling, the amount of media attention it garnered was surprising. From trade press newsletters to the Wall Street Journal, the revenue ruling was viewed as a tax-free road map to monetizing billions of dollars worth of corporate real estate. After some reflection, however, it is apparent this is not the case.

After providing background on Revenue Rulings 2001-29 and 73-236, the author discusses planning. To the extent that a taxable C corporation with significant real estate holdings is distributing nondeductible dividends, it may be worth considering the REIT structure. In addition, the real estate may be diluting higher growth earnings of the parent corporation, which could be better reflected if the real estate were spun off in a separate entity. The real estate also may be capable of attracting better equity or debt financing in a separate REIT vehicle than if it is retained in the parent entity. (D.L. Brandon, 95 Journal of Taxation 92.)

"When does self-employment tax take root on farm rents?" (2001). T.D. Englebrecht & J.D. Smullen, 66 Practical Tax Strategies 277. (*Digested under* Self-Employment Tax, page 194.)

REAL ESTATE TAXES

(*See* State Taxes)

REDEMPTIONS

(*See also* Dividends and Distributions; Estates and Estate Tax; Reorganizations)

"Avoiding the attribution rules in redemptions by estates and trusts" (2001). It is frequently desirable to redeem stock owned by an estate or trust. However, because of the close family relationships often involved in such cases and the consequent application of the stock attribution rules, it may be difficult to qualify the redemption as an exchange transaction taxable as a capital gain rather than as ordinary income. In certain circumstances, the estate or trust may avoid family attribution in order to qualify a redemption for capital gain treatment. But the rules can be complex and confusing, and have been the subject of misinterpretation and misapplication in the past. This article provides a road map for the type of redemptions that may be accomplished without running afoul of the attribution rules.

After reviewing the stock attribution rules applicable to estates and trusts, the author discusses the tax treatment of redemptions. Under Section 302(a), a redemption of stock is treated as an exchange of stock by the redeemed shareholder, resulting in capital gain rather than a dividend taxable as ordinary income, if the transaction complies with Section 302(b)(1), Section 302(b)(2), Section 302(b)(3), or Section 302(b)(4).

Then, the author considers Section 303 redemptions. Section 303 provides exchange (rather than dividend) treatment upon the redemption of stock from an estate-shareholder if the stock is included in the gross estate for estate tax purposes, and has a value exceeding 35 percent of the decedent's gross estate (less certain expenses and deductions under Section 2053 or Section 2054). Section 303 applies only to the extent that the redemption distribution does not exceed the amount of estate, inheritance, legacy, and succession taxes paid by the estate, plus allowable funeral and administrative expenses paid by the estate.

Finally, the author addresses avoiding dividend treatment on a redemption by an estate or trust under Section 302. In attempting to avoid dividend treatment for a redemption under Section 302, the problem often plaguing an estate or trust is that the attribution rules may make it difficult or impossible to achieve a sufficient reduction of ownership interest to satisfy the requirements of Section 302. (R.W. Harris, 28 Estate Planning 317.)

"Basis recovery not limited to basis of actual shares redeemed" (2001). In FSA 200111004, the IRS concluded that Section 304, as amended by the Taxpayer Relief Act of 1997, does not limit a shareholder's basis

recovery to only the basis of the shares actually redeemed. At issue in this FSA was the effect of the language of an amendment to Section 304(a)(1) and whether that language manifested congressional intent to limit the shareholder's basis recovery. (95 Journal of Taxation 56.)

"Regulations clarify tax on divorce-related stock redemption" (2001). 67 Practical Tax Strategies 254. (*Digested under* Husband and Wife—Divorce and Separation, page 79.)

"Regulations clarify tax on stock redemptions incident to divorce" (2001). T.R. Koski, 67 Practical Tax Strategies 282. (*Digested under* Husband and Wife—Divorce and Separation, page 79.)

REFUNDS

(*See* Procedure—Refunds)

RELATED TAXPAYERS

(*See* Affiliated Corporations; Allocations Among Related Taxpayers; Partners and Partnerships)

REORGANIZATIONS

(*See also* Affiliated Corporations; Bankruptcy; Dividends and Distributions; Redemptions)

"CFC restructuring and disposition—how international provisions alter the general rules" (2001). J.M. Calianno & B.J. Gregoire, 12 Journal of International Taxation, No. 10, 34. (*Digested under* Foreign Corporations, Persons, and Partnerships, page 56.)

"Creative transactional planning using the partnership merger and division regula-

tions" (2001). B.D. Rubin & A.M. Whiteway, 95 Journal of Taxation 133. (*Digested under* Partners and Partnerships—In General, page 135.)

"Final regulations on allocation of purchase price to assets affect actual and deemed sales" (2001). Final regulations under Sections 338 and 1060 provide rules for determining the amount realized and the amount of basis allocated to each asset transferred in a deemed or actual asset acquisition.

First, the authors provide background on qualified stock purchases (QSPs). A purchasing corporation can elect to treat a stock acquisition as a purchase of the underlying assets if it acquires 80 percent of the total voting power and 80 percent of the total value of the stock of a target corporation by purchase within a twelve-month period (i.e., a QSP). If a Section 338 election is made, the target is treated as if: (1) old target sold all of its assets at fair market value (FMV) and (2) new target purchased all of the assets as of the beginning of the day after the acquisition date. There are two types of elections that can be made under Section 338.

Then, the authors address Section 338(g) elections. The final regulations provide a general model of the transactions deemed to occur if a Section 338(g) election is made. Under Regulation § 1.338-1(a), the transactions specified in the final regulations are to be treated as if they actually occurred, and any resulting tax consequences are to be taken into account.

Under the Section 338(g) election model, old target is treated as transferring all of its assets to an unrelated person in exchange for consideration that includes the assumption of, or taking subject to, liabilities. New target is treated as acquiring all of its assets from an unrelated person in exchange for consideration that includes the assumption of, or taking subject to, liabilities. In a Section 338(h)(10) election, old target also is deemed to liquidate following the deemed asset sale.

Regulation § 1.338-1(a)(2) also clarifies that other rules of law apply to the deemed transaction as if the parties actually had

engaged in it, eliminating any uncertainty that may have existed under the former regulations as to tax consequences for old target and new target (such as income and deduction) in addition to old target's gain or loss realized on its deemed sale of assets. In addition, the characterization as a deemed asset sale apparently would apply for purposes of fifteen-year amortization under Section 197.

New target generally is treated as a new corporation that is not related to old target for purposes of Subtitle A. Regulation § 1.338-1(b)(2), however, contains a list of exceptions, i.e., Code sections for purposes of which old target and new target are considered the same corporation notwithstanding the deemed asset sale between the two (primarily affecting retirement plans and similar provisions).

Then, the authors address the Section 338(h)(10) model. Regulation § 1.338 (h)(10)-1 details the qualification rules and consequences of the Section 338(h)(10) election and provides a model on which taxation of the Section 338(h)(10) election is based. In a Section 338(h)(10) transaction old target is deemed to sell its assets to new target, distribute the proceeds to its shareholders, and cease to exist. In addition, this regulation clarifies several issues associated with a Section 338(h)(10) election, including: (1) whether old target's distribution of the sale proceeds and any retained assets is deemed to be a liquidation; (2) special S corporation issues; and (3) whether the installment method is available and may be applied to tiered targets.

Finally, the authors consider miscellaneous changes (affecting the test for relatedness, the anti-abuse rule, the next-day rule, the voting stock requirement, and definitions) and the impact of Section 1060 in regard to a series of related transactions, asymmetrical transfers, multiple trades or businesses, transaction costs, written allocation agreements, covenants entered by the seller, and like-kind exchanges. (C.E. MacNeil, A. Sargent & S.R. Wegener, 95 Journal of Taxation 15.)

"Final regulations on partnership mergers and divisions" (2001). Final regulations (Regulation §§ 1.708-1(c) and 1.708-1(d)) were recently issued on partnership mergers and divisions. The regulations were finalized substantially as proposed, with some interesting comments and revisions. (3 Business Entities, No. 2, 51.)

"Final regulations under Section 708 on partnership mergers and divisions" (2001). W.H. Caudill & C.J. Lallo, 3 Business Entities, No. 5, 6. (*Digested under* Partners and Partnerships—In General, page 138.)

"International aspects of Section 355 transactions" (2001). J.M. Calianno, 12 Journal of International Taxation, No. 1, 12. (*Digested under* Foreign Corporations, Persons, and Partnerships, page 58.)

"IRS lists factors for disregarding circular flows of cash" (2001). In FSA 200106004, the IRS has concluded that not all circular flows of cash occurring as part of a plan of reorganization for restructuring a corporate group may be disregarded under the circular flow of cash doctrine. (94 Journal of Taxation 313.)

"IRS reissues Section 355(e) proposed regulations as temporary—be careful what you wish for" (2001). The "second round" of proposed regulations issued under Section 355(e) focused on defining the circumstances in which an acquisition and a spinoff would be seen as part of a prohibited plan (or series of related transactions), and was exceedingly well-received. The proposed regulations had no practical impact, however—except, perhaps, as insight into what the IRS's ruling position might be—until such time as they might be finalized. Accordingly, practitioners advising their clients were left to navigate this complex provision armed only with the existing authority: cryptic statutory language and the equally opaque legislative history that accompanied its enactment.

In response to this void, the IRS took the unusual step of converting the proposed regulations into temporary regulations. As a result, advisers now possess a comprehensive document that they can employ to assist clients in judging whether an acquisition that follows or precedes an otherwise qualifying spinoff will be amalgamated with that spinoff for purposes of Section 355(e).

This might not be the salutary development that, at first blush, it seems to be. The IRS's ruling position, with respect to transactions that occurred before the proposed regulations were upgraded to authority status, seemed to be unusually liberal. Now that the IRS, with respect to its ruling responsibilities, is bound by the provisions of the temporary regulations, it is entirely possible that the same transactions, evaluated in the sometimes harsh light of the temporary regulations, would not elicit the same favorable response.

First, the author discusses the temporary regulations. The temporary regulations are identical in almost all respects to the proposed regulations, which were issued to implement the most contentious aspect of the "anti-*Morris Trust*" provisions that are manifested in Section 355(e). This is the portion of the statute that inquires whether a spinoff, which otherwise qualifies under Section 355(a), is part of a plan (or series of related transactions) pursuant to which one or more persons acquire stock representing a 50 percent (or greater) interest—measured by ownership of stock possessing the requisite voting power or value of all classes of stock—in either the distributing or distributed corporation.

Then, the author addresses the impact of the IRS's position in Letter Rulings 200104024, 200115001, 200133035, 200131003, and 200125011 as well as TD 8960. While the conversion of the proposed regulations into temporary regulations is generally viewed as a positive development since it arms practitioners with the concrete guidance they will need to effectively advise their clients with regard to the plan issue that is at the heart of Section 355(e), a study of the rulings issued by the IRS in the period prior to that conversion suggests that this may turn out to be a Pyrrhic victory.

The rulings indicate that the IRS has been willing to ignore evidence that an acquisition and distribution were parts of a plan in circumstances where, most notably, the parties were able to represent that the spinoff would have occurred at the same time and in a similar form regardless of the ensuing acquisition—in short, where the steps were not mutually interdependent. With the advent of TD 8960, however, this ruling flexibility likely will be lost as the IRS undoubtedly will shape its ruling policy around the presence or absence of the factors set forth in the temporary regulations that tend to show that the steps were component parts of a single plan. (R. Willens, 95 Journal of Taxation 197.)

"IRS reproposes anti-Morris trust regulations" (2001). On January 2, 2001, the IRS withdrew some very controversial proposed regulations under Section 355(e) interpreting the concept of "a plan or series of related transactions" and replaced them with a set of new proposed regulations. In so doing, the IRS substantially modified both the structure of the regulations themselves and the reach of the rules interpreting this aspect of Section 355(e) and, in general, removed the most offensive components of the previous set of proposed regulations.

After reviewing the history of Section 355(e) and the original proposed regulations, the authors discuss the new proposed regulations in detail. In general, the new proposed regulations focus on clarifying which acquisitions of distributing or controlled stock are part of a "plan or series of related transactions." Although there are no bright lines drawn in these regulations, they do provide safe harbors that taxpayers may rely upon. The new regulations drop the basic approach of the initial proposed regulations, which attempted to define a plan, and instead, adopt a weighing approach similar to the analysis involved when determining whether a distribution satisfies the device requirement.

The new proposed regulations take a facts-and-circumstances approach to the determination of the existence of a plan, but then set forth: (1) a nonexclusive list of factors that tend to demonstrate the existence of a plan; (2) a nonexclusive list of factors that tend to demonstrate the absence of a

plan; and (3) several safe harbors that can be relied on to conclude that there is no plan. In addition, several examples help to clarify the approach taken in the regulations.

Then, the authors provide commentary on the new proposed regulations. The IRS has managed to give practitioners enough guidance to advise clients with a reasonable degree of certainty in most transactions. As a practical matter, practitioners will be able to advise clients that if they respect a six-month "stand still" period just prior to, and after, a spin-off, they can be very confident in their ability to satisfy the proposed regulations. However, the proposed regulations build in enough flexibility so that the IRS can effectively police the area based on events occurring in close proximity to the spin-off, even if not specifically contemplated at the time of the distribution.

There are aspects of the proposed regulations that must be clarified before they are finalized—in particular the "reasonable certainty" provision in the operating rules and the rules relating to general public trading. But on the whole they are a very positive step in the right direction. (W. Galanis & H. Sobol, 3 Business Entities, No. 1, 4.)

"IRS treats multistep acquisition as a single merger" (2001). In Revenue Ruling 2001-46, the IRS has ruled that the merger of a subsidiary into a target corporation, followed by the merger of the target into the acquiring parent, is a single statutory merger of the target into the parent. That merger is a tax-free reorganization under Section 368(a)(1)(A). (67 Practical Tax Strategies 381.)

"Leveraged buy-out effected by transitory corporation treated as redemption and acquiror's liabilities treated as incurred by target" (2001). FSA 200126001 involves the characterization under the step-transaction doctrine of a leveraged buy-out effected through a transitory acquisition corporation. (3 Business Entities, No. 5, 55.)

"Merger of S corporations does not terminate S elections" (2001). 3 Business Entities, No. 4, 52. (*Digested under* S Corporations, page 187.)

177

"Presumptions of golden parachute proposed regulations rebutted by mergers' facts" (2001). In Letter Ruling 200110009, the issue was the effect of two mergers on the Section 280G excess parachute payment rules. (94 Journal of Taxation 374.)

"Putting tiered entities into a foreign holding company structure using check-the-box" (2001). The creation of a foreign holding company structure combined with international check-the-box tax planning involves interesting issues under subchapter C, especially when foreign tiered structures are transferred outbound. Characterizing the liquidation of the top-tier entity as an asset reorganization may avoid the gain recognition agreement (GRA) requirement under Section 367(a). Characterizing the bottom tiers as separate asset reorganizations may have the benefit of avoiding the potential application of the "yet-to-be-explained" anti-abuse rule under Section 367(e)(2).

After providing background and introducing a hypothetical for discussion, the author considers the application of the check-the-box regulations, including the current state of check-the-box planning, and outbound transfers. Regulation §§ 301.7701-1 through 301.7701-4 were issued to simplify entity classification by permitting a taxpayer to choose to be treated as a corporation, partnership, or disregarded entity. The regulations allow "eligible entities" to choose among various entity classifications. An entity is eligible unless it is included in a per se list; the regulations contain separate per se lists for domestic and foreign entities.

As a response to perceived abuse by U.S. multinationals using the check-the-box regulations to avoid subpart F income, early in 1998 the IRS issued Notice 98-11 and Temporary Regulation §§ 1.954-1T, 1.954-2T, and 1.954-9T. These rules were aimed at curbing the use of foreign hybrid branches in international tax planning. On June 19, 1998, in Notice 98-35, the IRS announced that the temporary regulations would be removed and that the proposed regulations relating to hybrid transactions would be reproposed with new dates of applicability. This was done to give Congress the opportunity to think more about the issues raised by hybrid transactions. On July 9, 1999, Notice 98-35 was withdrawn and new proposed regulations were issued on hybrid branch transactions that will be effective five years after they are finalized. The thrust of the proposed regulations is to treat, under certain circumstances, hybrid branches as controlled foreign corporations (CFCs) for purposes of protecting subpart F. To date, these rules have not been finalized.

Moreover, in another attempt to safeguard the subpart F regime, in November 1999 the IRS issued proposed regulations that, in certain circumstances, would invalidate a check-the-box election made for a foreign eligible entity.

Then, the author addresses reorganization requirements. For a reorganization to qualify as tax-free under Section 368, the statutory requirements must be met, as well as the regulatory requirements of: (1) business purpose; (2) continuity of business enterprise; and (3) continuity of proprietary interest.

Finally, the author considers Section 367 issues. The possibilities for avoiding U.S. tax on transfers involving foreign corporations are circumscribed by Section 367, which provides complex rules covering various situations (outbound transfers, inbound transfers, foreign divisive transactions, etc.). (P. Grube, 94 Journal of Taxation 5.)

"State apportionment factor consequences of Section 338(h)(10) election" (2001). D.A. Fruchtman, 3 Business Entities, No. 3, 30. (*Digested under* State Taxes—In General, page 202.)

"Tax consequences of converting stock options in a spinoff" (2001). No gain or loss will be recognized by a corporation or its option holders on the conversion of options pursuant to its spin off of a business division into a new corporation, according to Letter Ruling 200120030. Further, the substitution of the current outstanding options with either adjusted options in the existing corporation or new options in the new corporation will not constitute a modification, extension, or renewal of the outstanding options in the existing corporation. (95 Journal of Taxation 119.)

"Tax-free reorganization despite postacquisition asset sale" (2001). According to Revenue Ruling 2001-25, a target company may sell some of its assets following its acquisition in a triangular reorganization, without running afoul of the tax-free reorganization rules. (67 Practical Tax Strategies 62.)

"The real spin on the new spinoff ruling— should corporate-owned real estate be put into REITs?" (2001). D.L. Brandon, 95 Journal of Taxation 92. (*Digested under* Real Estate, page 173.)

"The re-proposed 'anti-*Morris Trust*' regulations are vastly improved, but some aspects remain vague" (2001). After background on the demise of the *Morris Trust* structure, the author considers the guidance provided by the proposed regulations on determining when a prohibited plan exists, safe harbors, and events that are—and are not—part of a plan. The question posed by Section 355(e) is whether an acquisition preceding or following a distribution (to which Section 355 otherwise applies) is part of a plan (or series of related transactions) that includes such distribution. Proposed Regulation § 1.355-7(b)(1) tells us that such a plan will be found where, with respect to an acquisition following a distribution, either the distributing corporation, the controlled corporation, or any of their respective controlling shareholders" intended, on the date of distribution, that "the acquisition" or a "similar acquisition" occur in connection with the distribution. Where an acquisition precedes a distribution, a prohibited plan will be found if any of the previously named parties intended, on the date of acquisition, that a distribution occur in connection with the acquisition.

Thus, the proposed regulations clear up a question that has vexed practitioners since the enactment of Section 355(e): Exactly whose intent is relevant in assessing whether the separation and acquisition events are sufficiently connected?

In light of the fact that the operation of Section 355(e) turns, ultimately, on a finding that certain persons harbored certain intentions, the analysis devised by the proposed regulations is a relatively familiar step-transaction doctrine approach to determining whether formally separate transactions (the distribution and acquisition) can be amalgamated and treated as a single transaction. In most cases where something as elusive as intent is sought to be gauged, objective indicia bearing on such intent are examined and, based on an equitable weighing of such indicia, a judgment is rendered with respect to the ultimate question.

The heart of the new rules is found in Proposed Regulation § 1.355-7(f), which provides six safe harbors, the satisfaction of any of which will mean, conclusively, that the events being evaluated are not part of a prohibited plan. Where the safe harbors are not satisfied, Proposed Regulation § 1.355-7(d) provides a "factors" approach. Paragraph (d)(2) enumerates nine facts and circumstances "tending to show" that the distribution and acquisition are part of such a plan; Proposed Regulation § 1.355-7(d)(3), in turn, provides a series of countervailing factors the presence of which tends to show that the events were not so connected.

Where none of the safe harbors are available, yet an acquisition follows a distribution or a distribution follows an acquisition, the facts and circumstances must be closely examined to ascertain whether there is evidence of an intention on the part of the distributing corporation, the controlled corporation, or any controlling shareholder thereof, on the date of the distribution or acquisition, that the events occurred in connection with one another.

Then, the author explores the application of the proposed regulations, using five examples. (R. Willens, 94 Journal of Taxation 69.)

"The Section 368 revenue ruling trilogy— below the surface, seismic shifts in IRS policy" (2001). Over a span of just ten days in May 2001, the IRS issued three revenue rulings dealing with—at least on the surface—relatively narrow and circumscribed aspects of the Section 368 reorganization provisions. A closer look, however, reveals that the reasoning employed by the IRS to reach the result in each ruling suggests that these pronouncements extend well beyond their unique facts. In fact, it seems reasonably clear that the IRS has chosen, through the mechanism of this trilogy of rulings, to comment on, respectively, the *Groman/Bashford* doctrine, the substantially all the assets test, and the continuing vitality of the *Kimbell-Diamond* rule. Accordingly, these rulings have implications, most notably for planning business combinations, that will reverberate throughout the mergers and acquisitions community.

First, the author discusses Revenue Ruling 2001-24 and the *Groman/Bashford* doctrine. It can be fairly argued that Revenue Ruling 2001-24 establishes, conclusively, the primacy of the continuity of business enterprise (COBE) rules with respect to the implications of an asset alienation following an otherwise qualifying reorganization and eliminates what can only be described as the reign of terror imposed by the *Groman/Bashford* line of reasoning.

Under the *Groman/Bashford* doctrine, the continuity of interest requirement, necessary for any acquisitive transaction to qualify as a reorganization, is not satisfied where the acquired assets reside in a "remote" entity, that is, an entity other than the corporation the stock of which was issued in the transaction.

Then, the author addresses Revenue Ruling 2001-25. This ruling, in conjunction with Revenue Ruling 88-48, establishes that the venerable substantially all (the assets) requirement is not purely a quantitative guideline but, instead, as a qualitative matter, seeks only to ensure that divisive transactions (the nature of which may have been redefined by Letter Ruling 200040023) cannot partake of the benefits of the law's acquisitive reorganization provisions.

Finally, the author considers Revenue Ruling 2001-26. Revenue Ruling 2001-26 arguably reinstates, to a limited extent anyway, the all-but-extinct *Kimbell-Diamond* doctrine. The ruling cites, with obvious approval, a decision that employed the *Kim-bell-Diamond* doctrine to treat an acquisition of stock (which, viewed independently, did not qualify as a reorganization), followed by a preplanned upstream merger, as a direct acquisition by the acquiring corporation of the properties of the target via a "statutory merger" as that term is used in Section 368(a)(1)(A). (R. Willens, 95 Journal of Taxation 5.)

"Trio of rulings foster tax-free triangular reorganizations" (2001). IRS guidance will make it easier for acquisitions structured as triangular mergers to qualify for nonrecognition treatment.

First, the authors provide background on triangular mergers. In a triangular merger, the corporation seeking to effect the acquisition uses a controlled subsidiary to consummate the transaction. In a forward triangular merger, the corporation to be acquired is merged into a subsidiary of the acquiring corporation, with the subsidiary surviving. In a reverse triangular merger, a subsidiary of the acquiring corporation is merged into the corporation to be acquired, with the latter corporation surviving as a new subsidiary of the acquiring corporation.

Next, the authors consider the requirements for forward triangular mergers to qualify as reorganizations. A forward triangular merger qualifies as a reorganization if it meets the statutory requirements in Section 368(a)(2)(D). That section permits a subsidiary of the acquiror to acquire the target in a merger (with the subsidiary surviving), using the acquiror's stock as part or all of the consideration. (Note that Section 368(a)(2)(D) refers to the controlled subsidiary in a forward triangular merger as the "acquiring corporation;" in this article, "acquiror" refers to the parent controlling the subsidiary involved in the merger.)

The acquiror's ownership of the subsidiary (the "controlled subsidiary") must meet the control test. Three additional requirements must also be satisfied: (1) the controlled subsidiary must acquire "substantially all" of the target's property; (2) no stock of the controlled subsidiary may be used in the transaction; and (3) the transaction must have been such as to qualify as a Type A reorganization if the target had been merged into the acquiror.

Then, the authors address the requirements for reverse triangular mergers. To qualify as a reorganization, a reverse triangular merger must meet two requirements in Section 368(a)(2)(E): (1) the target must hold substantially all of the properties formerly held by both the target and the controlled subsidiary and (2) in the transaction, the former shareholders of the target must exchange target stock meeting the control test for the acquiror's voting stock.

Finally, the authors turn to the IRS guidance provided in Revenue Rulings 2001-24, 2001-25, and 2001-26. This series of rulings is quite favorable for taxpayers and their advisors. In Revenue Ruling 2001-24, the IRS allows an acquiror to use a first-tier subsidiary to effect a forward triangular merger, and then contribute the stock of that subsidiary to another first-tier subsidiary without jeopardizing the reorganization status of the merger. Interestingly, in that ruling, the IRS prevents the step-transaction doctrine from working to the detriment of taxpayers.

In Revenue Ruling 2001-25, the IRS extended its view of the substantially-all requirement from the Type C reorganization context to the reverse triangular merger context, permitting a postacquisition cash sale of up to 50 percent of the target's assets. As a result, it ruled that a postacquisition sale of assets by the target would not preclude reorganization status for the transaction there at issue, where the target retained the sales proceeds.

The IRS's conclusion in Revenue Ruling 2001-26 demonstrates its willingness to allow taxpayers to use the step transaction in their favor. There, the IRS allowed an integrated transaction structured as a stock-for-stock tender offer followed by a reverse triangular merger to qualify as a reorganization, whether the tender offer was conducted at the level of the acquiror or its controlled subsidiary.

Tax advisors should view these three rulings as particularly taxpayer-friendly in that they add flexibility to using triangular mergers in acquisitive reorganizations. (M.R.

Martin & J.E. Tierney, 67 Practical Tax Strategies 290.)

"Vacation pay in asset and deemed asset sales: a half-baked trap for the unwary" **(2001).** R.W. Harris & B.J. Verhoeven, 3 Business Entities, No. 6, 22. (*Digested under* Fringe Benefits, page 68.)

RESEARCH EXPENDITURES

"Design expenses had to pass uncertainty test to qualify as R&E expenditures" **(2001).** In FSA 200125019, the IRS concluded that a footwear company's design expenses are research or experimental (R&E) expenditures only if they are attributable to activities to eliminate uncertainty in the product's development. (95 Journal of Taxation 182.)

"IRS offers guidance on using suspended research credits" **(2001).** The IRS, in Notice 2001-29, has provided additional guidance to corporate taxpayers that may request extensions of time to file their income tax returns for tax years that include expired research credit suspension periods. (66 Practical Tax Strategies 376.)

"R&D limited partnership not allowed Section 174 deduction because it was an investor" **(2001).** In *I-Tech R&D Limited Partnership* (2001), the Tax Court disallowed a partnership's current deduction under Section 174 for substantial research and experimental expenditures incurred by the partnership from 1984 through 1986 on the ground that the expenditures were not incurred by the taxpayer in connection with operation of a trade or business. (3 Business Entities, No. 3, 63.)

"Recent developments tinker with the research credit" **(2001).** A credit for increasing research and development expenditures was added to the federal income tax law in 1981 (currently Section 41). The credit was set to expire in 1985 so that Congress could evaluate its efficiency. Since 1985, a pattern of expiration and reinstatement has existed

181

for this credit. On June 30, 1999, the credit expired for the tenth time since it first expired in 1985. In December 1999, Congress extended the credit through June 30, 2004, but with some timing restrictions.

After reviewing the details of the credit's extension, modification, and clarification the author focuses on the Section 41 final regulations. As promised on the 2000 Treasury/IRS Business Plan, final regulations under Section 41 were issued in December 2000. The final regulations include several examples that explain the definitions and rules pertaining to gross receipts, discovering information, process of experimentation, shrinking back, internal-use software, and documentation.

Then, the author explores case law attempts to define "qualified research." Finally, the author discusses holidays, vacation, and other leave; controlled groups; funded research and government contracts; supplies versus depreciable property; contract research expenses; adjustments for certain acquisitions; severance/separation pay; revocation of the alternative incremental research credit election; guidance on software; and issues that remain regarding the "discovering information" requirement. (A. Nellen, 66 Practical Tax Strategies 152.)

"Some shoe design costs can qualify as research expenditures" (2001). The IRS has held, in FSA 200125019, that expenditures incurred by a taxpayer's design department for the development, modification, and improvement of athletic footwear can be research and experimental (R&E) expenditures. (67 Practical Tax Strategies 118.)

"Tax treatment of website development costs: not exactly point and click" (2001). D.E. Hardesty, 94 Journal of Taxation 140. (*Digested under* Computers, page 29.)

"The perennially controversial R&D credit regulations—when will taxpayers get the final word?" (2001). Long-awaited final regulations under Section 41 relating to the computation of the research (R&D) credit and to the definition of qualified research were issued on January 3, 2001.

After providing background on the R&D credit, the authors discuss the discovery test. One of the most controversial aspects of the final regulations concerns the discovery requirement. To qualify for the research credit, Section 41(d)(1)(B) requires that a taxpayer undertake research "for the purpose of discovering information (1) which is technological in nature and (2) the application of which is intended to be useful in the development of a new or improved business component of the taxpayer. . . ." The proposed regulations defined the phrase "discovering information" as "obtaining knowledge that exceeds, expands, or refines the common knowledge of skilled professionals in a particular field of technology or science."

This language was modified in the final rules. Regulation § 1.41-4(a)(3) refers to the common knowledge of skilled professionals in a "particular field of science or engineering." The regulations drop any reference to "technology," apparently in the belief that this change clarifies the definition.

Then, the authors consider documentation requirements. The final regulations include a documentation requirement that was not in the proposed regulations but, according to the Preamble to TD 8930, is intended to be less burdensome than a rule in the proposed regulations requiring taxpayers to record the results of their experiments. The new requirement, in Regulation § 1.41-4(d)(1), provides that no credit will be allowed unless the taxpayer prepares documentation, before or during the early stages of the research project, that describes the principal questions to be answered and the information the taxpayer seeks to obtain to meet the "common knowledge" standard. This documentation must be retained on paper or electronically in the manner prescribed under applicable guidance (revenue rulings, etc.).

Finally, the authors address the process of experimentation, internal-use software, and other notable provisions of the final regulations. (J.S. Wong & S. Ryan, 94 Journal of Taxation 203.)

RESIDENCE

(*See* Personal Residence)

RETURN PREPARERS

(*See* Tax Practice and Practitioners)

RESIDENT ALIENS

(*See* Foreign Corporations, Persons, and Partnerships)

ROLLOVERS

(*See* Pension and Profit-Sharing Plans—Distributions)

S

S CORPORATIONS

"'Anti-abuse' provisions for S corporation ESOPs become law" (2001). 3 Business Entities, No. 4, 49. (*Digested under* Pension and Profit-Sharing Plans—Employee Stock Ownership Plans (ESOPs), page 159.)

"Application of built-in gain tax to S corporations that become REITs" (2001). On May 30, 2001, the IRS released two private letter rulings—Letter Ruling 200134022 and Letter Ruling 200134023—that deal with situations in which a C corporation with appreciated assets converted to S corporation status and, within the ten-year recognition period under Section 1374, became a real estate investment trust (REIT). (3 Business Entities, No. 6, 40.)

"Corporate officer was employee of S corporation" (2001). In *Barron, CPA, Ltd*, (2001), a special trial judge of the Tax Court determined that an individual was an employee for federal employment tax purposes of an S corporation that provided accounting services. (3 Business Entities, No. 2, 56.)

"Corporation electing S status after initial S election transition period subject to built-in gain tax" (2001). In *Colorado Gas Compression, Inc.* (2001), the Tax Court addressed a unique set of facts regarding transition-period relief from the Section 1374 built-in gain tax. (3 Business Entities, No. 3, 59.)

"Corporation not deemed a successor corporation for purposes of five-year prohibition on reelection of S status" (2001). In Letter Ruling 200130031, the IRS ruled that a corporation was not a "successor corporation" for purposes of the five-year prohibition on reelection of S corporation status under Section 1362(g). (3 Business Entities, No. 5, 60.)

"Courts follow Supreme Court lead on effect of COD income on S corporation

basis" (2001). In *Gitlitz* (2001), the Supreme Court reversed the Tenth Circuit, and held that income from discharge of indebtedness (COD income) that is excluded from the gross income of an S corporation under Section 108(a), passes through to the S corporation's shareholders and increases their stock basis under Section 1367. This article discusses post-*Gitlitz* judicial developments concerning this issue. (3 Business Entities, No. 3, 56.)

"Disposition frees up suspended passive losses despite S election" (2001). In *St. Charles Investment Co.* (2000), the Tenth Circuit has reversed the Tax Court and held that an S corporation can deduct passive-activity losses, which were suspended while it was a closely held C corporation, in the year it disposed of the activity that gave rise to the losses. The issue was before the court as a matter of first impression, and has not been addressed by any other circuit. (66 Practical Tax Strategies 61.)

"Disproportionate S corporation distributions do not create second class of stock" (2001). In Letter Ruling 200125091, the IRS ruled that disproportionate distributions made by an S corporation to its shareholders and subsequent steps taken to equalize the distributions would not terminate the corporation's S election. (3 Business Entities, No. 5, 59.)

"Eighth Circuit concurs that no shareholder basis increase for bank loan to S corporation" (2001). In *Bean* (2001), the Eighth Circuit affirmed a Tax Court decision that shareholders of an S corporation were not entitled to increase their bases in the corporation's stock for certain bank loans to the corporation. (3 Business Entities, No. 6, 42.)

"ESOP's distribution of S corporation stock, followed by rollover to IRA, did not terminate S election where company immediately repurchased its stock" (2001). In

Letter Ruling 200122034, the IRS ruled that a corporation's S status would not terminate if an employee stock ownership plan (ESOP) distributed the corporation's stock to a plan beneficiary, the beneficiary rolled the stock into its IRA, and the corporation immediately bought back its stock. (3 Business Entities, No. 4, 52.)

"Final Section 338 regulations respond favorably to comments on S corporation issues" (2001). In February 2001, the IRS issued final regulations relating to deemed and actual asset acquisitions under Sections 338 and 1060. The final regulations generally are effective as of March 16, 2001. Among other things, the final regulations reflect several favorable changes relating to S corporations in response to comments that were received. Two key changes relate to acquisitions of S corporation stock for which Section 338(h)(10) elections are made. Very generally, if such an election is made, the S corporation is treated as selling its assets and then liquidating (even though the S corporation shareholders in reality sold their stock). (3 Business Entities, No. 2, 54.)

"Foreign tax credit planning for S corporations" (2001). S. Soltis & P.C. Lau, 3 Business Entities, No. 3, 36. (*Digested under* Foreign Tax Credit, page 65.)

"In calculating Section 7519 payment, S corporation with tax year other than required tax year must include gain from one-time sale of business assets" (2001). Letter Ruling 200129021 involves an S corporation that elected under Section 444(a) to have a tax year other than its required tax year. (3 Business Entities, No. 5, 60.)

"Ineligible corporation provided inadvertent invalid election relief" (2001). Letter Ruling 200107030 deals with a request for inadvertent invalid election relief in a somewhat unusual fact situation. (3 Business Entities, No. 3, 57.)

"IRS denies early S reelection to corporation that voluntarily revoked S election" (2001). In Letter Ruling 200108023, the IRS refused to allow a former S corporation to reelect S status before the end of the five-tax-year waiting period imposed by Section 1362(g). (3 Business Entities, No. 3, 57.)

"IRS issues favorable guidance on built-in gain tax and natural resources" (2001). On October 9, 2001, the IRS issued an advance copy of a revenue ruling that provides welcome guidance to taxpayers in the natural resources industries. Revenue Ruling 2001-50 deals with the application of the Section 1374 built-in gain tax to certain transactions involving timber, coal, and domestic iron ore. (3 Business Entities, No. 6, 39.)

"IRS proposes regulations on qualification of ESBTs as S corporation shareholders" (2001). On December 29, 2000, the IRS issued long-awaited proposed regulations relating to electing small business trusts (ESBTs) and S corporations under Sections 641 and 1361 as amended by the Small Business Job Protection Act of 1996. Temporary regulations were also issued under Section 444 relating to the election of a tax year other than a required tax year when an S corporation has an ESBT or a tax-exempt trust as a shareholder.

For most practitioners, the proposed regulations provide welcome guidance and address the most asked questions about ESBTs. The eligibility of partial grantor trusts to elect ESBT status is a major breakthrough for S corporation planners, although reporting and compliance for such trusts under the bifurcated approach required under the proposed regulations may bring complaints from tax return preparers. (C.W. Hall, III, 3 Business Entities, No. 2, 28.)

"IRS provides guidance on ESBTs and estimated taxes" (2001). On February 22, 2001, the IRS issued an advance copy of Notice 2001-25. The Notice addresses an estimated tax issue that arose as a result of the publication of proposed regulations in December 2000 regarding electing small business trusts (ESBTs). (3 Business Entities, No. 2, 55.)

"IRS rules that arbitration award does not create second class of stock" (2001). In

Letter Ruling 200103061, the IRS ruled that an arbitration award, and payments made pursuant to the award, did not create a second class of stock under Section 1361(b)(1)(D). (3 Business Entities, No. 3, 60.)

"IRS rules that termination would be inadvertent if conversion of S corporation to limited partnership terminated S election" (2001). In Letter Ruling 200119040, the IRS ruled that if an S corporation's conversion from a state corporation to a state limited partnership created a second class of stock under Section 1361(b)(1)(D) so as to terminate its S election, the consequent termination of the company's S election would be inadvertent within the meaning of Section 1362(f). (3 Business Entities, No. 5, 58.)

"Legislation favorable to tax-exempt shareholders of S corporations introduced" (2001). Rep. Baird (D-WA) and Rep. Ryan (R-WI) have introduced a bill (H.R. 2846) to "provide comparable unrelated business taxable income treatment to tax-exempt organizations which hold interests in S corporations to the treatment as is provided to such organizations for interests held in partnerships." (3 Business Entities, No. 6, 41.)

"Letter ruling applies basis adjustment rules to S corporation shareholders receiving liquidating distributions over more than one tax year" (2001). Letter Ruling 200106009 addresses the computation of gain or loss to shareholders of an S corporation that will be liquidated pursuant to a plan of liquidation contemplating sales of assets and liquidating distributions over a period spanning more than one tax year. (3 Business Entities, No. 3, 59.)

"Merger of S corporations does not terminate S elections" (2001). In Letter Ruling 200112053, the IRS addressed a situation where six S corporations proposed to merge into another S corporation pursuant to an agreement of merger and applicable state law. (3 Business Entities, No. 4, 52.)

"New IRS guidance provides fresh impetus for using electing small business trusts" **(2001).** Proposed regulations, as well as new temporary regulations, implement the provisions governing electing small business trusts (ESBTs), which have been permitted to be S corporation shareholders since the enactment of the Small Business Job Protection Act of 1996. Under the proposed regulations, during any period when there is no potential current beneficiary of an ESBT the trust itself will be treated as the shareholder.

First, the author discusses the impact of the proposed regulations, including grantor trusts, interests acquired by purchase, ESBT beneficiaries, ESBT elections, conversions, taxing the trust, and revocation and termination. ESBTs were intended by Congress to provide S corporation shareholders with an additional vehicle for holding their stock. The new rules flesh out the mechanics of the ESBT election, operation, and termination (including the tax consequences of the grantor portion, S portion, and non-S portion of the trust), and clarify the definitions of "beneficiary" and "eligible current beneficiary." The new proposed guidance dealing with ESBTs would amend Regulation §§ 1.641-1, 1.1361-1, 1.1362-6(b), and 1.1377-1.

Then, the author addresses the temporary regulations. The new temporary regulations modify the existing temporary regulations under Section 444 that permit an S corporation to use a fiscal year ending in September, October, or November if a required payment is made. (S.S. Traum, 94 Journal of Taxation 285.)

"No basis increase for guaranteeing S corporation debt" (2001). Shareholders of an S corporation could not use debt guarantees to increase their basis in order to deduct passed-through losses, according to the Tax Court in *Estate of Bean* (2000). (66 Practical Tax Strategies 63.)

"Ownership of S corporation by LLCs and limited partnerships does not terminate S election" (2001). In Letter Ruling 200107025, the IRS ruled that the proposed restructuring of an S corporation such that its shares would be owned by three limited liability companies and three limited partnerships would not terminate the corporation's S status under Section 1362(d)(2)(A). (3 Business Entities, No. 3, 61.)

"Proposed regulations on ESBTs: more guidance for family trusts owning S stock" (2001).

Legislation creating the electing small business trust (ESBT) enabled family trusts to be eligible S corporation shareholders. Proposed regulations provide clarification regarding the elements of an ESBT, the ESBT election, and taxation of an ESBT.

The multigenerational family trust is a keystone of a well-designed estate plan for holding private business interests. The proposed regulations to the ESBT provisions reflect an effort on the part of the IRS to facilitate these objectives. While some parts of the ESBT regulations may be questioned, the overall product will greatly assist estate tax planners and tax advisors.

After providing background, the authors consider the interim ESBT guidance. Shortly after the effective date of the legislation creating the ESBT, the IRS issued Notice 97-12 to provide the proper procedures for a trustee (and not the potential current beneficiaries) to follow in making the ESBT election. In addition to listing the required information to be submitted with the election, the Notice specified that the ESBT election must be filed within the periods set forth for qualified subchapter S trusts (QSST) elections—i.e., generally within the sixteen-day-and-two-month period beginning on the day that the stock is transferred to the trust.

Then, the authors address the ESBT proposed regulations. The IRS issued proposed regulations to the ESBT provisions on December 29, 2000. The bulk of the proposed regulations are contained in two parts: (1) Proposed Regulation § 1.1361-1(m) sets forth the core terms and definitions of "ESBT" and rules for making and maintaining an ESBT election and (2) Proposed Regulation § 1.641(c)-1 sets forth the rules for taxation of an ESBT. The proposed regulations override the interim guidance that was provided by the IRS on (1) making the ESBT election; (2) defining "beneficiary" and "potential current beneficiary";

(3) trust conversions; (4) revocation of ESBT status; and (5) taxation of distributions to ESBT beneficiaries.

Finally, the authors explore the definitions of "ESBT beneficiary" and "ESBT potential current beneficiary," the application to grantor trusts, making the ESBT election, allocation of tax items, ESBT taxation, estimated tax, termination or revocation of an ESBT election, additional issues, and proposed legislation. (J.D. August & J.J. Kulunas, 28 Estate Planning 459.)

"QSST elections for testamentary trusts—proposed regulations issued" (2001).

On August 23, 2001, the IRS issued proposed regulations relating to the qualified subchapter S trust election for testamentary trusts. (3 Business Entities, No. 6, 41.)

"Sales or exchanges of interests in pass thrus" (2001).

D.M. O'Leary, 3 Business Entities, No. 1, 34. (*Digested under* Partners and Partnerships—In General, page 143.)

"S corporation may deduct suspended PALs incurred while it was a C corporation" (2001).

In *St. Charles Investment Co.* (2000), the Tenth Circuit reversed the Tax Court in holding that losses suspended as passive activity losses (PALs) while the corporation was a closely held C corporation could be deducted by the corporation in the year it became an S corporation and disposed of its interest in the passive activity generating the suspended losses. (3 Business Entities, No. 1, 56.)

"S corporation's issuance of nonvoting common will not result in additional class of stock" (2001).

The IRS has ruled that an S corporation's issuance of nonvoting common stock to key employees, and the payment of bonuses to those employees, will not cause the S corporation to have more than one class of stock under Section 1361. At issue in Letter Ruling 200118046 was whether the terms and conditions related to the issuance of nonvoting common stock would create another class of stock within the meaning of Section 1361 and thereby make the corporation ineligible for S corporation status. (95 Journal of Taxation 55.)

"S election subjected corporation to LIFO recapture" (2001). The Tax Court in *Coggin Automotive Corp.* (2000) held that a C corporation that elected S corporation status as part of a restructuring plan was required to include in its gross income its ratable share of the LIFO recapture amount under Section 1363(d). (66 Practical Tax Strategies 60.)

"Seventh Circuit affirms holding that shareholder's participation interest did not increase basis in S corporation" (2001). In *Grojean* (2001), the Seventh Circuit found that the Tax Court did not commit a clear error in characterizing a shareholder's participation interest in a loan made by a bank to an S corporation as a guaranty. (3 Business Entities, No. 4, 51.)

"Shareholder's participation interest in loan to S corporation was guarantee" (2001). The Seventh Circuit has affirmed the Tax Court in *Grojean* (2001), holding that a shareholder's participation interest in a loan to his S corporation was a guarantee. Therefore, he was not entitled to include the participation interest in his S corporation stock basis for purposes of deducting losses passed through from the corporation. (67 Practical Tax Strategies 51.)

"Sixth Circuit affirms capitalization of expenses relating to S election" (2001). In *United Dairy Farmers, Inc.* (2001), the Sixth Circuit affirmed a district court decision that held that certain accounting expenses relating to an S corporation election should have been capitalized, rather than expensed. (3 Business Entities, No. 6, 42.)

"Small business corporation status not terminated by administrative dissolution and reincorporation" (2001). In Letter Rulings 200114029 and 200123058, the IRS addressed a situation in which an S corporation discovered that it had been administratively dissolved by the state because it had failed to file its annual corporate report. Upon learning of the dissolution, the corporation immediately reincorporated in the state. In both of the rulings, the IRS concluded that the company's status as a small business corporation had not terminated and that the company was not required to apply for a new employer identification number. (3 Business Entities, No. 4, 52.)

"Spillover basis rule of Sections 1367 and 1368 applies in Section 304 transaction" (2001). In Letter Ruling 200110004, the IRS ruled that the amendment to Section 304(a) made by the Taxpayer Relief Act of 1997 did not result in the application of a segregated basis rule in place of the spillover basis rule of Sections 1367 and 1368. (3 Business Entities, No. 3, 55.)

"Subchapter S Modernization Act of 2001 introduced" (2001). Two bills were introduced in the House and Senate on July 19, 2001, as the Subchapter S Modernization Act of 2001. The Act would expand the flexibility and usefulness of S corporations. (3 Business Entities, No. 5, 57.)

"Subchapter S reform initiatives" (2001). In March 2001, discussions were held in Washington concerning the reintroduction of the Subchapter S Revision Act of 1999, sponsored by Senator Orrin Hatch and Representative Clay Shaw. Senator Hatch and Representative Shaw are seeking comments on the Subchapter S Revision Act, which contains a number of provisions that will greatly expand the usefulness and flexibility of S corporations. (3 Business Entities, No. 3, 54.)

"Supreme Court hands taxpayers a victory in *Gitlitz*, but will Congress take it away?" (2001). Ending years of controversy, the Supreme Court in *Gitlitz* (2001) finally resolved the question whether the shareholders of an insolvent S corporation are entitled to increase their stock basis as a result of excluded cancellation of debt (COD) income. In its 8-1 decision for the taxpayers, the court emphatically rejected the IRS's "policy" arguments and relied, instead, on the plain language of the statute.

Although the technical issue decided in *Gitlitz* was a narrow one, the decision is likely to be very important for taxpayers and tax practitioners. The statutory language in question produced a result that could be viewed as a windfall for the taxpayer, i.e., COD income was excluded and the taxpayer was entitled to a basis increase. The Supreme Court concluded, however, that if the statutory language is clear, Congress's mandate must be followed.

First, the author discusses the Code. The controversy in *Gitlitz* was the result of clear, albeit convoluted, rules contained in several sections of the Code. Section 108(a)(1)(B) provides an exclusion for COD income realized by an insolvent taxpayer. Nevertheless, the exclusion of COD income is not a "free lunch"—if the taxpayer has tax attributes such as net operating losses (NOLs), capital loss carryforwards, passive loss carryforwards, and basis, they must be reduced under Section 108(b). In order to prevent attribute reduction from occurring before the attributes can offset any other taxable income realized by the taxpayer during the tax year, Section 108(b)(4)(A) provides that attribute reduction does not occur until after the determination of the tax imposed for the tax year of the discharge, i.e., until after the close of the tax year in which the COD income is excluded.

Then, the author considers the Supreme Court opinion in *Gitlitz*, which dealt, in turn, with the arguments made by the IRS and the reasoning set forth by the Tenth Circuit. In the Supreme Court, the IRS adopted as its primary position the argument that had been rejected by the Tax Court (on summary judgment) in *Winn* (1997), i.e., that the COD income of an insolvent S corporation is not an "item of income" and, thus, never passes through to the shareholders. The Supreme Court had no difficulty concluding that this argument was inconsistent with a plain reading of the statute.

The Supreme Court's resolution of the specific issue that was contested by the parties in *Gitlitz* is not likely to be of great historical significance; Congress will likely reverse the result by statute in the near future. (R.M. Lipton, 94 Journal of Taxation 133.)

"Supreme Court hands windfall to owners of insolvent S corporations" (2001). In January 2001, the Supreme Court decided *Gitlitz*, resolving a conflict involving the Tax Court and five circuit courts regarding the interplay of the cancellation-of-debt provisions of Section 108 and the passthrough rules of subchapter S. Somewhat surprisingly, the Supreme Court adopted an approach that resolved the conflict in the broadest way possible in favor of taxpayers, even though this resolution apparently results in a windfall that was likely neither foreseen nor intended by Congress.

First, the authors provide background on the interplay between Section 108 and subchapter S. Determining the proper application of Section 108 in the case of a bankrupt or insolvent S corporation has resulted in various approaches among the Tax Court and several circuit courts.

Then, the authors address the Supreme Court. In *Gitlitz*, an opinion authored by Justice Thomas, to which only Justice Breyer dissented, the Supreme Court ruled in favor of the taxpayers, adopting essentially the approach taken by the Third Circuit in *Farley* (2000).

By holding that an S corporation's excluded cancellation of debt (COD) income passes through to give shareholders a basis increase in their S corporation stock, and that attribute reduction on account of such excluded COD income occurs in the year following the year of the discharge, the Supreme Court adopted a taxpayer-favorable approach that resolved the various conflicts among the Tax Court and five circuit courts. Since no circuit court had previously followed the Tax Court's position that COD income does not pass through to give shareholders a basis increase in their S corporation stock, the Supreme Court majority's resolution of the passthrough issue was not surprising. Since only one of the four circuit courts—in *Farley*—(plus one district court) to consider the issue had adopted the position that attribute reduction occurs in the year following the year of discharge, however, the Supreme Court's resolution of the sequencing or timing issue was surprising.

It is interesting to note that the *Gitlitz* decision casts grave doubt on the validity of Regulation § 1.1366-1(a)(2)(viii), at least insofar as excluded COD income is concerned. Under that regulation, COD income does not meet the definition of "tax-exempt" income and, therefore, does not pass through to the S corporation's shareholders because it is not "permanently" exempt from tax, but only "tax-deferred." The Supreme Court, however, rejected this analysis in *Gitlitz*, finding that Section 1366(a)(1)(A) is worded broadly enough to allow the passthrough of tax-deferred as well as tax-exempt income.

Although only two courts had previously found that the attribute reduction required by Section 108(b) occurs in the year following the year of the discharge, the Supreme Court found that the Code's plain text mandated this result. But according to the authors, it is not clear that this result can be found in the plain text of the Code. Although Section 1017 clearly mandates such a result, the language of Section 108(d)(4)(A) in the S corporation context is not equally as clear. (M.R. Martin & J.E. Tierney, 66 Practical Tax Strategies 202.)

"Supreme Court, reversing Tenth Circuit, holds that excluded COD income increases stock basis of S corporation shareholders" (2001). In *Gitlitz* (2001), the Supreme Court reversed the Tenth Circuit, and held that income from discharge of indebtedness (COD income) that is excluded from the gross income of an S corporation under Section 108(a), passes through to the S corporation's shareholders and increases their stock bases under Section 1367. (3 Business Entities, No. 1, 53.)

"Suspended passive activity losses survive S election" (2001). In *St. Charles Investment Co.* (2000), the Tenth Circuit considered the issue of whether suspended passive activity losses may be carried forward when a corporation converts from a closely held C corporation to an S corporation. In deciding this issue of first impression, the court reached a conclusion in favor of the corporation (and implicitly, its shareholders) based

on what it considered to be the plain meaning of the statute.

After providing background on the passive activity loss rules of Section 469 and the tension between these rules and Section 1371(b)(1), the authors discuss the Tenth Circuit's reasoning. Although the court acknowledged that it was a windfall for the shareholders to claim a deduction for losses that were incurred by St. Charles before it had become an S corporation, it found that the language of the statute nonetheless mandated such a result. In contrast, the Tax Court had found that the "clear import" of Section 1371(b)(1) was to prevent shareholders of an S corporation from claiming deductions for losses incurred by a C corporation, noting that the S corporation shareholders should not be entitled to claim a deduction for a loss incurred by another taxpayer.

Thus, this case is another example of how it may be possible to convince a court that the Code mandates a particular tax result, even though the result may produce an apparent windfall for the taxpayer. (M.R. Martin & J.E. Tierney, 66 Practical Tax Strategies 273.)

"Take steps to maximize shareholder basis in S corporations" (2001). One advantage of the S corporation election is the passthrough to shareholders of corporate net losses. Deduction of these passthrough losses, however, is subject to several limitations at the shareholder level, the principal one of which is that the losses cannot exceed the shareholder's adjusted basis in his or her stock and in debt owed to the shareholder by the corporation (the "basis limitation"). The basis limitation is similar to the at-risk limitation of Section 465. The importance of the basis limitation is increased by the downturn in the economy and the heightened possibility of business and investment losses.

If the S election terminates, any deductions suspended under the basis limitation are treated as incurred on the last day of any posttermination transition period. These suspended deductions are allowed only to the extent of the shareholder's basis in his or her stock on the last day of each posttermination transition period. (Shareholder basis in debt thus no longer expands the basis limitation after termination.) The curtain falls at the end of the posttermination transition period, and any remaining suspended losses may no longer be deducted in subsequent C or S years. For this reason, retroactive restoration of the terminated election under Section 1362(f) may be a valuable alternative.

After providing background on the effect of insufficient basis, the authors discuss how to ensure sufficient basis. A shareholder normally wants to ensure that deductions are not suspended because of his or her insufficient basis. Several approaches may be taken to ensure sufficient basis and avoid suspended deductions. Such approaches include: (1) making an additional investment in stock or debt; (2) avoiding indirect debt; and (3) accelerating income and deferring deductions.

Then, the authors address additional investments in stock. Problems, involving excess liabilities, appreciated property, and dual-basis property, may arise when certain kinds of properties are contributed to the corporation in a nonrecognition exchange under Section 351.

Finally, the authors consider the income tax effect of acquiring stock from related parties. (L.L. Bravenec & E.L. Bravenec, 67 Practical Tax Strategies 210.)

"Tax considerations in choice of entity decision" (2001). The author's chart sets out the tax considerations in the choice of entity decision. A business may choose to operate as either a C corporation, an S corporation, a limited liability company (LLC), a limited partnership, or a general partnership. In addition, an LLC may choose to be taxed as either a corporation or as a partnership. The chart assumes that the LLC will be taxed as a partnership.

A C corporation, an LLC, and an S corporation provide all of their owners with limited liability for state law purposes. A limited partnership also provides all of its owners, except for the general partner, with limited liability. Therefore, the choice between the different types of entities often comes down to tax considerations. (M.A. McNulty, 3 Business Entities, No. 5, 16.)

"Tax Court allows basis increase for some, but not all, of corporation's shareholders attributable to loans made to S corporation" (2001). In *Cox* (2001), the Tax Court held that a shareholder could increase his basis in an S corporation by amounts he had borrowed from a bank and subsequently transferred to the corporation, but denied the corporation's other two shareholders a basis increase for such amounts. (3 Business Entities, No. 5, 58.)

"Tax Court holds that shareholder may not increase basis as the result of guarantee, but applies *Selfe* analysis" (2001). In *Jackson* (2001), the Tax Court, in a case appealable to the Eleventh Circuit, held that a shareholder could not increase his basis in an S corporation by reason of the guarantee of certain indebtedness of the corporation. (3 Business Entities, No. 3, 60.)

"Temporary regulations classify ESBTs, qualified plan trusts, and 501(c)(3) trusts as not constituting deferral entities" (2001). Temporary regulations were issued on December 28, 2000, that provide that an electing small business trust (ESBT), a qualified pension trust (including an ESOP), or a tax-exempt Section 501(c)(3) trust are not "deferral entities" for purposes of Section 444. The effect of the temporary regulations is that an S corporation will not be precluded from using Section 444 to adopt or change to a tax year with a deferral period simply because the S corporation has an ESBT, qualified pension trust, or a Section 501(c)(3) trust as a shareholder. (3 Business Entities, No. 1, 57.)

"The built-in gains tax revisited: fifteen years later" (2001). Section 1374 imposes a corporate-level tax on the built-in gains of S corporations that were previously C corporations. Section 1374 applies to built-in gains recognized by a corporation during the ten-year period following its conversion to S status. The tax rate is presently 35 percent (the highest rate of tax imposed under

Section 11(b)) of the S corporation's "net recognized built-in gain."

Regulation § 1.1374-2(a) provides that a corporation's "net recognized built-in gain" for any tax year is the lesser of: (1) the corporation's taxable income (using all rules applicable to C corporations) considering only its recognized built-in gain, recognized built-in loss, and recognized built-in gain carryover (the "pre-limitation amount"); (2) the corporation's taxable income determined as if it were a C corporation computed without the benefit of the dividends-received deduction or the deduction for net operating loss carryovers (the "taxable income limitation"); or (3) the amount by which the corporation's net unrealized built-in gain (NUBIG) exceeds its net recognized built-in gain for all prior tax years ("the NUBIG limitation").

"Recognized built-in gain" means any gain recognized during the ten-year recognition period, beginning on the effective date of the corporation's S election, from the disposition of any asset except to the extent that (1) the S corporation can establish that the asset disposed of was not held by it as of the effective date of its S election or (2) such asset's built-in gain (the excess of the fair market value of the asset over the corporation's adjusted tax basis in the asset) as of the effective date of the S election was less than the gain recognized by the corporation on the disposition.

Similarly, "recognized built-in loss" means any loss recognized during the ten-year recognition period on the disposition of any asset to the extent that the S corporation can show that (1) such asset was held by it as of the effective date of its conversion to S status and (2) the loss recognized does not exceed the amount of such asset's built-in loss (the excess of the corporation's adjusted tax basis in the asset over the asset's fair market value) as of the effective date of the corporation's S election.

In computing the Section 1374 built-in gains tax, a corporation's net recognized built-in gain is reduced by any net operating loss carryforwards and any capital loss carryforwards arising in a tax year during which the corporation was a C corporation, and the tax computed under Section 1374 may be reduced by business and alternative minimum tax credit carryforwards arising from years in which the corporation was a C corporation.

After discussing the computation of built-in gains tax, the author addresses case law and planning strategies. Although the built-in gains tax imposed under Section 1374 poses a significant hurdle to a corporation desiring to convert from C to S status, there now exists sufficient guidance in interpreting the built-in gains tax to allow the informed practitioner to fashion both preconversion and postconversion planning to either minimize or eliminate the converting corporation's exposure to the built-in gains tax. (S.R. Looney, 3 Business Entities, No. 2, 12.)

"The new extraterritorial income exclusion for S corporations" (2001). S. Soltis & P.C. Lau, 3 Business Entities, No. 2, 40. (*Digested under* Foreign Corporations, Persons, and Partnerships, page 64.)

"The subchapter S discharge of indebtedness issue: Supreme Court picks law over equity" (2001). In an eight-to-one decision written by Justice Thomas in *Gitlitz* (2001), the Supreme Court decisively concluded that the plain language of the Code must prevail over a perceived double tax benefit obtained by S corporation shareholders. Prior to the Supreme Court's decision, the Tax Court had consistently held that S corporation shareholders were not entitled to use tax-exempt cancellation of debt (COD) to reduce shareholder income from non–S corporation sources, thereby ruling in favor of the IRS.

On appeals from the Tax Court, the Tenth Circuit in *Nelson* (1999), the Sixth Circuit in *Gaudiano* (2000), and the Seventh Circuit in *Witzel* (2000) also found solutions aimed at preventing a windfall by requiring the taxpayer to offset COD income against suspended losses at the corporate level. The circuit courts expressed a clear concern with a double tax benefit obtained by S corporation shareholders and the need to interpret the statute to eliminate that benefit.

However, the Third Circuit in *Farley* (2000), the Eleventh Circuit in *Pugh Jr.* (2000), and the Oregon Federal District Court in *Hogue* (2000), ruled that the plain language of the statute required a result permitting the taxpayer to exclude COD from income and use that COD under the subchapter S rules to increase shareholder basis and apply any suspended losses to offset other shareholder income.

Then, the author discusses *Gitlitz*. In *Gitlitz*, the Supreme Court endorsed the statutory right of shareholders of an insolvent S corporation to use nontaxed discharge of indebtedness (COD) income to increase the bases of their stock in the corporation, and then use their increased bases in the stock to apply suspended S corporation losses to offset other income of the shareholders. The decision resolves a major conflict that has split the Circuit Courts of Appeal since 1994, when the IRS first attempted to prevent S corporation shareholders from obtaining a windfall by combining Sections 108, 1366, and 1367. (R.A. Shaw, 3 Business Entities, No. 3, 4.)

SELF-EMPLOYMENT TAX

"When does self-employment tax take root on farm rents?" (2001). Typically, farmers are self-employed business people, and under Section 1401, self-employment tax is imposed on an individual's self-employment income. Consequently, a farm operator's net earnings are generally subject to self-employment tax. On the other hand, rental income is generally not subject to self-employment tax. Suppose, however, an owner of farmland rents the land to someone else, but continues to perform farming services. The Eighth Circuit has reversed and remanded Tax Court decisions that cash rental income of farmers was taxable under Section 1402(a)(1) as self-employment earnings. The cases involved rentals to related parties. (T.D. Englebrecht & J.D. Smullen, 66 Practical Tax Strategies 277.)

SPECIAL-USE VALUATION

(*See* Valuation of Property—Special-Use Valuation)

STATE TAXES

In General

"Achieving low-cost relocations or expansions in the electronics industry" (2001).
Electronics companies seek locations with an available labor pool, advanced infrastructure, and market proximity. In fact, the need for an abundant supply of technologically skilled workers is often the driving concern for both "electronic manufacturing services" (EMS) and "original equipment manufacturers" (OEM), businesses seeking a workforce with advanced educational backgrounds and productivity. Most positions, including those involving the manufacturing process, require a computer-literate workforce. In this industry of frequent innovation, close proximity to colleges and universities is a must. These institutions provide not only a potential labor pool but also the ability to network with academia and collaborate on research and development. New technology with strategic economic and security implications make innovation a perpetual force that drives the EMS sector.

For the electronic industry, the workforce's preference for placing a high priority on qualify of life can further limit the number of potential sites. Since this workforce is in such great demand, these individuals can afford to be selective about where they live and work. Increasingly, however, as states and cities strive to create their own high-tech clusters, skilled labor pools, once located in California's "Silicon Valley," Boston, and Seattle, now are accumulating throughout the United States.

Generally, the more highly concentrated the electronic cluster, the more expensive it is to do business in that location. Therefore, each company must balance cost considerations with workforce, infrastructure, and market access to derive a short list of possible areas in which to relocate or expand. As companies begin to narrow the search through assessing available real estate and more-detailed location screenings, incentive opportunities, as well as other strategies, which can elevate one jurisdiction over another in the final analysis often are overlooked.

There are two general categories of business incentives: statutory and discretionary. Statutory incentives are available from governing bodies to all companies that apply, subject to certain qualifying criteria, which can include site location, nature of the business conducted, capital investment, job creation, or retention. Most states offer incentives through programs, such as enterprise zones, to spur investment and job creation. The benefits of locating in an enterprise zone vary, but typically include hiring credits and grants and investment credits and grants. State governments may provide training grants as a statutory incentive program, which may offset thousands of dollars in training costs for each participating employee. To obtain these incentives, companies must know that incentive programs exist and must be willing to commit resources necessary to comply with the requirements.

State and local governments employ discretionary incentives as tools to encourage capital investment and job creation, especially in competitive location decisions. Discretionary incentives include such benefits as infrastructure grants, low-cost financing, free or subsidized land, fee waivers, and tax abatements and deferrals, as well as in-kind assistance, such as expedited permitting. For discretionary incentives, timing is critical in determining the magnitude of incentives that can be secured.

It is important to implement an incentive strategy prior to making a final site selection. Such an approach allows time to implement appropriate recordkeeping to help the company achieve the statutory incentive benefits to which it is entitled. Timing also is critical in determining the magnitude of discretionary incentives that may be secured. Here, the overriding reason is that the basic purpose of discretionary incentives is to influence location decisions that are competitive among two or more jurisdictions.

With early consideration in the planning process, there are strategies to lower costs through facility designing and organizational restructuring measures. Companies planning for a new facility should consult with their engineers, consultants, and tax services pro-

195

viders about such potential cost reduction strategies. Ultimately, a successful location decision rests on finding a suitable match between a business and a community. Just as businesses need employees, communities need jobs. Just as businesses need infrastructure, communities need taxpayers. It is as simple as that—a mutual investment. Finding a community willing to offer the types of incentives a company needs is not only a cost-saving opportunity but also a signal of long-term synergy between that business and the community. (E.F. Sexton & J.S. Wong, 10 Journal of Multistate Taxation and Incentives, No. 10, 22.)

"A framework for conducting state tax research on the Internet" (2001). P.D. Callister, 11 Journal of Multistate Taxation and Incentives, No. 7, 26. (*Digested under* Computers, page 28.)

"A questionable methodology: including external costs of sales in property valuations" (2001). J.L. Terwilliger, 11 Journal of Multistate Taxation and Incentives, No. 7, 14. (*Digested under* Valuation of Property—In General, page 261.)

"Courts weigh in on 'highest and best use' and other valuation issues" (2001). In two recent, major property tax cases in the neighboring states of New York and New Jersey, the courts considered a variety of perplexing valuation issues in arriving at decisions with significantly different results, as discussed in this article. In the New York case, *Xerox* (1999), the taxpayer won almost $17 million in refunds, plus $2.5 million per year in future tax savings. In the New Jersey case, *ML Plainsboro* (1999), the taxpayer was seeking $15 million in refunds, but lost $5.6 million. The taxpayers in each case made essentially the same argument, that property should be valued using comparable sales rather than the cost approach. (J.F. Janata, 10 Journal of Multistate Taxation and Incentives, No. 9, 14.)

"Federal and state tax consequences of synthetic leasing—multiple benefits, minimal risks" (2001). S.G. Frost & P. Carman,

95 Journal of Taxation 361. (*Digested under* Real Estate, page 171.)

"Growth in the new economy: state initiatives target technology-based business" (2001). For several years, many states have been seeking to lure technology-based companies to locate in their particular jurisdiction. In determining the appropriate incentives to offer, state officials must consider the unique requirements of technology-based companies, including the critical need for talent to fill jobs and a knowledge-based workforce with certain skill sets, the need for sophisticated infrastructure, proximity to similar businesses, and technology-savvy locations. The actions taken by states include modifying existing incentive laws or enacting new incentives to target the industry, and instituting policy changes to address issues important to the technology sector.

One example of the way states have modified existing incentives to target technology-based businesses is reflected in recent job and investment tax credit legislation, which has been expanded to include industries such as telecommunications. In addition to amending existing incentives laws, many states have enacted new legislation to provide technology-based companies with additional reasons to locate in their jurisdiction. The article describes the New E-Conomy Transformation Act of 2000 (NET 2000), an aggressive effort by the District of Columbia to provide tax exemptions, reductions, and credits, as well as financing assistance that would place the District at the forefront of jurisdictions with targeted incentives for technology companies. The numerous benefits offered to new and existing "qualified technology companies," many of them discussed in the article, may dramatically reduce operating costs for eligible businesses in the District.

Incentives offered by other states are summarized briefly, including Florida, Georgia, Hawaii, Illinois, Kansas, Maine, Mississippi, New Jersey, New Mexico, North Carolina, Virginia, and Texas.

In addition to incentives legislation, the article describes various other policy changes and initiatives that states have established to target technology-based companies. The many examples in the article demonstrate that states have come to understand the need to focus on technology-based companies that provide high-paying jobs and economic growth. (J.H. DeVries & T.L. King, 11 Journal of Multistate Taxation and Incentives, No. 4, 14.)

"High-tech and growing? Here's the incentive to look where you're going" (2001). Despite criticism by those who believe incentives are corporate welfare, state and local governments continue to attract high-tech companies by offering tax and business incentives. Currently, high-tech companies seem to be concentrated in areas such as Silicon Valley, Dallas, Boston, and Washington, D.C. America's small to mid-size cities, however, are now aggressively competing with their larger counterparts to attract high-tech firms, and some states are getting into the game. As states and communities seek job expansion and relocation, they have become more interested in diversifying their economic climate by attracting businesses across all industries, including high technology. The majority of state and local governments, however, are still statutorily hindered by old-economy laws that prevent them from providing attractive incentive packages to high-tech companies.

A perfect example of how aggressive, targeted marketing can help a city pave the way for attracting high-tech businesses is found in the story of Austin, Texas, which has transformed itself into one of the most vibrant technology regions in the United States with a $20 million package of incentives, described in the article.

Traditional tax credits may not benefit high-tech companies because, when such credits are nonrefundable, they may be used only to offset tax liabilities, which many start-ups do not generate. Accordingly, the high-tech tailored incentives some states and cities now offer are nonincome based, such as refundable job credits, up-front training grants, low-interest financing, and assistance in finding investors. Some states are lowering the minimum capital investment or new job creation required to qualify for tax incentives. Others have created innovative financing programs that assist high-tech companies in securing up-front capital so they "hit the ground running." Business incentives such as New Jersey's Business Employment Incentive Program, which issues cash payments to employers associated with new jobs created, work well for high-tech companies still a few years away from profitability as defined by the tax code. Contrary to the majority of states, Ohio offers refundable tax credits for new job creation, programs that work well for high-tech companies by providing a credit that offsets business costs.

Unlike traditional industries, such as manufacturing, a high-tech company's greatest assets are people rather than capital equipment or stocks. Training and high-tech education are critical to the success of high-tech companies, making training grants one of the most popular incentives states can offer. Through its Technology Enhancement Certification for Hoosiers Fund (TECH Fund), Indiana provides grants to companies to train information technology workers in cutting-edge software development, systems networking, engineering, and other advanced e-business applications. Illinois provides its Industrial Training Program to assist Illinois employers in upgrading the skills of existing as well as new workers.

To stay ahead in the new economy, states and cities must use every economic development tool available to protect their economic future. Incentives will be key as competition for a high-tech identity heats up. (P.A. Naumoff & B.R. Smith, 11 Journal of Multistate Taxation and Incentives, No. 8, 12.)

"Incentives: setting the course from negotiation to compliance to receipt of benefits" (2001). Early in the incentive negotiation process, it is critical to provide a summary of the opportunities that may be available and to enlist the support of those disciplines and individuals within the organization that will directly affect the level of the incentives negotiated, received, and reported. The operations personnel should clearly understand what is expected of the company to achieve the benefit and participate in regular meetings attended, as well by all of the disciplines involved in executing the project. Negotiations in the economic development arena are fluid, and project parameters can change, bureaucratic requirements can change, and other hurdles can arise.

In many cases, economic incentive compliance is based on statutes that may be quite dogmatic in providing compliance requirements. Early in the process, establish proper systems to provide for the capture of appropriate and relevant information to support a statutory system with little or no room for variation. However, many incentives are granted under statutes that do not clearly define compliance requirements or that do not provide for the reporting of data that a local authority may deem vital. Such incentives are not adequately negotiated without carefully negotiating the details in agreements or contracts executed between the granting jurisdiction and the incentive recipient.

Recapture of incentive benefits by a community, also known as clawback, may occur after some default by the company. To allow greater flexibility before clawbacks commence, the company may wish to negotiate for cure periods or extensions. In many cases, communities may grant incentives conditioned upon the company's providing a "payment in lieu of taxes" (PILOT) to the granting jurisdiction or to an affected entity, such as a school district. The company may seek to include in the agreement a PILOT calculation method that results in reduction of the company's contributions when benefits decrease and an increase when benefits expand.

In connection with the incentive negotiation process, a simple matrix that provides a brief overview of the project, including key project parameters, is helpful in keeping constituents focused on the promised deliverables, as well as in providing an overall legend that matches incentives to project parameters that will become the essence of the compliance process. The matrix should include (1) a description of each incentive; (2) the anticipated range of benefit; (3) the status of the negotiation for each incentive;

and (4) pending actions or next steps. An added benefit in this type of approach is that it elicits a sense of ownership by each project team member and provides a catalyst to help achieve the desired result—maximum cooperation toward mutual goals.

The article focuses on the need for follow-through and what that entails, as well as the compliance aspect of the incentive process, including the negotiation of compliance requirements. A successful negotiation that results in maximum benefit to the company and the community is the ultimate goal of the economic development process. To ensure this result, team participation and support is one of the essential elements required, and incentives may rise and fall on the back of compliance. The economic development coordinator must take the initiative in enlisting team support to ensure that the incentives are realized, and in assembling that support to deliver the desired result.

The following approach, while not a guarantee, will provide reasonable insurance against lost or reduced incentives resulting from a lack of understanding of both the incentives and the compliance process:

- Establish/understand the project parameters.
- Agree only to what the company is sure it can deliver.
- Understand the criteria for the incentives.
- Provide education and information in a concise, meaningful format to the project team and support staff.
- Communicate requirements.
- Maintain open lines of communication.
- Prepare for hurdles—they will appear when least expected.
- Build support for the incentive process.
- Negotiate compliance requirements when possible.
- Review the negotiated incentive package with appropriate staff.
- Ensure that proper compliance systems are in place to support the incentive.
- Follow through.

(C.A. Caponi & L.J. Kramer, 10 Journal of Multistate Taxation and Incentives, No. 9, 22.)

"Intangible holding companies: There is life after *Geoffrey*" (2001). Many corporations that own significant intangible assets are seeking to reduce their state tax liabilities by transferring their trademarks and other intellectual property to intangible holding companies (IHCs) located in states that exempt such companies from corporate tax. Under the typical scenario, the corporation pays royalty or license fees to the IHC, which loans the money back to the operating company at market rates of interest. The result of these maneuvers is that the operating companies significantly reduce their taxable state income through deductions for interest and royalties paid to the IHC. The IHC, in addition to avoiding tax in its home state, is not subject to tax in the operating company's state because (presumably) it has no physical presence there.

In *Geoffrey* (S. Carolina 1993), South Carolina successfully imposed tax on a foreign IHC on the theory that the IHC had "economic nexus" with the state because its intangible property was in use there. The *Geoffrey* decision broke new ground in that it stepped away from the historical "physical presence" standard of determining nexus.

Many commentators have questioned the legal underpinnings of this decision. The U.S. Supreme Court denied certiorari, leaving unresolved the issue of whether a state may impose an income tax on a foreign corporation with no physical presence in the state. The decision has been formally embraced by Arkansas, Florida, Iowa, Massachusetts, New Jersey, and Wisconsin, and informally by several others. Other states have refused to assert nexus based on *Geoffrey*, including Alabama, Illinois, Maryland, Michigan, New Mexico, New York, and Tennessee.

Many states that continue to apply the U.S. Supreme Court's *Quill* (1992) physical presence test in determining corporate income tax nexus have asserted jurisdiction over foreign corporations based on "attributional nexus," whereby the activities of an agent in the state are attributed to a principal located outside the state. Instead of taxing the IHC as a separate entity, some states have required IHCs to file combined reports with the operating companies, with varying degrees of success described in the article. As another form of attack, both Ohio and Connecticut have adopted legislation that prohibits deductions for interest and royalties paid to IHCs.

Used correctly, an IHC can produce both business and tax benefits, but several steps should be taken to try to secure the intended tax consequences. The company must have an independent business purpose for creating the IHC. Several possible nontax goals mentioned in the article include protecting the transferred intangibles from the claims of the parent's creditors, incorporating in a favorable jurisdiction, and averting hostile takeovers. The companies should establish an arm's-length royalty agreement that reflects the true value of the intangible personal property.

It is important to maintain separate corporate identities for the operating company and the IHC, preferably with separate directors, officers, and employees. The IHC should establish a Delaware presence, including office space, bank account, telephone listing, and, if appropriate, employees. Viewed together, these steps may help to establish a corporate structure that will be respected by state tax administrators and the courts. (P.R. Comeau, T.P. Noonan & A.B. Sabol, 10 Journal of Multistate Taxation and Incentives, No. 9, 6.)

"Nexus revisited: current domestic and international tax issues in e-commerce" (2001). While many e-commerce companies are dropping along the wayside, the revolutionary distribution channel that e-commerce promises to be is alive and well. Following the U.S. Supreme Court's unwillingness in 1992 to set a bright-line test for nexus in *Quill*, many state departments of revenue and state courts have issued rulings that set diverse levels of nexus for different taxes in various jurisdictions. For years, various taxing authorities have claimed that a remote vendor has an obligation to pay its sales tax or collect its use tax because the government is "maintaining a civilized society" or "protecting a market" that the vendor is exploiting. In determining nexus, the governing language often includes phrases like "minimum contacts" and "substantial nexus," which are very ambiguous. Thus, interpretations and analyses vary from state to state.

Agency nexus employs the principles of agency law to impute the activities of in-state "actors" or "agents" to the out-of-state "principal"/taxpayer for purposes of establishing the taxpayer's nexus with the state. Since more agency nexus cases will be targeted specifically to e-business in the future, the article suggests an understanding of each state's definition of "agency" might be a clue to the direction of future rulings and cases. Economic nexus—a connection based on some economic presence, e.g., the existence of the vendor's customers in the state—may be the arena in which the states will take their claim on remote business conducted electronically. In 1993 in *Geoffrey*, the South Carolina Supreme Court found that nexus can be established through the existence of intangibles—in this case, trade names—used in the state. *Geoffrey* sidestepped the *Quill* decision, which involved sales/use taxation rather than income tax.

In *America Online*, a 2001 Tennessee case, the Chancery Court concluded that nothing short of an office, employees, or agents in Tennessee will cause a taxpayer to have nexus in that state. At the other end of the spectrum, under a new law, Arkansas is taking a much more aggressive stance, providing that Internet, mail order, and similar vendors are responsible for collecting sales tax if both of the following conditions exist that provide a reason to treat the in-state retailer as an agent of the remote vendor:

1. The vendor holds a substantial ownership interest, directly or through a subsidiary, in a retailer maintaining sales locations in Arkansas.

2. The vendor sells the same or substantially similar line of products as the Arkansas retailer under the same or substantially similar business name, or the facilities or employees of the Arkansas retailer are used to advertise or promote sales by the vendor to Arkansas purchasers. Nevertheless, the physical presence requirement of *Quill* may provide a basis for overturning the Arkansas statute.

Some states take the position that an out-of-state entity may be subject to tax based on its economic integration with an entity operating in the state as a unitary business. Generally, as long as one business does not accept returns or provide services for the other, and each company maintains separate accounts, does not integrate operations or management, and does not hold itself out to the public to be an affiliate of the other, the state will find it difficult to use the unitary concept to "pierce the corporate veil."

The Multistate Tax Commission (MTC) has concluded that the industry practice of remote computer vendors' providing warranty repairs through in-state third-party service providers creates nexus for imposing use tax collection responsibility and for income, franchise, or similar tax purposes in the state where the repair services are performed. How the courts will view on-line training and on-line customer care remains an open question. To identify, with regard to affiliate and agency nexus, a business's potential consumption tax exposure, tax planners need to know how the company solicits and acquires customers, receives and processes orders, processes payments, procures goods, fulfills orders, deals with returns, handles customer service issues, and interacts with strategic-alliance partners and third-party service providers.

The article summarizes various bills that have been proposed in Congress to address Internet taxation issues. The author argues the case for extension of the moratorium on taxation of Internet sales. The moratorium was enacted to enable a new business paradigm to develop, which still is nowhere near being firmly situated as a standard channel of distribution among companies. The article also offers suggestions for avoiding nexus, including having third parties completely handle warranties and servicing. To avoid affiliate and agency nexus, keep each company's operations as separate as possible by maintaining separate offices and employees, and using arm's-length pricing. Clearly, a holistic approach to tax planning is necessary, especially in light of the uncertainties presented by electronic commerce. (G. Mauro, 11 Journal of Multistate Taxation and Incentives, No. 5, 22.)

"Privacy issues may add to the debate over state taxation of e-commerce" (2001). In the global debate on the taxation of e-commerce, no issue has received more attention than state sales-and-use taxes in the United States. The primary reason for this heated debate likely stems from the perceived significant financial stakes. Sales-and-use taxes provide the states with a very substantial source of revenue, and anything that potentially threatens this revenue is of great concern to state and local taxing authorities.

As a result of this perceived importance, various e-commerce initiatives have focused primarily on sales-and-use taxes, including the Internet Tax Freedom Act (ITFA), the federal Advisory Commission on Electronic Commerce (established under the ITFA), and the National Tax Association's Commerce Tax Project. In addition, most discussions relating to other types of taxes have been framed using sales-and-use tax concepts and problems. Besides the significant financial motivation, this focus is due also to the complexity of sales-and-use taxation resulting from widely varying state and local tax schemes. The United States has a significantly greater number of state, county, and local jurisdictions imposing sales-and-use taxes than do most other industrialized nations. Therefore, the jurisdictional and collection issues apply to a very geographically diverse group of state citizens, thus increasing the collection and enforcement complexities.

A key element of the rapid growth of the Internet has been free and open access, and many of its supporters hypothesize that any government regulation (e.g., privacy law or taxation) will stifle Internet expansion. Every time someone connects to the Internet and accesses the Web, information about that person and that person's surfing habits is probably being collected. This occurs through direct methods (such as voluntarily filling out forms), as well as by indirect methods (when Websites harvest personal information via "click stream" data and "cookies"). The author envisions that Websites could some day start using a uniform cookie system that would allow all companies to exchange data about a user's complete surfing habits, creating an Internet in which privacy was nearly absent. In a recent poll, consumer trust emerged as e-commerce's biggest barrier to growth. Many consider this involuntary data collection to be the dominant privacy issue on the Internet. Therefore, the privacy problems might significantly hinder e-commerce from reaching its full potential.

Exploring privacy's legal framework in the United States, the article notes that these rights are not specifically guaranteed in any one set of legislation, but instead by a patchwork of federal and state constitutional, statutory, and case law. The U.S. Constitution recognizes no specific right to privacy. The First and Fourth Amendments protect some types of information; however, constitutional protections generally apply only to governmental infringements, not those by private parties. The Fifth Amendment limits the government's ability to collect incriminating information from an individual in a variety of contexts, although private papers are not covered. The First Amendment protects speech, both commercial and noncommercial, and the press. Anyone maintaining a Website or posting material on the Internet may be considered a "publisher."

The article mentions that many state constitutions provide privacy protection beyond that of the U.S. Constitution and gives some examples. Major statutory protections directed at specific industries or population groups also are discussed in more detail, including collecting personal information about children; limiting the federal government's collection and use of federal agency records containing personal information; prohibiting governmental authorities from accessing financial records; and limiting release of information to the government by online service providers.

201

The most significant characteristic of privacy and Internet taxation seems to be that there is no consensus about the proper actions needed to protect revenue, privacy, and the growth of the Internet. The chief concern among privacy advocates is that an avalanche of personal information would be available by enacting a taxing regime, a fear with regard to governmental agencies that is not true. However, informational privacy might be breached by private information aggregators, compiling and distributing the bits of personal data existing throughout the Internet. Some device or regulatory regime would have to exist to prevent private, third-party processors from collecting, aggregating, or selling their data.

Private enterprise working together with a well-thought-out governmental regulatory regime to protect consumer privacy, along with consumer awareness, should serve to protect consumers' privacy concerns in cyberspace. Finally, the article concludes it is highly unlikely that a multistate sales-and-use tax system for e-commerce will be adopted anytime soon because of the costs of administration and the current economic slowdown added to the difficulties associated with creating a legal framework consistent with the states' privacy laws. (P.W. Gillet, Jr., 11 Journal of Multistate Taxation and Incentives, No. 6, 12.)

"State apportionment factor consequences of Section 338(h)(10) election" (2001). Under Section 338(h)(10), a seller of at least 80 percent of the stock of a corporation that is a subsidiary in a consolidated group, an affiliated but unconsolidated subsidiary corporation, or an S corporation may, when requested by the purchaser, elect to have the transaction deemed a sale of the target corporation's assets for federal income tax purposes.

Following the election, the seller will not recognize gain on the sale of the stock, but the target will recognize gain on the deemed sale of its assets. The effect of the election on the amount of gain recognized on the sale depends upon the seller's and target's particular circumstances. In addition, for S corporation shareholders the character of the gain to the selling shareholders could be affected. In all cases, however, the election makes the gain recognizable on the target's return for the short period ending with the date of the sale, instead of to the seller on its return for the full year in which the sale occurred.

In general, purchasers will desire an (h)(10) election when the purchased assets' fair market value exceeds their combined adjusted bases. The purchaser will obtain a step-up in the assets' basis, which it uses to determine its future depreciation and amortization deductions. However, taxpayers making an (h)(10) election should not assume that the election will be followed in determining the selling and target corporations' state apportionment factors.

First, the author discusses possible apportionment factor treatments. The states' published rulings in this area have tended to focus on whether the states follow the federal election for purposes of determining apportionable income. However, even when it is known that a state follows the federal treatment in determining apportionable income, important issues remain in the determination of the state taxable income(s) of the selling taxpayers. One such issue is the apportionment factor treatment of the election.

Then, the author considers specific states' treatments. The treatment of the election for apportionment factor purposes was analyzed in a Massachusetts Appellate Tax Board decision and has also been addressed in rulings by Florida, Texas, and Virginia. (D.A. Fruchtman, 3 Business Entities, No. 3, 30.)

"State nonconformity to federal legislation could complicate REIT planning" (2001). The state tax treatment of real estate investment trusts (REITs) generally follows the corresponding federal treatment. Conformity is typically achieved through a state's incorporation of the Internal Revenue Code by reference. In states that incorporate the Code as of a specific date, however, there is often a lag between the time a federal tax change becomes effective for federal and state purposes. Accordingly, taxpayers should not be surprised to learn that recent federal legislation relaxing certain rules for REITs may not be adopted in some states. As a result, otherwise valid federal REITs may be disqualified in some states.

First, the authors discuss the Tax Relief Extension Act (TREA). TREA amends portions of the federal REIT provisions, which are located in subchapter M of the Code.

In a state that does not recognize TREA or the Code as amended by TREA, REITs that are planning to create a taxable REIT subsidiary (TRS)—an entity created by TREA—will be creating an entity that does not qualify under that state's REIT laws. If a state has in effect an earlier version of the Code (prior to TREA), a REIT that complies with all the Code requirements for REITs could now violate that state's definition of "REIT."

For example, a REIT may now own 100 percent of a TRS for federal income tax purposes. However, in a state that adopts a pre-TREA version of the Code, the ownership of the TRS would flatly violate the 10 percent asset diversification rule. This would result in a REIT that is valid for federal but not state income tax purposes.

State nonconformity with TREA is generally unintentional. Most states update their Code references periodically and are probably in nonconformity with TREA only inadvertently. Nevertheless, this nonconformity has made at least some taxpayers hesitant to implement the new TRS structure. (S.D. Smith, S. Amitay & J.K. Stewart, 3 Business Entities, No. 1, 30.)

"States follow federal lead in offering incentives for hiring targeted workers" (2001). The federal government has long had a program designed to encourage employers to hire those employees that for many generations were stuck in a vicious cycle of welfare dependence. Prior to 1994, the major federal jobs program was the targeted jobs tax credit. As this program was about to expire, the federal government, working in cooperation with state representatives as well as industry leaders, crafted a new program more focused on providing an incentive to employers to hire qualified individuals. As

currently enacted, under the work opportunity tax credit (WOTC), employers may claim a tax credit of up to $2,400 for each qualified new certified employee who is a member of one of the following eight targeted groups:

1. Families receiving aid in connection with a state program approved under the Social Security Act.

2. Qualified veterans.

3. Economically disadvantaged ex-felons.

4. High-risk youth (i.e., ages 18 through 24 residing in an empowerment zone or enterprise community).

5. Vocational rehabilitation referrals.

6. Qualified summer youth employees.

7. Qualified food stamp recipients, ages 18 through 24.

8. Qualified Supplemental Security Income recipients.

Also under the WOTC program, an alternative incentive, the "welfare to work credit" (W2W), took effect after 1997, providing employers with a higher credit for employing and retaining long-term family-assistance recipients. Although the WOTC and W2W credits are federal tax programs, certifications for qualified employees are issued through state agencies. Accordingly, the certification process may vary from state to state.

In addition to the federal tax credits, various states offer incentives for businesses hiring disadvantaged or other targeted employees. Many of these state programs are patterned after the federal WOTC and W2W initiatives. The state hiring incentives can be very lucrative, with credits ranging from $500 to $26,000 per qualified employee. The states are fairly consistent with regard to the criteria that employees must meet in order to qualify under the various programs, which follow the same general guidelines established for qualifying under the WOTC and the W2W tax credits. The article provides some examples of state incentive programs for hiring targeted workers and, where applicable, notes some of the differences between the particular state incentive and the corresponding federal tax credit. An exhibit highlights and summarizes credits offered by Arizona, California, Maryland, New York,

Rhode Island, South Carolina, and Virginia. The exhibit is supplemented by a short discussion of each state credit, explaining the qualifications, computation, and recapture provisions.

As the article demonstrates, it is not difficult to qualify for most state hiring incentives, which do not require a net increase in employment overall or from year to year. Any taxpayer that regularly or consistently hires new employees should consider the potential of securing these incentives. The benefits generally are available to any employer regardless of the company's predominant business activity. In addition, most of these hiring incentives have significant carryforward provisions, so that benefits may be realized at a later date. To some extent, the hiring credits may be administratively burdensome, but by establishing appropriate procedures, employers can facilitate the process for obtaining those incentives. (P.J. Herrera & R.M. Bortnick, 10 Journal of Multistate Taxation and Incentives, No. 10, 12.)

"State tax implications of the new federal innocent spouse rules" (2001). When a joint return is filed, each spouse is jointly and severally liable for the tax liability for the year. Therefore, when that liability is either understated or otherwise unpaid, the IRS can proceed against either spouse for collection. Too often, however, the spouse not actually responsible for the tax liability is the spouse easiest to locate and, consequently, is the one who ends up being liable for the taxes. Seeking to prevent such unfair situations, in 1971 Congress enacted IRC Section 6013(e), the "innocent spouse rules," which were liberalized under IRC Section 6015 in 1998. Three avenues are now available for claiming relief from joint and several tax liability:

1. Innocent spouse relief
2. Separate liability election.
3. Equitable relief.

Each method has its own set of conditions that must be satisfied. Since the enactment of Section 6015, several states have adopted the federal provisions for determining when similar relief will be granted at the state level. Other states have adopted modified versions and still others have developed their own innocent spouse rules. The article first examines the requirements for obtaining relief under Section 6015.

For the IRS to consider granting a request for innocent spouse relief, the following five conditions must be met: (1) the requesting spouse must have filed a joint return with the nonrequesting spouse; (2) the return reflects an understatement of tax attributable to an erroneous item of the nonrequesting spouse; (3) on signing the return, the requesting spouse did not know, and had no reason to know, that the understatement existed; (4) based on the facts and circumstances, it would be inequitable to hold the requesting spouse liable for the tax deficiency resulting from the understatement; and (5) the requesting spouse elects innocent spouse relief within two years after the IRS first began collection activities with respect to the requesting spouse.

A requesting spouse who fails to satisfy any one of these five conditions will be denied relief under Section 6015(b). While the first, second, and fifth conditions are fairly straightforward, the article provides further explanation of how to satisfy the third and fourth requirements. The courts differentiate between knowledge of understated or omitted income and knowledge of overstated deductions or credits.

A second alternative for escaping joint and several liability on a jointly filed tax return is for a spouse to elect to allocate the deficiency based on each spouse's share, on a separate-return basis, of the items taken into account in computing the deficiency (Section 6015(c)). To be eligible for the separate liability election, the spouses must have filed a joint return, the spouses must be divorced or legally separated at the time the election is filed, and the requesting spouse elects separate liability treatment within two years after the IRS first began collection activities with respect to the requesting spouse.

Separate liability election is not available where the IRS demonstrates that assets were transferred between spouses as part of a fraudulent scheme or for any portion of a deficiency where the electing spouse had *actual* knowledge of the item that gave rise to the deficiency (a narrower standard than the "had no reason to know" standard of Section 6015(b)). The article discusses several Tax Court cases that explored these requirements.

Under Section 6015(f), the IRS may grant relief from joint and several tax liability when the requesting spouse qualifies under neither Section 6015(b) nor Section 6015(c) *and* the IRS determines that it would be inequitable to hold the requesting spouse liable for the joint tax liability, provided certain threshold conditions are met and the spouses are divorced or legally separated, the requesting spouse believed the nonrequesting spouse would pay the tax liability, and the requesting spouse would suffer economic hardship if relief were not granted. Revenue Procedure 2000-15 provides a list of these conditions as well as positive factors that weigh in favor of granting equitable relief and negative factors that weigh against it.

State laws vary widely with regard to providing innocent spouses with relief from joint and several tax liability, although many follow the federal lead. A table in the article groups the states into eight general categories, ranging from those offering innocent spouse relief that mirrors the federal statutory model of Section 6015 or its predecessor statute, to states that grant relief based on independent factors (perhaps with some reference to the IRC), to states offering no innocent spouse relief but where such protection has been proposed, to states that have rejected proposed innocent spouse relief, and states that do not impose a tax on individual income. The article also discusses special rules for spouses living in community property states and the specific filing procedures for taxpayers seeking relief from joint liability. (L.M. Johnson & B. Clements, 10 Journal of Multistate Taxation and Incentives, No. 10, 4.)

"State tax nexus issues—the decades-old debate continues in the shadow of the Internet" (2001). The California State Board of Equalization decision in *Borders Online, Inc.* (2001) concerning Borders books, which has stores in the state, as well as a separate company engaging in online sales over the Internet, is sure to focus additional attention on the complex questions that arise in the context of state taxation of out-of-state entities doing some business or merely having customers in the state. Whether the type of tax involved is sales and use or corporate income and franchise, practitioners must consider the potential consequences of the slightest connection.

The California statute imposes the duty to collect and remit tax on any person who, among other things, has a representative or independent contractor "selling" tangible personal property in California on the person's behalf. The Board concluded that the availability of return-for-refund at California stores was a significant selling advantage accruing to Borders Online; accordingly, Borders Stores was performing "selling" activities in California for Borders Online. In the context of constitutional requirements, the Board found that the standard of "substantial physical presence" had been met because Borders Stores' physical plant and personnel could be attributed to Borders Online. (A.R. Rosen & M.A. Connell, 95 Journal of Taxation 303.)

"State tax treatment of LLCs and RLLPs: update for 2001" (2001). This latest update of the limited liability company (LLC)/ registered limited liability partnership (RLLP) charts sets out the various differences in the way these entities are treated by the fifty states and the District of Columbia. Tax considerations, such as entity-level taxes, conformity with the federal income tax classification rules, and potential entity-level withholding requirements, are discussed, as well as nontax elements, such as restrictions on the availability of entity forms for certain professionals and the extent of liability protection afforded to partners of LLPs. (B.P. Ely & P.C. Bond, 11 Journal of Multistate Taxation and Incentives, No. 2, 26; B.P. Ely & C.R. Grissom, 3 Business Entities, No. 4, 14.)

"State unrelated business income taxes pose compliance issues for exempt organizations" (2001). Unrelated business income tax

(UBIT) is imposed at the federal level on tax-exempt organizations that engage in a trade or business that is substantially unrelated to the organization's exempt purpose. Most practitioners are aware of federal filing requirements and make every effort to comply with the federal UBIT rules. State income tax filing and related compliance requirements, however, are sometimes overlooked. An exhibit in the article presents a summary of some typical requirements in selected jurisdictions, including Arizona, California, Delaware, the District of Columbia, Georgia, Illinois, Massachusetts, New Jersey, New York, and Utah.

A tax-exempt organization that generates federal unrelated business taxable income should periodically review its business activities to determine whether it is in compliance with state income tax (and perhaps sales-and-use tax) laws. This review should consider the specific states where the organization might be conducting business, including states in which the organization owns or leases real or personal property, employees perform services, the organization carries on fundraising activities, and other direct connections. In addition to business activities, exempt organizations should review their investments to determine whether they create additional state income tax filing requirements. As the article indicates, the question of state requirements can be somewhat complex and typically requires a thorough analysis of state income tax statutes, regulations, rulings, and other authoritative guidance.

Another important consideration is the relative ease in which states can identify—and potentially audit—investors in partnerships. Tax-exempt organizations that invest in partnerships may want to obtain assurances that unrelated business taxable income on a state-by-state basis will be provided timely and in a reasonable format.

Organizations should also analyze any available exceptions. For example, a tax-exempt organization may not be required to file a state income tax return if its only activity in the taxing state is through an investment in a limited partnership that does business within the state's borders. However,

in addition to state UBIT requirements, exempt organizations should be aware of the possible need to request state income tax exemption letters and file state information returns.

If the tax-exempt organization may have a significant state tax filing liability, the organization should consider negotiating a voluntary compliance agreement with the affected states in order to mitigate the costs. Typically such agreements are negotiated by a professional representative on behalf of the delinquent taxpayer without initially disclosing the taxpayer's identity. In exchange for an organization's voluntarily registering with the taxing authorities and paying taxes on a prospective basis, most states are willing to waive all penalties and assess only a portion of the tax attributable to the prior years. (W. Gentilesco & J.M. Buehler, 11 Journal of Multistate Taxation and Incentives, No. 2, 6.)

"Streamlined sales tax project seeks to expand collection of tax by remote vendors" (2001).

There is widespread concern among state and local governments that, as electronic commerce becomes more prevalent, sales-and-use tax revenues will erode because of the greater proportion of transactions conducted with remote sellers that do not have nexus in the buyer's tax jurisdiction. The Streamlined Sales Tax Project for the 21st Century (SSTP) is an initiative in which nearly forty state governments are working to develop a system for voluntary tax collection by remote vendors. SSTP participants also are concerned that the complexity and administrative burden faced by remote sellers creates a major barrier to sales tax collection. In addition, the advent of e-commerce and the proliferation of new business models makes the determination of whether a seller has nexus with a taxing jurisdiction both more difficult and more uncertain.

In December 2000, representatives from the SSTP's participating states approved a model Uniform Sales and Use Tax Administration Act (the Uniform Act) as well as a Streamlined Sales and Use Tax Agreement (the Agreement). The Act sets out various requirements that the Agreement must satisfy for the state to become a signatory or "member state." These cross requirements appear designed to ensure that member states' sales-and-use tax systems conform to the SSTP protocols.

The SSTP—at least initially—seeks voluntary compliance by offering remote sellers various incentives to participate. States that participate in the system will be required to adopt certain simplifications to their sales tax schemes. The Agreement requires that each member state have only one state rate that applies to all taxable goods and services, as well as one sales tax rate or one use tax rate per local taxing jurisdiction. Each state generally has a different tax base, and local jurisdictions may have tax bases that differ from the state's. The draft agreement contains several provisions aimed at conforming tax bases by standardizing definitions of products that commonly are subject to special sales tax treatment, establishing a common state and local tax base, and providing limitations on timing and frequency of change. The Agreement also aims to simplify tax administration and compliance among the states and to standardize the administration of exemptions.

One of the main objectives behind the creation of the SSTP and the Streamlined Agreement is to encourage remote sellers to voluntarily collect sales-and-use tax. The incentives include tax amnesty and monetary allowances. The Agreement provides that registration of the SSTP program and the collection and remittance of sales-and-use taxes in the member states will not be a factor in determining whether a seller has nexus with a member state *for any tax.*

A hallmark of the SSTP proposal is the harnessing of technology to ease the administrative burden of tax compliance. The centerpoint of the system is the use of "certified service providers," third parties that will have primary responsibility not only for calculating the tax but also for collecting, reporting, and remitting the tax. Under the agreement registered sellers will be required to use certified tax compliance software via three different options, described in more detail in the article.

The SSTP is conducting a pilot project to test automated tax compliance systems. The project involves a test of the technology only, and the participating states have not adopted any changes to the sales-and-use tax laws as part of the trial run. Privacy also has been identified as one of the aspects of the certified service provider (CSP) model that the SSTP is testing in the pilot project. The Uniform Act specifically requires that all member states adopt a standard policy for CSPs that will protect consumers' privacy and keep tax information confidential.

Achieving uniformity among the myriad taxing jurisdictions is a significant component of the SSTP's agenda. The Agreement requires member states to adopt uniform sourcing rules.

By easing the administrative burden of remote sales tax collection, some observers believe that the states will be able to convince either Congress or the U.S. Supreme Court to permit mandatory collection by remote sellers without a physical presence. The primary components of the sales tax project include developing uniform standards, streamlining rates, streamlining administration, using technology to simplify calculation, reporting, and remitting tax, and providing incentives for remote sellers to voluntarily collect sales tax regardless of whether they have nexus in the taxing jurisdiction.

Neither the National Tax Association's Communications and Electronic Commerce Tax Project nor the Internet Tax Freedom Act's Advisory Commission on Electronic Commerce was able to achieve consensus on the tax treatment of electronic commerce. It remains to be seen whether the states themselves—via the SSTP—will be successful in their attempt to expand the collection of sales-and-use taxes by remote sellers. (S.M. Edwards, 11 Journal of Multistate Taxation and Incentives, No. 5, 6.)

"Tax credits for job creation and training: employment-based incentives that work" (2001). Tax credits for job creation and employee training can be a valuable method of encouraging economic development. In contrast to some other programs, the granting of income tax credits allows economic development authorities to avoid expenditures of limited funds to attract business. Although states forgo some revenue by offering tax credits, that scenario may be better than the revenue effect of losing an entire business expansion project. By lowering the operating costs for businesses and creating opportunities for citizens, states can create an attractive business environment through a tax regime that includes training and job credits. Workers get worthwhile jobs, communities benefit from reduced social costs, and businesses profit from the ability to add and train employees at lower marginal cost.

One common form of assistance, income tax credits, often engenders particular issues, especially when these credits are nonrefundable. States that offer employment credits, however, generally allow taxpayers to carry forward unused credits. In addition, taxpayers may be able to secure credits retroactively for open tax years by filing amended returns. States have begun to broaden their employment credit programs, once targeted at manufacturing and corporate headquarters, as their economies have shifted toward technology-intensive fields. However, since economic development rules may not fully reflect the interpretations of state departments of revenue that issue tax credits, the article recommends that applicants strictly comply with any state agency responsible for the employment-based tax credit.

Another incentive, training credits, reward employers for investing in improvements to "human capital," by providing an effective, practical tool to combat labor shortages, underemployment, and outmoded skills. Training credits may be available for employer-sponsored job instruction, basic skills training, and tuition reimbursement. Claiming credits for employer-sponsored training typically requires strict adherence to the certification and recordkeeping requirements. Calculating the allowable costs of a training program may not be straightforward, since many states distinguish between what a company records as training expenses and the costs eligible in computing the training tax credit. The amount of credit, of course,

differs by state, as do other considerations, such as eligible employees and creditable expenses. Some states permit credits for "basic skills" training in an effort to reduce the pool of unskilled labor, extending the credit to include secondary and post-secondary tuition, as well as youth vocational education.

One of the most common tax credit incentives is the income tax credit many states grant to employers for creating jobs. This tax benefit has proven to be an effective tool to assist in attracting businesses to a region. Although state job tax credits are sometimes modeled on the former federal "targeted jobs tax credit," there is considerable variance among particular programs. For example, eligibility often is limited to specific targeted industries and some jurisdictions impose an investment threshold in conjunction with job creation.

Taxpayers must consider various limitations when determining the level of jobs eligible for the credit, since the intention is to stimulate an increase in *net* new jobs during a given period. In an effort to encourage the creation of *quality* jobs, many states have adopted various prerequisites— for example, restricting the definition of "eligible new jobs" to full-time employees, or setting some minimum qualified wage. Many states vary job creation thresholds and benefit levels with the extent of economic development in a particular locale. The rationale behind creating tiers or priority funding areas is to steer new investment into less developed parts of the state by reducing the cost of doing business in these areas. Job tax credits often are available over several years. Also, some states require taxpayers to maintain the increase in jobs for a year prior to claiming the credit. Some states allow taxpayers to choose the tax against which to claim job tax credits, and the article suggests that taxpayers be aware of this flexibility and assess the potential for increased benefit.

Tax credits for job creation and employee training can be a valuable method encouraging economic development. Although states forgo some revenue by offering tax credits, that scenario may be better than the revenue effect of losing an entire business expansion project. By lowering the operating costs for businesses and creating opportunities for citizens, states can create an attractive business environment through a tax regime that includes training and job credits. (M.L. Benton, 11 Journal of Multistate Taxation and Incentives, No. 3, 6.)

"What nonprofits should look for as states consider Internet taxation" (2001). In reality, the "taxation of the Internet" encompasses three primary commercial segments or categories:

(1) Taxation of access to the Internet itself. One example would be levying an excise tax on the fees charged by an Internet service provider to allow its customer to gain access to the Internet through the provider's switch connection.

(2) Taxation of various directly Web-related services to build and maintain Internet infrastructure. This includes telecommunications devices, database sites, computer servers, switching mechanisms, advertising, and Website maintenance.

(3) Taxation of transactions in which tangible personal property and, to some extent, intellectual property changes hands via orders placed online but physically delivered to the customer. This is potentially the largest source of tax revenue.

First, the author discusses the current framework for taxation. The taxation of sales of products and services—the third and most potentially lucrative category of Internet taxation—is determined by the law of the various states as limited by federal constitutional principles, which have generally arisen under legislative and judicial analysis of catalog sales.

Virtually every sales tax system has complementary "use tax" provisions. Without the use tax, the customer could be tempted to "forum shop" to avoid sales taxes. This hurts the government, because of the loss of revenue, as well as the local vendor who would be at a competitive disadvantage. It is this use tax concept and its application that is at the heart of the current debate.

Then, the author discusses the work of the Advisory Commission on Electronic

Commerce and issues for nonprofits. The Internet has strained the legal system's ability to deal with the application and enforcement of tax laws. It has also strained the political process that will have to make the needed changes in that system. This was shown by the work of the nineteen-member Advisory Commission on Electronic Commerce mandated by the Internet Tax Freedom Act.

The viewpoint of nonprofit organizations was essentially left out of the Commission debate on Internet taxation, but the issues and implications for nonprofits could be far-reaching. Every nonprofit organization needs to monitor these activities. They should band together to have a significant voice in any process that may be created to address these issues in the future. Nonprofit organizations cannot count on industry or governmental representatives to carry their issues and concerns to the final legislative vehicle. (N.H. Wright, 12 Journal of Taxation of Exempt Organizations 155.)

Alabama

"Are interstate sales of personal property subject to sales tax?" (2001). The U.S. Supreme Court's denial of certiorari in *Valhalla* in 2000 dashed the last hope for a big payoff for numerous consultants, accountants, and lawyers, who had filed use tax refund claims and a subsequent class-action suit, relying on a supposed "loophole" that an Alabama administrative law judge (ALJ) found in the state's sales-and-use tax law. The claims were based on the theory that interstate sales of goods delivered in Alabama were sales that "closed" in Alabama and, thus, were subject to the state's sales tax. Under a statutory exception to Alabama's use tax, as then written, transactions subject to sales tax were exempt from use tax. Thus, an Alabama customer could escape both the sales tax and the use tax on interstate purchases from vendors that did not have nexus with Alabama. Many taxpayers filed refund claims for all use tax paid. Those claims were rigorously audited by the state and no "loophole" refunds were paid.

The article presents the background administrative proceedings in which the ALJ's rationale evolved. In *Rawhide*, a 1985 administrative proceeding, and *Rush Hospital* (1993), the ALJ concluded that title to the property transferred on delivery in Alabama, and, accordingly, the Alabama use tax could not apply because these transactions were subject to sales tax. The Department of Revenue did not appeal the ALJ's decision in *Rush Hospital* but, nevertheless, continued to assess use tax on interstate transactions. Referring to the *Rawhide* and *Rush Hospital* situations as a "loophole," the ALJ suggested that Alabama close the loophole by legislation or regulations.

The Alabama legislature failed to take action. In *Bluegrass Bit* (1997), the ALJ again applied sales tax and not use tax, noting that Alabama had adopted the Uniform Commercial Code's definition of "sale" as "the passing of title from the seller to the buyer for a price." Under Alabama law, title generally passes when the seller completes delivery of the sales item by the seller or the seller's agent. The law also designated that a common carrier and the U.S. Postal Service are deemed to be the seller's agents, so that sales by an Alabama retailer that are delivered by mail or common carrier to the purchaser outside of Alabama would be closed outside of Alabama and thus not subject to Alabama tax.

The ALJ applied the "loophole" view to f.o.b. origin sales in 1985, finding *Oxmore Press* subject to Alabama sales tax on telephone directories that it printed and delivered to a Birmingham, Alabama, post office for shipment to South Central Bell's customers in other states. According to the ALJ, under Alabama's statutes, "the controlling factor would be delivery, unless the parties explicitly agreed otherwise." In the ALJ's "loophole" view, all interstate transactions are subject to sales tax. A sale that is f.o.b. origin is subject to sales tax in the state of origin. A sale that is f.o.b. destination is subject to sales tax in the destination state. Under this view, the author notes, there would seem to be no constitutional purpose for use tax because all transactions are subject to sales tax.

The Alabama Department of Revenue followed a traditional use tax approach, assessing use tax, not sales tax, against either the seller or the consumer on all transactions shipped into Alabama from outside the state. The author claims that the ALJ's "loophole" was of limited application and did not apply to all transactions. Nevertheless, the ALJ's *Bluegrass Bit* decision triggered substantial refund claims.

Four months after the ALJ's decision in *Bluegrass Bit*, the legislature amended the Alabama code to limit the use tax exemption to property on which Alabama sales tax is paid by the consumer to a person licensed under the state's sales tax law. Highly motivated litigants immediately filed a class-action suit in *Valhalla* in 2000. The trial court held that the statute was impermissibly retroactive and sought to enjoin Alabama from enforcing it during the period in dispute. The Department of Revenue appealed. The appellate court concluded that the legislature's intent in enacting the statute was to clarify that current law exempts from use tax only that property sold at retail in Alabama on which sales tax was paid. Further, the court noted that the legitimate legislative end behind the new statute was to close a perceived loophole in Alabama's existing sales-and-use tax statutes.

In fact, the author concludes, there never was a real loophole. The correct interpretation of the original code section is that sales tax does not apply to interstate transactions because the U.S. Constitution, as interpreted by the Alabama code, prohibits taxation of transactions taking place in interstate commerce. The immediate significance of the *Valhalla* decision is that all use tax refund claims based on the "loophole" are denied. The issue of lasting significance is the clash between the "loophole" position of the Alabama ALJ and the "traditional" position of the Department of Revenue. Adopting the "loophole" application of sales tax could open the door for assessment of both sales tax and use tax on the same transaction, widespread tax avoidance, tax shifting, and conflicts between states. (J.W.

Compton, 11 Journal of Multistate Taxation and Incentives, No. 1, 14.)

Arizona

"Extension, other changes for Arizona Enterprise Zone Program" (2001). Arizona's Governor signed legislation in 2001 that delays repeal of the Arizona Enterprise Zone program until June 30, 2006. The bill also (1) expands the program to include businesses with some retail sales; (2) adds investment requirements for small manufacturing businesses based on the population of the county or city where the business is located; (3) adds annual reporting requirements; and (4) provides that termination of an enterprise zone designation will not affect carryovers of the credit for increased employment in an enterprise zone. (11 Journal of Multistate Taxation and Incentives, No. 8, 27.)

Arkansas

"Special incentives for at least one steel manufacturer" (2001). In 2001, Arkansas enacted legislation to provide some tax breaks to "qualified steel manufacturers," including a sales tax exemption, an increase in the net operating loss deduction carryforward period, and other recycling credit benefits. The article suggests that these special incentives were enacted primarily to keep a local steel mill from taking its expansion plans out of state. (11 Journal of Multistate Taxation and Incentives, No. 3, 33.)

California

"California audits the manufacturer's investment credit: a look at the major issues" (2001). According to taxpayers and the California Franchise Tax Board (FTB) staff, field audits of that state's manufacturer's investment credit (MIC) have begun in earnest. The MIC statute provides that a "qualified taxpayer" for purposes of the

credit is one whose activities fall within Standard Industrial Classification (SIC) Codes for manufacturing or software development. Property generally must be tangible personal property that is depreciable, primarily used in manufacturing or a related process, and placed in service in California after 1993. The taxpayer generally must have paid sales or use tax on the cost of the qualified property, which also must be chargeable to the taxpayer's capital account. Based on experiences of taxpayers that have completed audits by the FTB and on FTB attorneys' statements, major audit issues involve taxpayer qualification, qualified costs, qualified property, and the leasing of property.

One common problem area involves qualified taxpayers who construct or acquire property used for pollution control, since the real property elements do not qualify. Since general administrative services do not qualify, taxpayers involved in manufacturing cannot include computers or software used to track or measure inventory. According to the FTB, equipment categories that taxpayers may mistakenly consider to be qualified property for purposes of the MIC include communications equipment, security equipment, fire prevention or warning systems, loading and storage equipment, and transportation equipment.

Identification of Section 1245(a) property in the manufacturing setting often proves difficult. In examining whether any particular asset is an inherently permanent structure rather than Section 1245 tangible personal property, the FTB proposes to use the factors in *Whiteco Industries*, a 1975 U.S. Tax Court decision, which are listed in the article. In addition to the "qualified taxpayer" requirement (e.g., the taxpayer's activities must fall within the SIC Codes in Division D, manufacturing), a significant dispute exists between taxpayers and the FTB concerning the use of the SIC Manual in determining whether a business qualified for the MIC, several examples of which are provided. If certain assets are used for more than one purpose, the FTB will bifurcate the elements so that the portion of the asset primarily used in manufacturing may be eligible for the MIC. Some of the most common issues arising from field audits concern whether a particular item is tangible personal property or whether the property is used as part of manufacturing or a related process. One area of dispute concerns the use of tangible personal property in research and development, because some taxpayers believe that the FTB audit staff applies a very narrow definition of "R&D."

The most significant audit issues with regard to leasing involve the specific rules that must be followed in order to ensure that purchases qualify for the MIC. Under either a capital or operating lease, the lessee, not the lessor, may claim the MIC, and the sales-and-use tax treatment of a lease is used to analyze the transaction for purposes of MIC availability. For an operating lease to qualify for the MIC, the lessor must elect to pay the sales tax on the acquisition of the property rather than on the lease payment stream.

The article offers the following pointers to taxpayers and their professional advisors: The cost of qualified property can be subject to the MIC only if California sales-or-use tax has been paid, directly or indirectly, on that cost, and the cost is properly chargeable to the taxpayer's capital account. "Qualified property" is tangible personal property that is used primarily in manufacturing or a related process. Buildings and other real property (except for special-purpose buildings), as well as intangible property, do not qualify for the MIC. In connection with a third-party construction contract, the FTB places the burden on the taxpayer to show the breakdown between, e.g., charges for MIC-qualified direct labor and the nonqualified portion of the bill representing the contractor's overhead and profit. Capitalized direct costs of labor qualify for the MIC, but indirect labor costs do not.

The lack of a dialogue or process to resolve MIC issues with taxpayers has led some to describe the audits as "aggressive." Critical in the audit scenario is the maintenance of adequate records so that the taxpayer can successfully substantiate the MIC claims. (C. Micheli & M.D. Herbert, 11 Journal of Multistate Taxation and Incentives, No. 4, 24.)

"How much do California's manufacturing tax incentives cost?—a look at taxpayer usage" (2001). California offers two alternative benefits—an income tax credit and a sales tax exemption—in connection with the purchase of certain specified property used in manufacturing activities. This article examines taxpayers' actual use of the benefits, particularly in comparison to the original and revised revenue estimates developed when the legislature enacted these provisions. (C. Micheli, 11 Journal of Multistate Taxation and Incentives, No. 1, 24.)

Colorado

"Enterprise zone sales tax exemption incorporated former federal ITC limit" (2001). In *Cray Computer Corp.* (2001), the Colorado Supreme Court held that purchases of used machinery qualify under the state's enterprise zone sales tax exemption. According to the court, however, the exemption statute incorporates the $150,000 limitation for qualified used business property under the former federal investment tax credit (ITC). Thus, Cray Computer Corp., the taxpayer, was liable for both state and county sales tax on all but $150,000 of the $6.6 million price of used machinery that it sold to another company. (11 Journal of Multistate Taxation and Incentives, No. 3, 34.)

"State offers agricultural development incentives" (2001). New legislation applicable to tax years beginning after 2000 authorizes the Colorado Agricultural Value-Added Development Board to offer eligible agricultural cooperatives tax credits, grants, loans, loan guarantees, and equity investments of up to $2 million per project. These benefits encourage rural agricultural business projects that add value to Colorado agricultural products. (11 Journal of Multistate Taxation and Incentives, No. 8, 28.)

"State Supreme Court expands credit in upholding use tax on test cars" (2001). In *General Motors* (1999), the Colorado Supreme Court upheld Denver's use tax imposed on cars shipped from the out-of-state factories of General Motors (GM) to the GM facility in Denver for testing purposes, subject to credits for any sales-or-use taxes paid to other cities and states on the cars or car parts. (10 Journal of Multistate Taxation and Incentives, No. 9, 29.)

Connecticut

"Court bars automatic disallowance of FSC commission expense" (2001). In *Eastman Kodak* (2000), the Connecticut Superior Court, in a matter of first impression, held that the Connecticut Department of Revenue Service's (DRS) automatic disallowance, under the corporation business tax, of deductions for 8/23rds of the commission expenses incurred by a taxpayer for sales made by a related "foreign sales corporation" (FSC) was not supported either by statute or by a properly promulgated regulation. (11 Journal of Multistate Taxation and Incentives, No. 1, 13.)

"High court says software customization is taxable computer service" (2001). In *Andersen Consulting* (2001), the Connecticut Supreme Court reversed the superior court and held that developing customized software represented taxable computer and data processing services, rather than the sale of intangible property. In its opinion, the court considered the impact of legislation, adopted during the pendency of the appeal, that was designed to retroactively reverse the result reached by the trial court. The decision and the related legislation will have significant implications for the taxation of computer software transactions in Connecticut. (11 Journal of Multistate Taxation and Incentives, No. 7, 38.)

"Labor Department issues regulations for incentive tax credit hiring program" (2001). The Connecticut Department of Labor has adopted regulations governing the state's incentive tax credit program for hiring certain welfare recipients. (11 Journal of Multistate Taxation and Incentives, No. 3, 35.)

District of Columbia

"New incentives encourage pollution clean-up" (2001). New tax credits offsetting business franchise and real property taxes will be offered in the District of Columbia in connection with the clean-up and redevelopment of contaminated property. The legislation (effective June 15, 2001) also expands the use of tax increment financing already offered in the District as a means of encouraging economic development, now applicable to contaminated property areas. A tax-free "environmental savings account" may be used to accumulate funds for use in connection with such clean-up and redevelopment. (11 Journal of Multistate Taxation and Incentives, No. 8, 29.)

Florida

"Legislature amends enterprise zone incentive laws" (2001). Florida enacted legislation in 2001 intended to promote economic development by amending various enterprise zone tax incentives and jobs tax credits, and creating a new sales-and-use tax "community contribution credit." (11 Journal of Multistate Taxation and Incentives, No. 8, 30.)

Illinois

"Court rules short-term investment income was not apportionable" (2001). In *Home Interiors & Gifts, Inc.* (2000), the Illinois Appellate Court held that the state's Department of Revenue may not tax, on an apportioned basis, a nonresident corporation's interest income from short-term investments except to the extent that the investments are actually used as working capital in the corporation's business. *Home Interiors* is significant because it places real limits on Illinois' power to tax an out-of-state business on interest income generated by investment accounts not used as working capital. (11 Journal of Multistate Taxation and Incentives, No. 6, 30.)

"Illinois job tax credit gives state the 'EDGE' in relocations and expansions" (2001). After years of losing companies to other states, Illinois seeks to curb this trend by offering its own, more attractive tax incentive, the Economic Development for a Growing Economy Tax Credit Act (EDGE). Administered by the Illinois Department of Commerce and Community Affairs (DCCA), the EDGE tax credit provides a nonrefundable credit against the state corporate income tax based on the personal income tax payments of newly hired employees. The program empowers DCCA to determine both the length of the subsidy and the amount of the personal income tax payments that are applied to the credit.

Since EDGE's inception in 1999, the latest statistics indicate that the tax credit has been successful in creating and retaining Illinois jobs. In May 2001, Boeing announced that it will relocate its corporate headquarters from Seattle to Chicago. To illustrate why various companies, including Boeing, have taken advantage of the Illinois EDGE tax credit, the article examines the program's background and the qualifications and application process for the credit, as well as some specific EDGE "success stories."

To qualify for the Illinois EDGE tax credit, a company must either invest $5 million in capital improvements to be placed in service in Illinois and employ at least twenty-five new employees in Illinois as a direct result of the project; or invest capital and create new jobs in Illinois in amounts to be expressly specified by DCCA and another state agency. The terms "new employee" and "full-time" employee, as defined under the credit, are discussed in the article.

If a taxpayer believes it may qualify for the EDGE tax credit, it must submit a written application that includes, among other things, a project summary, site map, description of employees to be hired, detailed description of the investment in capital improvements, and evidence that, if not for the credit, the project would not occur in Illinois. The state's review committee must consider whether the project will make the required investment, hire the required number of employees, is economically sound, and result in an overall positive fiscal impact on the state. Another major limitation with regard to the EDGE tax credit is that it is not available for Illinois companies that seek to relocate within the state, which would encourage cities in Illinois to compete against one another for existing companies, rather than create new jobs.

As a result of its EDGE tax credit, Illinois now can compete on a level playing field with other states that have enacted similar programs. While not necessarily the sole reason for a company's relocating to or expanding in Illinois, the state's EDGE credit program certainly is one tool among many other financial incentives that DCCA has used to encourage companies to make new investments in people and capital in Illinois. In light of DCCA's most recent victory in convincing Boeing to relocate its headquarters to Illinois, surely many other businesses will look to benefit from the EDGE tax credit in the future. (D.A. Hughes & B.W. Wong, 11 Journal of Multistate Taxation and Incentives, No. 5, 14.)

Kansas

"Incentives for electric generation facilities" (2001). In 2001 Kansas enacted a pair of laws intended to encourage the construction of electric generation facilities. The legislation permits certain "independent power producer property" to be excluded from the definition of "public utility." It also allows electric generation facilities that are still under construction to receive favorable accounting treatment. Finally, the new legislation creates property tax exemptions related to the construction of electric generation facilities and pollution control devices used at those facilities. (11 Journal of Multistate Taxation and Incentives, No. 8, 33.)

"Loan in takeover-defense tactic results in nonbusiness interest" (2001). In *Kroger Co.* (2000), the Kansas Supreme Court applied the "transactional test" in ruling that a non-Kansas corporation's interest costs incurred in defending against a hostile takeover were nonbusiness expenses allocable to the state of its domicile and therefore nondeductible in Kansas. The U.S. Supreme Court denied certiorari and, thus, let the decision stand. (11 Journal of Multistate Taxation and Incentives, No. 6, 33.)

"Multistate, family controlled businesses found to be unitary" (2001). In *Broce Construction Co.* (2000), the Kansas Court of Appeals held that multistate corporations that were involved in the same general line of business (in this case, highway construction) were engaged in a unitary business. The Court of Appeals noted that each company in *Broce* was engaged in the same general line of business in each state, many of the same people served as officers or directors of each company, intercompany financing, leasing, and loan arrangements were in place, and employees were transferred among the companies. (11 Journal of Multistate Taxation and Incentives, No. 6, 31.)

"Substantial nexus required a greater physical presence" (2001). In *Matter of Intercard* (2000), the Kansas Supreme Court affirmed the decision of the Kansas Board of Tax Appeals, ruling that the taxpayer's contacts with the state were isolated and sporadic and did not create substantial nexus. The circumstances turned out to be somewhat taxpayer-friendly, in that visits by technicians lasted for a total of forty-four hours over three months. Furthermore, the taxpayer did not engage in sales solicitations in the state and did not send any other employees or sales agents into Kansas during the audit period. (11 Journal of Multistate Taxation and Incentives, No. 7, 40.)

Louisiana

"Court clarifies constitutional limit on enacting exemptions" (2001). Since 1991, an exclusion from Louisiana's state sales-and-use tax has been in effect for tangible personal property purchased for rental. By express provision, the exclusion did not apply to local sales-and-use taxes. In 1999, however, the legislature enacted a similar exclusion for local taxes that was to be phased in over four years.

In *Louisiana Municipal Association* (2000), an association of political subdivisions filed suit against the state seeking to have the 1999 legislation declared unconstitutional. The basis for the plaintiff's position was a provision of the Louisiana Constitution, which, in part, prohibits, in a regular session of the legislature held in an odd-numbered year, the enactment of a measure legislating with regard to tax exemptions, exclusions, deductions, or credits. Based on this provision, the trial court found that the statute was unconstitutional. The state appealed directly to the Louisiana Supreme Court, which reversed the trial court's decision. (11 Journal of Multistate Taxation and Incentives, No. 1, 21.)

Maryland

"Out-of-state affiliate defeats state's nexus claims" (2001). In *MCI International Telecommunications* (1999), the Maryland Tax Court held that only if an out-of-state corporation with no presence in Maryland is a "phantom" entity (i.e., lacking economic substance), may the Department of Assessment and Taxation attribute nexus to the out-of-state corporation based solely on the activities of an in-state affiliate. (10 Journal of Multistate Taxation and Incentives, No. 10, 32.)

"State enacts tax incentives promoting clean, efficient energy" (2001). In 2000 Maryland enacted the Clean Energy Incentive Act that (1) grants state income tax credits for the purchase of specified solar energy property and for the use of qualified energy resources to produce electricity; (2) offers sales-and-use tax exemptions for purchases of certain electric appliances that meet or exceed applicable federal energy star efficiency guidelines and specified energy-efficient heating and cooling equipment and fuel cell electric generating equipment; and (3) provides a motor vehicle excise tax credit for the purchase of qualified electric vehicles

215

and hybrid vehicles. (11 Journal of Multistate Taxation and Incentives, No. 3, 36.)

Michigan

"Court's decision in *Meijer, Inc.* may render Michigan's property tax obsolete" (2001). In Michigan the townships, counties, and schools are financed primarily through property taxes and state aid. The provision of additional public services, such as police and fire, also depend heavily on the property tax. The Michigan general property tax may be in the process of being rendered obsolete by contemporary judicial construction that arguably contradicts the long-standing common understanding of the meaning of the constitutional term "true cash value" as used in assessing large unique industrial property. Because the general property tax is the largest revenue producer among all Michigan's state and local taxes, this possibility must be taken very seriously. One recent property tax decision may have equated the "true cash value" on which the property tax is assessed with a "market value" concept that does not recognize the economic market facts leading to the construction of such multi-billion-dollar facilities.

In its 2000 *Meijer* decision, the Michigan Court of Appeals reversed the Michigan Tax Tribunal's carefully reasoned 1993 and 1994 "cash value" determinations with respect to a 189,000-square-foot combined grocery and soft-goods retail store. The appellate court concluded that the Tribunal erred when it failed to make its own determination of, and to deduct because of, the functional obsolescence due to "modification costs" that would be made by a "typical purchaser." Since many new industrial facilities are specifically designed to suit their owner's needs and therefore will have diminished utility appeal to anyone other than their owner-occupant, application of the *Meijer* decision would result in a ludicrous situation where a new modern facility would be worth significantly less than its replacement cost. If this analysis is adopted, the identity of the purchaser is critically important.

The analysis of *Meijer* in the article points out several limitations and raises some criticisms. First, the appellate court did not treat the subject real property improvements as unique and ignored an earlier court decision that did. In *Meijer* the Tax Tribunal adopted a replacement cost that replaced only the utility that a "typical purchaser" would value the subject, not the utility of the subject to its owner-occupant. This approach would require those establishing Michigan "true cash value" for a new building to delete the construction cost of all features that might not have utility to a typical purchaser. Unfortunately, the city did not appeal the Tribunal's implied conclusion that the owner-occupant could not be deemed a hypothetical purchaser.

In *Meijer*, the Tax Tribunal cited for authority the Michigan Supreme Court's 1982 decision in *First Federal*, which not only rendered valueless in the Michigan General Property Tax Act "cash value" context all building features unique to the owner-occupant but also required the deduction of the cost of removing such building features that a "typical" purchaser would not want. The court of appeals also assumed that the *First Federal* decision was precedential and would preclude inclusion of the cost of building features of utility to the owner because they would not add to the cash value or selling price of the property to another retailer. If this rationale is generally applied to unique and special purpose industrial properties, their value could be further reduced by the cost of removing features specifically designed to suit the current owner's image or business.

The article contends that *Meijer* is distinguishable from *First Federal* because it did not deal with a special-purpose or unique-type property. Furthermore, if there is no market in which assessable property can be valued through the sales or income approaches to value, the Michigan Supreme Court has repeatedly established that the property tax evaluator must look to a hypothetical market and to a hypothetical buyer to determine what would be paid to purchase the property to put it to its highest and best use. The evaluator has no reason to conclude, nor is there any justification for the conclusion that the hypothetical purchaser would not be willing to pay for special and unique features designed to suit the operation of the property at its highest and best use. Indeed, the author reasons, common sense and logic suggest that this should be the result.

If the rationale of the court of appeals in *Meijer* is generally applied to unique and special-purpose industrial properties, then much of the cost of brand-new such facilities may not be reflected in their property tax "true cash value." The ultimate objective and policy of a general property tax must be to distribute the tax burden proportionately and equitably. When the property tax is generally perceived as unfair and not uniform in its distribution of the tax burden, its days as the mainstay of local government finance will be numbered. (S.J. McKim III, 11 Journal of Multistate Taxation and Incentives, No. 2, 12.)

Minnesota

"Court upholds taxing statutory residents' out-of-state income" (2001). In *Stelzner* (2001), the Minnesota Supreme Court held that taxing a statutory resident's entire income that was generated primarily outside the state did not violate the Commerce Clause. (11 Journal of Multistate Taxation and Incentives, No. 2, 38.)

"Nonresident's in-state managerial services now taxable" (2001). In *Benda* (1999), the Minnesota Supreme Court held that a nonresident who performed managerial and administrative services for his employer in Minnesota for several days during the year was not subject to tax on the portion of his salary attributable to the work performed instate. The court concluded that such managerial activities did not constitute "personal or professional services" under Minnesota's statutes, the income from which is subject to tax. However, the legislature amended the statute to subject such income to taxation in the future. The new law is effective for wages received after May 16, 2000, and,

thus, refund opportunities for managers still may exist. (11 Journal of Multistate Taxation and Incentives, No. 4, 33.)

Mississippi

"Incentives aid major manufacturer and its suppliers" (2001). New Mississippi tax incentives, which are intended to entice a major motor vehicle manufacturer to locate in Mississippi, include income tax credits for jobs created by the enterprise that operates the plant, as well as by certain suppliers located on the plant site. Sales tax exemptions are available for various equipment and utility and repair services sold or leased to the manufacturer, and for materials, machinery, and equipment used in the construction of the plant. The legislation also offers protection from special local property taxes and certain exemptions if a municipality should expand its boundaries to include the plant site. Income tax credits also will apply for jobs created by the plant operator and for certain suppliers located on the plant site. Qualified businesses will benefit from various sales-and-use tax exemptions enacted as part of the new legislation. (11 Journal of Multistate Taxation and Incentives, No. 3, 37.)

Missouri

"Liberal postdeprivation remedy for void statewide local use tax" (2001). In *North Supply Co.* (2000), the Missouri Supreme Court found that the taxpayer should have been permitted to pursue a "clear and certain" postdeprivation remedy despite the existence of other, predeprivation remedies. The decision is a good example of the court's sensitivity to making sure a taxpayer has a fair and adequate remedy when a tax is determined invalid. (11 Journal of Multistate Taxation and Incentives, No. 1, 31.)

"Some creative uses for Missouri's state tax credit programs" (2001). Missouri is one of many states that use income tax credits as a popular means to implement and stimulate business development in the state. In recent years, Missouri has been particularly generous in providing a large variety of income tax credits as incentives to promote economic development projects, research and development activities, business expansion, low-income and other affordable housing, job training, the rehabilitation of abandoned or historic properties, and similar programs. Over the past decade, Missouri's incentive programs have provided numerous taxpayers with hundreds of millions of dollars of tax credits to further these objectives.

Missouri imposes constitutional limitations on the total revenues that the state can collect and spend without requiring voter approval. Sections of the Missouri Constitution, nicknamed the "Hancock Amendment," provide that the ratio of state government revenue to total Missouri personal income, as determined at the time of the amendment's adoption in 1980, must remain substantially unchanged unless state voters specifically approve new tax increases. To the extent that the revenue collected in any year exceeds a calculated amount by more than 1 percent, the state must refund the excess to the corporations and individual taxpayers based on the income taxes paid during the preceding fiscal year. Revenues exceeded Hancock limitations for fiscal years ended June 30, 1995, and 1996, 1997, 1998, and 1999. However, taxpayers who used income tax credits to reduce their income tax liabilities for the relevant computation periods also had their Hancock refunds proportionately reduced or eliminated.

In *Missouri Merchants and Manufacturers Association*, a 2001 Missouri Supreme Court case, the plaintiffs claimed that the total Hancock refund was understated by the hundreds of millions of dollars of tax credits the state had granted. The court concluded that only "refundable" income tax credits that exceeded the taxpayer's income tax liability for the year had to be added back to revenue. Although the *Missouri Merchants and Manufacturers* decision was very disappointing to Missouri's taxpayers, the Missouri Supreme Court's ratification of the Department of Revenue's treatment of income tax credits with regard to the tax liabilities they can offset can be useful for future planning purposes. Unlike most other states' tax credit programs, many of Missouri's credits are transferable; taxpayers that generate credits but cannot use them (e.g., because of NOLs) may sell the credits to other taxpayers that can use them. Purchaser taxpayers can pay their taxes at a discount, offsetting a dollar of tax liability with a credit bought for less than one dollar. The seller gets cash in exchange for a tax credit it otherwise may not be able to use for years or not use at all.

Because income tax credits extinguish the tax liability when the credit is used, the liability disappears as if it had never existed. Potential underpayment penalties and interest are extinguished as well. The article provides an example of one of Missouri's most successful transferable tax credit programs in its historic preservation tax credit, applicable to expenditures incurred after January 1, 1998. The state tax credit scheme loosely parallels the comparable federal incentive program that encourages real estate developers and property owners to restore, rather than abandon or demolish, historically significant buildings.

The historic preservation credits may be used to offset either personal or corporate income taxes, or the state's financial institutions tax. To the extent that the credits exceed the taxpayer's tax liability for the year, they may be carried back to offset all open years' tax liabilities (typically, three years), or carried forward for ten years. The state will permit taxpayers to immediately amend their most-recent three years' tax returns to carry back historic preservation tax credits *that are used on returns filed before 2002*. However, the preferential carryback treatment will not be available for returns filed in later years, for which taxpayers must first offset their tax liabilities for the year in which the tax credits are issued before being able to use the credits for carryback purposes. (J.M. Lohman & J.P. Barrie, 11 Journal of Multistate Taxation and Incentives, No. 6, 6.)

Montana

"Property tax breaks for remodeling of commercial buildings" (2001). New Montana legislation effective for property tax years beginning after 2000 offers property tax exemptions and abatements intended to encourage the remodeling, reconstruction, or expansion of an existing commercial building or structure that results in an increase in the building's taxable value by at least 5 percent. To be eligible for the tax benefits, the building must not have been used in a business for at least six months immediately preceding the date of application for approval by the governing body of the locality where the reconstruction takes place. (11 Journal of Multistate Taxation and Incentives, No. 8, 34.)

Nebraska

"New tax credits for business relocation and expansion" (2001). The Invest Nebraska Act, which was enacted in 2001, provides tax credits to encourage new businesses to locate, and existing businesses to expand, in Nebraska. An eligible business that meets any of the required levels of employment and investment will be entitled to a wage benefit credit. The wage benefit credit is a specified percentage of the total compensation paid to the company's new employees at the project. Meeting specified higher levels of job creation and investment allows a company to choose instead an investment tax credit. The company must state in its application for benefits which option it will seek. A company failing to comply for the entire entitlement period may be subject to credit recapture or disallowance. (11 Journal of Multistate Taxation and Incentives, No. 8, 35.)

New Hampshire

"New local property tax exemption for some new construction" (2001). New legislation in New Hampshire, effective April 1, 2001, through March 31, 2006, provides certain municipalities in economically depressed areas with a construction property tax exemption intended to encourage new construction, rehabilitation, and property improvements for public accommodation and industrial use. An eligible municipality wishing to adopt the new exemption must follow certain procedures specified in the new law, which differ depending on whether the municipality is a town or a city. (11 Journal of Multistate Taxation and Incentives, No. 3, 39.)

New Mexico

"New tax credits aimed at promoting research and development" (2001). In an effort to encourage technology-based businesses to engage in research, development, and experimentation in New Mexico, the state has enacted the Technology Jobs Tax Credit Act, providing a jobs tax credit to both individual and business taxpayers. The basic credit is 4 percent of qualified research expenditures, higher payrolls may produce an additional 4 percent credit, and various taxes may be offset. (11 Journal of Multistate Taxation and Incentives, No. 3, 41.)

"Tax Department adopts new rule for determining place of sale" (2001). A hearing officer for the New Mexico Taxation and Revenue Department ruled in *Apple Computer* (2000) that a sale occurs in New Mexico when a seller completes all acts necessary to complete its performance under the sales agreement. The hearing officer rejected the taxpayer's argument that a sale of tangible personal property occurs at the place title passes from the seller to the buyer. (11 Journal of Multistate Taxation and Incentives, No. 6, 46.)

New York

"Court applies standard for facial unconstitutionality" (2001). In *Tennessee Gas Pipeline Co.* (2000), the New York Appellate Division looked to both the language of the statute and case law to decide that New

219

York's "natural gas import tax" (NGIT) was constitutional. The court held that even though there may be some instances in which the NGIT may burden interstate commerce, that was not enough to declare the taxing statute unconstitutional on its face. Unless a challenging party can prove that the statute is invalid in all circumstances, such a challenge will fail. (10 Journal of Multistate Taxation and Incentives, No. 10, 30.)

"Dairy co-op denied packaging exemption for milk crates" (2001). In *Upstate Farms Cooperatives* (2001), the New York State Tax Appeals Tribunal ruled that purchases of milk crates by a milk processor and distributor for use in delivering milk to its customers were not exempt from sales tax under the exception for packaging materials. (11 Journal of Multistate Taxation and Incentives, No. 5, 45.)

"New York's empire zones take economic development incentives to the next level" (2001). In 1986, New York State created its Economic Development Zone (EDZ) Program, offering tax credits to promote the development of new businesses and the expansion of existing businesses in areas characterized by persistent and pervasive poverty, high unemployment, minimal job creation, and shrinking tax bases. Effective generally for tax years beginning after 2000, New York amended its tax laws to provide benefits under the Empire Zones Program Act (the Act), which also transformed the existing "Economic Development Zones" into "Empire Zones."

Currently, fifty-six areas throughout New York State are officially designated as Empire Zones. The Act adds new incentives for businesses that locate or expand in the Zones and meet the definition of a "Qualified Empire Zone Enterprise" (QEZE). A QEZE is a business enterprise that is certified as eligible to receive benefits under Article 18-B of the New York General Municipal Law, and which qualifies by meeting an annual "employment test." All these new benefits are discussed in greater detail in the article.

Effective for tax years beginning after 2000, a QEZE is allowed to claim a credit against corporate franchise (income) tax for a percentage of the tax attributable to the zone enterprise. As a result, most new general business corporations that began operations in a zone and operate only within the zones can reduce their income/franchise tax liability to zero during the first ten tax years of benefit eligibility. Effective for tax years beginning after 2000, a QEZE may claim a refundable credit against its New York franchise (income) tax for "eligible real property taxes." This credit also is available to a sole proprietor of a QEZE or a member of a partnership or limited liability company that is a QEZE.

Although not a new credit, New York's wage tax credit has been enhanced for tax years beginning after 2000 so that the credit now is double that which was offered for prior tax years. The enhanced wage tax credit generally is $1,500 per full-time employee hired to fill a new job, but it doubles to $3,000 per employee hired from certain targeted, economically disadvantaged groups. The wage tax credit is available for up to five consecutive years for QEZEs that hire full-time employees in newly created jobs.

QEZEs that create jobs and make new investments in qualified tangible property in the Empire Zone may qualify for tax credits of up to 19 percent of the cost or other basis, for federal income tax purposes, of the eligible investment. The basic Empire Zone 10 percent investment tax credit, generally applicable to investments in depreciable property in a Zone, may be increased by 90 percent over three years (via the Empire Zone employment incentive credit) merely by increasing the company's Empire Zone workforce by 1 percent.

Effective March 1, 2001, certain purchases and uses of tangible personal property and services (including utility services) by a QEZE within an Empire Zone are exempt from New York State's 4 percent sales-and-use tax and from the additional 0.25 percent tax imposed within New York City and certain surrounding counties for a period of ten years. The exemptions do not apply to

220

any locally imposed sales-and-use taxes unless the locality imposing the levy chooses to provide an exemption.

Various energy incentives may be available to eligible businesses that locate or are established in certain Empire Zones and create new jobs or make new investments there. Furthermore, businesses or home-owners who construct, alter, install, or improve real property located within an Empire Zone may be eligible for a partial exemption from real property taxes for up to ten years.

In January 2001, New York's Governor unveiled an unprecedented $1 billion high-technology and biotechnology plan to support the state in seeking to become a world leader in university-based research, business creation, and job development in those fields. The plan would fund three high-technology "Centers of Excellence" to directly link university researchers with business and industry leaders.

New York has undertaken numerous steps over the past several years to create a less-burdensome taxing environment in which to do business. The opportunity for both new and expanding businesses to operate in New York virtually free of all state and local taxes, along with the benefits of refundable tax credits, property tax exemptions, and utility discounts, are inducements that any company looking to expand its workforce and make new capital investments should examine before finalizing a location decision. (M. Grella & A.E. Westerlund, 11 Journal of Multistate Taxation and Incentives, No. 7, 6.)

"No refund for company financing vendors' now-bad A/R including tax" (2001). In *General Electric Capital* (2000), a finance company, General Electric Capital Corp (GECC), claimed refunds of sales taxes remitted to New York by unrelated third-party vendors where the finance company became the assignee of the vendors' credit card accounts receivable that subsequently became worthless debts. The sales tax refund claimed by GECC was attributable to the taxable sales the credit card customers charged but did not pay. The administrative law judge in this New York Division of Tax

Appeals case rejected the finance company's claim because the company had not made the original sales on which the tax was imposed. (11 Journal of Multistate Taxation and Incentives, No. 1, 22.)

North Carolina

"North Carolina enters the Delaware intangible holding company fracas" (2001). Final Decision No. 97-990, issued in 2000 by the North Carolina Secretary of Revenue, found that an out-of-state corporation with no physical presence in North Carolina that licensed trademarks to a related company with retail operations in the state was conducting business in the state and therefore subject to the state's corporate income and franchise taxes. The taxpayer in the decision was a Delaware corporation that licensed trademarks to retail affiliates in North Carolina, and then loaned the royalty funds back to the retail companies at a market rate of interest. The retail companies deducted the royalty payments and the interest expense on their North Carolina corporate tax returns. The decision recognized the Department of Revenue's long-standing position that the term "doing business" in North Carolina included the owning, renting, or operating of business or income-producing property in the state, including trademarks, trade names, and other intangibles.

The cornerstone of the decision was the theory that federal trademark law, specifically the Lanham Act, requires the regulation and control of the use of the trademark by the owner in order to prevent abandonment and loss. Under the "related company" doctrine, the legitimate, controlled use of the trademarks by the licensee inures to the benefit of the licensor, preventing their abandonment and loss. The taxpayers insisted that none of the trademark protection activities that they performed took place in North Carolina, thus precluding the state's imposition of corporate taxes. In contrast, the Department argued that the assessments were supported by the regulation and the taxpayers were operating a business in the state. And under the Lanham Act, these protection activities performed by the related companies created an agency relationship whereby the employees of the retail companies performed trademark protection activities on behalf of and for the benefit of the licensors.

The decision contained a detailed summary of the issues raised by the parties under the U.S. Constitution and related U.S. Supreme Court decisions. The Due Process Clause of the U.S. Constitution requires that, first, some minimal connection must exist between a taxpayer's interstate activities and the state seeking to impose a tax and, second, some relationship must exist between the income the state is seeking to tax and the taxpayer's in-state operations. The Department argued that the activities of both the taxpayers and the retail companies acting on the taxpayers' behalf met the minimum contact requirements of the Due Process Clause. Emphasizing the absence of any taxpayer-owned real or tangible personal property or employees in North Carolina, the taxpayers argued, on Commerce Clause grounds, that their lack of physical presence precluded the state from imposing tax. The Department argued a different interpretation, that, when income taxes are at issue, the test for establishing nexus under the Commerce Clause is substantial nexus, not physical presence. The licensing agreements and the required trademark protection activities established an agency relationship sufficient to satisfy physical presence.

A bill introduced on April 5, 2001, would require an add-back of intangible expense and interest costs that are paid to a related company and would impose substantial penalties for failure to comply. However, the issues addressed in Final Decision No. 97-990 remain highly controversial and unsettled and have created a dilemma for taxpayers and practitioners. Until the decision is modified or overturned, a nondomiciled corporation's licensing of trademarks to a North Carolina entity may establish taxable nexus and subject the nondomiciliary corporation to the state's corporate income and franchise taxes. The Due Process and Commerce Clause arguments are being raised in several forums, and are likely to beg for resolution by the U.S. Supreme Court. In the meantime, tax practitioners and corporations with multistate activities must step lightly through the minefields of state taxation. (M.A. Hannah & C.W. Hall III, 11 Journal of Multistate Taxation and Incentives, No. 4, 6.)

"The apportionability of liquidation gain in light of *Lenox, Inc.*" (2001). The taxpayer in *Lenox* (2000), a decision of the North Carolina Court of Appeals, was a manufacturer of consumer products that did business in several states, including North Carolina. After selling a special operating division devoted exclusively to the making and selling of fine jewelry in 1988, the taxpayer distributed the sale funds to its parent, allocating the resulting gain from the sales transaction to New Jersey, its commercial domicile. The North Carolina Department of Revenue took exception, contending that the gain was apportionable "business income," arising from transactions and activity in the regular course of the corporation's trade or business, and included income from tangible and intangible property if the acquisition, management, and/or disposition of the property constituted integral parts of the corporation's regular trade or business operations.

This definition is modeled after the one found in the Uniform Division of Income for Tax Purposes Act (UDITPA). As have courts in the majority of states adopting UDITPA, North Carolina courts have ruled that this "business income" definition consists of two tests—a transactional test that asks if an income-producing transaction took place as a regular part of the taxpayer's business and a functional test that seeks a nexus or connection between an income- producing asset and the taxpayer's regular business operations.

In considering whether the gain from a liquidating disposition of assets that the taxpayer had used in producing business income is necessarily also business income under the functional test, the *Lenox* court reviewed case law from courts in other UDITPA states. The court surveyed opinions from Kansas, New Mexico, Pennsylvania, and Illinois that proposed that gain from a liquidating disposition is not necessarily business income under the functional test even though the assets that the taxpayer has sold may have been used in producing business income. The state supreme court suggested that liquidating dispositions do not produce business income under the functional test because such transactions represent a means of terminating, rather than advancing, the taxpayer's regular trade or business. In one court's view, the taxpayer's failure to reinvest sale proceeds in the business was evidence that the taxpayer had not disposed of the asset as an integral part of its business. If the cases reviewed by the court in *Lenox* *implicitly* acknowledge that, when it comes to the functional test, the nature of a liquidating disposition trumps the nexus between an income-producing asset and the taxpayer's regular business operations, at least two decisions *explicitly* embrace this view. In *Polaroid* (1998), the North Carolina Supreme Court expressly noted that cases involving liquidating dispositions "are in a category by themselves."

In *Lenox*, after surveying the cases discussed in the article, the North Carolina Court of Appeals returned to the facts at hand. The court noted that Lenox's sale represented the complete termination of the taxpayer's involvement in the fine jewelry business. In addition, the sales proceeds were immediately distributed to the taxpayer's corporate parent and not reinvested in continuing operations. Thus, the court concluded that the totality of the circumstances compelled the conclusion that the liquidation gain was not business income under the functional test.

After *Lenox*, the view that gains from the disposition of capital assets are always subject to apportionment needs to be reexamined. Indeed, in the aftermath of the North Carolina appellate court's opinion, the message to taxpayers in liquidating disposition cases is that the gain is not always business income. (J.M. Goodman & B.L. Browdy, 11 Journal of Multistate Taxation and Incentives, No. 1, 6.)

Ohio

"Court rules on taxability of in-store advertising" (2001). In *TV Fanfare Publications* (1999), the Ohio Supreme Court held that a "production charge" for *creating* advertising material to be placed on supermarket shopping carts and other supermarket property was subject to Ohio's use tax, but that an "advertising service charge" for *placing* the advertising material on the carts and in the supermarkets was not subject to tax. (10 Journal of Multistate Taxation and Incentives, No. 10, 27.)

"Limit on foreign-dividend deduction was unconstitutional" (2001). In *Emerson Electric* (2000), the Ohio Supreme Court held that the state's taxing scheme, which permitted a corporation to deduct 100 percent of the dividends received from domestic subsidiaries but only 85 percent of the dividends received from foreign (i.e., non-U.S.) subsidiaries, violated the Foreign Commerce Clause of the U.S. Constitution. (11 Journal of Multistate Taxation and Incentives, No. 1, 46.)

"Machinery used to weigh, sort goods was exempt packaging equipment" (2001). In *Newfield Publications* (1999), the Ohio Supreme Court held that a series of machines that were integral and essential parts of the vendor's equipment used in placing packaged merchandise into bulk packages for shipment to a mail house, and ultimately to customers, was exempt from sales and use taxes. (10 Journal of Multistate Taxation and Incentives, No. 10, 29.)

"Tax credit, property exemption were not corporate favoritism" (2001). In *Cuno v. DaimlerChrysler* (2001), an Ohio federal district court sided with DaimlerChrysler in upholding the legality of $280 million in tax benefits it received primarily as an inducement for the automaker to keep operating in Toledo, Ohio. The eighteen plaintiffs claimed that Ohio's statutory tax incentive schemes "compel a conclusion of corporate favoritism" that violates the Equal Protection Clause of the Ohio Constitution and the

Commerce Clause of the U.S. Constitution. The federal district court disagreed, finding a legitimate state interest with a rational nexus to the credit and exemption, and no violation of equal protection. (11 Journal of Multistate Taxation and Incentives, No. 8, 40.)

Oklahoma

"Tax increment financing and similar incentives stimulate Oklahoma's economy" (2001). "Tax increment financing" is a financial technique intended to stimulate economic activity in a designated geographic area that otherwise would have limited growth potential. In essence, this procedure allows the government to segregate or apportion new or incremental property taxes and other levies that are generated primarily as a result of a specific development project to pay for public improvements associated with the project. Prior to the project's implementation, a "baseline" assessed value is established for all real and personal property in the district. The subsequent increase in value over the baseline that results from the improvements to the property in the district generates the incremental taxes that can be used to fund the project on a "pay-as-you-go basis" or to pay debt service on bonds issued to finance the improvements. Under a tax increment financing plan, the regular taxing entities typically are guaranteed as much tax revenue from the area as they receive in the base year. Once the financial obligations of tax increment financing are satisfied, substantially increased tax revenues should be available for the taxing entities in the area.

Tax increment financing was implemented in Oklahoma in 1990 when the voters approved a new provision, Section 6C, in Article X of the state constitution, authorizing specific political subdivisions (cities, towns, counties) to use local taxes and fees for "assistance in development financing" to encourage historic preservation and development in areas of economic stagnation or decline. The Local Development Act authorizes Oklahoma's towns, cities, and counties, after notice and hearing, to designate tax increment districts and approve project plans. In addition, the Act provides for the issuance of debt in the form of bonds or "other obligations" to finance project costs and provides details for retirement of these obligations from incremental revenues that the subdivision receives as a result of the project being financed. The article describes how several towns and cities in Oklahoma have used tax increment financing in distressed areas within their jurisdictions and to create areas that will attract economic development, including purchases of land and making site improvements. In 2000, the state legislature modified the Local Development Act to clarify its application, subsequent to a state supreme court ruling that Oklahoma City's Health Sciences Center Park's long-term debt arrangements were not properly authorized.

Two other, related, but different incentives that may be used by Oklahoma political jurisdictions are incentive districts and urban redevelopment or renewal districts. An incentive district is created as a reaction to a business's location or relocation and specifically benefits a business via tax relief. Several Oklahoma communities have used incentive districts for historical preservation, blight diffusion, and simply to get a business to come to town.

The Urban Renewal Act set out a method to use certain ad valorem tax revenues to pay costs resulting from urban redevelopment efforts within municipalities by allowing the legislature to allocate a portion of new ad valorem taxes derived from increased value within a tax increment district, regardless of the taxing entity. The County Excise Board was mandated by legislation to allocate a percentage of these taxes to be used for urban renewal and redevelopment if a city or town within the county performed certain steps to establish the urban renewal project and created a tax incremental allocation district and requested that the taxes be set aside annually. Since the Urban Renewal Act results in a smaller possibility of funds being available for community and economic development than does the Local Development Act, its use has become less frequent.

Today's competitive economic development environment requires communities to employ financing tools to enhance their appeal as a suitable place for business. In addition, community development in connection with revitalization, creation of employment opportunities, and dealing with population growth will be enhanced through more frequent use of tax increment financing. As more increment districts are formed and tested in Oklahoma, the state's evolving law should become clearer, and thus more conducive to use. (B. Vincent, 11 Journal of Multistate Taxation and Incentives, No. 3, 14.)

Oregon

"State expands pollution control facility incentives" (2001). Under legislation effective October 6, 2001, Oregon has expanded its pollution control facility credit allowed against corporate and personal income taxes and the property tax exemption provisions relating to pollution control facilities. The new law extends the carryover period for unexpired tax credits and also modifies the calculation of the maximum credit allowed in any one tax year. The requirements necessary for a certificate to be effective for tax relief must be fulfilled prior to 2008, instead of 2002, as required by the prior law. (11 Journal of Multistate Taxation and Incentives, No. 8, 42.)

Pennsylvania

"Commonwealth revises statute, gives up on basic UDITPA income division" (2001). Although Pennsylvania essentially adopted the apportionment and allocation of income provisions of the Uniform Division of Income for Tax Purposes Act (UDITPA), in Act 2001-23 the state has attempted to resolve the business/nonbusiness income debate that frequently arises in multistate corporate franchise and income taxation. In a change made retroactive to tax years beginning after 1998, the Commonwealth rewrote the UDITPA-like definitions of "business

income" and "nonbusiness income" to eliminate any distinction between the two types of income and returned to a pure apportionment regime. (11 Journal of Multistate Taxation and Incentives, No. 6, 34.)

"Court orders retroactive remedy for severed invalid exemption" (2001). The litigation in *Annenberg*, which has produced five judicial opinions to date, was sent back to Montgomery County for further proceedings by the Pennsylvania Supreme Court in 2000. The statute contested by the taxpayer in this case allows Pennsylvania's 67 counties to impose a tax on Pennsylvania-resident holders of specified intangible personal property (primarily securities) but expressly exempts from the tax shares of stock in corporations that transact business in Pennsylvania.

The State Supreme Court held that the tax was unconstitutional and violated the Interstate Commerce Clause. The court also found the exemption clause severable from the tax statute, so that counties were free to impose tax on all stock. The requirement that retrospective relief be provided carries problems, because the options for that relief are unclear. A decision will have to be made whether to impose the tax retrospectively on all shares of stock or to repeal the county imposition of personal property tax partially (on shares of stock only) or entirely (on all intangibles). (11 Journal of Multistate Taxation and Incentives, No. 1, 29.)

"Developers denied a second round of property tax incentives" (2001). According to the Pennsylvania Supreme Court's ruling in *Lincoln Philadelphia Realty* (2000), several real estate developers that had received real property tax exemptions under a program to encourage construction in economically depressed areas could not later seek larger exemptions even though the city ordinance authorizing the original exemptions may not have followed statutory guidelines. The court denied the taxpayers' appeals, finding that they missed the deadlines for appealing the original decisions. The court also rejected two seemingly contradictory challenges regarding the authority and independence of the Board of Revision. (11 Journal of Multistate Taxation and Incentives, No. 3, 42.)

"Governor announces twelve new Keystone Opportunity Zones" (2001). In 2001, the Governor of Pennsylvania announced the creation of twelve new Keystone Opportunity Zones under an expansion of the state's existing economic development program. The expanded program also contains tax incentives for banks, insurance companies, and utilities, and provides a job tax credit for certain types of utilities that did not receive full tax relief under the original program. (11 Journal of Multistate Taxation and Incentives, No. 8, 42.)

South Carolina

"New corporate tax moratorium for creating new jobs" (2001). Under South Carolina legislation enacted in 2000, for tax years beginning after 1999, a corporate taxpayer that, within a five-year period, creates and maintains at least 100 new, full-time jobs at a qualified facility in certain counties in the state is allowed a ten-year moratorium on a portion of its South Carolina corporate income taxes. A fifteen-year moratorium applies if the taxpayer creates and maintains at least 200 new, full-time jobs. The determination of what is a new, full-time job, a qualified facility, the seven qualified counties, and certain other rules are defined in the job-credit tax statute and summarized in the article. (11 Journal of Multistate Taxation and Incentives, No. 3, 44.)

Tennessee

"Tax applied to aircraft fuel used in interstate commerce" (2001). In *American Airlines* (2000), the Tennessee Court of Appeals affirmed the imposition of use tax on aircraft fuel that was piped into Tennessee and used by an airline for flights to out-of-state destinations. (11 Journal of Multistate Taxation and Incentives, No. 5, 48.)

Texas

"Court says physical presence needed for franchise tax nexus" (2001). In *Rylander v. Bandag Licensing Corp.* (2000), the Texas Court of Appeals heldthat an out-of-state intangible holding company that licenses intellectual property in the state did not have franchise tax nexus where its sole contact with Texas was the holding of a certificate of authority (COA) to do business in the state. The appellate court ruled that the mere possession of the COA was not an "activity" and therefore insufficient to satisfy the "substantial nexus" requirement under the Commerce Clause, which requires a physical presence in the taxing state. As interpreted by the Texas courts, the mere holding of a COA also was insufficient as a contact to meet the "minimum connection" requirement under the Due Process Clause. (11 Journal of Multistate Taxation and Incentives, No. 1, 48.)

Utah

"Tenth Circuit agrees 4R Act voids state's Eleventh Amendment immunity" (2001). In *Union Pacific* (1999), the Tenth Circuit Court of Appeals held that the Eleventh Amendment did not provide Utah immunity from lawsuits under the Railroad Revitalization and Regulatory Reform Act of 1976 (the 4R Act), which authorizes rail carriers to challenge a state tax as discriminatory. (11 Journal of Multistate Taxation and Incentives, No. 1, 32.)

Washington

"Taxpayer should have claimed benefits despite apparent ineligibility" (2001). In *CPC Partnership*, a 2001 Washington Board of Tax Appeals ruling, taxpayers who had failed to apply for tax incentives because they thought they did not qualify for benefits could not rely on the doctrines of equitable estoppel or unjust enrichment to get refunds when a court decision made it appear that they would be eligible for the programs. (11

Journal of Multistate Taxation and Incentives, No. 8, 44.)

STATUTE OF LIMITATIONS

(*See* Assessment and Collection—Statute of Limitations)

STOCK OPTIONS

"Affiliates must share value of compensatory stock options as compensation cost" (2001). Under Regulation § 1.482-7, the value of compensatory stock options is a compensation cost that must be shared with affiliates under a qualified cost-sharing arrangement, according to FSA 200103024. (94 Journal of Taxation 250.)

"Beware of AMT on incentive stock options" (2001). L.M. Kaplan, 67 Practical Tax Strategies 260. (*Digested under* Alternative Minimum Tax, page 5.)

"Employees of controlled partnership (electing to be taxed as a corporation) may participate in parent corporation's employee stock-purchase plan" (2001). Letter Ruling 200046013 addresses the application of the employment relationship requirements of Regulation § 1.421-7(h) to a Section 423 Employee Stock Purchase Plan adopted by a corporation utilizing check-the-box entities in its corporate structure. (3 Business Entities, No. 1, 58.)

"Grant under stock incentive plan met the requirements for performance-based exception" (2001). 95 Journal of Taxation 313. (*Digested under* Compensation for Personal Services, page 26.)

"Pledge of stock options provides charitable deduction for corporation" (2001). A corporation is entitled to a charitable contribution deduction for the pledge of an option to a foundation, according to Letter Ruling 200141019. (95 Journal of Taxation 374.)

"Statutory stock options avoid withholding—for now" (2001). 66 Practical Tax Strategies 254. (*Digested under* Withholding of Tax, page 270.)

"Tax consequences of converting stock options in a spinoff" (2001). 95 Journal of Taxation 119. (*Digested under* Reorganizations, page 178.)

STOCK REDEMPTIONS

(*See* Redemptions)

SUBCHAPTER S

(*See* S Corporations)

SUBSIDIARIES

(*See* Affiliated Corporations)

T

TAXABLE YEAR

(*See* Accounting Methods)

TAXATION, GENERALLY

"New law offers tax relief for individuals—but only temporarily" (2001). The Economic Growth and Tax Relief Reconciliation Act of 2001 (the Act) contains a wide array of tax cuts, but many are phased in and all the provisions terminate no later than 2011.

First, the author discusses tax rate reductions, personal exemptions, and itemized deductions. The Act creates a new 10 percent regular income tax bracket and reduces the rates of upper income tax brackets. No reduction is otherwise provided for the 15 percent bracket. The Act reduces and eventually eliminates the phase-out of the personal exemption for upper-income taxpayers. The Act reduces and eventually eliminates the overall limitation on itemized deductions for all taxpayers.

Then, the author addresses tax benefits relating to children, marriage penalty relief, education incentives, IRAs, and alternative minimum tax. (R.E. Ward, 67 Practical Tax Strategies 30.)

"Numerous inflation-adjusted thresholds rise in 2001" (2001). Some important tax thresholds and filing figures have increased in 2001 because of inflation indexing, according to Revenue Procedure 2001-13 (and clarified by Notice 2001-12). (66 Practical Tax Strategies 117.)

"Roundup of tax developments from the year that was" (2001). Election year politics provided much in the way of promised tax reforms and benefits but little in the way of legislation. Congress voted to provide relief for the so-called marriage penalty by expanding the lower tax brackets and liberalizing the earned income tax credit. President Clinton, however, vetoed this bill on August 5, 2000. In addition, Congress voted to repeal the federal estate and gift tax over a ten-year period but this bill was also vetoed by the President on August 31, 2000. As of the writing of this article, the House had voted to repeal the foreign sales corporation (FSC) provisions and enact broader exclusions for extraterritorial income. The House's action was prompted by a World Trade Organization ruling that the FSC provisions were an illegal export subsidy. The proposed provisions have been criticized by many European trading partners, and it remains to be seen what the final resolution of this issue will entail.

Legislation was passed that, for instance, extended various provisions, including the research and experimentation tax credit and provided for the use of certain nonrefundable credits, such as the education and child care credits against alternative minimum tax (AMT) liability. In addition, this legislation also sharply curtailed the availability of the installment method of accounting. Moreover, various judicial and administrative developments occurred that affect numerous taxpayers.

First, the author discusses gross income for individuals. Four cases highlighted the split of authority that exists with respect to whether an attorney's share of a contingent fee was includable in the taxpayer's gross income.

Then, the author addresses developments concerning tax accounting, corporations (including S corporations), partnerships, and real estate. (M.A. Melone, 66 Practical Tax Strategies 25.)

"Selected highlights of the Economic Growth and Tax Relief Reconciliation Act of 2001" (2001). The highlights of the Economic Growth and Tax Relief Reconciliation Act of 2001 (the Act) covered in this article represent only a portion of the numerous amendments, additions, and repeal of provisions of the Code contained in the Act. Learning, understanding, and applying all of the various provisions of the Act as they become effective over the next ten years, as well as keeping abreast of additional changes that will certainly be enacted, will present a major challenge to tax professionals. In addition, the widespread skepticism that Congress will allow the entire Act to sunset on December 31, 2010, will make tax planning particularly difficult. Planning around the estate, gift, and generation-skipping transfer (GST) taxes has always been complicated, and it has been made even more so by the complexity of the Act and the uncertainty as to what the rules will be over the long term.

First, the author discusses income tax provisions for individuals. The income tax provisions for individuals in the Act include tax rate reduction, refunds, repeal of the phase-out of itemized deductions and personal exemptions, alternative minimum tax and marriage penalty relief, the child tax credit, adoption and education tax benefits, student loans, and IRAs.

Then, the author addresses estate, gift, and GST tax provisions. Although there has been extensive media coverage about the repeal of the death taxes, in reality, the estate tax and the GST tax have been repealed only for one year, 2010. The gift tax has not been repealed and continues in effect even after the repeal of the estate tax and the GST tax. (D.C. Treich, 3 Business Entities, No. 5, 30.)

TAX-EXEMPT ORGANIZATIONS

(*See also* Charitable Contributions)

In General

"Defunct organization cannot challenge revocation of exemption" (2001). In *Abraham Lincoln Opportunity Foundation* (ALOF) (2001), the Eleventh Circuit upheld the dismissal of a suit by ALOF challenging the IRS's revocation of its Section 501(c)(3) status after it had already been dissolved. (13 Taxation of Exempts 104.)

"For-profit sub okayed, but rent payments from sub to public charity parent will be taxable" (2001). A tax-exempt organization often wishes to establish a business activity that complements its charitable purpose but would not necessarily be considered a "charitable function," or that may be a business venture unrelated to the charity's primary activities. According to Letter Ruling 200132040, a tax-exempt organization can establish a for-profit subsidiary in these situations to operate the business without adversely affecting the parent organization's Section 501(c)(3) exempt status. (95 Journal of Taxation 253.)

"How to establish donor-advised funds and community foundations" (2001). The controversy over the roles of for-profits that set up donor-advised funds is less important than the ambiguities of what rules the IRS will apply to them.

First, the author provides background on community foundations and donor-advised funds, including their advantages and disadvantages. The 1990s saw a donor-advised fund surpass all but two other charities in annual donations and, not coincidentally, saw the IRS change from mounting an attack to recognizing a permanent new charitable vehicle. The 2000s are likely to see massive growth in the donor-advised fund segment of the nonprofit world, not by drawing donations away from other nonprofits, but by attracting a growing portion of the $41 trillion wealth transfer over the years 1998 through 2052. This should be welcomed, not feared.

Then, the author considers community foundation requirements, and donor-advised fund requirements. There are two tests that must be met for a "community trust." The first deals with the parts and is generally referred to as the component part test. The second, referring to the whole, is called the single entity test. The component part test incorporates the private foundation rules of Regulation § 1.507-2(a)(8), adapted to apply to the community foundation. The reasoning is that a fund with a material restriction is not a component part, and that a gift with a material restriction is not a completed gift. The requirements are extensive.

There have been a number of IRS private letter rulings involving funds sponsored by community foundations, as well as rulings involving free-standing donor-advised funds. In other rulings, the IRS has dealt with community foundations without ruling on donor-advised funds specifically.

The IRS says that it reviews donor-advised funds using the principles similar to the material restriction or condition requirements of Regulation § 1.507-2(a)(8), but does not expressly refer to the rest of the component part test or the single entity test. The IRS elsewhere has said that both groups are subject to the same rules, and has referred to similar but unclear rules. These rules are fairly similar to the Administration's Green Book proposals in February 2000.

Finally, the author provides guidance on establishing a community foundation or donor-advised fund and addresses possible legislation or rules. (W.R. Bird, 13 Taxation of Exempts 68.)

"Internet guidance should reconcile old law with a new medium" (2001). On October 16, 2000, the IRS published Announcement 2000-84, giving notice that the IRS is "considering the necessity of issuing guidance that would clarify the application of the Internal Revenue Code to the use of the Internet by exempt organizations." The announcement states that the IRS "has made no final decision concerning the need for additional guidance," and that it may conclude that no further guidance is necessary. In short, the IRS is asking for guidance about whether to issue guidance.

The announcement is unique because it seeks guidance on the application of a variety of different Code provisions to a single technological medium—the Internet. The authors are not aware of any other situation in which the IRS has focused its inquiry on a specific method of conveying information as opposed to a particular Code section or sections. This announcement is testament to the dramatic influence that the Internet has had on the work of exempt organizations.

In the announcement, the IRS asks for guidance in each of the following areas: (1) whether guidance is required at all; (2) general considerations about how we think about a Website; (3) political and lobbying activities; (4) unrelated business income tax (UBIT); and (5) solicitation of charitable contributions and disclosure by charities. In each of the substantive areas, the IRS identifies some specific questions, but also asks the public to pose questions and consider issues that the IRS has not asked.

After providing background on the announcement, the authors argue that the IRS should provide guidance, by issuing at least two detailed revenue rulings, one in the area of lobbying and political activity and one in the area of UBIT.

Then, the authors address general considerations about web sites, UBIT, and charitable solicitations. (R.A. Wexler & A.M. Anderson, 12 Journal of Taxation of Exempt Organizations 187.)

"IRS takes hard line on Section 501(c)(3) bonds and exempt status" (2001). E.M. Mills, 13 Taxation of Exempts 45. (*Digested under* Bonds, Debentures, and Notes, page 9.)

"Looking back to assess the *United Cancer Council* case" (2001). The Seventh Circuit decision in *United Cancer Council* (1999) has influenced both state laws on charitable solicitation and temporary regulations on intermediate sanctions.

First, the author discusses the case. The United Cancer Council (UCC) was organized in 1963, but did not receive its tax-exempt status until 1969. In 1984, UCC operated on a budget of $35,000 and, according to the summary of facts in the Seventh Circuit's decision, was on the verge of bankruptcy. The board of directors retained The Watson & Hughey Company (W&H), a direct mail consultant that specialized in raising funds for small charitable organizations. The negotiations between UCC and W&H culminated in an "arm's-length" agreement.

Because of UCC's weak financial position, the committee of the board that negotiated the agreement wanted W&H to "front the expenses" to conduct the fundraising campaign. In return for assuming the risk, W&H was given "exclusivity" during the term of a five-year contract, as well as co-ownership of the list of donors to be produced by the fundraising campaign. UCC's right to use the list was restricted to appeals to its own donors, but W&H's right to use the list was unrestricted. During the term of the contract, W&H raised $28.7 million at a cost of $26.5 million.

The contract expired on May 30, 1989, leaving UCC with a substantial, valuable donor list and the opportunity to negotiate a contract with another direct marketing consultant. UCC seized the opportunity, but the venture was far from successful. UCC was forced to file in bankruptcy on June 1, 1990. Shortly thereafter, the IRS revoked UCC's tax-exempt status retroactively to the date the organization signed the contract with W&H. UCC challenged the retroactive revocation in the Tax Court. After a lengthy trial and a very long wait, a decision was issued in December 1997.

The Tax Court upheld the IRS's revocation on the sole basis that UCC had allowed its assets to "inure" to the benefit of W&H. Finding W&H to be an "insider," Judge Chabot endorsed the IRS's private inurement argument. Clearly controversial, the decision of the Tax Court was welcomed by many and criticized by others.

The UCC appealed to the Seventh Circuit. The heart of the appeal was the challenge to the determination that an "outsider" could become an "insider" as the result of a contractual advantage, and thereby have the doctrine of inurement applied to UCC.

While the decision was reversed on the issue of inurement, it was remanded to the Tax Court on the issue of private benefit. The Tax Court did not reach a decision on that theory, and the case had proceeded no further when the parties entered into a closing agreement. Although the case is now over, its effect is still being felt.

Then, the author addresses the impact of the case. When the IRS pursued the revocation of UCC's tax-exempt status, the organization was already in bankruptcy, and perhaps the IRS believed the revocation would not be challenged. The IRS's victory in the Tax Court was dramatically reversed by the Seventh Circuit's decision, but what it lost in court it may have won in reality. The industry took note of the facts and circumstances of the *UCC* case, as did other regulatory agencies and the states. Therefore, it can be said that the *UCC* case prompted changes, mostly of a positive nature, relative to industry practices and regulatory oversight of the fundraising process. (E. Copilevitz, 13 Taxation of Exempts 63.)

"Separate exemption applications not needed for single-member LLCs owned by exempt support organization" (2001). 95 Journal of Taxation 248. (*Digested under* Limited Liability Companies, page 123.)

"The commerciality doctrine is a judicial border patrol for charities' activities" (2001). The commerciality doctrine is a judge-made tool that can be used against charitable activities with a commercial "hue."

First, the author discusses the organizational and operational tests under Section 501(c)(3), the framework in which the IRS can raise the commerciality doctrine, and the "feeder" rules. To be exempt as a Section 501(c)(3) charity, an organization must meet both organizational and operational tests.

With minimal guidance, almost every organization can pass the organizational test. The operational test, however, is much more subjective and provides the framework in which the IRS can raise the commerciality doctrine.

Even though the commerciality doctrine is a creation of case law, some statutory rules provide a good background for analyzing the doctrine. Section 502, for example, sets out the general rule that an organization operating a trade or business for profit as a "feeder" for a tax-exempt organization will not qualify as tax-exempt itself, even though all its profits support the charity.

Then, the author addresses the origin of the commerciality doctrine in case law, contemporary case law, and contemporary application of the doctrine. In 1991, the Seventh Circuit explored the contemporary use of the commerciality doctrine in *Living Faith, Inc.* In that case, a Seventh-Day Adventist organization operated vegetarian restaurants and health food stores in furtherance of church doctrine. Given the commercial character of its restaurants, however, the IRS, the Tax Court, and the Seventh Circuit agreed that the organization should be denied exempt status, concluding that it "conducts its operations with a substantial commercial purpose." Despite the organization's religious hue, the Seventh Circuit supported use of the commerciality doctrine. (J.R. Walker, 12 Journal of Taxation of Exempt Organizations 209.)

"The evolving use of limited liability companies by tax-exempt organizations" (2001). R.W. Friz, 13 Taxation of Exempts 112. (*Digested under* Limited Liability Companies, page 123.)

"VEBA's return of assets did not cause retroactive loss of exemption, penalty" (2001). The IRS concluded in Letter Ruling 200126034 that a VEBA's return of assets to its tax-exempt sponsoring employer did not cause the retroactive revocation of the VEBA's exempt status under Section 501(c)(9), did not trigger the Section 4976 excise tax, and did not result in unrelated business taxable income to either the sponsoring employer or the VEBA. (95 Journal of Taxation 185.)

"What nonprofits should look for as states consider Internet taxation" (2001). N.H. Wright, 12 Journal of Taxation of Exempt Organizations 155. (*Digested under* State Taxes—In General, page 209.)

Colleges, Universities, and Other Educational Institutions

"Treasury issues proposed regulations on information reporting for education credits and student loan interest" (2001). N.J. Foran, 12 Journal of Taxation of Exempt Organizations 161. (*Digested under* Tax-Exempt Organizations—Disclosure and Information Reporting, page 236.)

Compensation and Benefits

"A selective review of the intermediate sanctions temporary regulations—generally, improved all around" (2001). In brief, the law states that if a transaction between an "applicable tax-exempt organization" and a "disqualified person" confers an "excess benefit" on the disqualified person, he or she is liable for an excise tax equal to 25 percent of the excess benefit or 200 percent of the excess benefit if the transaction is not "corrected" in a timely manner.

Furthermore, "organization managers" who knowingly "participate" in the transaction can be held personally liable for an excise tax equal to 10 percent of the excess benefit, up to $10,000. Under Section 4958(d)(1) liability is joint and several, and under Temporary Regulation § 53.4958-IT(f) covered transactions include all those occurring after September 13, 1995.

The legislative history and the 1998 proposed regulations contained two safe harbors that help mitigate the potentially punitive effects of the law: (1) An organization can invoke a "rebuttable presumption of reasonableness" if an "authorized body" of the organization approves the transaction in advance, relies on "appropriate data" regarding comparability, and "adequately documents" the basis for its findings. (2) Similarly, "organization managers" can protect themselves from liability for the 10 percent/$10,000 excise tax by relying on a "reasoned written opinion" of certain professionals.

Through these safe harbors, the organization and its managers (but not the disqualified person) can help insulate themselves from liability for intermediate sanctions.

After providing background, the author discusses the new temporary regulations. After thirteen pages of commentary in the Preamble, including responses to several proposals made with respect to the 1998 proposed regulations, the temporary regulations are organized as follows: (1) taxes on excess benefit transactions, including, inter alia, definitions of "excess benefit," "organization manager," and "participation," and rules governing joint and several liability, statutes of limitation, and effective dates (Temporary Regulation § 53.4958-1T); (2) definition of "applicable tax-exempt organization" (Temporary Regulation § 53.4958-2T); (3) definition of "disqualified person" (Temporary Regulation § 53.4958-3T); (4) "excess benefit transaction," including a definition, exclusions, and the "initial contract rule" (Temporary Regulation § 53.4958-4T); (5) rebuttable presumption of reasonableness (Temporary Regulation § 53.4958-6T); (6) correction (Temporary Regulation § 53.4958-7T); and (7) special rules, including those governing church tax inquiries under Section 7611 (Temporary Regulation § 53.4958-8T).

Another section has been reserved for future regulations governing revenue-sharing arrangements. The IRS has touted the temporary regulations as an easy-to-use "road map" for avoiding inurement. Whether or not this proves true, the temporary regulations certainly are comprehensive albeit with a few glaring omissions.

An examination of what the IRS has done—and failed to do—to guide exempt organizations toward compliance with the intermediate sanctions law reveals that many of the more restrictive provisions of the proposed regulations have been liberalized,

particularly the rules regarding the operation of the rebuttable presumption of reasonableness.

Then, the author turns to enforcement, Form 990, and public relations. Some mixed messages are coming from Washington on the subject of enforcement. On the one hand, there have been indications that fewer resources are available for exempt organization (EO) audits. On the other hand, the IRS already has imposed intermediate sanctions in a few notable cases.

Any practitioner who has reviewed a Form 990 recently is painfully aware that EOs must disclose: (1) whether they engaged in or became aware of any excess benefit transaction during the year and (2) the amount of excise taxes their organization managers or disqualified persons were required to pay during the year. (P.S. Kaufmann, 94 Journal of Taxation 301.)

"Temporary regulations provide window of opportunity on intermediate sanctions" (2001). On January 10, 2001, the IRS issued temporary regulations under what are commonly known as the intermediate sanction rules of Section 4958. The temporary regulations, which expand on the previously issued proposed regulations concerning the penalty excise tax, took effect on the same day and will remain in effect through January 9, 2004. This gives organizations a window of opportunity to implement safe-harbor procedures concerning any business deal or compensation agreements that they may currently have in place or may enter into.

The temporary regulations make important modifications to the circumstances that can lead to imposition of these penalty taxes. The policies and procedures an organization previously adopted to maintain compliance with the prior version of these rules should be reviewed in light of these changes. For many organizations, compliance with the requirements prescribed in the temporary regulations may be less burdensome than the level of effort necessary to meet previous standards. The temporary regulations reiterate that the intermediate sanctions penalty excise taxes will not affect the substantive standards for tax exemption under Section 501(c)(3) or Section 501(c)(4).

First, the author discusses who and what actions are affected. The intermediate sanctions penalize individuals with positions of substantial influence over certain tax-exempt organizations (disqualified persons) who use their leverage to receive undue financial benefits (in excess benefit transactions). Any person who was in a position to exercise substantial influence over the affairs of the tax-exempt entity at any time during a five-year period ending on the date of the excess benefit transaction will be treated as a disqualified person.

Then, the author addresses safe harbors. Various provisions within the temporary regulations may be interpreted as safe harbors because they provide clear guidance on actions that an organization may take to protect itself from being subject to the intermediate sanctions penalties.

Finally, the author considers other rules, including those applicable to revenue-sharing and a second-tier tax. The law does not specifically state when an excess benefit transaction occurs, but the temporary regulations provide that it occurs on the date that the disqualified person receives the economic benefit. In the case of deferred compensation, the date is the last day of the tax year of the disqualified person during which the benefit is earned and vested. (J.M. Buehler, 13 Taxation of Exempts 3.)

Disclosure and Information Reporting

"New campaign finance disclosure law hits the wrong target" (2001). On July 1, 2000, President Clinton signed legislation (P.L. 106-230, "the Act") designed to require certain political organizations to disclose activities they had not previously had to disclose. These groups, frequently referred to as stealth political action committees (PACs), are creatures of the Code, existing in the nether territory between the IRS's definition of "political activity" and the more narrow definition used by the Federal Election Commission (FEC).

The Act was designed to shine the light on these groups, many of which were said to be taking in barrels full of corporate cash, using it to influence elections, and not reporting a dime of it. It was enacted without any real consideration or debate in Congress, however. Not unexpectedly, it includes some disastrous unintended consequences.

After providing background, the author discusses the Act and its consequences—both intended and unintended. The Act is divided into three sections: (1) required notification of Section 527 status; (2) disclosures by political organizations; and (3) return requirements relating to Section 527 organizations.

One unintended consequence of great consequence to leaders of state associations is the requirement that a number of "non-stealth" state and local political organizations comply with the Act. Thus, the Act creates new, duplicative disclosure requirements for these state entities that already disclose their activities to their own state election authorities. This application to about 10,000 political organizations only serves to obscure the real focus of the Act—organizations that seek to influence the outcome of federal elections without being forced to disclose their activities to the FEC. (G. Constantine, 12 Journal of Taxation of Exempt Organizations 150.)

"The Internet brings 'cyber-accountability' to the nonprofit sector" (2001). The dozens of pages of information returns that exempt organizations must file have been turned into millions of pages of information that can be used by the general public to assess the organizations' performance.

First, the author discusses disclosure requirements and Form 990. Since the enactment of the Revenue Act of 1987, tax-exempt entities have been required to disclose financial information to interested parties who request permission to inspect copies of the organizations' annual Forms 990 (Return of Organization Exempt from Income Tax). These disclosure requirements, combined with regulatory oversight by the IRS, clearly provide some measure of organizational accountability to various constituencies, including current and prospective donors, organization employees and patrons, other exempt entities, and the citizenry at large.

Then, the author considers cyber-accountability and accountability Websites, including GuideStar. One of the newest and most comprehensive Websites aimed at promoting cyber-accountability in the nonprofit sector is the GuideStar site (www.guidestar.org), developed and operated by Philanthropic Research, Inc. (PRI), a Section 501(c)(3) tax-exempt entity based in Williamsburg, VA. PRI was founded in 1994 with a mission "to revolutionize philanthropy and nonprofit practice with information."

Finally, the author explores potential uses of web information. The information now available on the Internet about charitable organizations may be used in a variety of ways to promote greater accountability in the nonprofit sector. (C.K. Craig, 13 Taxation of Exempts 82.)

"Treasury issues proposed regulations on information reporting for education credits and student loan interest" (2001). Proposed regulations concern the Section 6050S information reporting requirements for education credits and qualified education loan interest. Although the proposed regulations apply to information returns and statements required to be filed or furnished after 2001, they may be relied on until the final regulations are issued.

After providing background, the author discusses qualified tuition and related expenses (QTRE) reporting. An information form (Form 1098-T) must be filed with the IRS for each individual for whom QTRE payments are received or for whom reimbursements or refunds are made. A substitute form may be used if it meets the requirements of Revenue Procedure 98-37. The information form may also be filed magnetically according to the rules of Section 6011(e) and Regulation § 301.6011-2.

The QTRE reporting requirements have been significantly expanded. It is important for those affected by the reporting requirements to review their compliance programs to ensure that they will comply with the regulations when they become effective. Failure to comply with the regulations could result in significant penalties.

Then, the author addresses education loan interest reporting. An information form (Form 1098-E, "Student Loan Interest Statement") must be filed with the IRS for each payor. A substitute form may be used if it meets the requirements of Revenue Procedure 98-37. The form may also be filed magnetically according to the rules of Section 6011(e) and Regulation § 301.6011-2. The qualified education loan (QEL) interest reporting requirements are similar to those that have been in place. (N.J. Foran, 12 Journal of Taxation of Exempt Organizations 161.)

Hospitals and Other Health Care Organizations

"An HMO wins the insurance battle, but will HMOs lose the war?" (2001). One of the market-driven creations of health maintenance organizations (HMOs) is the "point of service" (POS) plan, which is a response to consumer demands for flexibility that allows the enrollee to select his or her provider of choice rather than being locked into a panel. The level of coverage (and level of co-payments that enrollees must make for their care) is then determined by that choice, i.e., it is determined by the point at which services are sought. When the point of service selected is outside of the network panel of providers, the payment for those services often resembles true indemnity insurance.

After providing background, the author addresses Technical Advice Memorandum 200033046 and the lessons to be learned from it. Technical Advice Memorandum 200033046 carries the IRS position on HMO exemption and POS products to the next logical step. In the IRS's analysis, physician compensation determines whether there is commercial-type insurance activity. This is true in the sense of loss or denial of exemption and in the less drastic determination of whether a particular coverage plan results in unrelated business income (UBI) under Section 501(m).

Although the facts were different in Technical Advice Memorandum 200033046, the implication is that the POS premium allocable to in-network care may not be commercial-type insurance if the in-network physicians providing the care are at substantial financial risk for the cost of the enrollees' care. It remains unclear, however, whether any arrangement other than capitation or complying with the virtual safe harbor (15 percent discount and 15 percent withhold) will be persuasive with the IRS. Finally, even though Technical Advice Memorandum 200033046 adds another key chapter in the explanation of exemption issues for HMOs, additional chapters remain to be written. (G.M. Griffith, 12 Journal of Taxation of Exempt Organizations 145.)

"Applying Section 382 to loss corporation affiliates of exempt organizations" (2001). In a private letter ruling, the IRS concluded that loss corporations owned by affiliates of three tax-exempt health care systems did not undergo an ownership change for purposes of Section 382(g) when the parents of the three systems combined. Thus, the surviving system was able to avoid the Section 382 restrictions on using the affiliates' net operating losses (NOLs) that would have applied had the IRS ruled differently.

Letter Ruling 200028005 signifies a willingness on the part of the IRS to be flexible in its interpretation of Section 382 in nontraditional contexts. Given the degree of consolidation that has taken place in recent years within the health care industry, the conclusion reached in this ruling could apply to similarly situated organizations, even though the private ruling carries no precedential weight for other taxpayers. (R.J. Mason, M.V. Rountree & H.A. Levenson, 12 Journal of Taxation of Exempt Organizations 139.)

"Exempt HMO's insurance income is taxable under subchapter L" (2001). The IRS ruled in Technical Advice Memorandum 200033046 that an exempt HMO provided commercial-type insurance within the mean-

ing of Section 501(m) through its point-of-service (POS) plan. The IRS also ruled that the insurance was an insubstantial portion of the HMO's total activities and the resulting income should be calculated under subchapter L and not as Section 511 unrelated business income. (94 Journal of Taxation 60.)

"Global capitation and risk pool arrangements did not threaten health care provider's tax-exempt status" (2001). The issue in Letter Ruling 200044039 was whether an exempt health care provider system engaged in commercial-type insurance activities within the meaning of Section 501(m) by entering into global capitated risk agreements with insurance companies and health maintenance organizations. The IRS ruled that it did not, and also ruled that risk pool arrangements incorporated into the global capitation agreements did not result in private inurement or impermissible private benefit. (94 Journal of Taxation 57.)

"Medical billing arrangement between clinic and exempt health system is not a partnership" (2001). In Letter Ruling 200139005, the IRS ruled that a billing arrangement between a medical clinic and a subsidiary of a tax-exempt health system was not a partnership for federal tax purposes. (95 Journal of Taxation 376.)

"Restoring the charitable exemption of the Great Plains Health Alliance" (2001). Technical Advice Memorandum 9822004 was issued in October 1997, followed by the revocation of Great Plains Health Alliance's (GPHA's) income tax exemption on March 2, 1998. The Technical Advice Memorandum contained numerous misstatements of fact and law and reached conclusions not supported by the facts. One of the erroneous conclusions was that the individuals working within the leased hospitals were, in fact, employees of those governmental hospitals and not of GPHA. The Technical Advice Memorandum concluded that GPHA was not engaged in providing charitable services but only in providing management.

After providing background on GPHA, the author discusses the process of reestablishing GPHA's exemption. The apparently needless IRS action on the exemption, and the process of reestablishing that exemption, were a source of considerable frustration to the officers and board members of GPHA. On the other hand, the outcome is a stronger organizational structure and a clearer form of lease agreement, as well as the clarification of a number of the relationships within the organization and among its employees. (H.P. Elwood, 13 Taxation of Exempts 150.)

"Ruling approves a 'good' health care joint venture" (2001). In Letter Ruling 200118054, the IRS concluded that a non-profit health care system parent would not jeopardize its exemption or incur unrelated business income by participating in a limited liability company to own and operate an ambulatory surgery center previously owned and operated by the nonprofit system. (13 Taxation of Exempts 33.)

"The de-evolution of the community benefit standard for health care organizations" (2001). After decades under the community benefit standard, charity care appears to be a new test for the exemption of health care organizations.

First, the author provides background on the community benefit standard. In Revenue Ruling 69-545, the IRS recognized that the term "charitable" is used in Section 501(c)(3) in its generally accepted legal sense and that the term includes the promotion of health for the benefit of the community. An organization need not reach every member of the community, nor offer its services to the indigent, to be promoting health for the benefit of the community. Instead, an organization will be found to promote health for the benefit of a community within the meaning of Section 501(c)(3) if its activities serve a sufficiently large and indefinite class of individuals so that the community is interested in enforcement of the charitable trust.

Then, the author discusses the de-evolution of the standard. FSA 200110030 remains the most recent IRS pronouncement

with respect to the community benefit standard. In this pronouncement, the IRS clearly (but incorrectly) states that charity care is a requirement for exemption under the community benefit standard. While an FSA may not supersede a revenue ruling, the mere presence of incorrect legal analysis like the one in FSA 200110030 will result in unnecessary time and expense for the IRS and tax-exempt health care organizations during the course of an audit. (R.C. Louthian III, 13 Taxation of Exempts 118.)

Political Organizations and Activities

"How campaign finance reform legislation would affect tax-exempt organizations" (2001). On April 2, 2001, the Senate passed the McCain-Feingold "Bipartisan Campaign Reform Act of 2001." The passage was a major victory for campaign finance reform supporters, as the Senate had in the past proved to be the insurmountable barrier to reform efforts. Supporters in the House moved quickly to try to take advantage of the momentum created by that vote in their attempt to pass H.R. 2356, introduced by Reps. Chris Shays (R-Conn.) and Marty Meehan (D-Mass.), which closely matched the Senate bill. Attempts to have a floor vote on a House campaign finance reform bill failed in July 2001, however.

First, the author discusses current law. Federal election-related activities are governed by the Federal Election Campaign Act of 1971 (FECA) and the Federal Election Commission's (FEC's) regulations.

Then, the author addresses the legislation. Recent campaign finance reform bills, including the revised Shays-Meehan bill, address both party soft money and sham ads. While provisions relating to the former have attracted the lion's share of media attention, it is the attempts to regulate the latter that would have the most direct effect on tax-exempt organizations.

The Shays-Meehan bill appears to have the best chance of becoming law and therefore is the focus of discussion in the article. It is very similar to the McCain-Feingold bill that passed the Senate in April 2001, and the similarity is intentional. Campaign finance reform supporters hope to avoid a House-Senate conference, which they believe could very well be fatal to the bills in their entirety or to the provisions they consider most important. Their plan is to have the House pass a bill that then would stand a reasonable chance of achieving Senate passage unchanged.

Finally, the author explores open issues on electioneering communications, including constitutional issues. (L.H. Mayer, 13 Taxation of Exempts 131.)

"New campaign finance disclosure law hits the wrong target" (2001). G. Constantine, 12 Journal of Taxation of Exempt Organizations 150. (*Digested under* Tax-Exempt Organizations—Disclosure and Information Reporting, page 235.)

"What guidance is needed—and not needed—for political and lobbying activities on the Internet" (2001). On October 16, 2000, the IRS published Announcement 2000-84, giving notice that the IRS is considering the necessity of issuing guidance that would clarify the application of the Code to the use of the Internet by tax-exempt organizations. In the announcement, the IRS asks for guidance in each of the following areas: (1) whether guidance is required at all; (2) general considerations about how we think about a Website; (3) political and lobbying activities, (4) unrelated business income tax (UBIT); and (5) solicitation of charitable contributions and disclosure by charities. This article focuses on political and lobbying activities.

The IRS has posed seven specific questions seeking guidance; the first two questions focus on political activity and the remainder on lobbying. The preface to these questions on electioneering and lobbying refers to "charitable organizations described in Section 501(c)(3)." The specific questions are directed toward Section 501(c)(3) organizations. The IRS could have asked specific questions directed toward Section 501(c)(4) or Section 527 organizations. It did not; however, any guidance issued with respect to Section 501(c)(3) organizations

will, necessarily, affect the analysis for Section 501(c)(4) organizations and Section 527 organizations as well.

Then, the authors address each of the seven questions in the request for guidance. (R.A. Wexler & A.M. Anderson, 12 Journal of Taxation of Exempt Organizations 260.)

Private Foundations

"Assessing the options for terminating private foundation status" (2001). Involuntary terminations of private foundation status are a sanction, but the various types of voluntary terminations may help an organization adapt to its changing needs.

First, the author provides brief definitions of the terms and sanctions uniquely applicable to this area as an aid to understanding the issues involved in an entity ceasing to be a private charity.

Then, the author considers involuntary terminations. The ultimate penalty for failure to play by the excise tax rules Congress designed to curtail private foundation activities is an involuntary termination and imposition of a "third-tier tax." When there have been willful acts or failures to act that are either repeated or flagrant, and those acts or failures have resulted in the imposition of the first- and second-tier sanctions under a provision of Chapter 42 (specifically, Sections 4941 through 4945), the IRS can notify the foundation that it is liable for a termination tax.

Finally, the author considers voluntary terminations. When the directors or trustees decide, for whatever reason, that they cannot continue to sustain the life of a private foundation, they can terminate or dispose of all of the foundation's assets in several ways that will not subject the foundation to the termination tax.

The first method requires no advance IRS approval—the foundation can simply give away all of its assets to one or more Section 509(a)(1) public charities. Though not listed in the statute, the IRS has agreed in private rulings that a foundation can undertake this type of termination when distributing its assets to a Section 509(a)(2) or

239

Section 509(a)(3) organization. The foundation can also convert itself into a public charity by virtue of activities it will begin to conduct. It can begin to operate as a church, school, or hospital, or it can seek public funding that will equal at least one third of its annual revenue. Lastly, a private foundation can contribute its assets to one or more other private foundations.

A foundation also can relinquish its private foundation status by giving notice to the IRS and paying the termination tax. (J. Blazek, 12 Journal of Taxation of Exempt Organizations 199.)

"Grantmaking to foreign organizations aided by a 'simplified' procedure" (2001). The primary concern for a private foundation when making grants to foreign organizations is to ensure that the grant does not run afoul of the taxable expenditure rules. Revenue Procedure 92-94 provides foundation managers with a safe-harbor procedure.

First, the author provides an overview of the rules regarding expenditures and responsibility. Generally, a grant to an organization is a taxable expenditure unless: (1) the grant is made to an organization described in Section 509(a)(1), Section 509(a)(2), or Section 509(a)(3); (2) it is made to a private operating foundation; or (3) the private foundation exercises "expenditure responsibility" regarding the grant. Substantial paperwork requirements must be met to satisfy the expenditure responsibility requirements.

An individual cannot make a donation to a charity organized abroad and receive a charitable contribution deduction. An individual can, however, establish a private foundation, receive a charitable deduction, and, through the foundation, make grants to foreign organizations that will not be deemed as taxable expenditures.

Then, the author discusses the simplified procedure. The safe-harbor procedure provided in Revenue Procedure 92-94, if followed, ensures compliance with the "good-faith determination" and "reasonable judgment" requirements of the regulations. A foundation is deemed to have satisfied the requirements of Revenue Procedure 92-94 if it bases its good-faith determination and reasonable judgment on a "currently qualified" affidavit obtained from the foreign organization. The affidavit itself must be in English, and provide substantially the information set out in the form affidavit provided by the revenue procedure. (M.S. Kutzin, 12 Journal of Taxation of Exempt Organizations 181.)

"Mutual fund investment and intercompany transactions were not self-dealing" (2001). The IRS has concluded in Letter Ruling 200116047 that a private operating foundation's investment in mutual funds managed by a disqualified person and intercompany transactions between the foundation and disqualified persons were not self-dealing under Section 4941. (95 Journal of Taxation 185.)

"Outdated regulations hamper foundations making foreign program-related investments" (2001). Grantmaking and concepts of charity have changed and expanded over the thirty-odd years since program-related investments were first envisioned. The business world and economic realities have also changed during that time. Today, there is considerably more grant-making in foreign countries by U.S. charities than there was thirty years ago. One of the eleven projects on the IRS's guidance priority list for 2000 was guidance on private foundations' assistance to foreign entities. That need continues.

After providing background on the rules pertaining to making program-related investments, the author argues that the time has come to bring the program-related investment regulations into the twenty-first century. According to the author, the IRS should issue some new global examples, or otherwise provide reliable guidance to private foundations that want to make program-related investments in or through foreign for-profit organizations—including financial intermediaries, irrespective of their form of legal organization—to accomplish relief of the poor, economic development in poor regions, environmental protection, and similar charitable purposes worldwide.

Private foundations will not develop all of the innovative programs necessary for twenty-first century philanthropy unless they receive such further assurances. The IRS took the first step in 1972. The time has come to take another. (D.S. Chernoff, 12 *Journal of Taxation of Exempt Organizations* 249.)

"The benefits of establishing a private foundation in Delaware" (2001). Income, gift, and estate tax motives encourage many donors to form foundations. In addition, nontax motives have played a large part in the proliferation of family foundations. Nontax benefits include: (1) the ability to involve children and grandchildren in the family's charitable-giving process; (2) flexibility through the grant-making process; (3) the donor's ability to maintain legal control over the charitable assets; (4) preservation of the donor's anonymity; and (5) the relative ease of forming and administering a private foundation.

After considering the advantages of private foundations, the authors discuss why foundations should be corporations, not trusts, and why a Delaware nonprofit corporation may be the best choice. A donor should consider creating his private foundation as a Delaware nonprofit corporation because Delaware law provides: (1) clear guidance on the fiduciary duties applicable to directors; (2) flexible standards of corporate governance; and (3) minimal governmental interference with the activities of charitable entities.

Finally, the authors address how Delaware charitable trusts can benefit private foundations. A donor might create a charitable lead trust or a charitable remainder trust as a funding vehicle for the private foundation. (W.D. Sparks, II & R.W. Nenno, 28 *Estate Planning* 110.)

"The emergence of 'venture philanthropy' raises new tax issues" (2001). There is no precisely articulated or widely accepted definition of "venture philanthropy" (VP). Self-identified venture philanthropists emphasize capacity-building for their grantees, such as staff training and strategic planning. They generally commit to long-term relationships with grant recipients, and often become deeply involved with grantee operations. Some require representation on a grantee's board as a condition of funding. Others play significant roles with grantee organizations by providing high-level volunteer services.

New economy donors often suggest that they are more willing to take risks than traditional grantmakers. They may also spread risks among "investor groups" in which a number of grantmakers collectively support a grantee. Venture philanthropists may also be more mindful of harmonizing investment portfolios with programmatic goals than their predecessors.

First, the author discusses the use of the private foundation model for venture philanthropists. For many new economy philanthropists, a desire for full control over their charitable giving is the most salient factor in selecting a legal structure. Consequently, the model of choice is frequently a Section 501(c)(3) organization classified as a private foundation, which allows unfettered control by its founders.

Then, the author considers the supporting organization model. The unfavorable charitable contribution rules and heavy regulation of private foundations have led some new economy donors to choose other legal structures. Section 509(a)(3) supporting organizations are popular alternatives. By establishing a supporting organization relationship with an existing public charity or charities, it is possible for a donor to create a Section 501(c)(3) organization that itself qualifies as a public charity, thereby avoiding the complex issues described in the article with respect to private foundations.

Finally, the author turns to donor-advised fund models. Not all venture philanthropy involves a high net-worth donor or family pursuing charitable goals through a new entity. Collaborative efforts also abound. One innovative model is a pooled structure, in which a relatively small group of entrepreneurs, often with relatively modest contributions, combine their assets to "invest" in grantees in a coordinated fashion. This can be done through a private foundation, but a donor-advised fund at a community foundation or other public charity is often more cost-effective and easier to administer. (L. Woods, 13 Taxation of Exempts 51.)

Religious Organizations

"Exclusion for housing allowance no longer limited to fair market rental value" (2001). In *Warren* (2000), an unexpected decision, the Tax Court has held that a housing allowance is nontaxable for income tax reporting purposes under Section 107 as long as it is used to pay for housing-related expenses, even if the amount of the allowance exceeds the fair rental value of the housing.

After providing background, the author analyzes the decision. In *Warren*, the Tax Court rejected the IRS's position that the parsonage exclusion under Section 107(2) may not exceed the lesser of: (1) the amount used to provide a home or (2) the fair market rental value of the home. Instead, the court held that the exclusion is limited only to the actual amount used to provide a home and the amount designated by the employer. The court rejected the annual "fair rental value" test that the IRS adopted in 1971, which limited nontaxable housing allowances for ministers who own their homes to the annual rental value of their home. The IRS filed an appeal on September 26, 2000. (B.A. Miller, 12 Journal of Taxation of Exempt Organizations 276.)

"'Pervasively sectarian' institutions may now qualify for tax-exempt financing" (2001). As a result of Supreme Court cases decided in the 1970s, certain religious institutions deemed to be "pervasively sectarian" have not been allowed to obtain exempt bond financing. More recent Supreme Court cases have moved away from the "pervasively sectarian" analysis, however. Instead, the court has adopted an analysis that no longer focuses on the motives and actions of the aid recipient, but instead focuses on those of the government. This new focus could permit a "pervasively sectarian" institution to participate in exempt bond financing if the institution otherwise qualifies for the financing, without regard to its religious character, and if the financing is used for activities that serve a qualifying secular objective.

First, the author discusses this shift in the case law. Like many complex areas of the law, the shift in doctrine has not been clear or emphatic. Instead, the shift has developed in a series of cases both at the Supreme Court level and in lower courts. Before last year, the case law established a clear trend away from the "pervasively sectarian" analysis, but did not reject the analysis in a context that would apply to exempt bond financing. This lack of clarity continued to prevent many religious institutions from obtaining the "unqualified opinion" of bond counsel necessary to issue exempt bonds.

In *Mitchell v. Helms* (2000), however, the Supreme Court emphatically rejected the "pervasively sectarian" analysis. Following this decision, a federal district court substantially redefined the "pervasively sectarian" analysis to permit a religious college to receive direct cash grants from the government. The analysis followed in these cases should make it easier for religious institutions, particularly institutions of higher education, to obtain exempt bond financing.

Although the *Mitchell* decision does not directly address exempt bond financing for religious institutions, the analysis in the decision leaves little, if any, room for applying the "pervasively sectarian" test to such financing. Without that test, participation in exempt bond financing by a religious organization would be subject only to some form of nondiscrimination analysis. As a result, religious institutions that might previously have been deemed "pervasively sectarian" would generally qualify for exempt bond financing, assuming they provide qualifying services that satisfy secular standards. (S.J. Lark, 12 Journal of Taxation of Exempt Organizations 173.)

"Revenue from product sales by religious organizations may be taxable" (2001). S.J. Lark, 13 Taxation of Exempts 94. (*Digested* *under* Tax-Exempt Organizations—Unrelated Business Income Tax, page 244.)

Unrelated Business Income Tax

"Gaming activities can land a tax bill for tax-exempts" (2001). When tax-exempt organizations sponsor gaming activities, they may subject themselves to a tax on unrelated business income or to a variety of excise taxes. Tax-exempt organizations conducting gaming activities may be subject to an occupational tax and a wagering excise tax under Sections 4411 and 4401, respectively.

After providing background, the author discusses unrelated business taxable income (UBTI), the bingo exclusion, the public entertainment activities exclusion, and the volunteer labor exclusion. Income from regularly conducted gaming activities is treated as UBTI unless a specific exclusion applies. Section 513(f) provides an exclusion from UBTI for any income from bingo games. Section 513(d) provides that income from qualified public entertainment activities by qualified organizations is not UBTI. The term "unrelated trade or business" does not include any trade or business in which substantially all the work in carrying on the trade or business is performed for the organization without compensation.

Then, the author turns to recordkeeping. Exempt organizations are required to keep the same types of books and records that would be maintained by any other business organizations.

Finally, the author addresses information returns, and taxes on wagering. (L.R. Garrison, 67 Practical Tax Strategies 23.)

"Income from lease of broadcasting tower is taxable to university" (2001). Reversing a favorable prior ruling, the IRS has found in Letter Ruling 200104031 that a university's income from the rental of space on a broadcasting tower was not rent from real property under Section 512(b)(3), and was unrelated business taxable income under Section 512(a)(1). (94 Journal of Taxation 315.)

"Keeping ahead of the UBIT consequences of a gift shop" (2001). Exempt organizations contemplating opening or expanding product sales activities would be well-advised to invest some time at the outset addressing the relatedness of the merchandise to the organization's exempt purposes and establishing systems for tracking revenues, costs, and overhead associated with unrelated items.

First, the author discusses the definition of "substantially related." For most organizations, the key hurdle to excluding gift shop sales from unrelated business income (UBI) is demonstrating that the activity of selling is substantially related to the exercise or performance of the organization's exempt functions. Under Section 513(a), the conduct of a trade or business is not deemed substantially related merely because the activity produces income that is later used or spent in carrying out the organization's exempt purposes. Rather, the Code focuses on the manner in which the income is earned.

Then, the author addresses the business of art and the IRS's treatment of sales of different lines of merchandise as separate activities for purposes of the relatedness test of Regulation § 1.513-1(d). The operation of a gift shop represents multiple, similar activities, each of which has its own potential for generating UBI, depending on the facts and circumstances of each item sold.

Finally, the author addresses the treatment of various types of items including reproductions and adaptations, souvenirs, educational toys and teaching items for children, interpretations of objects rather than replicas, collectibles and mementoes, books and audio media, convenience and sundry items, paper products, ornaments and decorations, and engraving services; the practical application of inventory analysis, catalog and off-site stores, expense allocation, and nonsales revenue. (S.R. Bills, 13 Taxation of Exempts 35.)

"Legislation favorable to tax-exempt shareholders of S corporations introduced" (2001). 3 Business Entities, No. 6, 41. (*Digested under* S Corporations, page 187.)

"Revenue from product sales by religious organizations may be taxable" (2001). Although the sale of products by religious organizations may provide a valuable source of revenue, it may also create unrelated business income tax (UBIT) liability under Sections 511 through 513. Unfortunately, the regulations and applicable case law do not provide clear guidance regarding which products sold by a religious organization may give rise to UBIT liability.

First, the author provides background on UBIT, including the "relatedness" criteria for product sales. Whether any particular product "contributes importantly" to the mission of a religious organization is a subjective inquiry. As a result, it may be difficult in many instances for a religious organization to determine with certainty whether its product sales activities may give rise to UBIT liability.

Then, the author provides an analytical framework for assessing UBIT risk. Applying the framework set forth in this article may give religious organizations a better sense of the tax liability risk associated with their current and planned activities. Further, religious organizations may be able to reduce the risk of UBIT liability by incorporating into their product sales activities, to the extent possible, the relatedness criteria. (S.J. Lark, 13 Taxation of Exempts 94.)

"State unrelated business income taxes pose compliance issues for exempt organizations" (2001). W. Gentilesco & J.M. Buehler, 11 Journal of Multistate Taxation and Incentives, No. 2, 6. (*Digested under* State Taxes—In General, page 205.)

TAX PRACTICE AND PRACTITIONERS

(*See also* Interest and Penalties; Tax Shelters)

"Updated IRS guidance on disclosures that avoid penalties" (2001). 12 Journal of International Taxation, No. 2, 4. (*Digested under* Interest and Penalties, page 89.)

TAX SHELTERS

"Are individual tax shelters the 'competence test' for IRS and practitioners?" (2001). Budget and personnel problems plaguing an IRS in the throes of a congressionally mandated reorganization may have encouraged some taxpayers to play the audit lottery. Those individuals who have been persuaded by tax shelter promoters to invest in schemes that are potentially subject to attack for lacking a business purpose or on similar grounds may find themselves aggressively pursued, however. Practitioners with clients suddenly thinking the better of such investments will have significant issues to deal with.

After providing background on investment in tax shelters, the author discusses malpractice. If a lawyer fails to preserve the statute of limitations on the taxpayer's claim against the promoter, the lawyer should expect to become the target of the taxpayer's wrath when the time comes to pay a substantial deficiency, interest, and penalties, and the claim against the promoter is barred.

Next, the author considers invalidating exculpatory agreements. One of the common strategies in tax shelter promotion is to include an exculpatory provision protecting the promoter.

Then, the author addresses penalties. Frequently in these shelter transactions taxpayers have been informed that there is some exposure to a 20-percent penalty, but assured that the risk is acceptable. As a business matter, a 20-percent penalty seems a small risk given the overwhelming odds of success of the audit lottery. What taxpayers rarely understand is the real possibility of a 40-percent penalty. The 40-percent valuation-overstatement penalty of Section 6662(h) applies where the value or the adjusted basis of any property is overstated by more than 400 percent.

Defending against penalties presents a potential hidden danger. Both penalties—the 20 percent and the 40 percent—may be excused pursuant to the reasonable cause and good faith provisions of Section 6664(c). The pitfall is that merely asserting the excuse of the penalty risks waiver of the attorney-client privilege in the transaction.

Finally, the author turns to the economic substance and business purpose test. The overriding determinant of the success of the vast majority of tax shelter transactions will be how the economic substance and business purpose test is to be applied. (P.J. Sax, 95 Journal of Taxation 231.)

"Corporate tax shelter attacks—the government is on a roll" (2001). The IRS's attack on tax shelters has proceeded on two fronts: (1) victory in court (see, e.g., the Tax Court decision in *Salina Partnership, LP* and the Delaware federal district court decision in *CM Holdings, Inc.* (2000)) and (2) "listing" as tax shelters the specific transactions described in three Notices—Notice 2001-17, Notice 2001-16, and Notice 2000-61. A fourth notice states that customary leveraged lease transactions will not be subject to the registration and list-maintenance rules for tax shelters (Notice 2001-18). (R.D. Lorence, 12 Journal of International Taxation, No. 4, 53.)

"Corporate tax shelters: a never-ending series" (2001). Corporate tax shelters have been much in the news—at the appellate court level, at the IRS, and in Congress. The reader may well feel that this is a never-ending subject. The author of this article has certainly come to think so.

Most surprising in recent events are the two blows suffered by the government at the appellate court level, discussed in this article. We are left without a coherent view of what constitutes a sham transaction motivated solely by tax considerations. Indeed, even within the same panel of the Eleventh Circuit, there seems to be no agreement on this subject. (R.D. Lorence, 12 Journal of International Taxation, No. 10, 10.)

"Guidance on tax shelter registration penalty" (2001). ILM 200112003 offers guidance regarding the Section 6707 penalty consequences for a promoter's failure to register a tax shelter under Section 6111. (66 Practical Tax Strategies 304.)

"LILO transaction lacks economic substance" (2001). In what appears to be part of the continuing scrutiny of lease-in/lease-out (LILO) transactions, the IRS has issued field service advice in which it concluded that a LILO transaction lacked economic substance. Thus, in FSA 200105003, the IRS disallowed deductions for interest, rent, and transaction fees related to the transaction. (94 Journal of Taxation 314.)

"No statute of limitations on penalty for failing to register a tax shelter" (2001). 94 Journal of Taxation 375. (*Digested under Assessment and Collection—Statute of Limitations, page 8.*)

"Risks and rewards of tax shelter investments" (2001). A variety of tax shelter arrangements generate valuable deductions, although when tax deferral is involved, those shelters are likely to produce taxable income years down the road.

After providing background, the authors discuss leverage. Leverage enables investors to make a relatively low cash outlay to garner substantial gains and other benefits. The benefits of leverage occur, for example, when an investment of only a modest down payment in real estate triggers depreciation or tax credits. Regular or nonrecourse debt (for real estate) is used to finance the balance of the transaction. With recourse financing, investors carry personal and unlimited liability for the debt, while nonrecourse financing limits personal liability to the specific assets acquired.

Then, the authors address the benefits of tax deferral and permanent reduction in taxes, as well as the risks of tax shelters. The tax credits generated by a tax shelter reduce an investor's tax liability. If the recapture provisions can be avoided, this reduction is permanent.

245

One of the major risks in any tax shelter investment is its lack of economic substance. IRS regulations have attempted to clarify the economic substance doctrine by requiring a comparison between the present value of an activity's expected pretax profits and its tax benefits.

Finally, the authors consider the impact of the passive activity limitations and the at-risk rules. (S. Harrington, J.J. Connors & K. Milani, 67 Practical Tax Strategies 218.)

"The IRS gets aggressive: why taxpayers need to pay attention to FSAs" (2001). The IRS has become particularly aggressive with respect to transactions that it perceives as having a tax-avoidance component. In these situations, the IRS has advanced a variety of legal arguments to deny the claimed tax benefits. Recent field service advice (FSAs) highlight three such arguments: The IRS has used the substance-over-form doctrine to disregard the literal language of a statute or recharacterize the facts of a transaction; in other cases it has gone in the opposite direction and sought to hold a taxpayer to its chosen form even if the substance of the transaction might be otherwise; and it also has applied Section 482 in nontraditional ways to deny a taxpayer's claimed treatment. In some cases the IRS has asserted a variety of theories.

First, the authors discuss the substance-over-form theory. In one category of FSAs the IRS has asserted the substance-over-form doctrine. This broad doctrine has many applications, affording the IRS many opportunities to challenge a transaction. Under this doctrine, the IRS has: (1) applied a law's presumed intent over its literal language; (2) rearranged or disregarded steps of a transaction and recharacterized transactions; (3) asserted agency and alter ego theories; and (4) invoked anti-abuse provisions of the Code, such as Section 269. Underlying all of these arguments is the IRS's skepticism about a transaction's nontax purpose, the taxpayer's arguments notwithstanding.

In many of these FSAs, the IRS simply asserts that a transaction is not really what the taxpayer claims it is. While this type of dispute is almost as old as the income tax

law itself, the Third Circuit tax shelter decision in *ACM Partnership* (1998) seems to have emboldened the IRS in this area. Like *ACM*, recurring features of these FSAs are the presence of a tainted promoter and no, or flimsy, evidence that the taxpayer was interested in making, or could have made, a pretax profit.

Then, the authors address the form-over-substance theory. The IRS's resolve to assert the substance-over-form doctrine is matched by its resolve to assert an opposite "form over substance" doctrine. "Form over substance" FSAs assert that a taxpayer should be bound to the form of a transaction it has chosen, and that a taxpayer generally cannot affirmatively employ the substance over form doctrine to its advantage. Like its employment of substance over form, the IRS has asserted the form-over-substance doctrine liberally, especially where it believes a taxpayer has taken some undue advantage of the tax law.

Finally, the authors consider reallocations. The IRS has been active in seeking to apply Section 482. That section provides the IRS with broad discretion to reallocate gross income, deductions, credits, or allowances wherever two or more organizations, trades, or businesses are owned or controlled directly or indirectly by the "same interests." Given this broad authority, it is not surprising that the IRS frequently invokes Section 482 in respect of transactions involving related entities. In recent FSAs, however, the IRS has invoked Section 482 in the far less common scenario of transactions among unrelated entities in which a nonrecognition provision of the Code is at issue.

A common feature of these FSAs, like the *ACM* case, is the presence of a tainted promoter and the perceived lack of business purpose for the transaction in question. (D.L. Forst & B.W.S. Bassett, 95 Journal of Taxation 42.)

"Yet another LILO deal found by IRS to lack economic substance" (2001). In FSA 200112020, another "lease-in/lease-out" (LILO) arrangement was found by the IRS to lack economic substance and was therefore disregarded for tax purposes. (94 Journal of Taxation 376.)

THEFT LOSSES

(*See* Losses)

TRANSFER PRICING

(*See* International Taxation)

TRAVEL AND ENTERTAINMENT EXPENSES

(*See* Business Expenses—Travel and Entertainment)

TRUSTS AND TRUST TAXATION

(*See also* Charitable Contributions; Estate Planning; Estates and Estate Tax; Gifts and Gift Tax; Marital Deduction; Valuation of Property)

"Charitable remainder trusts: Final regulations on prevention of abuse of CRTs" **(2001).** On January 5, 2001, the IRS issued final regulations designed to prevent what the IRS perceived as an abusive use of the charitable remainder trust (CRT). The final regulations modify the application of Section 664 in characterizing distributions from a CRT. The final regulations are effective as to distributions made by a CRT after October 18, 1999.

After providing background, the authors discuss the impact of the final regulations, including deemed sales, unrelated business taxable income (UBTI), payment of the annuity/unitrust amount, and transactions prior to the effective date. Although the CRT is a legislatively blessed tax shelter, the IRS

is on the attack against what it perceives to be inappropriate tax avoidance. The final regulations seek to eliminate what would otherwise be characterized in the hands of the recipients as a tax-free distribution of corpus from the CRT by treating certain distributions as if there had been a sale by the CRT. The final regulations clarify whether a deemed sale by a CRT would generate UBTI. Annuity/unitrust payment provisions are applicable to distributions made on or after January 5, 2001. (S.J. Schlesinger & D.L. Mark, 28 Estate Planning 185.)

"Charitable remainder trusts require more than good drafting" **(2001).** Not only must the trust document be properly worded, but the trust provisions must be carried out; otherwise, the charitable deduction can be lost.

First, the authors discuss the basic rules applicable to charitable remainder annuity trusts (CRATs) and charitable remainder unitrusts (CRUTs). Concrete rules in Section 664 must be adhered to in setting up and operating a CRAT or CRUT.

Then, the authors address the impact of the Tax Court decision in *Atkinson* (2000), a case of first impression in the area of CRAT/CRUT operation. If a CRAT or CRUT is not constructed and administered in accordance with Section 664, the trust can be disqualified as a CRAT or CRUT and any tax benefits lost. This was the unfortunate result in *Atkinson*. (C.J. Langstraat & A.M. Cagle, 66 Practical Tax Strategies 94.)

"Diversification and other investment issues of charitable and other trusts" **(2001).** The National Conference of Commissioners on Uniform State Laws approved the Uniform Prudent Investor Act (the Act) in 1994. The Act considers diversification as generally appropriate, yet permits a trustee to make a reasonable determination not to diversify.

First, the authors discuss case law. In *Estate of Rowe* (2000), the Appellate Division, Third Department of the New York State Supreme Court entered an order affirming the decision of the Otsego County Surrogate's Court upholding the removal of the bank-trustee for its negligent conduct for failing to diversify trust assets, and assessing a surcharge against the trustee based on capital lost by the trust.

In *Estate of Janes* (1997), the New York Court of Appeals affirmed the order of the Appellate Division that found that the Surrogate's Court, after trial, properly imposed liability on the corporate fiduciary for its initial imprudent failure to diversify, as well as for its subsequent indifference, inaction, and failure to make full and complete disclosure in its management of the estate.

In *Estate of Saxton* (2000), the New York Appellate Division entered an order modifying the decree of the Broome County Surrogate's Court by reversing so much of the decree as established the amount of the surcharge against the bank-trustee, and otherwise affirming the Surrogate's Court's determination holding the bank liable for its failure to diversify investments held in the trust (not a charitable trust).

Then, the authors discuss the requirements of the Act. (S.J. Schlesinger & D.L. Mark, 28 Estate Planning 87.)

"Divorce can permit division of CRUT without adverse tax consequences" (2001). A husband and wife's division of their two-life (consecutive) charitable remainder unitrust (CRUT) as part of their marital property settlement was held in Letter Ruling 200120016 not to have caused the old or new trusts to fail to qualify under Section 664, and did not result in either gift or income taxes. (95 Journal of Taxation 117.)

"Final regulations approve certain changes in grandfathered GST trusts" (2001). Final regulations specify modifications that may be made to a grandfathered generation-skipping transfer (GST) trust without causing the trust to lose its GST tax-exempt status.

After providing background on trusts that have grandfathered GST status, the authors discuss the final regulations. In the final regulations, the IRS maintained its course set forth in the proposed regulations to provide the four safe-harbor provisions that carve out actions or modifications that do not cause a trust to lose its grandfathered GST status. The fourth safe harbor is a catch-all provision that may protect an action that fails to meet one or more of the criteria for the first three safe harbors.

Then, the authors analyze planning opportunities and pitfalls under the final regulations. Planning opportunities are offered by conversion to minimum unitrust interests and division of sprinkling trusts. (J.B. O'Grady & J.S. Stringer, 28 Estate Planning 526.)

"How proposed regulations on the definition of "income" affect total return trusts" (2001). Before using total return trusts, practitioners should carefully analyze the impact of the new proposed regulations that revise the definition of "trust income."

First, the author provides an overview of the proposed regulations. On February 14, 2001, the IRS issued proposed regulations that revise the definition of "income" under Section 643(b) to take into account changes in the definition of "trust accounting income" under state laws. A Treasury Department official has publicly said that this regulation project considers how total return trusts and the equitable adjustment provision of the 1997 Revised Uniform Principal and Income Act (UPIA) will affect federal tax provisions. The proposed regulations also clarify the situations in which capital gains are included in distributable net income (DNI) under Section 643(a)(3). Moreover, the proposed regulations make conforming amendments affecting ordinary trusts, pooled income funds, charitable remainder trusts (CRTs), marital deduction trusts, and trusts that are exempt from generation-skipping transfer (GST) taxes.

Then, the author considers the impact of the proposed regulations, the effect on other trusts (including marital deduction trusts, qualified domestic trusts, and GST tax trusts), and other tax provisions not addressed by the proposed regulations (regarding charitable deduction limitations, private foundations, information reporting, subchapter S, foreign trusts, and collateral consequences of using total return trusts).

While a total return trust is a dynamic, revolutionizing estate planning tool, total return trusts have certain tax consequences that practitioners should analyze carefully.

Before using total return trusts, practitioners should consider the proposed regulations that revise the definition of "income" to take into account governing instruments or state laws that define "trust accounting income" as a unitrust amount or permit the trustee to make adjustments between income and principal. Practitioners should also consider the tax consequences of a total return trust under other existing federal tax provisions not addressed by the proposed regulations. (L. Howell-Smith, 28 Estate Planning 308.)

"IRS issues new regulations for charitable trusts" (2001). On January 4, 2001, the IRS issued final regulations to address perceived abuses with respect to charitable remainder trusts (CRTs) and charitable lead trusts (CLTs). The proposed regulations concerning accelerated CRTs were issued October 18, 1999, and were extremely controversial. The final regulations were issued in TD 8926. The proposed regulations addressing the "vulture" CLT were issued April 5, 2000. The final CLT regulations were issued in TD 8923. While there were some modifications in both sets of final regulations, the proposed regulations were essentially issued in final form.

First, the author discusses CRTs. The final CRT regulations target trusts that are used to eliminate capital gain on the sale of appreciated assets.

Then, the author considers CLTs. The new regulations on CLTs address the period of the lead interest. In general, the term of the lead interest must be either a specified term of years or the life or lives of individuals living at the date of the transfer. The proposed regulations provided that the lives that can be used as measuring lives for the charitable term are limited to the donor, the donor's spouse, and a lineal ancestor of all beneficiaries. The final regulations expand on the proposed regulations to permit the spouse of a lineal ancestor to be the measuring life. Thus, stepchildren and step-grandchildren may be the remainder beneficiaries. (C.D. Duronio, 12 Journal of Taxation of Exempt Organizations 226.)

"IRS proposes regulations on qualification of ESBTs as S corporation shareholders" (2001). C.W. Hall, III, 3 Business Entities, No. 2, 28. (*Digested under* S Corporations, page 186.)

"IRS provides guidance on ESBTs and estimated taxes" (2001). 3 Business Entities, No. 2, 55. (*Digested under* S Corporations, page 186.)

"Judicial reformation of trusts—the drafting tool of last resort" (2001). Judicial reformation of irrevocable trusts is, of course, nothing new. In recent years, this "drafting tool" has been used with far greater frequency. Probably the principal reason for this is the complex and ever-changing maze of tax laws and investment vehicles that contemporary trustees must negotiate. Indeed, the pace of change seems only to accelerate, and consequently, the occasions when trust provisions no longer fit the needs of the beneficiaries or the intent of the settlor undoubtedly will become even more common.

First, the authors discuss procedure. Trust reformations normally can be accomplished only by order of a trial court in a judicial proceeding that is valid under state law. The court must have subject matter and personal jurisdiction over a trust and its beneficiaries. Jurisdiction over a trust can exist simultaneously in many states. A state's jurisdiction may be based on the fact that a single trustee or beneficiary resides in the state, trust property has a situs in the state, the grantor of the trust was a resident of the state when the trust was created or became irrevocable, or the trust expressly invokes the jurisdiction of the state's courts.

Because multiple states frequently have jurisdiction over the same trust, proceedings occasionally may be commenced involving the same trust in more than one state at the same time.

Then, the authors consider substantive rules. Historically, as a matter of substantive law, reformation has not been allowed when it is sought merely because the trustee or beneficiaries or even the grantor are no longer pleased with the trust's contents.

249

Before reformation will be granted, it must be established that: (1) a change in circumstances has occurred that (2) was not anticipated or foreseen by the creator of the trust; and that (3) results in a frustration of an important purpose of the trust. Traditionally, a second ground for reformation is clear and convincing evidence that a trust or a provision within a trust was based on a mistake of fact or law on the part of the trust creator. In practice, many state courts are willing to modify or reform irrevocable trusts where all parties are in agreement and no clear intention of the settlor is violated by the change.

Finally, the authors address tax issues, fiduciary issues, and contemporary challenges. (D.R. Hodgman & D.C. Blickenstaff, 28 Estate Planning 287.)

"Key issues to consider when drafting life insurance trusts" (2001). Irrevocable life insurance trusts (ILITs), with their inherent leveraging through "cheap" dollars (i.e., premiums), are a valuable planning tool to deal with the payment of estate taxes and provide liquidity to a deceased grantor's estate. Because ILITs are irrevocable, however, estate planners should consider, as circumstances and client desires may warrant, developing a flexible document with regard to *Crummey* withdrawal rights, potential generation-skipping transfer (GST) tax issues, and coordination of the client's other estate planning documents with the ILIT.

First, the author discusses key provisions regarding *Crummey* withdrawal rights. A *Crummey* withdrawal right granted to each beneficiary—when used in conjunction with the annual gift tax exclusion under Section 2503(b)—allows the grantor's payment of insurance premiums to the ILIT to be gift tax-free.

Then, the author addresses key GST tax provisions. Except when an ILIT is a Section 2642(c) or Section 2503(c) generation-skipping trust, every ILIT has potential GST tax exposure. Therefore, every time a transfer to the trust is made, a decision must be made whether GST exemption will be allocated to the ILIT on a timely filed gift tax return via the required Notice of Allocation attachment.

Finally, the author considers additional provisions. Other provisions to think about when drafting an ILIT address avoiding potentially adverse tax consequences to the ILIT beneficiaries, and coordinating the ILIT with the grantor's other estate planning documents. (S.V. Grassi, Jr., 28 Estate Planning 217.)

"Measuring life for charitable lead trusts restricted" (2001). Final regulations seek to prevent the abusive use of charitable lead trusts as vehicles for generating charitable deductions in excess of what passes to charity. (66 Practical Tax Strategies 184.)

"New IRS guidance provides fresh impetus for using electing small business trusts" (2001). S.S. Traum, 94 Journal of Taxation 285. (*Digested under* S Corporations, page 187.)

"New regulations sanction 'accelerated' charitable lead trusts" (2001). Substantial opportunities to leverage and accelerate transfers of value to descendants are available to persons whose actual life expectancies are significantly shorter than their actuarial life expectancies.

A charitable lead trust (CLT) is one of the most opportunistic mechanisms for achieving such leverage. Final regulations sanction the use of CLTs to accelerate the transfer of wealth to descendants whose relationships to the donor fall within a narrow, but reasonable, ambit.

First, the author provides background on CLTs, including the "accelerated" CLT and the "ghoul" CLT. A charitable lead trust is an irrevocable arrangement that provides for payment at least annually of an annuity or unitrust amount to a qualified charitable organization for a term of years or a period measured by the life or lives of one or more individuals living at the time the trust is created. Upon termination of the specified charitable interest, the trust assets generally are distributed to, or held in further trust for the benefit of, noncharitable beneficiaries.

Then, the author addresses the final regulations. The final regulations effectively end the use of "ghoul" CLTs that leveraged the valuation advantages under the tables through the use of an unrelated person who was seriously ill but not "terminally ill" within the meaning of Section 7520 as a measuring life for a charitable term interest. However, the final regulations sanction the use of such an "accelerated" lead trust if the person selected as the measuring life is traditionally considered a member of the remainder beneficiary's family. Although planners may find the use of such an "accelerated" lead trust difficult to discuss with families, the tax advantages of such an arrangement may be so significant that the planner should not overlook his or her ethical obligation to consider this strategy under appropriate circumstances. (R.D. Van Dolson, 28 Estate Planning 162.)

"No resulting trust in home maintained by same-sex couple" (2001). 28 Estate Planning 28. (*Digested under* Personal Residence, page 162.)

"Planning for U.S. beneficiaries of foreign trusts under recent regulations" (2001). 1996 was a watershed year for estate planning with foreign trusts, and the year 2000 saw the IRS issue long-awaited proposed regulations in addition to finalizing certain proposed and temporary regulations issued in 1997 and 1999. All of these developments affect the taxation of foreign trusts with U.S. beneficiaries and transfers to foreign trusts by U.S. persons.

During the year 2000, the IRS issued proposed regulations under Sections 679 and 684 and final regulations under Section 672(f). It also issued final regulations under Section 671, defining the term "grantor" for purposes of U.S. income taxation of estates, trusts, and beneficiaries. Consequently, practitioners have a clearer idea of what aspects of international estate planning are still tax-effective when either a U.S. grantor or a U.S. beneficiary is involved.

This article analyzes how to create a tax-efficient trust for a U.S. beneficiary under the new regulations by examining which foreign trusts are treated as having a U.S. beneficiary, what constitutes a transfer

to a foreign trust, who is deemed to be the grantor of a foreign trust, and when gain is required to be recognized.

After providing background, the author discusses outbound foreign trusts. The term "outbound trust" refers to a foreign trust created by a U.S. person, as well as to a domestic trust that becomes foreign. The proposed regulations under Section 679, issued on August 2, 2000, offer clarification as to when a foreign trust will be treated as having a U.S. beneficiary and what constitutes a transfer to a foreign trust (or estate) by a U.S. person.

Then, the author considers when a foreign trust will be treated as having a U.S. beneficiary. The proposed regulations under Section 679 take a very broad approach in determining whether a foreign trust created by a U.S. person is deemed to have a U.S. beneficiary. A foreign trust will be treated as having a U.S. beneficiary if any part of the income or corpus of the trust could be paid to or for the direct or indirect benefit of a U.S. person either during the taxable year of the U.S. transferor or upon termination of the trust if it is terminated within that transferor's taxable year.

Finally, the author addresses what constitutes a transfer to a foreign trust, who is a grantor, recognition of gain on transfer, preimmigration trusts, reporting requirements, and inbound foreign trusts. (S.D. Harrington, 28 Estate Planning 258.)

"Planning to meet a range of donor needs with 'flip' charitable remainder unitrusts" (2001). Under Section 664, a charitable remainder trust (CRT) is a trust that provides for the distribution of a specified payment at least annually to one or more persons, at least one of which must be a noncharitable beneficiary. The payment period must be for the life or lives of the individual beneficiaries (all of whom must be living at the time the trust is created) or for a term of years, not in excess of twenty years. At the termination of the noncharitable interest or interests, the remainder must either be held in a continuing trust for charitable purposes, or paid to or for the use of one or more charitable organizations described in Section 170(c).

After providing background on CRTs and types of CRTs, including charitable remainder unitrusts (CRUTs), the author discusses the regulations. The regulations under Section 664 address a number of matters of concern to the IRS involving perceived abuses of the CRT rules. The regulations also clarify certain matters that had previously been addressed in private letter rulings, including the use of "flip" unitrusts.

Then, the author considers planning strategies. Making the flip unitrust widely available has provided a variety of planning opportunities for donors and their advisors in connection with establishing a CRT. Income tax planning is no longer the sole focus; instead, donors must also focus on more long-term needs and goals. This places a responsibility on planned giving officers and other advisors to delve into those needs and goals with the prospective donor, and to examine all of the possible structures for a proposed CRT. (M.A.W. McKinnon, 12 Journal of Taxation of Exempt Organizations 253.)

"Proposed regulations clarify treating revocable trust as part of estate" (2001). Section 645 permits an executor and a trustee to elect that a qualified revocable trust be treated and taxed as part of a decedent's estate for income tax purposes. The IRS has issued proposed regulations that provide: (1) procedures for making the Section 645 election; (2) rules regarding the tax treatment while the election is in effect; (3) rules for terminating the election; and (4) clarification of the reporting rules. When finalized, the proposed regulations will replace the procedures for making the Section 645 election in Revenue Procedure 98-13.

First, the authors discuss the benefit of election. The Section 645 election makes available to trusts some of the income tax advantages traditionally available only to estates.

Then, the authors address interim guidance, qualified revocable trusts, making the election, taxpayer identification numbers, income tax burdens, and the effective date. The proposed regulations are to be effective

when finalized. In the meantime, the guidance provided in Revenue Procedure 98-13 should be followed. (M. Kove & J.M. Kosakow, 28 Estate Planning 169.)

"Proposed regulations let revocable trust be treated as part of estate" (2001). The IRS has issued proposed regulations, relating to the election under Section 645 to have certain revocable trusts treated as part of an estate for tax purposes. (66 Practical Tax Strategies 184.)

"Proposed regulations on ESBTs: more guidance for family trusts owning S stock" (2001). J.D. August & J.J. Kulunas, 28 Estate Planning 459. (*Digested under* S Corporations, page 188.)

"Proposed regulations update definition of 'trust income'" (2001). The IRS has issued proposed regulations, revising the definition of "income" under Section 643(b) to take into account recent trends in trust accounting practices. (66 Practical Tax Strategies 296.)

"QSST elections for testamentary trusts—proposed regulations issued" (2001). 3 Business Entities, No. 6, 41. (*Digested under* S Corporations, page 188.)

"Spousal interests in GRATs not exempt from gift tax" (2001). 67 Practical Tax Strategies 376. (*Digested under* Gifts and Gift Tax, page 75.)

"Tax consequences of outstanding trust liabilities when grantor status terminates" (2001). The use of "defective grantor trusts" has become a commonplace part of the wealth transfer process. Such trusts are an integral part of estate planning techniques that include sales to grantor trusts. In the context of such sales, commentators have discussed at length the detrimental income tax consequences that may result if the grantor dies before the note issued by the grantor trust to the grantor has been fully discharged. There has been very little—if any—discussion, however, of the detrimental income tax and estate tax consequences that may result if a grantor trust has any outstanding liabilities when grantor trust status is terminated (by reason of the grantor's death or otherwise).

After reviewing the advantages of grantor trusts, the authors discuss the consequences of grantor trust status termination. When a grantor trust's status as a disregarded entity terminates and its separate existence for tax purposes is respected, any liability owed by the trust—whether to the grantor or to a third party—will suddenly become the trust's. The result in many instances will be that the grantor is relieved of an obligation and thereby will recognize capital gain, triggering income tax and very often additional estate tax.

Then the authors suggest ways of avoiding problems upon termination. Suggestions include: (1) paying off debt as soon as possible; (2) being aware of third-party borrowing; (3) being aware of hidden debt; and (4) considering whether or not to elect out of installment sale treatment. (D.V. Dunn & D.A. Handler, 95 Journal of Taxation 49.)

"The aftermath of *Walton*: the rehabilitation of the fixed-term, zeroed-out GRAT" (2001). The fixed-term, zeroed-out grantor retained annuity trust (GRAT) is an extremely valuable estate planning tool for individuals who want to transfer property to family members without paying gift tax. It has recently been made more desirable by the scheduled increase in the gift tax exemption and the uncertain future of the federal transfer tax system. At the same time, the tax consequences of a properly structured fixed-term GRAT have become somewhat less uncertain by reason of the Tax Court's invalidation of Regulation § 25.2702-3(e), Example 5 in *Walton* (2000). That decision, coupled with the government's failure to appeal it, will encourage the use of GRATs and the claim that Example 5 does not apply to increase the size of the resulting taxable gift.

Nevertheless, it is crucial that estate planners not become careless or over-confident. Those who intend to rely on *Walton* must take care to use fixed-term GRATs structured to fit within the holding of *Walton* and to warn their clients that the IRS has not yet revoked Example 5 or acquiesced in the

decision (even if the government's failure to appeal that decision suggests a recognition of the weakness of the position taken in Example 5). Moreover, the decision to recommend a fixed-term, zeroed-out GRAT is the beginning, not the end, of any recommendation. The remaining decisions, including those relating to the length of the GRAT, and the identity (and perhaps the terms) of the remainder beneficiary also must be made to fit within the balance of the client's estate plan. (C.S. McCaffrey, L.L. Plaine & P.H. Schneider, 95 Journal of Taxation 325.)

"The Delaware tax trap and the abolition of the rule against perpetuities" (2001). This article discusses the relationship between the Delaware Tax Trap and the abolition of the rule against perpetuities. The principal premise of the author is that in some states, a beneficiary of a dynasty trust can safely exercise a nongeneral power of appointment to create a successive power of appointment without running afoul of the Delaware Tax Trap, while in other states this cannot be done without causing gift or estate tax liability.

After providing background on powers of appointment and the rule against perpetuities, the author discusses the Delaware Tax Trap, the Code, and regulations. The Powers of Appointment Act of 1951 added Sections 811(f)(4) and 1000(c)(4) to the Internal Revenue Code of 1939. These sections, the predecessors to Sections 2041(a)(3) and 2514(d) of the current Code, were enacted in response to the perceived Delaware problem.

Eventually, Sections 2041(a)(3) and 2514(d) became known as the Delaware Tax Trap because a beneficiary of a trust established in Delaware could inadvertently subject the trust property to gift or estate tax if the trust gave a beneficiary a nongeneral power of appointment that was exercised to create a successive nongeneral power of appointment. On the other hand, this trap might prove advantageous where it is better to subject the trust property to a nonskip beneficiary's gift or estate tax rate as opposed to having the trust assets subjected to generation-skipping transfer (GST) tax (for instance, if insufficient GST exemption was allocated to the trust).

Then, the author discusses implications for states that have abolished the rule against perpetuities but have not adopted a rule against the suspension of the power of alienation, and states that may have avoided or stumbled into the Delaware Tax Trap. Practitioners should keep in mind the relationship between Sections 2041(a)(3) and 2514(d) and the applicable perpetuities rule when drafting a dynasty trust that gives a beneficiary the ability to exercise a nongeneral power of appointment to create a successive nongeneral power of appointment. (S.E. Greer, 28 Estate Planning 68.)

"The impact of choice of trustee and powers of grantor and beneficiary" (2001). Because of the increasing international mobility of trustees, grantors, and beneficiaries as well as the trend toward more global investment management, planners should exercise caution to preserve the domestic trust status of the trusts they draft, unless, of course, treatment as a foreign trust is intended.

After providing background, the author discusses the final regulations, effective February 2, 1999, which made significant modifications with respect to the control test requiring that a U.S. person, not just a U.S. fiduciary, control all substantial decisions of a trust. Under the final regulations, control means having the power, by vote or otherwise, to make all the substantial decisions of the trust, with no other person having the power to veto any of the substantial decisions.

The final regulations made two changes to the provisions of the proposed regulations with respect to substantial decisions. First, the final regulations expanded the meaning of the term "substantial decisions." Second, the final regulations continue to treat investment decisions as substantial decisions, but provide that if a U.S. person hires an investment advisor, the investment decisions made by the investment advisor will be treated as substantial decisions made by the U.S. person if the U.S. person can terminate the investment advisor's power to make investment decisions at will. (S.L. Shier, 28 Estate Planning 172.)

"The integrated offshore intentionally defective grantor trust" (2001). The combination of one or two intentionally defective irrevocable trusts (IDITs) (husband and wife) with a family limited partnership (FLP) is probably the single most powerful tool for reducing, over time, a client's taxable estate to zero and transferring the entire amount to the client's children.

First, the authors provide background on the basic technique. As with all estate planning tools, there are advantages and disadvantages to the IDIT. One of the greatest advantages of the IDIT is that flexibility that occurs when the trust can be toggled between grantor and nongrantor status for income tax purposes. With proper planning, the toggle switch provides a much greater ability to properly time the reduction to zero of a client's taxable estate.

The main problem with the more traditional toggle switches is that the IRS may argue there is an implied agreement, or characterize the trust as a perpetual grantor trust, with the result that the corpus will be included in the grantor's federal estate.

Then, the author discusses the use of the integrated offshore IDIT. The integrated offshore IDIT offers a new approach for turning grantor trust status on and off. The trustee and grantor are not required to work in harmony to toggle the switch. Instead, either the trustee or the grantor alone can be given the power to control the toggle switch by making the IDIT a foreign trust for tax purposes (grantor trust status on) or a domestic trust for tax purposes (grantor trust status off). Further, there may be other nontax reasons for changing the IDIT from a domestic trust to a foreign trust, such as asset protection or to avoid the rule against perpetuities. For these reasons, an estate planner should consider the option of the integrated offshore IDIT as an alternative to the more traditional methods to create a toggle switch. (M. Merric & E.D. Brown, 95 Journal of Taxation 277.)

254

"The latest state legislation governing total return unitrusts" (2001). The IRS issued proposed regulations on February 15, 2001, approving both the power to adjust between principal and income contained in the Uniform Principal and Income Act (UPAIA), and the total return unitrust approach, under consideration in a number of states. These proposed regulations have a positive impact on planning for purposes of (1) the marital deduction; (2) conversion of a generation-skipping transfer (GST) grandfathered trust; and (3) qualification for qualified domestic trusts (QDOTs). Moreover, incidental to the unitrust approach, the proposed regulations approved the use of an ordering rule in which short- and long-term capital gains would be a part of distributable net income (DNI) for income tax purposes. But those good things would be available only to trustees and estate planners in states that have adopted these new concepts in connection with their principal and income rules.

After providing background, the authors discuss the importance of change by the states. Those states that do not initiate change will not have the benefit of that change even for trusts drafted in the future. Why? Because the concept of income, in order to be considered such for federal tax purposes, must not be a fundamental departure from existing state law. Hence, an attempt to draft a power for a trustee to adjust without the existence of a state statutory power will fail for marital deduction purposes. So also will a total return unitrust, unless the trust is drafted based on distributing the unitrust amount or income, whichever is greater. Consequently, the proposed regulations have kick-started statutory reform across the country because no forward-thinking state wants its trust businesses to be at a competitive disadvantage.

Next, the authors consider Delaware law. On June 21, 2001, Delaware became the first state in the country to enact a statute expressly allowing trustees of income trusts to convert their regime to one using the total return unitrust (TRU) concept.

Then, the authors turn to other states' legislation and other approaches. Unlike the Delaware statute, the New York, Missouri, and Pennsylvania proposals all contain both the power to adjust and a separate unitrust section. The rationale in having both is that no one of the two solutions is optimal for all trusts. There are trusts and families for which the greater flexibility of the power to adjust is superior, and there are trusts and families for which the unitrust is superior.

Interest in TRU statutes has been shown in Maryland, Colorado, Texas, Iowa, Alaska, Maine, Massachusetts, Ohio, California, Florida, Illinois, and others. (R.B. Wolf & S.R. Leimberg, 28 Estate Planning 474.)

"The overall tax impact of accumulating versus distributing trust income" (2001). Although the high income tax rates applicable to trusts might seem to argue in favor of distributing trust income to the beneficiaries, rather than accumulating it in the trust, this may not be the wisest strategy.

The most tax-advantaged distributions may conflict with certain practical objectives of the trust and the practical objectives of the testator/grantor's estate plan, generally. Nevertheless, the trustee of any trust that provides for the discretionary accumulation of income should consider the relative advantages and disadvantages of accumulation versus distribution. This analysis should focus on both transfer tax and income tax ramifications. In particular, a desire for short-term income tax savings should not, per se, take precedence over the often ultimately larger transfer tax benefits of forgoing those savings. (S.B. Sherman, 28 Estate Planning 83.)

"The quest for the zeroed-out GRAT:" *Walton* says it can be done" (2001). By declaring Example 5 invalid in *Walton* (2000), the Tax Court gives estate planners the opportunity to create the long sought-after zeroed-out grantor retained annuity trust (GRAT). Such a trust has the potential to pass property to descendants free of all transfer taxes if sufficient appreciation occurs in the GRAT property.

After providing background on Section 2702 and Regulation § 25.2702-(3)(e), Example 5, the author discusses *Walton*. On April 7, 1993, Mrs. Walton transferred Wal-

Mart stock worth slightly more than $200 million to two GRATs, and retained the right to annuity payments for two years. Significantly, both GRATs provided that if Mrs. Walton died before the end of the two-year term, any remaining annuity payments were to be made to her estate. She took the position that the annuities were therefore payable in all events for the entire two-year term, and valued them as term annuities with no actuarial reduction for the possibility that she might not survive the term. On audit, the IRS applied the rationale of Example 5 and asserted that Mrs. Walton had in fact made a gift of more than $7.6 million.

Then, the author addresses planning strategies after *Walton*. The essential requirement to have an annuity valued as a term interest, and not as an annuity for the shorter of the life of the grantor or the selected term, is that the annuity be payable in all events for the full term. In *Walton*, that requirement was satisfied by reason of the annuity being payable to the grantor's estate if she failed to survive the term. That may be the only way the annuity can safely be said to be payable for the entire term, although the Tax Court seemed to suggest that if a GRAT were ''simply silent'' concerning the status of annuity payments after the grantor's death, those remaining payments would be made to the grantor's estate as a matter of property law. (J.J. Caulfield, 28 Estate Planning 251.)

''Transfer of punitive damages to charity does not avoid all tax'' (2001). Taxpayers who received punitive damages in a personal injury lawsuit were not required to include in their income under the anticipatory-assignment-of-income doctrine the portion of the award that they transferred to a tax-exempt charitable trust, but were required to include the portion of the award that their attorney retained under a contingency fee agreement, according to Letter Ruling 200107019. (66 Practical Tax Strategies 250.)

''Trust's advisory fees subject to 2 percent-of-AGI deduction floor'' (2001). The Federal Circuit affirmed the Court of Federal Claims in *Mellon Bank N.A.* (2001), holding that a trust's deductions of fees paid for outside investment strategy advice and other services were subject to the 2 percent floor on miscellaneous itemized deductions. (67 Practical Tax Strategies 310.)

''What are the implications when a lawyer serves as trustee?'' (2001). Trustees are in demand, and lawyers are often asked to serve as fiduciaries. This article analyzes the implications of such an arrangement, and also examines alternatives, including the use of professional, independent, individual fiduciaries.

First, the author discusses the responses of lawyers to the heightened demand for fiduciaries. Given a lawyer-centric planning process, clients often ask their estate planning lawyer to serve as fiduciary. To be sure, many lawyers do. And in some locales, notably Boston, most of the larger firms not only provide fiduciaries but have also expanded into offering asset management for clients.

It is at least as common for lawyers to decline the role, though. Troublesome issues related to service as a fiduciary involve conflict of interest and relevant expertise. Many lawyers have decided that the very real possibility of being accused of conflict of interest or lack of expertise is simply not worth the fees associated with acting as a fiduciary.

Then, the author considers alternatives. Several aspects of the problems of conflict of interest and risk of liability can be mitigated by better drafting of trust provisions and documents. The risk of an individual trustee's lack of expertise can also be spread, primarily via co-fiduciaries with different perspectives, who each add value through a particular specialty. (T.C. Gaspard, 28 Estate Planning 542.)

''When income isn't 'income'—the impact of the new proposed regulations under Section 643'' (2001). Proposed regulations dramatically revise the definition of ''income'' under Section 643(b) and clarify the situations in which capital gains of a trust are included in distributable net income (DNI) under Section 643(a). These proposals are arguably the most important IRS pronouncements affecting trust administration in recent years.

In recognizing the prevalence of total return investing under modern portfolio theory and the prudent investor legislation enacted by most states, the IRS has provided that nonconventional definitions of "income" enacted (or proposed to be enacted) by many states, such as statutory unitrusts or equitable adjustments under the Uniform Principal and Income Act, will not cause a trust to fail to qualify for favorable tax treatment under the various marital trust provisions, or under other provisions of the Code. Furthermore, the IRS recognizes that the amount distributable to an income beneficiary will in many situations be greater than the traditionally computed trust accounting income, and the proposed regulations provide guidance, albeit somewhat unclear, on whether and under what circumstances that additional amount will be taxed to the beneficiary rather than the trust.

After providing background on the tension between income and principal, the significance of the definition of "income," and the taxation of trusts and beneficiaries, the authors discuss the definitions of "income" and "DNI" under the proposed regulations. Section 643(b), the source of authority for the definition of "income" in the proposed regulations, provides substantial flexibility since it looks solely to the terms of the governing instrument and state law. Proposed Regulation § 1.643(b)-1 provides that for purposes of the taxation of estates, trusts (other than grantor trusts), and beneficiaries, generally, the definition of "income" continues to be determined under traditional principles of income and principal, allocating ordinary income to trust accounting income and capital gain to principal. If local law permits a different allocation, however, trust provisions following that law will be respected for tax purposes if local law provides for a reasonable apportionment between the income and remainder beneficiaries of the total return of the trust for the year.

Proposed Regulation § 1.643(a)-3(a) states the traditional rule that capital gain ordinarily will be excluded from DNI. (This mirrors the default provision of Proposed Regulation § 1.643(b)-1, which provides that trust provisions that depart fundamentally from traditional principles of income and principal generally will not be recognized.) Proposed Regulation § 1.643(a)-3(b) addresses the treatment of capital gain under standards that are more consistent with practices under the Prudent Investor Act.

Then, the authors consider the effect on the marital deduction and charitable deduction. Proposed Regulation §§ 20.2056(b)-5(f)(1) and 1.2523(e)-1(f)(1) specify that the requirement that a spouse be entitled to all of the income from a general power of appointment trust or a qualified terminable interest property (QTIP) trust will be met if the spouse is entitled to income as defined by a state statute that provides for a reasonable apportionment between the income and remainder beneficiaries of the total return of the trust and that meets the requirements of Proposed Regulation § 1.643(b)-1.

Two types of charitable vehicles that are exempt from income tax permit a noncharitable individual to have an income interest: (1) net income charitable remainder unitrusts (NICRUTs) and (2) pooled income funds. The proposed regulations have limited application with respect to these charitable vehicles.

Finally, the authors turn to grandfathered generation-skipping transfer (GST) tax trusts. (B.A. Sloan, T.R. Harris & G.L. Cushing, 94 Journal of Taxation 325.)

"Y2K—a vintage year for GRATs" (2001).

The year 2000 was an important year for grantor retained annuity trusts (GRATs), which are typically used to reduce the amount of a taxable gift, by reserving to the donor an annuity interest payable from the transferred assets for a term of years. During the year 2000, the IRS prohibited the use of certain loans and similar arrangements to satisfy the annuity obligation, the Tax Court in *Cook* struck down the use of certain contingent spousal interests to inflate the gift tax value of the reserved annuity interest, and the Tax Court in *Walton* declared invalid the notorious Example 5, by which the IRS

257

attempted to deflate artificially the gift tax value of the grantor's reserved annuity interest.

Each of these developments bears examination by any estate planner who is contemplating the use of a GRAT to reduce a client's wealth transfer taxes. (H.M. Zaritsky, 28 Estate Planning 144.)

U

UNRELATED BUSINESS INCOME TAX

(*See* Tax-Exempt Organizations—Unrelated Business Income Tax)

V

VALUATION OF PROPERTY

(See also Charitable Contributions; Estate Planning; Estates and Estate Tax; Gifts and Gift Tax; Marital Deduction; Partners and Partnerships; Trusts and Trust Taxation)

In General

"A questionable methodology: including external costs of sales in property valuations" **(2001).** An ad valorem tax is a tax imposed on property or an article of commerce in proportion to its value, as determined by an assessment or appraisal. The value of tangible personal property for ad valorem tax purposes can be markedly different depending on where the property is reported for tax purposes and how property appraisers and the courts determine taxable value.

Under the constitutional or statutory guidelines of states that levy taxes on tangible personal property, the property generally must be uniformly valued at a "just value" or "market value." Sales tax, freight, and other shipping costs, as well as installation costs, all may serve to drive up the asset's basis, and thus the initial valuation for property tax purposes. The article notes another disparity, that use tax, which serves as a counterpart to the sales tax, is not added to the value of tangible personal property for property tax assessments. Adding external costs to the value of property seems unconstitutional at both the state and the federal levels because it violates the notion of uniform and just valuation for all property similarly situated within a state. Surprisingly, only a handful of states have considered the issue and, of those, only two found that inclusion of external costs of sale constitutes excessive taxation to the purchaser.

In *Wal-Mart Stores, Inc. v. Mazourek* (2000), the Florida Court of Appeals for the Fifth District concluded that the $2 million in sales taxes the retail chain paid when it purchased stores should not be included in the valuation of property for ad valorem tax purposes, since these costs add nothing to the actual value of the property. The Kansas Supreme Court reached a similar conclusion in *McGraw Fertilizer* (1997) and generally rejected the inclusion of external costs, noting that a disparity could exist between two taxpayers owning identical pieces of equipment but with different reported values for that equipment. This disparity was in direct conflict with the uniformity section of the Kansas Constitution, which requires that all property be taxed the same as other property within the same taxing jurisdiction. However, in *Wal-Mart Stores, Inc. v. Todora* (2001), Florida's Second District found to the contrary, that under the cost approach, the inclusion of external costs of sales does not upset the presumption of correctness.

A review of decisions in South Carolina, California, Colorado, and Maryland illustrates how external costs of sale of an asset can be attributed incorrectly, in the author's opinion, to the value of the asset itself. These holdings take circuitous routes to reach the same outcome and result in economic consequences that help larger businesses at the expense of their smaller competitors.

The article observes that many state constitutions have similar provisions to ensure equity and fairness in the imposition of the tax burden. However, when courts examine whether the *methodology* used accomplishes this, all too often the focus is at a fairly topical level—is the appraisal method selected statutorily acceptable and used in a consistent manner? The courts fail to delve below the surface, to review whether the selected valuation method achieves uniformity of taxation.

Depreciation, including physical depreciation, functional obsolescence, technological obsolescence, and economic obsolescence, allows for the taxable value of an asset to be reduced over time in recognition of the declining worth the asset has in the marketplace or in the production of income to the taxpayer reporting the asset for ad valorem tax purposes. Though depreciation might, over time, mitigate the excessive valuation of tangible personal property, it does not cure the problem. The declining value of the assets, no matter how far along the depreciation scale it may be, still reflects a basis that is premised on an inflated value.

The article concludes that taxpayers should not be penalized simply for owning property that may be assessed at a value significantly higher than the same type of property owned by others. Permitting the inclusion of external costs of sale in property valuations penalizes smaller businesses and other taxpayers that lack the economic clout to use more complex and advantageous purchasing systems.

Taxpayers seeking to contest their property valuations based on the inclusion of external costs would do well to persuade their taxing authorities to adopt the analysis used by the Kansas Supreme Court in *McGraw Fertilizer*. There, the court recognized that uniformity in taxation can exist only where true market values are returned, absent the external costs of sale. State courts in California, Colorado, Maryland, and South Carolina may wish to reconsider their decisions, especially in light of the adverse economic consequences that might result. Otherwise, savvy manufacturers may capitalize on this difference in taxable values when it comes to relocate or expand capital-intensive production facilities. (J.L. Terwilliger, 11 Journal of Multistate Taxation and Incentives, No. 7, 14.)

"Contingent annuity interest did not reduce taxable GRAT transfer" (2001). According to the Tax Court in *Schott* (2001), the taxpayers could not value their retained interest in grantor retained annuity trusts (GRATs) as dual-life annuities, rather than single-life annuities. Doing so would have

lowered the taxable gift. (67 Practical Tax Strategies 57.)

"Courts weigh in on 'highest and best use' and other valuation issues" (2001). J.F. Janata, 10 Journal of Multistate Taxation and Incentives, No. 9, 14. (*Digested under* State Taxes—In General, page 196.)

"Defined value gifts: Does IRS have it all wrong?" (2001). Clients who wish to make lifetime gifts often are deterred by a practical economic concern: how to limit the value of what is given away to the amount that they intend to give and no more. This intended limitation has both a tax and a nontax element to it. This issue is even more vexing when the client wants to give subjectively valued assets, particularly with respect to limiting the gift tax value.

One method of gift giving that many clients consider is a formula gift that is tied to both the total value that they intend to give and the value of the gift property as finally determined for gift tax purposes. This article discusses so-called defined value gifts in the context of FSA 200122011 (the FSA) and a pending Tax Court case—*McCord*.

First, the author provides background on the FSA and *McCord*. In the FSA, the IRS considered whether a formula clause that allocates additional value to a charitable donee in the event the value of the transferred property is redetermined for federal transfer tax purposes will be respected for federal transfer tax purposes. The IRS answered that the formula clause should not be given effect for federal tax purposes.

The facts of the FSA supposedly are those of a docketed Tax Court case, *McCord*, that was tried in Houston before Judge Foley on May 7, 2001, and still awaited decision at press time. The taxpayer's version of the facts in *McCord* differs significantly from the facts set forth by the IRS in the FSA.

Then, the author considers whether, in light of the FSA, use of a formula for transfer tax purposes is still safe and provides commentary on relevant authorities, the IRS step-transaction argument, design of defined gift transactions, and the effect of an intervening purchase of the charity's interests. A careful reading of the FSA clearly indicates that the IRS is concerned only about the use of formulae for gift tax purposes, and maybe only where the exact tranche gift technique is used. Nevertheless, the IRS rationale for a blanket disregard of gift tax formulae for a defined value gift cannot withstand much intellectual scrutiny. Proponents of the defined value gift point to the regulations and published rulings that expressly sanction the use of values as finally determined for tax purposes.

Finally, the author explores the second issue raised in the FSA: whether the amount of a transfer may be reduced by the actuarial value of the estate taxes attributable to the potential Section 2035(c) [now 2035(b)] inclusion in the donors' gross estates. Not surprisingly, the IRS answered this question as follows: "The amount of the gift may not be reduced by the actuarial value of the potential estate taxes because the fact of inclusion and the amount of any estate tax attributable thereto is too speculative." (L.P. Hood, Jr., 28 Estate Planning 582.)

"Donees' agreement to pay future tax did not reduce gift's value" (2001). An agreement by transferees of a gift of stock to assume liability for any additional gift taxes or estate taxes assessed, and related expenses, does not create a lien or encumbrance on the stock reducing its value for gift tax purposes, ruled a Virginia federal district court in *Frank Armstrong, Jr. Trust* (2001). At the time of the agreement, the imposition of such taxes and liabilities was too speculative. (28 Estate Planning 329.)

"Family limited partnership gifts get limited valuation discounts" (2001). The Tax Court has held, in *Estate of Jones* (2001), that transfers a father made to family limited partnerships were not taxable gifts and the value of limited partnership interests that he subsequently transferred by gift should be reduced by lack-of-marketability and secondary market discounts. (66 Practical Tax Strategies 293.)

"Family limited partnerships: the open issues" (2001). J.A. Bogdanski, 28 Estate Planning 282. (*Digested under* Partners and Partnerships—Family Limited Partnerships, page 146.)

"Invalid regulation overvalued taxable GRAT gift" (2001). The Tax Court rejected the IRS's valuation of gifts that took the form of remainder interests in grantor retained annuity trusts (GRATs) in *Walton* (2001). In reaching its conclusion, the court held that Regulation § 25.2702-3(e), Example 5 is an invalid interpretation of Section 2702. (66 Practical Tax Strategies 232.)

"Late alternate valuation election forced estate to value property at the date of death" (2001). The estate must value all the property included in the gross estate as of the date of the decedent's death because the executor made an alternate valuation date election more than eighteen months after the statutorily permissible period expired, the Tax Court ruled in *Estate of Eddy* (2000). According to the court, the IRS does not have discretionary authority under Revenue Procedure 92-85 to allow an executor to make an untimely election to use the alternate valuation date when Section 2032 provides that an alternate valuation election must be made on either the due date of the return or the due date of the return including extensions. In addition, since the executor failed to make the alternate valuation election within the one year prescribed by law, alternate valuation was precluded. (28 Estate Planning 26.)

"Lottery payments valued using actuarial tables" (2001). The Tax Court has held, in *Estate of Gribauskas* (2001), that an interest held by a decedent at his death, consisting of annual installments of a lottery prize, must be valued for estate tax purposes as an annuity using the actuarial tables prescribed under Section 7520. (66 Practical Tax Strategies 298.)

"Ninth Circuit reverses Tax Court, and rules no premium for minority voting stock" (2001). The per share value of a minority interest in a company's voting stock was no greater than the value of a share of nonvoting stock, the Ninth Circuit ruled in *Estate of Simplot* (2001). (28 Estate Planning 441.)

"No swing vote premium on minority interest in family business" (2001). The Tax Court decision in *Estate of True* (2001) indicates that the IRS's concept of a swing vote premium may well not be applicable to the transfer of a minority interest in a closely held business owned entirely by a single family.

First, the author provides background on the IRS's position on the minority interest discount and the swing vote premium. The IRS has introduced the swing vote premium as part of its fight against the minority interest discount. According to the swing vote premium, no discount for lack of control is appropriate when a minority interest has a swing vote characteristic.

Since the Tax Court decision in *Winkler* (1989), the IRS has ruled privately that the swing vote characteristic may apply to the transfer of common stock in a closely held corporation in which all of the outstanding stock is held by a single family.

Then, the author addresses *Estate of True*. The Tax Court relied on established precedent prescribing that, in determining whether a minority interest discount applies, the court cannot assume the hypothetical buyer is a member of the transferor's family, but the court is free to assume that the hypothetical buyer would recognize the actual identity of the other partners. Given these assumptions, the Tax Court found it unlikely that a member of the decedent's family would join forces with an unrelated purchaser to gain voting control of the partnership. (P.J. Walsh, 67 Practical Tax Strategies 324.)

"Post-death certainties do not count in valuing estate" (2001). In a case of first impression, the Eleventh Circuit has held that an estate's deduction for a claim against the estate must be based on its date-of-death estimated value, not what the estate later actually paid, according to *Estate of O'Neal* (2001). (67 Practical Tax Strategies 240.)

"Post-death events not considered in valuing deduction" (2001). The Tenth Circuit has reversed the Tax Court in *Estate of McMorris* (2001), holding that events occurring after a decedent's death may not be considered in determining an estate's deduction for income taxes owed by the decedent at the time of death. (66 Practical Tax Strategies 293.)

"Purported oral options did not reduce property values" (2001). Properties that were owned by a decedent at her date of death were not encumbered by oral options that extended existing leases on the properties and, therefore, the estate was not entitled to reduce the value of the decedent's interest in the properties for estate tax purposes, according to the Tax Court in *Estate of Edwards* (2001). (67 Practical Tax Strategies 241.)

"Redemption agreement did not reduce taxable value" (2001). The Tax Court held in *Estate of Schwan* (2001) that the value for estate tax purposes of stock bequeathed to a foundation under an arrangement that required the stock be redeemed was not necessarily the redemption price. (67 Practical Tax Strategies 190.)

"Stock owned outright and in marital trust aggregated" (2001). In FSA 200119013, the IRS has concluded that for valuation purposes, stock in a closely held company that a decedent owned outright should be aggregated with shares over which he had a testamentary general power of appointment. (67 Practical Tax Strategies 56.)

"Subsequent litigation cannot alter amount of claim deducted" (2001). 28 Estate Planning 548. (*Digested under* Estates and Estate Tax—In General, page 53.)

"The burden of proving fair market value" (2001). The traditional rules on the burden of proof in federal tax cases were changed in 1998. Section 7491 was added to the Code following a round of public congressional criticism of the IRS. Under that Code section, the government bears the burden of proof in court as to any factual issue if the taxpayer: (1) introduces credible evidence with respect to that issue; (2) complies with any legal requirements to substantiate any item; (3) has maintained all records required by law; and (4) has cooperated with reasonable IRS requests for witnesses, information, documents, meetings, and interviews.

After providing background on the rules regarding proof of fair market value, the author discusses the Ninth Circuit response. In 2001, three surprising decisions by the Ninth Circuit—*Morrissey*, *Simplot*, and *Mitchell*—indicated that in most valuation cases, the IRS may have had the burden of proof even before the enactment of Section 7491. In all three of the cases, the government had largely prevailed in the Tax Court; in all three, the Ninth Circuit reversed, holding that the government had, and failed to carry, the burden of proving fair market value. (J.A. Bogdanski, 28 Estate Planning 618.)

"Valuation adjustments applicable to transfers of family business interests" (2001). The use of estate planning transfer techniques combined with the application of valuation discounts to closely held business interests should make possible the successful transition of a business at a nominal transfer tax cost.

First, the author discusses valuing the closely held business, including valuation adjustments applicable to partial interests—lack of marketability or liquidity discounts, lack of control/minority interest discounts, premiums for voting privileges, key-person discounts, and discounts attributable to built-in capital gains. Once the fair market value of the entire business has been determined, valuation discounts should be applied to partial interests in the business to reflect the fact that a willing buyer may agree only to pay less than the pro rata portion of the value of the entire entity, if certain other factors that suppress or reduce the earning power are present. Moreover, a premium may be applicable to reflect a control position. Courts have consistently held that several types of valuation adjustments may apply in valuing partial interests in closely held businesses.

Then, the author addresses posttransaction valuation adjustments and achieving finality for lifetime transfers of partial interests in a closely held business. It would be wise for a taxpayer to hire qualified professional appraisers to substantiate the valuation adjustments attributable to transferred closely held business interests. Nevertheless, there is always the risk that, on audit, the IRS will request an adjustment of the valuation discounts originally reported. Frequently, there is a negotiation with the IRS resulting in a settlement concerning the allowable discounts.

Because of the uncertainty surrounding the valuation of transfers of closely held business interests, it is advantageous to achieve finality with the IRS regarding the transaction as soon as possible. If a transfer is adequately disclosed on a gift tax return and the period of limitations on assessment of gift tax has expired, the value of the gift cannot be adjusted for purposes of determining prior taxable gifts and the current gift tax liability, and the value of the gift cannot be adjusted for purposes of determining adjusted taxable gifts and the estate tax liability.

Finally, the author turns to litigating valuation cases before the Tax Court. If a taxpayer has a valuation dispute with the IRS that cannot be settled, the taxpayer generally has two choices. The taxpayer can either: (1) pay the tax deficiency and sue in federal district court for a refund or (2) refuse to pay the deficiency currently and litigate the case before the Tax Court. (N.H. Weinberg, 28 Estate Planning 268.)

"Valuation based on partial restoration despite insurance expectation" (2001). When a decedent died owning a residence that was in the process of being rebuilt following a fire, the property's value for estate tax purposes was based on its condition on the decedent's date of death, according to the Tax Court in *Estate of Bull* (2001). The value did not take into account an expected insurance recovery. (66 Practical Tax Strategies 381.)

"Valuation developments highlight the importance of appraisals" (2001). The role of appraisers in estate and gift tax controversies has been highlighted by recent developments, making the proper selection of an appraiser and a thorough understanding of the appraiser's work-product more critical to an estate planner's own value to the client.

First, the author discusses the impact of a trilogy of Tax Court valuation cases, decided in the last quarter of 2000—*Shepherd*, *Estate of Strangi*, and *Knight*. The three cases all identify problems with the values claimed by the taxpayers, and all three cases result in significantly higher transfer tax values than the taxpayers claimed—generally as a result of smaller valuation discounts than the taxpayers had claimed. As a result, the cases will undoubtedly be hailed as "victories" for the tax collector.

For the most part, though, it is clear from the court's opinions that the taxpayers' disappointments were attributed either to the taxpayers' failure to structure or implement the transactions with proper care, or to the taxpayers' valuation experts' failure to explain their valuation conclusions in a careful and understandable fashion. Both of these failures should be avoidable with proper knowledge of the applicable rules and attention to their application, including careful attention to the appraisal process and the appraiser's report.

Then, the author discusses the impact of this trilogy of cases on the selecting and working with appraisers, the pros and cons of assembling a team of appraisers, and the cost of an appraisal. Recent substantive and procedural developments have made it more likely that valuation controversies will continue to beset estate planners, while at the same time placing a greater premium on care in the engagement and follow-up of appraisers. It often takes time and costs money to do the best job possible. But it is prudent to try. (R.D. Aucutt, 28 Estate Planning 299.)

"Valuation discount for tax on built-in capital gain" (2001). The Fifth Circuit has vacated the judgment of the Tax Court in *Estate of Jameson* (2001), and remanded the case to allow a discount for built-in capital gains when valuing stock in a privately held

holding company. (67 Practical Tax Strategies 375.)

"Value of deceased partner's minority interest is discounted for estate tax purposes" (2001). On remand from the Fifth Circuit, a Texas federal district court in *Adams* (2001) determined that discounts for lack of control, lack of marketability, and lack of diversification applied to value an assignee's interest in a partnership for estate tax purposes. (3 Business Entities, No. 6, 36.)

Special-Use Valuation

"Tax Court clarifies requirements for special-use valuation" (2001). Special-use valuation of timberland, standing timber, and pastureland requires careful selection of comparable property and thorough analysis of the cash rental from the property, as the Tax Court decision in *Estate of Rogers* (2000) demonstrates. In *Rogers*, the Tax Court held that an estate was entitled to value a decedent's timberland and standing timber, as well as a parcel of pastureland that constituted "qualified woodland," pursuant to the special-use valuation formula method under Section 2032A(e)(7), because the estate provided leases of comparable land for the five most recent calendar years ending before the date of the decedent's death.

After considering the facts in *Rogers*, the authors discuss the valuation issues, including comparability of real properties and comparability of rental values.

Finally, the authors offer tips for the practitioner. Special-use valuation of qualifying timberland, standing timber, and pastureland under Section 2032A(e)(7) requires careful selection of comparable property and thorough analysis of the cash rental from the property. For timberland, comparable land should be of a similar size, topography, and soil type to that of the estate's subject property. Similarly, adjustments should be made to account for differences in location, land quality, or timber type and maturity. Comparable property should meet as many of the factors described in Regulation § 20.2032A-4(d) as possible. More importantly, the estate should provide detailed descriptions of the subject properties and the comparable properties when preparing the estate tax return.

When choosing comparable leased property, leases with rent escalation clauses will help the estate ensure that the leases represent the prevailing rents for that type of land during the statutory period. Both actual rents and the state and local property taxes should be explained and fully substantiated with original source data. (H.W. Neiswender & S.M. Wyatt, 28 Estate Planning 80.)

W

WITHHOLDING OF TAX

"A practical guide for new QIs" (2001). The IRS has provided guidance on a qualified intermediary's (QI's) withholding and information-reporting obligations in three notices—Notice 2001-4, Notice 2001-11, and Announcement 2001-15. Members of the banking community have greatly appreciated this guidance because many uncertainties regarding the new regulations have been clarified. Also, this guidance is significant because it demonstrates an attempt by the IRS to make the new withholding tax and QI rules workable. The IRS took into consideration several concerns of potential QIs and sought to fix these problems in a manner acceptable to the QI community.

First, the author discusses each of the three notices—Notice 2001-4, Notice 2001-11, and Announcement 2001-15. In response to comments regarding the implementation of the new regulations and the QI Agreement, the IRS issued guidance in Notice 2001-4 providing transitional relief for entities affected by the new rules (including both QIs and U.S. withholding agents), as well as clarification regarding the term "know your customer" (KYC).

Under the new regulations, as discussed in Notice 2001-11, financial institutions organized under the laws of a U.S. possession that act as intermediaries ("possessions financial institutions") are generally required to act as non-QIs (NQIs). Payments of U.S.-source income to NQIs are generally subject to 30 percent withholding (or 31 percent backup withholding for deposit interest and certain payments on short-term obligations) unless the NQI provides documentation from, and other information relating to, customers on whose behalf the NQI acts that supports a reduced withholding rate.

Announcement 2001-15 responds to concerns about implementing the new certification requirements contained in the new Form W-9 issued in December 2000. The IRS has made use of the form optional until July 1, 2001. The major change to Form W-9 is that a payee must now certify that he is a U.S. person (including a U.S. resident alien). Payors must use the revised Form W-9 for all new solicitations after June 30, 2001. A foreign person may not use a Form W-9 to furnish his taxpayer identification number (TIN) to the payor after December 31, 2000. Instead, foreign payees must use the appropriate Form W-8.

Then, the author addresses nonresident alien withholding and Form 1042-S reporting, and backup withholding and Form 1099 reporting. (D.M. Balaban, P.J. Connors, P. Marcovici, M.J. Michaels & T.A. O'Donnell, 12 Journal of International Taxation, No. 4, 12.)

"Braiding the rope: transitional relief for financial intermediaries and U.S. withholding agents under new regulations" (2001). In 1997, the IRS issued new regulations relating to the withholding, documentation, and information reporting of certain payments to foreign persons (the new regulations). The new rules, as amended in May 2000, became effective on January 1, 2001 (the effective date). The provisions of the new regulations relating to qualified intermediaries (QIs) are a key component of the new regulations. The IRS outlined the QI application procedures and the terms of the QI Agreement (the model QI Agreement) in Revenue Procedure 2000-12, which was released in January 2000.

First, the authors discuss Notice 2001-4 and transitional relief. With less than one month remaining before the effective date, questions regarding the implementation of the new regulations remained outstanding. In response to this problem, the IRS issued additional guidance regarding the new regulations in Notice 2001-4 (the Notice). The Notice provides transitional relief for entities affected by the new rules and addresses other issues such as recipient specific reporting by

269

trusts and foundations. It also clarifies the term "know your customer."

Then, the authors consider issuance of new versions of W-8 forms. (M.J. Michaels, D.M. Balaban, P.J. Connors, P. Marcovici & T.A. O'Donnell, 12 Journal of International Taxation, No. 2, 41.)

"Eligibility for reduced dividend withholding rate turns on record date" (2001). In TAM 200048011, the IRS ruled that the record date of stock ownership, not the date of payment, determines whether a foreign corporation qualifies for the lower tax treaty rate for withholding on U.S.-source dividends. (94 Journal of Taxation 184.)

"Notice 2001-43: relief under the new withholding and QI rules" (2001). Notice 2001-43 provides additional guidance on the implementation of the U.S. withholding tax and qualified intermediary (QI) rules that became effective as of January 1, 2001.

First, the authors discuss the broader permission for branches to apply home-country know-your-customer (KYC) rules. Pursuant to Notice 2001-43, relief is extended to situations in which the country where the branch is located is in the process of having its KYC rules approved. The Notice clarifies that the IRS will permit a branch of a financial institution to act as a QI if the branch is located in a country identified by the IRS as a jurisdiction awaiting approval of KYC rules provided the branch is part of an entity organized in a country that has acceptable KYC rules and the entity agrees to apply its home-country KYC rules to the branch. The branch will be permitted to act as a QI under this rule only for the period during which the jurisdiction where it is

located is identified as awaiting approval. After the IRS approves the KYC rules of the branch's jurisdiction, the branch must apply the KYC rules of that jurisdiction beginning on the date that an attachment to the QI agreement for the jurisdiction is posted on the IRS website.

Then, the authors address the Notice's provisions regarding: (1) additional clarification regarding the relief announced in December 2000 that is available to QI institutions in respect of non-U.S. grantor and simple trusts and foundations with no-U.S. beneficial owners; (2) further extension of the period to apply for QI status with retroactive effect to January 1, 2001; (3) an alternative convention for converting payments to non-U.S. currency into U.S. dollars; (4) a minimization of disclosure on certain treaty-based return positions; and (5) relief for nonqualified intermediaries (NQIs). (T.A. O'Donnell, M.J. Michaels, P. Marcovici & D.M. Balaban, 12 Journal of International Taxation, No. 9, 24.)

"Planning helps avert employer tip tax woes" (2001). R.A. Stein, 66 Practical Tax Strategies 337. (*Digested under* Compensation for Personal Services, page 26.)

"Statutory stock options avoid withholding—for now" (2001). Notice 2001-14 provides that the IRS will not assess FICA or FUTA tax on the exercise of any statutory stock option exercised before January 1, 2003. Similarly, the IRS will not treat the disposition of stock acquired by an employee pursuant to the exercise of the option as subject to income tax withholding. (66 Practical Tax Strategies 254.)

Y

YEAR DEDUCTIBLE

(*See* Accounting Methods)

YEAR, TAXABLE

(*See* Accounting Methods)

YEAR INCOME INCLUDABLE

(*See* Accounting Methods)

Table of IRC Sections

IRC §

382 . . . . 4, 131, 237	705 141
382(g) 237	706 3
401(a)(2) 152	707 149
401(a)(17) 153, 154	707(a)(2) 139
401(k) 156, 157, 158	707(a)(2)(B) 136, 139
402(g) 153	707(a)(2)(B)(iii) 136
403(b) 157, 158	707(c) 144
404 68	708 . . . . 138, 139, 176
404(a)(11) 68	708(b)(2)(B) 135
411(d)(6) 153, 156	731(a) 149
411(d)(6)(B)(i) 153	732(b) 140
414(v) 153, 154, 155	732(f) 138
415 . . . . 153, 154	737 135
423 227	737(a) 135
441 3	741 19
442 3	751 . . . . 19, 20
444 . . . . 186, 187, 192	751(a) 19
444(a) 186	752 . . . . 8, 148, 149
448 2	752(a) 145
457 . . . . 156, 157	754 . . . . 137, 144
465 . . . . 8, 191	811(f)(4) 253
469 191	863 . . . . 90, 92
469(a) 152	863(d) 92
482 . . . . 5, 90, 246	863(e) 92
501(c)(3) 9, 24, 25, 124, 192, 230, 231, 232,	864(e) 65
235, 236, 238, 239, 241	864(e)(5) 65
501(c)(4) 235, 239	864(e)(6) 65
501(c)(9) 233	872(b) 93
501(m) 237	877 93
502 233	881(a) 61
509(a)(1) 239, 240	882(a) 61
509(a)(2) 239, 240	883(a) 93
509(a)(3) 240	897 58
511–513 244	901 66
511(a) 25	902 . . . . 59, 65
512(a)(1) 243	902(d)(2)(E) 59
512(b)(3) 243	902(d)(4) 59
513(a) 243	903 66
513(d) 243	904 65
513(f) 243	904(d) 65
527 235	904(d)(3) 59, 65
529 . . . . 39, 40, 41	921–927 58
529(b)(1)(A) 41	936 114
531 36	941(a) 56
541 36	942(c) 65
641 186	943(c) 57
642(c) 43	943(d) 56
643(a) 256	951 114
643(a)(3) 248	951(a) 62
643(b) 248, 252, 256, 257	956 114
645 252	1000(c)(4) 253
664 . . . . 247, 248, 252	1017 191
672(f) 251	1031 . . . . 121, 122
679 251	1041 79
684 251	1059A 96, 97
691 145	1060 . . . . 175, 186
691(a) 54	1202 140
691(c) 53, 54, 144, 145	1221 125
704(b) 136, 149	1223 140
704(c) 136, 149	1231 . . . . 13, 17, 125
704(c)(1)(A) 136, 149	1245 211
704(c)(1)(B) 135	1245(a) 211

Table
of Articles

The Journal of Taxation

Accounting

Compensation and Benefits

Corporations and Shareholders

policy, *Robert Willens*, 95 JTAX 5, Jul01.

When service corporations liquidate as part of a change in form of entity—the problem of goodwill, *John C. Zimmerman*, 95 JTAX 110, Aug01.

Estates, Trusts, and Gifts

Creating an amicable estate plan for the decedent's children and the second spouse, *Peter B. Tiernan*, 94 JTAX 98, Feb01.

Estate planning changes in the 2001 Tax Act—more than you can count, *Jonathan G. Blattmachr & Lauren Y. Detzel*, 95 JTAX 74, Aug01.

Generation-skipping transfer tax planning after the 2001 Act: mostly good news, *Carol A. Harrington, Carlyn S. McCaffrey, Lloyd Leva Plaine, & Pam H. Schneider*, 95 JTAX 143, Sep01.

New IRS guidance provides fresh impetus for using electing small business trusts, *Sydney S. Traum*, 94 JTAX 285, May01.

Sometimes less is more: the estate tax tradeoffs involved in the family business elections, *John O. Everett, Nancy B. Nichols, David B. Davidson, & Jerome L. Lonnes*, 94 JTAX 338, Jun01.

Tax consequences of outstanding trust liabilities when grantor status terminates, *Deborah V. Dunn & David A. Handler*, 95 JTAX 49, Jul01.

The aftermath of *Walton*: the rehabilitation of the fixed-term, zeroed-out GRAT, *Carlyn S. McCaffrey, Lloyd Leva Plaine, & Pam H. Schneider*, 95 JTAX 325, Dec01.

The integrated offshore intentionally defective grantor trust, *Mark Merric & Edward D. Brown*, 95 JTAX 277, Nov01.

When income isn't "income"—the impact of the new Proposed Regulations under Section 643, *Barbara A. Sloan, T. Randolph Harris, & George L. Cushing*, 94 JTAX 325, Jun01.

Exempt Organizations

A selective review of the intermediate sanctions Temporary Regulations—generally, improved all around, *Pamela S. Kaufmann*, 94 JTAX 301, May01.

International

Guidance on tax attributes in Section 367(b) exchanges will make planning easier, *Vikram A. Gosain, Vickie R. Kraay, & Seth Goldstein*, 94 JTAX 242, Apr01.

Opportunities for the foreign investor in U.S. real estate—if planning comes first, *Michael Hirschfeld & Shaul Grossman*, 94 JTAX 36, Jan01.

Planning for foreign corporations using partnerships to take the plunge into U.S. markets, *Paul C. Lau & Sandra L. Soltis*, 94 JTAX 105, Feb01.

The extraterritorial income exclusion enhances the tax benefits once sought from FSCs, *Alan S. Lederman & Bobbe Hirsh*, 94 JTAX 174, Mar01.

Letter Rulings

Acquiring corporation may not deduct target's contingent liabilities, 94 JTAX 121, Feb01.

Adjustments to option prices did not affect status as performance-based compensation, 94 JTAX 184, Mar01.

Affiliates must share value of compensatory stock options as compensation cost, 94 JTAX 250, Apr01.

Agreement to name mall after company does not produce impermissible tenant services for REIT, 95 JTAX 375, Dec01.

Basis recovery not limited to basis of actual shares redeemed, 95 JTAX 56, Jul01.

"Benefits and burdens" approach used to determine where sales to foreign customers occurred, 94 JTAX 185, Mar01.

Cash element of contribution/dividend transaction ignored as attempt to create foreign tax credit, 95 JTAX 379, Dec01.

"Charitable lid" formula used in connection with FLP disregarded, 95 JTAX 116, Aug01.

Corporation may use tax book value to apportion interest expense, 94 JTAX 252, Apr01.

Credit advanced to foreign sub for inventory purchases was equity, not debt, 95 JTAX 312, Nov01.

Deductible performance-based compensation in a short tax year, 94 JTAX 122, Feb01.

Design expenses had to pass uncertainty test to qualify as R&E expenditures, 95 JTAX 182, Sep01.

Discharged unsecured debt is bad debt deduction for parent corporation, 94 JTAX 251, Apr01.

Divorce can permit division of CRUT without adverse tax consequences, 95 JTAX 117, Aug01.

Dual consolidated loss rules applied to bar use of foreign NOLs, 94 JTAX 186, Mar01.

Eligibility for reduced dividend withholding rate turns on record date, 94 JTAX 184, Mar01.

Exempt HMO's insurance income is taxable under Subchapter L, 94 JTAX 60, Jan01.

Partnerships, S Corporations, and Limited Liability Companies

tions, *Jeffrey A. Erickson & Roger F. Pillow*, 94 JTAX 261, May01.

New IRS guidance provides fresh impetus for using electing small business trusts, *Sydney S. Traum*, 94 JTAX 285, May01.

Partnership interest transfers under the holding period final regulations: opportunities and traps remain, *Sheldon I. Banoff*, 94 JTAX 211, Apr01.

Possible consequences of options to acquire partnership interests, *Christopher S. Armstrong & Matthew K. Cooper*, 94 JTAX 356, Jun01.

Rev. Proc. 2001-43, Section 83(b), and unvested profits interests—the final facet of *Diamond?*, *Glenn E. Mincey, Eric B. Sloan, & Sheldon I. Banoff*, 95 JTAX 205, Oct01.

Supreme Court hands taxpayers a victory in *Gitlitz*, but will Congress take it away?, *Richard M. Lipton*, 94 JTAX 133, Mar01.

Transfer of a partnership interest at death creates tough issues for the successor, *Sally M. Jones & David M. Maloney*, 94 JTAX 24, Jan01.

Personal

EGTRRA adds new tax benefits to planning for higher education expenses under Section 529, *Karen M. Stockmal*, 95 JTAX 238, Oct01.

Has the innocent spouse become the overprotected spouse? Reflections on recent cases, *Robert H. Feldman*, 94 JTAX 51, Jan01.

IRS, reversing course, issues new interim guidance for split-dollar life insurance, *A. Thomas Brisendine & Frank T. Scudere*, 94 JTAX 294, May01.

Operation of personal residence exclusion rules clarified in new Proposed Regulations, *William R. Simpson & Joseph L. Morris*, 94 JTAX 165, Mar01.

Potential reduction in capital gains tax rate requires new planning and new recordkeeping now, *Alan E. Weiner*, 94 JTAX 156, Mar01.

Taxation and the human body: an analysis of transactions involving kidneys, *Frederick R. Parker, Jr.*, 94 JTAX 367, Jun01.]

Procedure

Are individual tax shelters the "competence test" for IRS and practitioners?, *Paul J. Sax*, 95 JTAX 231, Oct01.

Final TEFRA audit and litigation regulations issued as IRS intensifies its focus on partnership audits, *Jonathan Z. Ackerman &*

Christopher P. La Puma, 95 JTAX 261, Nov01.

Has the innocent spouse become the overprotected spouse? Reflections on recent cases, *Robert H. Feldman*, 94 JTAX 51, Jan01.

IRS reverses its position on late returns and refund claims: the mailbox rule will apply, *Philip N. Jones*, 94 JTAX 81, Feb01.

IRS rolls out its new program to resolve ongoing issues before taxpayers file, *David R. Stubblefield*, 94 JTAX 197, Apr01.

The IRS gets aggressive: why taxpayers need to pay attention to FSAs, *David L. Forst & Barton W.S. Bassett*, 95 JTAX 42, Jul01.

Real Estate

Federal and state tax consequences of synthetic leasing—multiple benefits, minimal risks, *Steven G. Frost & Paul Carman*, 95 JTAX 361, Dec01.

Operation of personal residence exclusion rules clarified in new Proposed Regulations, *William R. Simpson & Joseph L. Morris*, 94 JTAX 165, Mar01.

Opportunities for the foreign investor in U.S. real estate—if planning comes first, *Michael Hirschfeld & Shaul Grossman*, 94 JTAX 36, Jan01.

Tax Court requires capitalization of payment for relief of a burdensome lease, *Dean Surkin*, 95 JTAX 298, Nov01.

The real spin on the new spinoff Ruling—should corporate-owned real estate be put into REITs?, *David L. Brandon*, 95 JTAX 92, Aug01.

Shop Talk

Attorneys liable for malpractice despite "substantial authority"!, 94 JTAX 124, Feb01.

California "fixes" LLC franchise taxes—at a price, 95 JTAX 382, Dec01.

Computing tax malpractice damages: the "interest differential," 94 JTAX 127, Feb01.

Confidentiality agreements for tax-savings products—are they unethical?, 94 JTAX 61, Jan01.

Corporation's directors face liability for CEO's tax benefits, 94 JTAX 63, Jan01.

Courts troubled by accounting firms acting as government tax auditors, 95 JTAX 62, Jul01.

Does IRS need "substantial authority" to bring cases against taxpayers?, 94 JTAX 256, Apr01.

Fourth Circuit's reversal in *Hillman* limits self-charged items; now what?, 95 JTAX 60, Jul01.

State and Local

Practical Tax Strategies

Accounting

Election lets taxpayers avoid mid-quarter convention for depreciation, 67 PTS 362, Dec01.

Final regulations on Section 467 rental agreements, 66 PTS 121, Feb01.

Flooring installer wins right to use cash method, 66 PTS 54, Jan01.

Fresh alternative to mutual funds offers tax benefit, *A. Seddik Meziani & James G.S. Yang*, 67 PTS 100, Aug01.

Full prepaid annual fees were income in the year billed, 67 PTS 306, Nov01.

Guidance on adopting and changing accounting periods, 67 PTS 115, Aug01.

IRS could require taxpayer to change accounting method, 67 PTS 366, Dec01.

IRS offers guidance on using suspended research credits, 66 PTS 376, Jun01.

IRS okays revoking election out of installment method, 66 PTS 236, Apr01.

IRS will not challenge contractors' use of the cash method, 66 PTS 309, May01.

Lump-sum payments made at lease inception were rent to lease purchaser, 66 PTS 122, Feb01.

No current deduction for property purchase to cancel lease, 66 PTS 56, Jan01.

On-line transactions intensify trader vs. investor question, *Jack Robinson & Richard S. Mark*, 66 PTS 80, Feb01.

Overpayments not income in year of receipt, 67 PTS 114, Aug01.

Payment under noncompetition agreement was disguised dividend, 67 PTS 363, Dec01.

Proposed Regulations on mid-contract changes in taxpayers, 66 PTS 236, Apr01.

Recent developments tinker with the research credit, *Annette Nellen*, 66 PTS 152, Mar01.

Resort owned by shareholders avoided entertainment facility rules, 66 PTS 55, Jan01.

Roundup of tax developments from the year that was, *Matthew A. Melone*, 66 PTS 25, Jan01.

Sale of goodwill partly converted into deductible compensation, 66 PTS 191, Mar01.

Section 179 speeds up deductions for equipment purchases, *Steven C. Colburn*, 66 PTS 361, Jun01.

Self-charged fees cannot offset passive income, 67 PTS 50, Jul01.

Single sale generates multiple types of capital gains, *Joe Walsh*, 67 PTS 14, Jul01.

Some shoe design costs can qualify as research expenditures, 67 PTS 118, Aug01.

Specific rules apply for opting out of MACRS, 67 PTS 364, Dec01.

Substantiation can be crucial for exception to passive loss rules, 67 PTS 119, Aug01.

Tax Court rejects de minimis expensing rule, 67 PTS 110, Aug01.

Unearth "farmer" status and harvest beneficial tax treatment, *Ted D. Englebrecht & Amie Moore*, 67 PTS 166, Sep01.

Upfront cash payments are taxable income upfront, 67 PTS 179, Sep01.

Bankruptcy

Claim not subordinated despite failure to collect from third party, 66 PTS 179, Mar01.

District court let bankruptcy court decide who gets funds, 67 PTS 112, Aug01.

IRS can set off otherwise exempt property, 66 PTS 178, Mar01.

Right to setoff trumps right to exempt property, 67 PTS 244, Oct01.

Compensation and Qualified Plans

Are points on first home worth paying with IRA funds, *Sidney J. Baxendale & Richard M. Walter*, 66 PTS 35, Jan01.

Backpay award creates current FICA tax liability, 67 PTS 54, Jul01.

Beware of AMT on incentive stock options, *Lisa M. Kaplan*, 67 PTS 260, Nov01.

Big compensation was reasonable under independent-investor test, 67 PTS 249, Oct01.

Cafeteria plan regulations expand mid-year election menu, *Barry Salkin*, 66 PTS 211, Apr01.

Cross-testing final regulations validate new comparability plans, *Michael S. Melbinger*, 67 PTS 132, Sep01.

Deferred compensation rewards and retains key employees, *Joseph R. Pozzuolo & Lisa Kaplan*, 66 PTS 85, Feb01.

Employee statement needed for employer to get FICA refund, 66 PTS 50, Jan01.

Employer's deduction can exceed income to employee for jet use, 67 PTS 127, Aug01.

Excess pension plan assets can be put to various uses, *Michael S. Melbinger & Jean M. Hahn*, 67 PTS 204, Oct01.

Final regulations clarify qualified transportation fringe benefit rules, 66 PTS 175, Mar01.

Formula-based compensation included disguised dividend, 67 PTS 126, Aug01.

Guidance on changes to qualified plan benefits limitations, 67 PTS 368, Dec01.

Guidance on effective dates for retirement plan rules, 67 PTS 248, Oct01.

How small is de minimis for fringe benefit exclusion?, 66 PTS 254, Apr01.

Income distributed to owner was compensation, 67 PTS 373, Dec01.

IRS revamps taxation of split-dollar arrangements, 66 PTS 173, Mar01.

IRS revises per-diem rates for travel reimbursements, 67 PTS 315, Nov01.

Mass transit commuting exclusion has mass appeal, *Theresa A. Cardello*, 67 PTS 349, Dec01.

Mortgage reduces marital deduction for joint property, 66 PS 233, Apr01.
No extra annual exclusions for reciprocal gifts, 67 PTS 120, Aug01.
No swing vote premium on minority interest in family business, *Peter J. Walsh*, 67 PTS 324, Dec01.
Post-death certainties do not count in valuing estate, 67 PTS 240, Oct01.
Post-death events not considered in valuing deduction, 66 PTS 293, May01.
Proposed regulations let revocable trust be treated as part of estate, 66 PTS 184, Mar01.
Proposed regulations update definition of trust income, 66 PTS 296, May01.
Purported oral options did not reduce property values, 67 PTS 241, Oct01.
Redemption agreement did not reduce taxable value, 67 PTS 190, Sep01.
Rental real estate gets installment payment break, 66 PTS 380, Jun01.
Save transfer taxes with family limited partnerships, *Peter J. Walsh*, 66 PTS 324, Jun01.
Settlement of nondeductible bequest got deduction, 67 PTS 303, Nov01.
Spousal interests in GRATs not exempt from gift tax, 67 PTS 376, Dec01.
Stock owned outright and in marital trust aggregated, 67 PTS 56, Jul01.
Structure generation-skipping gifts for tax savings, *Martin A. Goldberg*, 67 PTS 196, Oct01.
Transfer in exchange for self-canceling installment note was part gift, 67 PTS 121, Aug01.
Trust's advisory fees subject to 2%-of-AGI deduction floor, 67 PTS 310, Nov01.
Use of property after making gift kept it in estate, 67 PTS 304, Nov01.
Valuation based on partial restoration despite insurance expectation, 66 PTS 381, Jun01.
Valuation discount for tax on built-in capital gain, 67 PTS 375, Dec01.

Exempt Organizations

Gaming activities can land a tax bill for tax-exempts, *Larry R. Garrison*, 67 PTS 23, Jul01.

IRS Examination Questions

Accident insurance, 67 PTS 379, Dec01.
Automobile deductions, 66 PTS 378, Jun01.
Business incorporation, 66 PTS 316, May01.
Business vehicles, 66 PTS 252, Apr01.
Charitable contributions, 67 PTS 253, Oct01.
Child care credit, 67 PTS 378, Dec01.
Dividend reinvestment plan, 67 PTS 188, Sep01.

Estimated taxes, 66 PTS 58, Jan01; 67 PTS 252, Oct01.
Guaranteed payments, 66 PTS 252, Apr01.
Income recognition, 66 PTS 188, Mar01.
Installment sales, 67 PTS 124, Aug01.
Interest deductions, 67 PTS 316, Nov01.
Moving expenses, 66 PTS 59, Jan01.
Organizational expenses, 66 PTS 188, Mar01 67 PTS 188, Sep01.
Partnership losses, 67 PTS 60, Jul01.
Related-party transactions, 67 PTS 316, Nov01.
Repair vs. improvement, 66 PTS 124, Feb01.
Sale of partnership interest, 66 PTS 378, Jun01.
Scholarships, 66 PTS 124, Feb01.
S corporation distributions, 66 PTS 316, May01.
S corporation losses, 67 PTS 61, Jul01.
Section 179 deduction, 67 PTS 124, Aug01.
Stock basis, 66 PTS 58, Jan01.
Stock distributions, 66 PTS 125, Feb01.

Partnerships, S Corporations, and Limited Liability Companies

Assessment in single-member LLC's name is valid against owner, 67 PTS 182, Sep01.
Avoid tripping on family limited partnership trap, *Joseph R. Oliver & Charles A. Granstaff*, 66 PTS 268, May01.
Disposition frees up suspended passive losses despite S election, 66 PTS 61, Jan01.
Family limited partnership gifts get limited valuation discounts, 66 PTS 293, May01.
Final regulations issued for partnership allocation of nonrecourse liabilities, 66 PTS 62, Jan01.
Income distributed to owner was compensation, 67 PTS 373, Dec01.
Individual partners must be assessed for limitations period to run, 67 PTS 246, Oct01.
No basis increase for guaranteeing S corporation debt, 66 PTS 63, Jan01.
Partners must be individually assessed prior to collection activity, 66 PTS 373, Jun01.
Proposed Regulations on basis of corporate partner's interest in partnership, 66 PTS 248, Apr01.
Save transfer taxes with family limited partnerships, *Peter J. Walsh*, 66 PTS 324, Jun01.
S election subjected corporation to LIFO recapture, 66 PTS 60, Jan01.
Self-charged fees cannot offset passive income, 67 PTS 50, Jul01.
Shareholder's participation interest in loan to S corporation was guarantee, 67 PTS 51, Jul01.
Single sale generates multiple types of capital gains, *Joe Walsh*, 67 PTS 14, Jul01.
Special rules for partner in "trader" partnership, 66 PTS 308, May01.
Supreme Court hands windfall to owners of insolvent S corporations, *Mark R. Martin*

Embezzlement not reasonable cause for not filing, 66 PTS 289, May01.

Employee statement needed for employer to get FICA refund, 66 PTS 50, Jan01.

Equitable tolling of limitations period available only after RRA '98, 67 PTS 45, Jul01.

Erroneous tax abatement may be reversed, 66 PTS 372, Jun01.

Final determination withstands taxpayer's challenge, 66 PTS 47, Jan01.

Financial difficulties may be reasonable cause, 67 PTS 109, Aug01.

Fraud may extend employment tax return assessment, 66 PTS 240, Apr01.

Fuel excise tax credits are not limited by one-claim rule, 66 PTS 241, Apr01.

Guidance on tax shelter registration penalty, 66 PTS 304, May01.

How "ignorant" must innocent spouse be for tax relief, *Timothy R. Koski*, 66 PTS 4, Jan01.

Individual partners must be assessed for limitations period to run, 67 PTS 246, Oct01.

Innocent spouse relief granted for tax on inherited IRA, 66 PTS 301, May01.

Interest is refunded until due date not credit date, 67 PTS 244, Oct01.

IRS memo explains requirements for offer in compromise, 67 PTS 182, Sep01.

IRS offers guidance on using suspended research credits, 66 PTS 376, Jun01.

IRS provided sufficient detail to make deficiency notice valid, 67 PTS 176, Sep01.

IRS waived signature requirement on joint return, 66 PTS 178, Mar01.

IRS was wrong, but no attorney's fees awarded, 67 PTS 299, Nov01.

Liens and levies are separate collection actions, 67 PTS 245, Oct01.

Limitations period and latches did not prevent transferee liability, 66 PTS 241, Apr01.

Limitations period overrode by duty of consistency, 66 PTS 51, Jan01.

Limitations period strictly construed for wrongful levy suit, 66 PTS 108, Feb01.

Limitations period tolled during back-to-back bankruptcies, 66 PTS 110, Feb01.

"Mailbox rule" applied despite mailing instructions error, 66 PTS 244, Apr01.

Mailbox rule exception was not met, 67 PTS 302, Nov01.

Mental abuse may be duress for innocent spouse relief, 66 PTS 108, Feb01.

Must exhaust administrative remedies to get attorney's fees, 66 PTS 45, Jan01.

Partners must be individually assessed prior to collection activity, 66 PTS 373, Jun01.

Postmark date controls when determining if petition was timely, 66 PTS 45, Jan01.

Proposed Regulations clarify "innocent spouse" relief requirements, 66 PTS 245, Apr01.

Return with error was a valid claim for refund, 66 PTS 302, May01.

Special agents' good faith interpretation of law precludes damages, 67 PTS 44, Jul01.

Successful requests for innocent spouse relief, 66 PTS 375, Jun01.

Summons quashed based on attorney-client privilege, 66 PTS 290, May01.

Surviving corporation subject to transferee liability for tax debt, 67 PTS 359, Dec01.

Tax Court correct forum for income tax levy appeal, 67 PTS 360, Dec01.

Tax Court properly applied equitable recoupment doctrine, 67 PTS 318, Nov01.

Taxpayer not prevailing party so no litigation costs awarded, 67 PTS 174, Sep01.

Transferee liability imposed based on a fraudulent transfer, 66 PTS 181, Mar01.

Untimely suit prevents payment vs. deposit determination, 67 PTS 46, Jul01.

Waiver needed to obtain fuel credits, 66 PTS 290, May01.

What is "actual knowledge" for innocent spouse relief?, 66 PTS 44, Jan01.

Real Estate

Developer could allocate estimated costs to lots sold, 66 PTS 314, May01.

Final regulations exclude some construction allowances, 66 PTS 52, Jan01.

Final regulations on Section 467 rental agreements, 66 PTS 121, Feb01.

Find the right place for REITs in an investment portfolio, *Richard B. Toolson*, 67 PTS 92, Aug01.

Lease surrender payment is taxed as capital gain, 66 PTS 53, Jan01.

New safe harbor promotes reverse exchanges, *Bradley T. Borden*, 66 PTS 68, Feb01.

Proposed Regulations furnish home-sale exclusion guidance, *Michael Schlesinger*, 66 PTS 132, Mar01.

Putting home in trust reduced excludable gain, 66 PTS 182, Mar01.

Rental deductions are more restrictive at home, 67 PTS 184, Sep01.

Rental real estate gets installment payment break, 66 PTS 380, Jun01.

Renting home office to employer can reduce deductions, 67 PTS 184, Sep01.

When does self-employment tax take root on farm rents?, *Ted D. Englebrecht & Jacquelyn D. Smullen*, 66 PTS 277, May01.

Estate Planning

Estate Planning, Generally

Administration of a business interest held by an estate or trust, *Marc S. Bekerman &*

Charitable Contributions

Computers

Intuitive Estate Planner, Version 4.2, offers a wealth of helpful estate planning features, *Joseph G. Hodges, Jr.*, 28 EP 244, May01.

No-cost Internet resources for estate planners, *Donald H. Kelley*, 28 EP 45, Jan01.

Online fee-based services for estate planners, *Donald H. Kelley*, 28 EP 349, Jul01.

Generation-skipping Transfer Tax

Final regulations approve certain changes in grandfathered GST trusts, *John B. O'Grady & Jennifer Schooley Stringer*, 28 EP 526, Nov01.

Tips for preparing generation-skipping transfer tax returns, *Douglas R. Thornburg & Charles A. Lowenhaupt*, 28 EP 208, May01.

Gifts and Gift Tax

Adequate disclosure: its impact on gift tax return strategies, *Michael D. Mulligan*, 28 EP 3, Jan01.

Annual exclusion denied for reciprocal gifts, 28 EP 225, May01.

Defined value gifts: does IRS have it all wrong?, *L. Paul Hood, Jr.*, 28 EP 582, Dec01.

Gift giving allowed under power of attorney, 28 EP 123, Mar01.

Gift incomplete if check paid after donor's death, 28 EP 445, Sep01.

No annual exclusion for indirect gifts, rules Tax Court, 28 EP 223, May01.

Reciprocal trust doctrine was applied to gifts, 28 EP 553, Nov01.

Tax Court disallows use of SCIN, 28 EP 551, Nov01.

Transfer of assets to family partnership was not a taxable gift, 28 EP 118, Mar01.

Individual Retirement Accounts (IRAs) and Retirement Plans

Charitable estate planning with retirement benefits, *Sanford J. Schlesinger & Dana L. Mark*, 28 EP 390, Aug01.

How multi-generation IRA preserves cash flow for children, *Gerald J. Robinson*, 28 EP 22, Jan01.

IRS proposes new, liberalized minimum distribution regulations, *Richard S. Franklin & Robert T. Kleinknecht*, 28 EP 355, Aug01.

Insurance

Aggressive viatical settlement transactions: gambling on human lives, *Jeffrey A. Baskies & Brian J. Samuels*, 28 EP 76, Feb01.

COLI, BOLI, TOLI and "insurable interests," *Stephan R. Leimberg & Albert E. Gibbons*, 28 EP 333, Jul01.

Dealing with EGTRRA's impact on an insurance professional's practice, *Stephan R. Leimberg & Albert E. Gibbons*, 28 EP 403, Sep01.

Extracting hidden value from unwanted life insurance policies, *Morton P. Greenberg & John E. Mayer*, 28 EP 434, Sep01.

IRS ruling taxes plan as both split-dollar and interest-free loan, *Albert R. Kingan*, 28 EP 19, Jan01.

Key issues to consider when drafting life insurance trusts, *Sebastian V. Grassi, Jr.*, 28 EP 217, May01.

Life (insurance) after estate tax "repeal" or "reform," 28 EP 128, Mar01.

Notice 2001-10 will have dramatic effects on split-dollar arrangements, *Howard M. Zaritsky & Stephan R. Leimberg*, 28 EP 99, Mar01.

Premium financing: the last choice—not the first choice, *Stephan R. Leimberg & Albert E. Gibbons*, 28 EP 35, Jan01.

Proposed Regulations on the definition of trust income: the best thing for life insurance planning since sliced bread, *Stephan R. Leimberg & Albert E. Gibbons*, 28 EP 231, May01.

Typical life insurance planning mistakes and some suggested solutions, *Lawrence Brody & Lucinda A. Althauser*, 28 EP 51, Feb01.

Using life insurance and annuities for asset protection, *Peter Spero*, 28 EP 12, Jan01.

Marital Deduction

Marital deduction disallowed for potential increased annuity payments, 28 EP 443, Sep01.

No marital deduction for assets passing under settlement agreement, 28 EP 121, Mar01.

No marital deduction for property acquired in settlement of annuity, 28 EP 228, May01.

Trusts

Administration of a business interest held by an estate or trust, *Marc S. Bekerman & Steven S. Kirkpatrick*, 28 EP 536, Nov01.

Avoiding the attribution rules in redemptions by estates and trusts, *Richard W. Harris*, 28 EP 317, Jul01.

Charitable remainder trusts: final regulations on prevention of abuse of CRTs, *Sanford J.*

Valuation

The Journal of International Taxation

International Taxation, Generally

Argentina

Australia

Barbados

Still more German tax reforms, *Jorg Menger & Ilona Kahl*, 12 J INT TAX, No. 10, 26, Oct01.

Hong Kong

Hong Kong issues long-awaited guidance on taxation of stock options, *Sarah McGrath & Anne Shih*, 12 J INT TAX, No. 10, 54, Oct01.

Taxation of e-commerce in Hong Kong, *Sarah McGrath*, 12 J INT TAX, No. 12, 42, Dec01.

India

India cuts taxes, introduces transfer pricing legislation, 12 J INT TAX, No. 7, 13, Jul01.

Indonesia

Netherlands-Indonesia tax treaty still applies, 12 J INT TAX, No. 7, 15, Jul01.

Italy

Draft 2001 Italian corporate and tax reform unveiled, 12 J INT TAX, No. 10, 7, Oct01.

Italian CFC rules and Subpart F compared, *Andrea Silvestri*, 12 J INT TAX, No. 12, 20, Dec01.

2001 Italian budget lowers corporate tax, enhances tools to reduce tax burden, 12 J INT TAX, No. 7, 15, Jul01.

Mexico

Mexican tax reform—compliance, anti-avoidance, and economics, *Ricardo Suarez & Luis Coronado*, 12 J INT TAX, No. 4, 36, Apr01.

Partial Mexican withholding refund possible on dividends to U.S. companies, 12 J INT TAX, No. 10, 8, Oct01.

Netherlands

A guide to European holding companies—Part 2: Belgium, the Netherlands, and Spain, *Stanley C. Ruchelman, Ewout Van Asbeck, Guillermo Canalejo, Werner Heyvaert, Michael T. McGowan, & Stephan Neidhardt*, 12 J INT TAX, No. 1, 22, Jan01.

Netherlands announces policy objectives for conduit companies, *Michael Molenaars*

& Emile Bongers, 12 J INT TAX, No. 7, 61, Jul01.

Netherlands-Indonesia tax treaty still applies, 12 J INT TAX, No. 7, 15, Jul01.

Proposed amendments to Dutch fiscal unity regime revisited, 12 J INT TAX, No. 11, 13, Nov01.

Proposed changes to Dutch fiscal unity affect existing BV1/BV2 structures, 12 J INT TAX, No. 10, 9, Oct01.

Report recommends changes to Netherlands' corporate tax regime, *Michael Molenaars & Emile Bongers*, 12 J INT TAX, No. 10, 58, Oct01.

The Netherlands: 2000 tax wrap-up, *Harry B. Doornbosch & Stan Berings*, 12 J INT TAX, No. 8, 30, Aug01.

Portugal

Portugal introduces comprehensive transfer pricing rules, 12 J INT TAX, No. 7, 15, Jul01.

Puerto Rico

Prospects improve for use of R&D credit in Puerto Rico, *Robert S. Griggs*, 12 J INT TAX, No. 7, 57, Jul01.

Puerto Rico seeks new tax incentives to compensate for loss of Section 936, *Robert S. Griggs*, 12 J INT TAX, No. 11, 41, Nov01.

Russia

Russia's tax system overhaul includes clearer VAT rules, 12 J INT TAX, No. 1, 8, Jan01.

Singapore

Exchange of information in Singapore's tax treaties, *Tan How Teck*, 12 J INT TAX, No. 7, 50, Jul01.

Spain

A guide to European holding companies—Part 2: Belgium, the Netherlands, and Spain, *Stanley C. Ruchelman, Ewout Van Asbeck, Guillermo Canalejo, Werner Heyvaert, Michael T. McGowan, & Stephan Neidhardt*, 12 J INT TAX, No. 1, 22, Jan01.

Sweden

California

California audits the manufacturer's investment credit: a look at the major issues, *Chris Micheli & Michael D. Herbert*, 11 JMT, No. 4, 24, Jul01.

How much do California's manufacturing tax incentives cost?—a look at taxpayer usage, *Chris Micheli*, 11 JMT, No. 1, 24, Mar/Apr01.

Colorado

Enterprise zone sales tax exemption incorporated former federal ITC limit, 11 JMT, No. 3, 34, Jun01.

State offers agricultural development incentives, 11 JMT, No. 8, 28, Nov/Dec01.

State Supreme Court expands credit in upholding use tax on test cars, 10 JMT, No. 9, 29, Jan01.

Connecticut

Court bars automatic disallowance of FSC commission expense, 11 JMT, No. 1, 13, Mar/Apr01.

High court says software customization is taxable computer service, 11 JMT, No. 7, 38, Oct01.

Labor Department issues regulations for incentive tax credit hiring program, 11 JMT, No. 3, 35, Jun01.

District of Columbia

New incentives encourage pollution clean-up, 11 JMT, No. 8, 29, Nov/Dec01.

Florida

Legislature amends enterprise zone incentive laws, 11 JMT, No. 8, 30, Nov/Dec01.

Illinois

Court rules short-term investment income was not apportionable, 11 JMT, No. 6, 30, Sep01.

Illinois job tax credit gives state the "EDGE" in relocations and expansions, *David A. Hughes & Benjamin W. Wong*, 11 JMT, No. 5, 14, Aug01.

Kansas

Incentives for electric generation facilities, 11 JMT, No. 8, 33, Nov/Dec01.

Loan in takeover-defense tactic results in non-business interest, 11 JMT, No. 6, 33, Sep01.

Multistate, family controlled businesses found to be unitary, 11 JMT, No. 6, 31, Sep01.

Substantial nexus required a greater physical presence, 11 JMT, No. 7, 40, Oct01.

Louisiana

Court clarifies constitutional limit on enacting exemptions, 11 JMT, No. 1, 21, Mar/Apr01.

Maryland

Out-of-state affiliate defeats state's nexus claims, 10 JMT, No. 10, 32, Feb01.

State enacts tax incentives promoting clean, efficient energy, 11 JMT, No. 3, 36, Jun01.

Michigan

Court's decision in *Meijer, Inc.* may render Michigan's property tax obsolete, *Samuel J. McKim III*, 11 JMT, No. 2, 12, May01.

Minnesota

Court upholds taxing statutory residents' out-of-state income, 11 JMT, No. 2, 38, May01.

Nonresident's in-state managerial services now taxable, 11 JMT, No. 4, 33, Jul01.

Mississippi

Incentives aid major manufacturer and its suppliers, 11 JMT, No. 3, 37, Jun01.

Missouri

Liberal post-deprivation remedy for void state-wide local use tax, 11 JMT, No. 1, 31, Mar/Apr01.

Some creative uses for Missouri's state tax credit programs, *Janette M. Lohman & John P. Barrie*, 11 JMT, No. 6, 6, Sep01.

Montana

Tax incentives in the U.S. Virgin Islands improve under amended industrial development program, *Mark A. Opper & Betty W. McIntosh*, 11 JMT, No. 8, 6, Nov/Dec01.

Washington

Taxpayer should have claimed benefits despite apparent ineligibility, 11 JMT, No. 8, 44, Nov/Dec01.

Taxation of Exempts (The Journal of Taxation of Exempt Organizations)

Exempt Organizations, Generally

Applying Section 382 to loss corporation affiliates of exempt organizations, *Robert J. Mason, Mark V. Rountree, & Howard A. Levenson*, 12 JTEO 139, Jan/Feb01.

Defunct organization cannot challenge revocation of exemption, 13 JTEO 104, Sep/Oct01.

Internet guidance should reconcile old law with a new medium, *Robert A. Wexler & Alice M. Anderson*, 12 JTEO 187, Mar/Apr01.

IRS takes hard line on Section 501(c)(3) bonds and exempt status, *Elizabeth M. Mills*, 13 JTEO 45, Jul/Aug01.

Looking back to assess the *United Cancer Council* case, *Errol Copilevitz*, 13 JTEO 63, Sep/Oct01.

Temporary regulations provide window of opportunity on intermediate sanctions, *Janet M. Buehler*, 13 JTEO 3, Jul/Aug01.

The commerciality doctrine is a judicial border patrol for charities' activities, *James R. Walker*, 12 JTEO 209, Mar/Apr01.

The evolving use of limited liability companies by tax-exempt organizations, *Robert W. Friz*, 13 JTEO 112, Nov/Dec01.

What nonprofits should look for as states consider Internet taxation, *Norman H. Wright*, 12 JTEO 155, Jan/Feb01.

Accounting

FASB sets financial accounting standards for gifts through agents and intermediaries, *Maureen L. Thomas*, 12 JTEO 229, Mar/Apr01.

Charitable Contributions

Charitable fundraising involves more tax complexity than meets the eye, *John V. Woodhull & Vreni Jones*, 12 JTEO 213, Mar/Apr01.

Charitable gift planning after the 2001 Tax Act, *Carolyn D. Duronio*, 13 JTEO 146, Nov/Dec01.

Charitable giving tax bill leaves the House for an uncertain Senate future, 13 JTEO 92, Sep/Oct01.

Charting the interacting provisions of the charitable contribution deduction for individuals, *James L. Wittenbach & Ken Milani*, 13 JTEO 9, Jul/Aug01.

Charting the provisions of the charitable contribution deduction for corporations, *Ken Milani & James L. Wittenbach*, 13 JTEO 125, Nov/Dec01.

Congress repeals estate tax—for a while, 13 JTEO 48, Jul/Aug01.

FASB sets financial accounting standards for gifts through agents and intermediaries, *Maureen L. Thomas*, 12 JTEO 229, Mar/Apr01.

How to establish donor-advised funds and community foundations, *Wendell R. Bird*, 13 JTEO 68, Sep/Oct01.

IRS issues new regulations for charitable trusts, *Carolyn D. Duronio*, 12 JTEO 226, Mar/Apr01.

Let the donor beware of the charitable family limited partnership, *Carolyn D. Duronio*, 12 JTEO 272, May/Jun01.

Planning to meet a range of donor needs with "flip" charitable remainder unitrusts, *Michele A.W. McKinnon*, 12 JTEO 253, May/Jun01.

President Bush presents his tax plans for charitable giving, *Robert A. Boisture, Catherine E. Livingston, & Kristen A. Gurdin*, 12 JTEO 235, May/Jun01.

The tax consequences of accepting charitable contributions through a single-member LLC, *Catherine E. Livingston*, 13 JTEO 107, Nov/Dec01.

The who's who and what's what of charitable fundraisers, *John V. Woodhull & Vreni R. Jones*, 13 JTEO 23, Jul/Aug01.

Colleges, Universities, and Other Educational Institutions

Information statements can now be provided to taxpayers electronically, *Nancy J. Foran*, 13 JTEO 100, Sep/Oct01.

Treasury issues proposed regulations on information reporting for education credits and student loan interest, *Nancy J. Foran*, 12 JTEO 161, Jan/Feb01.

Compensation and Benefits

Exclusion for housing allowance no longer limited to fair market rental value, *Brad A. Miller,* 12 JTEO 276, May/Jun01.

Temporary regulations provide window of opportunity on intermediate sanctions, *Janet M. Buehler,* 13 JTEO 3, Jul/Aug01.

Disclosure and Information Reporting

Information statements can now be provided to taxpayers electronically, *Nancy J. Foran,* 13 JTEO 100, Sep/Oct01.

New campaign finance disclosure law hits the wrong target, *George Constantine,* 12 JTEO 150, Jan/Feb01.

The Internet brings "cyber-accountability" to the nonprofit sector, *Caroline K. Craig,* 13 JTEO 82, Sep/Oct01.

Treasury issues proposed regulations on information reporting for education credits and student loan interest, *Nancy J. Foran,* 12 JTEO 161, Jan/Feb01.

Hospitals and Other Health Care Organizations

An HMO wins the insurance battle, but will HMOs lose the war?, *Gerald M. Griffith,* 12 JTEO 145, Jan/Feb01.

Restoring the charitable exemption of the Great Plains Health Alliance, *H. Philip Elwood,* 13 JTEO 150, Nov/Dec01.

Ruling approves a "good" health care joint venture, 13 JTEO 33, Jul/Aug01.

The de-evolution of the community benefit standard for health care organizations, *Robert C. Louthian III,* 13 JTEO 118, Nov/Dec01.

Political Organizations and Activities

How campaign finance reform legislation would affect tax-exempt organizations, *Lloyd H. Mayer,* 13 JTEO 131, Nov/Dec01.

New campaign finance disclosure law hits the wrong target, *George Constantine,* 12 JTEO 150, Jan/Feb01.

What guidance is needed—and not needed—for political and lobbying activities on the Internet, *Robert A. Wexler & Alice M. Anderson,* 12 JTEO 260, May/Jun01.

Private Foundations

Assessing the options for terminating private foundation status, *Jody Blazek,* 12 JTEO 199, Mar/Apr01.

Grantmaking to foreign organizations aided by a "simplified" procedure, *Michael S. Kutzin,* 12 JTEO 181, Jan/Feb01.

Outdated regulations hamper foundations making foreign program-related investments, *David S. Chernoff,* 12 JTEO 249, May/Jun01.

The emergence of "venture philanthropy" raises new tax issues, *LaVerne Woods,* 13 JTEO 51, Sep/Oct01.

Religious Organizations

Exclusion for housing allowance no longer limited to fair market rental value, *Brad A. Miller,* 12 JTEO 276, May/Jun01.

"Pervasively sectarian" institutions may now qualify for tax-exempt financing, *Stuart J. Lark,* 12 JTEO 173, Jan/Feb01.

Revenue from product sales by religious organizations may be taxable, *Stuart J. Lark,* 13 JTEO 94, Sep/Oct01.

Unrelated Business Income Tax

Keeping ahead of the UBIT consequences of a gift shop, *Susan R. Bills,* 13 JTEO 35, Jul/Aug01.

Revenue from product sales by religious organizations may be taxable, *Stuart J. Lark,* 13 JTEO 94, Sep/Oct01.

Business Entities

Business Entities, Generally

Charles H. Egerton interviewed by Jerald David August, 3 BE, No. 4, 6, Jul/Aug01.

Checking-the-box constitutes plan of liquidation, 3 BE, No. 2, 56, Mar/Apr01.

Exchange accommodation titleholder and deferred Section 1031 exchanges, *Terence Floyd Cuff,* 3 BE, No. 1, 40, Jan/Feb01.

Farmer recognized discharge-of-indebtedness income on debt payoff, 3 BE, No. 2, 56, Mar/Apr01.

Foreign entities: proposed regulations under check-the-box rules, 3 BE, No. 2, 56, Mar/Apr01.

Jerald David August interviews Donald C. Alexander, Steve Glaze, and William J. Wilkins, 3 BE, No. 2, 4, Mar/Apr01.

New proposed revenue procedures on accounting periods, 3 BE, No. 4, 54, Jul/Aug01.

Proposed regulations on treatment of payments by domestic reverse hybrid entities, 3 BE, No. 4, 57, Jul/Aug01.

Personal Service Corporations

Real Estate Investment Trusts

S Corporations

IRS issues favorable guidance on built-in gain tax and natural resources, 3 BE, No. 6, 39, Nov/Dec01.

IRS issues letter ruling on plan to "incentivize" employees through dividend based distributions and transfers of nonvoting stock, 3 BE, No. 4, 51, Jul/Aug01.

IRS proposes regulations on qualification of ESBTs as S corporation shareholders, *C. Wells Hall, III*, 3 BE, No. 2, 28, Mar/Apr01.

IRS provides guidance on ESBTs and estimated taxes, 3 BE, No. 2, 55, Mar/Apr01.

IRS rules that arbitration award does not create second class of stock, 3 BE, No. 3, 60, May/Jun01.

IRS rules that termination would be inadvertent if conversion of S corporation to limited partnership terminated S election, 3 BE, No. 5, 58, Sep/Oct01.

Legislation favorable to tax-exempt shareholders of S corporations introduced, 3 BE, No. 6, 41, Nov/Dec01.

Letter ruling applies basis adjustment rules to S corporation shareholders receiving liquidating distributions over more than one tax year, 3 BE, No. 3, 59, May/Jun01.

Merger of S corporations does not terminate S elections, 3 BE, No. 4, 52, Jul/Aug01.

Ownership of S corporation by LLCs and limited partnerships does not terminate S election, 3 BE, No. 3, 61, May/Jun01.

QSST and S corporation elections not terminated when trust entered into various agreements with respect to S corporation stock, 3 BE, No. 6, 42, Nov/Dec01.

QSST elections for testamentary trusts — proposed regulations issued, 3 BE, No. 6, 41, Nov/Dec01.

S corporation may deduct suspended PALs incurred while it was a C corporation, 3 BE, No. 1, 56, Jan/Feb01.

Self-charged management fee not deductible against related nonpassive management fee income, 3 BE, No. 4, 52, Jul/Aug01.

Seventh Circuit affirms holding that shareholder's participation interest did not increase basis in S corporation, 3 BE, No. 4, 51, Jul/Aug01.

Sixth Circuit affirms capitalization of expenses relating to S election, 3 BE, No. 6, 42, Nov/Dec01.

Small business corporation status not terminated by administrative dissolution and reincorporation, 3 BE, No. 4, 52, Jul/Aug01.

Spillover basis rule of Sections 1367 and 1368 applies in Section 304 transaction, 3 BE, No. 3, 55, May/Jun01.

Subchapter S Modernization Act of 2001 introduced, 3 BE, No. 5, 57, Sep/Oct01.

Subchapter S reform initiatives, 3 BE, No. 3, 54, May/Jun01.

Supreme Court, reversing Tenth Circuit, holds that excluded COD income increases stock basis of S corporation shareholders, 3 BE, No. 1, 53, Jan/Feb01.

Tax Court allows basis increase for some, but not all, of corporation's shareholders attributable to loans made to S corporation, 3 BE, No. 5, 58, Sep/Oct01.

Tax Court holds that shareholder may not increase basis as the result of guarantee, but applies *Selfe* analysis, 3 BE, No. 3, 60, May/Jun01.

Temporary Regulations classify ESBTs, qualified plan trusts, and 501(c)(3) trusts as not constituting deferral entities, 3 BE, No. 1, 57, Jan/Feb01.

The built-in gains tax revisited: 15 years later, *Stephen R. Looney*, 3 BE, No. 2, 12, Mar/Apr01.

The new extraterritorial income exclusion for S corporations, *Sandra Soltis & Paul C. Lau*, 3 BE, No. 2, 40, Mar/Apr01.

The Subchapter S discharge of indebtedness issue: Supreme Court picks law over equity, *Richard A. Shaw*, 3 BE, No. 3, 4, May/Jun01.

JTD2